West Pointers *and the* Civil War

★ ★ ★

Civil War America

Gary W. Gallagher, editor

West Pointers *and the* Civil War

THE OLD ARMY IN WAR AND PEACE

★ ★ ★

Wayne Wei-siang Hsieh

THE UNIVERSITY OF NORTH CAROLINA PRESS
Chapel Hill

Designed and set by Rebecca Evans in Monotype Walbaum
Manufactured in the United States of America

The paper in this book meets the guidelines for permanence
and durability of the Committee on Production Guidelines for
Book Longevity of the Council on Library Resources.

The University of North Carolina Press has been a member
of the Green Press Initiative since 2003.

Library of Congress Cataloging-in-Publication Data
Hsieh, Wayne Wei-siang.
West Pointers and the Civil War : the old army
in war and peace / Wayne Wei-siang Hsieh.
p. cm. — (Civil War America)
Includes bibliographical references and index.
ISBN 978-0-8078-3278-3 (cloth : alk. paper)
1. United States — History, Military — To 1900. 2. United
States. Army — History — 19th century. 3. Military art and science —
United States — History — 19th century. 4. Mexican War, 1846–1848 —
Campaigns. 5. United States — History — Civil War, 1861–1865 — Campaigns.
6. Generals — United States — History — 19th century. 7. United States
Military Academy — Alumni and alumnae — Biography. I. Title.
E181.H79 2009   355.00973 — dc22   2009016646

Portions of this work appeared earlier, in somewhat different form, as
"'I Owe Virginia Little, My County Much': Robert E. Lee, the United States
Regular Army, and Unconditional Unionism," in *Crucible of the Civil War: Virginia
from Secession to Commemoration*, ed. Gary W. Gallagher, Edward L. Ayers, and
Andrew W. Torget (Charlottesville: University of Virginia Press, 2006), 35–57.

13 12 11 10 09   5 4 3 2 1

In memoriam

ISAAC JACOB MEYERS

(1979–2008)

★ ★ ★

In honor of

VETERANS OF OIF/OEF

CONTENTS

✦ ✦ ✦

TABLES, FIGURES, AND MAPS

★ ★ ★

ACKNOWLEDGMENTS

★ ★ ★

I have gathered innumerable debts in the long process of writing this book. First off, I should thank the staff of every archive and library listed in my bibliography. Such institutions provide indispensable services to historians, and although we frequently express our gratitude, we never thank them as thoroughly as they deserve. Special thanks should go to Michael Musick, recently retired from the National Archives; Dr. Richard Somers of the United States Army Military History Institute; and the delightful staff at the Special Collections wing of the United States Military Academy Library — most especially Susan Lintelmann, Alan Aimone, Deborah A. McKeon-Pogue, and Suzanne M. Christoff. As a historian of the old army, I am comforted to know that the documentary basis of the history of West Point is in good hands. Dr. Eugenia Kiesling allowed me to rent a room of her gracious home, and for that I am also thankful. Denise Ho also facilitated some research in Washington, D.C., by allowing me to apartment-sit in Rosslyn for a few weeks. The Huntington Library also provided a wonderful venue for the writing of the bulk of this study, both for its scenic gardens and for its thorough collection of Civil War–related books. This book was copyedited while I served on an interagency detail with the Department of State in Iraq. This meant that I had to rely on the gracious assistance of Keith Bohannon, Noel Harrison, LT Patrick Alfonzo, and Christopher Nichols to double-check some citations and points of fact. Chris was especially helpful on this front.

I have also benefited from substantial institutional support, which made this work possible. Thanks thus goes out to the Jacob K. Javits Fellowship program funded by the Department of Education, which supported my graduate study; the Whitney Humanities Center at Yale University for granting me a Andrew W. Mellon postdoctoral fellowship that gave me further support for the writing of this book; and the Naval Academy Research Council, whose SEED grants funded two summers of research and writing during my time here at the United States Naval Academy. Both the Whitney Humanities Center and the History Department at the Naval Academy have proved to be delightful places to work, and I can think of no other historian who has been blessed with better colleagues so early in his academic career.

Many individuals have also made fruitful comments on this work. They include the members of the Works in Progress Seminar at the History Department of the United States Naval Academy; Michael F. Holt and James W. Ceaser, both of the University of Virginia; J. E. Lendon, whose ruthless eye improved the introduction and conclusion a great deal; and my two outside readers who evaluated the manuscript for the publisher—Dr. Joseph Glatthaar and another historian who remains anonymous. Both made invaluable suggestions, and both represented the process of peer review working at its best. David Perry and the staff at the University of North Carolina Press also deserve obvious credit for seeing this book through. Any errors that remain are, of course, my own responsibility.

More broadly, I should thank my many teachers for making this book possible. Donald Kagan, The late (sadly) Henry Ashby Turner Jr., and David Brion Davis gave me as exemplary an undergraduate history education as anyone could desire, while Charles Hill and Norma Thompson did so much for my liberal education outside of the discipline of history. At Virginia, the aforementioned J. E. Lendon lent me both his wisdom and his friendship. My parents, of course, also deserve much thanks for making all these educational experiences possible. As does Noel Sugimura, an old friend from college, who has helped me fend off the more irascible elements of my personality.

Most importantly, however, I must thank my co-advisors, who did so much to midwife this work—Gary W. Gallagher and Edward L. Ayers, the former still at the University of Virginia, the latter now president of the University of Richmond. Both bore with my own version of graduate student angst, and without their wise counsel, I would never have completed my graduate education as fruitfully as I did. Both have provided ample support to my career, even in its more unconventional aspects, and both have set the highest possible bars for me in both scholarship and professional conduct.

Finally, the book is dedicated to representatives of two exemplary parts of what I, for lack of a better term, call American civilization. Isaac Meyers, a dear old friend, represented the best the world of humane letters offered. In his humanity, grace, and genteel learning, one saw the best of what the university has to offer. As a work of military history, however, this book by necessity concerns itself with very different aspects of the human experience, which are as unavoidable as they are unpleasant. But in the blood and muck of the battlefield, nobility and grandeur can still exist, and it is in that spirit that this book is also dedicated to the men and women of Operation Iraqi Freedom (OIF) and Operation Enduring Freedom (OEF). Special thanks go out to the "Bastards" of B Co/2-27 IN, "Coyote" CAT14 of 443 CA BN, and 3 BSTB, units whom the author worked especially closely with as a Department of Defense civilian detailed to the State Department in Iraq. Special thanks go out to SFC Patrick Bujold of CAT14, both MAJ Steven Sigloch and LTC Christopher Stenman of 3 BSTB, and, most especially, CPT Jason Honeycutt of the "Bastards." Like the old army, every man and woman in this modern successor to the regulars is a volunteer, and some even are graduates from West Point, ensuring that the long gray line continues to extend into the future. Their sacrifices have made, and continue to make, possible so many worthwhile parts of our national life, and it is to be hoped that these new guardians of the republic will not meet with the neglect faced by their old army predecessors.

West Pointers *and the* Civil War

★ ★ ★

INTRODUCTION

* * *

After Gen. Robert E. Lee's surrender to Lt. Gen. Ulysses S. Grant at Appomattox, Brig. Gen. Edward Porter Alexander, a senior Confederate artillerist, proposed to his commander that the army's men disband to their different home states. Alexander hoped to extract better terms from the victorious Federals — in effect, to resort to a guerrilla war, although Alexander dared not use those terms so explicitly. Lee refused, bluntly telling Alexander that "the men would have no rations & they would be under no discipline. They are already demoralized by four years of war. They would have to plunder & rob to procure subsistence. The country would be full of lawless bands in every part, & a state of society would ensue from which it would take the country years to recover. . . . And as for myself, while you young men might afford to go to bushwhacking, the only proper & dignified course for me would be to surrender myself & take the consequences of my actions."[1] Faced with that rebuke, Alexander meekly accepted his chief's course. After all, both Alexander and Lee, like most senior Union and Confederate commanders, had been veterans of an antebellum U.S. Army deeply suspicious of irregular warfare.

The orderly manner in which Lee surrendered his army to Grant, and his army's willingness to surrender when commanded to do so, showed how much the antebellum U.S. Army's patterns and habits of thought still remained among its veterans. In the midst of developments some historians have plausibly called revolutionary — emancipation, the Federal arming of slaves, serious Confederate proposals to do the same, and an unprecedented (in American history) centralization of power in both sections — both armies continued to fight in uniform, and under notions of hierarchy and discipline developed by regular army officers in what many have called the "old army." The social conservatism of the Confederacy's planter elite and its unwillingness to jeopardize slavery helped prevent the rise of a more substantial Confederate insurgency, but the old army backgrounds of the Confederate high command, including West Point graduate Jefferson Davis, also played an important part. It is telling that Lee, who did become something of a revolutionary when he called for the arming of slaves in 1864, never seriously contemplated a guerrilla-oriented strategy. Lee became willing to arm slaves, but like the leaders of the Union army, he intended that they remain bound to a military chain of command akin to the systems of disciplined hierarchy that marked almost all of Lee's entire adult life.

In committing themselves to a struggle of nation-state armies, both the Union and Confederate armies became dependent on the small group of regular army veterans who had monopolized professional military expertise in the antebellum army. These old army veterans thus dominated the command cadres of both contending military forces. The successes and the failures of those armies thus depended on the collision of old army methods with the difficult and trying circumstances presented by the Civil War, with its vast hosts of raw and untrained troops. Both old army leaders and citizen-soldier followers gradually improved their military dexterity, but the institutional legacies and circumstances shared by both sections prevented either army from gaining a marked superiority in military competence over one another. This in turn helps to explain the war's long and wearying course, as the armies pummeled one another, until the Union finally found leaders and methods capable of bringing the Confederate armies to heel. Political, social, and economic factors all, of course, played important roles in the final Union victory, but that victory could not come until the Federal armies found military answers to military problems. Lincoln summed it up in his second inaugural address, when he referred to "the progress of our arms, upon which all else chiefly depends."[2]

For the most part, northerners and southerners entered the Civil War with a set of cultural expectations rooted in an Anglo-American martial tradition that had glorified the civic and military virtue of the studiously unprofessional citizen-soldier; they ended the war with veteran troops as professional as any other Western military in the world, although almost all of the volunteers would quickly return to civilian life. Antebellum Americans had inherited from their English ancestors a profound suspicion of standing armies rooted in the military-backed absolutism of ancien régime France, the classical example of Rome's fall into an imperial autocracy backed by a professional standing army, various failed attempts to centralize English government in the seventeenth century, and the conflict that led to the American Revolution in the following century. Nevertheless, Civil War–era political leaders in both sections vied to vindicate their own respective nation-states, whether within their borders or on external battlefields, and that in turn required the reasonably effective monopoly on large-scale violence associated with the standing armies of nation-state Europe.

Unorganized citizen-soldiers and militia could and did serve as guerrillas during the Civil War, but both the Confederacy and the Union wanted to exercise a degree of authority over the disputed territory in question far beyond the uncertain control of dispersed guerrillas. The Confederate government had to raise large standing armies capable of fighting and defeating similar Union armies, not only as a goal in and of itself but also for the purpose of gaining European recognition of the Confederacy as a legitimate nation-state. Irregulars can harass and deny an enemy army total control over a territory, but they cannot themselves control the territory with any degree of permanence.[3] Union war aims in turn could hardly tolerate the presence of substantial Confederate field armies defying Federal authority.

The need to fight a nation-state war thus forced Americans to tolerate the special type of military expertise monopolized for the most part by graduates of the United States Military Academy at West Point. Before 1861, a political culture that did its best to answer questions of military policy with paeans to an overly idealized citizen-soldier militia had given a small cadre of regular army officers almost exclusive access to this vital type of knowledge. When a sectional war broke out, the raw and disorganized state of volunteer military forces dictated that both sides draw generals and drillmasters from the old army's leadership cadre. The distinctly impractical nature of antebellum martial culture allowed this leadership cadre to maintain its monopoly over the war's military leadership throughout the entire conflict. Because of cultural and ideological preferences, political leaders in both sections found themselves wholly unable to provide an alternative to the West Point conception of professional expertise that would not in turn lead to immediate defeat on the battlefield. Although both the Union and the Confederacy fought the Civil War to vindicate political orders that placed civil authority at the head of the state, they found themselves instead bound to the capricious foibles of a relative handful of old army men at the heads of their armies, holding positions of influence entirely out of proportion to either antebellum precedent or wartime preference.[4]

Antebellum American political culture made no provision for granting professional soldiers such a high level of social and political importance, and civilian political leaders still saw themselves as the undisputed masters of both war efforts. Even if they did not entirely subscribe to those ideals, political leaders had to pay far more lip service than did professional military leaders to wider civilian expectations regarding the nature of professional military expertise, the swiftness of operations, and the martial virtues of the citizen-soldier. In the Union, a heated domestic debate over war aims and emancipation caused frictions that did not exist in the Confederacy, because almost all white southerners in the Confederate states agreed on the need to protect slavery and the southern racial order.[5] This dispute over war aims, combined with the fact that most West Pointers were conservative Unionists hostile toward emancipation, created a situation where debates over military expertise in the North became a proxy for debates over Federal war aims.

Most importantly, Maj. Gen. George B. McClellan, the Army of the Potomac's first commander and an anti-emancipation member of the Democratic Party who ran for president in 1864, helped make congressional Republican leaders so distrustful of professional military expertise that the resulting civil-military friction in the Federal high command nearly compromised the overall northern war effort. Civil-military tensions in the Union war effort contributed to the lack of coordination between Federal generals that helped lead to the crushing defeat at Second Bull Run in August 1862, the dreary Mud March of the Army of the Potomac in January 1863, and the costly offensive operations of the Overland campaign in the spring of 1864 that nearly cost the Lincoln administration reelection in 1864. Grant, the Union commander of that campaign, felt compelled to use overly aggressive methods in part because of Republican perceptions that earlier commanders had been far too timid. Such frictions could have existed only by virtue of West Pointers' indispensable old army expertise, which had allowed McClellanite West Pointers to monopolize the leadership cadre of the Union's most important field army in the face of severe dissatisfaction among civilian political leaders.[6]

For all the high-quality scholarship that historians and commentators have lavished upon the American Civil War, the origins and workings of the military machinery that undergird the sectional conflict's armies remain imperfectly understood. How does one keep a field army supplied with the most basic of necessities? How does one move troops from one point to another under conditions of extreme stress, much less take an enemy position by storm? How does one train troops to use their weapons at a high-enough level of competence that they are a greater threat to their enemies than their comrades?[7] The guardians of the old army had a better idea of how to answer these sorts of basic questions than any other coherent group of Civil War Americans, but, perhaps most importantly, they knew from their time in the regular army that pious bromides to the inherent superiority of the citizen-soldier could not provide adequate answers. Their actual professional expertise, measured by the same European standards that the old army used as professional models, had more than its fair share of inadequacies, but their simple recognition of the practical importance of specialized military knowledge set them apart from their fellow countrymen.

We cannot understand this expertise without also comprehending the American profession of arms' long-standing roots in both American and European military practice, stretching back as far as the colonial period but most especially to the creation of a professional regular army in the United States after the War of 1812. These methods manifested themselves concretely in drill manuals, tactical review boards, ordnance department treatises on military equipment, and American officers' official missions to Europe. As a provincial army far removed from the foci of the Western art of war in Europe, the American profession of arms drew from Old World, and especially French, models and precedents. American soldiers in the Civil War carried muskets using a modified version of the minié bullet, named for its French inventor; marched in step to tactical manuals adapted from French drill regulations; and wore a visored cap, the kepi, of Gallic origin.

Even military historians of the Civil War have neglected to some degree these sorts of questions. The recent flood of Civil War battle studies, many prodigiously researched and admirably well written, has produced excellent empirical accounts of the ebb and flow of individual battles, but they have not cast as much light on other important questions regarding the war's military history. There is some truth to one academic's jibe — albeit one qualified by a real respect for the empirical strengths of tactical history — that much Civil War battle history should be likened to "the blood-and-guts equivalent of a Harlequin romance novel," but a better literary analogy would be the lengthy battle passages of Homer's *Iliad*.[8] Indeed, the continued popularity of biographies of Civil War generals fits the same heroic genre of history.

At base, in short, many battle studies and generals' biographies center around the memorialization of brave men and brave deeds. If one considers the physical experience of combat to be the most important or instructive aspect of the Civil War, then chronicling the exact movements of single regiments on a battlefield takes on a profound importance in and of itself. If it is in a field army commander's crucible of character where we find the most profound lessons of the war, then the Civil War general's biography is the genre of choice. These issues set apart the well-researched and well-written battle study from the Harlequin romance novel; the former concerns life, death, and violence among actual human beings who once walked the earth.[9]

A different sort of question exercises this study, however: how did the Union emerge triumphant and the Confederacy lose its struggle for independence?[10] Furthermore, this issue has implications for the question of *why* the Union emerged victorious. If we answered the question of why the North won without paying attention to the question of how each assumed cause actually brought about that result, it would be all too easy to assume a predetermined certainty for the final outcome. We could then ascribe that certain outcome to any one of a whole range of factors, from the Union's larger material resources to cultural peculiarities in the American South, without taking care to measure those assumptions against actual empirical evidence. Furthermore, focusing on the question of *how* forces us to understand the American Civil War on its own terms and not allow the conflict to become a battlefield proxy for later controversies.

Indeed, while popular military historians have generally focused on tactical history to the exclusion of other types of historical questions, the smaller community of Civil War military history based in the academy has suffered in many ways from the opposite problem of focusing too heavily on the Civil War's connections to World War I. Much of this scholarship, owing to the lasting influence of two British soldier-scholars, B. H. Liddell Hart and J. F. C. Fuller, hoped to find in the Civil War solutions to the First World War's problem of tactical stalemate, the origins of "total war," and larger lessons on technological change in warfare. Both also committed themselves to the primacy of the entrenched defensive during the Civil War. Liddell Hart cited the rifle-musket as making frontal attacks "an almost hopeless venture," while Fuller declared at one point that "in 1861–5 the rifle bullet was the lord of the battlefield as was the machine-gun bullet in 1914–18."[11] Both also saw in the Civil War the widespread mobilization of and attack on a nation's material and psychological resources that marked twentieth-century total war. Liddell Hart praised Sherman not only for finding a mobile solution to the indecisive tactical stalemate created by entrenchments and the rifle-musket but also for recognizing during his campaigns in Georgia and South Carolina "the essential influence of economic and psychological factors upon the course of such a [modern] war." Fuller emphasized the Civil War's relationship to the Industrial Revolution, calling it a "war born of steam-power, which changed not only the historical structure of nations but the traditional structure of armies. To-day we are faced by many similar changes; for it may be said without fear of contradiction that we are now living in the throes of the second industrial revolution, a most powerful sequel which is daily adding to the might of coal and steam the might of oil and electricity."[12]

Although an insistent concern over the transnational origins of the world wars stands to reason, it can and has imposed upon the American Civil War a frame of reference far removed from the actual conflict between 1861 and 1865. An international and broad-brush perspective toward the sectional conflict can cause as many distortions as the narrowest tactical history. For example, a recent wave of revisionist scholarship has challenged the long-standing consensus that the combination of rifle-muskets and hasty entrenchments dramatically increased the fighting power of soldiers fighting on the tactical defensive in a manner that foreshadowed the trench warfare of the western front. Much of the revisionist school focuses on engagement ranges for Civil War battles. If the revisionists are correct that most Civil War troops withheld their fire until attacking troops approached within 125 yards or less because of a combination of terrain limitations and tactical preference, then the 300-yard range of the new infantry arms (roughly treble that of smoothbore muskets) could have only limited effects on actual practice during the war.

The whole question of engagement ranges is something of a canard, however, and reflects an undue emphasis on debating the Civil War's similarities or lack thereof to World War I trench warfare, and whether the rifle-musket's increased range foreshadowed the machine gun. Even at a hundred yards, modern tests show that smoothbore shots would not regularly fall in a group size less than 3 feet across, compared to a 10.25-inch group size for a Model 1863 Springfield rifle-musket. At such a range, the smoothbore musket had a tolerable chance at hitting a soldier in a close-order line of battle, but it could not suffice for sniping and sharp-shooting. In the war's last year, many Civil War operations became marked by this sort of aimed fire among troops manning static trenches, and the improved accuracy of rifle-muskets, especially in those cases where the trench lines stood in close proximity, would have had a considerable impact. Factors rooted in the Civil War's own specific circumstances had a far greater influence on the war's conduct than raw technological factors, or the implications of a war fought half a century later.[13]

We can best understand the war on its own terms and explain its progress and development if we avoid linking the American conflict, whether by analogy or by claims for causation, to conflicts that occurred long after Appomattox. Carefully considered comparisons with later military conflicts may have some value, but simple chronology dictates that only events and processes that occurred before 1861 could have a real causal effect on the American conflict. For example, instead of comparing the Civil War to trench warfare during the First World War or the use of atomic weapons on Japan, it would be more fruitful to look at the Mexican War, which not only occurred fifteen years before the Civil War but also shared many of the same commanders and participants.

Indeed, historians have neglected tactical developments both before and after the Mexican War. Pre—Mexican War tactics have received almost no scholarly treatment, while the two leading historians of Civil War minor tactics, Perry D. Jamieson and Grady McWhiney, give too much weight to the adoption of the rifle-musket in explaining the increased movement rates and skirmishing of the new U.S. Army infantry tactics of the 1850s. Brent Nosworthy's more recent treatment ignores the important influence of a strong tradition of light infantry tactics in the American service that preexisted the Mexican War by several decades.[14] These authors also neglect the most important and most deceptively obvious aspect of the old army's tactical manuals: their simple existence. Whatever their merits or lack thereof, the old army had the only usable system of tactics in both contending sections at the outbreak of war, which more than anything else made them indispensable to the formation of the Union and Confederate armies. The brilliant successes of American arms during the Mexican War, made possible by a comprehensive program of professionalization between the end of the War of 1812 in 1814 and the outbreak of war in 1845, highlights the importance of basic military competence. In contrast, decidedly unprofessional U.S. forces had performed extremely poorly during the opening campaigns of the War of 1812.

Technology does have an influence on soldiers' morale, training, and cohesion, as does an individual soldier's preexisting social background and ideological beliefs; however, in wartime, military organizations themselves have a profound effect on the reactions and responses of soldiers in battle. Not only must a Civil War army's bureaucratic organization physically sustain an army in the field; it also must prepare and condition a soldier for battle with various forms of drill, depending on the particular unit. Early in the war, both Union and Confederate armies struggled to acquire a basic level of competence, but what saved both armies from disaster were their roughly equivalent levels of ineptitude and equally long processes of learning. Over time, both armies learned their business, but their identical starting points and their similar leadership cadres prevented either army from acquiring a decisive advantage over the other in terms of military competence.

This equilibrium of competence frequently stymied Civil War generals' efforts to destroy their opponents in climactic and Napoleonic battles of annihilation. Such decisive decisions required a marked superiority in resources or military ability that usually did not exist, with the possible exception of the Confederate Army of Tennessee's two crushing defeats at Franklin and Nashville late in the war. This equilibrium had a larger role in making Civil War battles "indecisive" than the technological imperatives of the rifle-musket paired with entrenchments. Furthermore, a close examination of individual battles shows that many frontal assaults failed to carry a position more from a failure of coordination among an army's senior officers than from the technical capabilities of the rifle-musket.[15] Indeed, the almost entirely unplanned and spontaneous attack on Missionary Ridge by Federal troops, four months after the supposedly absolute vindication of defensive tactics at Gettysburg in July 1863, succeeded because of the demoralized state of the defending Confederates, muddled orders, and poor engineering.

The human and organizational factors that created the preconditions for a long, grinding war, with heavy casualties on both sides, had profound implications for both sections' overall war efforts. In the North, the war's prolongation strengthened the hands of those opposed to slavery, making emancipation a politically plausible war measure, which ironically enough would not have been the case if the Union had won a short and decisive victory. In the Confederacy, the old army predilections of its army's generals helped foreclose any recourse to a widespread and calculated strategy of insurgency. While guerrillas did have a significant effect on Federal military operations, the Confederate leadership always intended to win the war along nation-state lines, with regularly organized armies that could obtain European recognition. The common old army origins of both sectional hosts not only prolonged but also limited Civil War violence—it laid the preconditions for the relative indecisiveness of Civil War battle, while doing much to limit that violence to an arena defined by Western nation-state notions of armies, uniforms, and battles. For that reason, among others, we ignore the old army at our own peril.

CHAPTER ONE

Colonials, Continentals, and Federals

The Origins of American Military Professionalism

★ ★ ★

The crucial formative years of the antebellum old army occurred in the twenty or so years after the end of the War of 1812 in 1815 — when Sylvanus Thayer carved into the high cliffs of West Point a military academy for posterity, when a then nationalist John C. Calhoun pushed through organizational forms that persisted for nearly a century, and when a cluster of professionally minded officers hardened by the War of 1812 used their senior command positions to preserve and advance the cause of "military science." These reformers set out to prevent a recurrence of the poor showing American arms exhibited during the first campaigns of the War of 1812. They had to struggle against a strong streak of antimilitarism in Anglo-American political culture and decades of precedent. In the end, their efforts would have to face the practical test of battle during the Mexican War.[1] That conflict would vindicate the virtues of military professionalism and give the old army the institutional strength and monopoly of expertise it would carry into the Civil War.

The brilliant military successes of American arms in the Mexican War, whatever one thinks of the war's moral significance, testifies most powerfully to the martial achievements of the old army's fathers. While the United States had floundered in the first years of the War of 1812, American troops won brilliant victories in the war with Mexico from the moment of its outbreak and conquered a continent-wide dominion in the process. The American victory had many causes, of course, but the presence of a hard core of regulars able and willing to convert the mere potential of military success into substantive fact played an important role.

Nevertheless, the old army that won the Mexican War and provided the institutional bedrock for both American armies during the Civil War could make no claims to perfection: its major flaws included an absence of large-unit training; a sometimes overly provincial attitude toward European, especially French, practice; and a conception of staff work so focused on logistics and financial accountability that it neglected those vital

areas of military organization which allow the different pieces of an army to maneuver and fight together in situations of extreme stress. A sometimes self-serving satisfaction with this organizational status quo and the unwillingness of Congress to provide larger amounts of material support caused the old army to bear these flaws throughout the rest of the antebellum period and thus into the Civil War. If we compare its competence to previous American armies and its contemporary rivals, however, the old army proved more than adequate.

This achievement impresses us all the more because there was nothing predetermined about the army's post–War of 1812 reforms. Although the militia continued to decline into decrepitude, the citizen-soldier ideal of Anglo-American republicanism had ancient roots in even more ancient hills, irrespective of the War of 1812. Most Americans saw Jackson's victory at New Orleans where militiamen defeated British regulars as yet another vindication of the citizen-soldier ideal (ignoring the early campaigns on the northern frontier and the capture of the national capital), and few would have comprehended their professional soldiery's preoccupation with European practice and method. Some remained openly hostile to professionalism — West Point in this period had to weather periodic charges of aristocratic privilege. In this sometimes-hostile environment, Congress restricted the army's size, so that in 1845, on the eve of the Mexican War, the old army numbered barely 8,509 men (826 officers and 7,683 enlisted men). Poor pay and difficult conditions resulted in severe rates of desertion, reaching as high as more than half of the year's enlistments in 1826. It is something of a wonder that Calhoun and the first generation of American military professionals had as much as success as they did.[2]

Their achievements did not spring self-begotten out of the humiliations of Bladensburg and Washington's fall to the British in 1814, however. The founders of the Continental army also had to contend with the powerful strain of antimilitarism in Anglo-American culture, which had frustrated earlier attempts at reform. The precedents the revolutionary generation set had a special and disproportionate influence because of the prestige they later held in American political culture and practice. Indeed, George Washington and Alexander Hamilton had established in their lifetimes the basic parameters for American military policy and thought throughout the nineteenth century: the primacy of civilian control, a dual military system based on a small core of regulars and a larger reserve of citizen-soldiers organized under federal supervision, a well-articulated system of military education, and an officer-heavy regular army designed to expand quickly in wartime. Not all of these ideas always found fruition, but among the nineteenth-century makers of American military policy, these ideas had tremendous influence, whatever specific measures different individuals endorsed or condemned.[3]

The nascent professionalism of Washington and Hamilton survived an ingrained Anglo-American suspicion of standing armies because of the inherent inadequacies of the militia system. First of all, the militia ideal of a citizen-soldier who would throw back any and all sorts of enemies in order to return immediately to the bosom of civilian society could not obtain the state-oriented objectives of American military policy from the Revolution onward. The political goals of all American wars between the Revolution and the Civil War included the vindication of one combatant's sovereign state control. That control took various forms, including but not limited to the founding of an independent American nation, the protection of national authority against foreign and domestic enemies, the conquest of large portions of Mexico, the Confederacy's vindication of its own existence, and the pacification of sometimes-hostile Indian peoples. In all these different circumstances, a professional military's institutional solidity proved indispensable. American governments wished to govern and control their conquests; the tendency of guerrillas and insurgents to slip out of the control of political elites and their inability to challenge directly massed regular forces made them inadequate tools for American nation-states.[4]

The militia's continuous decline also made the presence of some sort of standing army all but compulsory. In the more settled areas of British North America, citizens became increasingly reluctant to attend the muster days that kept the militia's training and competence at acceptable levels. Even aside from this organizational decline, the militia had always proved unsuitable for dealing with campaigns waged at any appreciable distance from the yeomanry's home communities, a problem with citizen-soldiers since at least the time of ancient Greece and Rome. The militia might still suffice for local defense forces, but in large-scale conflicts like the great North American wars for empire of the eighteenth century, British regulars had proved indispensable. In any conflict that might require a siege, expertise in artillery, or even the simple ability to maintain troops in the field over a long period of time, regulars would have to be available.

COLONIALS, CONTINENTALS, AND FEDERALS

Various problems with the militia became self-evident as early as Washington's siege of British-held Boston in 1775 and 1776. After their success at Lexington and Concord, New Englanders had flocked to Boston to invest the city. Unfortunately, sieges take time, and militiamen have homes to return to and cannot stay in the field indefinitely, so Washington found his army slowly melting away. In order to restore the situation, the Continental Congress created a Continental army in 1775, which served as an ersatz regular army. Both the militia and the Continentals played their part in defeating the British. Irregulars had their days of glory at Saratoga and in the much more partisan-driven southern campaigns, but even in the southern colonies, the war's final decisive blow came at the hands of a force composed of Continentals, French regulars, and a substantial French fleet during a siege operation at Yorktown.[5]

Conscious, perhaps overly so, of their own expertise, the officers of the Continental army became increasingly disenchanted during the war with both the failings of the militia and the perpetual suspicion they labored under from a political leadership openly hostile to standing armies. In fact, one of the many grievances of those Americans who revolted against the crown was the increasing use of British regulars in North America. Instead of the hated regulars, self-described "patriots" put their trust in a militia of citizen-soldiers — sturdy yeomen who would leave their plows, defeat overdrilled professionals with the flexible virtue of free men, and return to their farms after the danger had passed.[6] Resentful of civilian suspicions, the first American professionals in the Continental army and their later heirs defined themselves as much in opposition to the American militiaman as in concordance with European models of officership.

Furthermore, Continental army officers had substantive material grievances with the mismanagement of the Continental Congress. The Job-like winters of 1777–78 at Valley Forge and 1779–80 at Jockey Hollow near Morristown, where civilian ineptitude and indifference caused much of the suffering, alienated both officers and enlisted men. The gentlemen-officers of the Continentals possessed too many social airs to make common cause with their men in opposition to the Congress, but the rank and file of several state lines did participate in a few short-lived mutinies. In early 1783 some officers staged a pseudo-revolt of their own, the "Newburgh Conspiracy," in which they hoped to use scarcely veiled threats of coercion to compel Congress to approve the half-pay pensions most Continental officers saw as their just reward. Washington, by the sheer force of his personality and influence, quashed the movement and set a long-lived American precedent for civilian control of the military.[7]

With the advent of peace in 1783, and the Newburgh crisis resolved, the new nation also needed a new peacetime military policy. Washington, in perhaps the most important early state paper on American military policy, the famous "Sentiments on a Peace Establishment," laid out in 1783 many of the driving themes of American military policy and practice until the Civil War. Washington called for a small regular army to guard the frontiers against both the Indians and European powers, a well-organized and reformed militia to be used in time of war, a system of arsenals, and some provision for military education, especially with regard to engineering and artillery. Washington's conception of "a well organized Militia" never achieved fruition, although the federalized volunteers of the Mexican and Civil wars kept the citizen-soldier tradition alive.[8] The other three elements of Washington's proposals did eventually become a part of American military practice, however.

In the short term, Washington's ideas came to naught, despite similar proposals from Frederick William, Baron von Steuben, and Alexander Hamilton. The Indians on the frontier remained relatively quiescent, and the early Confederation government disbanded the Continental army in 1784, leaving eighty men at West Point to guard military stores.[9] The specter of impending anarchy raised by Shays's Rebellion in 1786 then helped spur on the movement that would result in the creation of the federal constitution. This new constitution increased the power of the central national government, and Congress received explicit authority to establish a navy and standing army, with the president as commander in chief. Furthermore, the federal government also had the authority to suppress some internal dissent.

Nevertheless, the new federal Congress showed no urgency in using its new constitutional powers to raise a standing army, and Secretary of War Henry Knox's attempt to institute a program of militia regularization and training under federal supervision and control proved almost wholly futile. Congress authorized a standing army of 1,216 men in 1790, but the measures proved inadequate, and in 1791 a small force of American troops on the Northwest frontier suffered a humiliating defeat (900 casualties out of 1,400 men) at the hands of Indians. The catastrophe compelled Congress to increase the army's size under Anthony Wayne, whom Washington recalled from civilian life to restore the young nation's military fortunes. Wayne proved up to the task and vindicated his regulars with the victory at Fallen Timbers in the summer of 1794.[10]

Increasing tensions with France during the Quasi-War of the late 1790s gave a further impetus to the military ambitions of the new Federalist Party. Many of the Federalist reforms proved stillborn in the end, but Hamilton developed two ideas that would be influential among American professionals until the Civil War and beyond: the expansible army concept and a system of military education that included both a basic school for all officers and specialized schools of application for individual branches.[11] The expansible army called for a top-heavy organization of officers and sergeants that would allow an army to "expand" in wartime by simply adding enlisted men to existing companies. Its advocates believed that the new wartime recruits could be quickly and efficiently integrated into the existing units under the command of already-seasoned leaders.

Hamilton's ideas on military education went hand in hand with this cadre system: "Since it is agreed, that we are not to keep on foot numerous forces instructed and disciplined, military science in its various branches ought to be cultivated, with peculiar care, in proper Nurseries; So that there may Always exist a sufficient body of it ready to be imparted and diffused, and a competent number of persons qualified to act as instructors to the additional troops, which events may successively require to be raised." Hamilton proposed a two-year fundamental school, which all officers were to attend, and separate artillery-engineering, infantry, cavalry, and naval branch schools.[12] The curriculum Thayer later established at West Point ended up making most officers go through what was essentially a four-year engineering school, but at times throughout the antebellum period the War Department would attempt to constitute branch schools of practice for artillery, infantry, and cavalry.

Hamilton's belief that "an army is in many respect a machine; of which the displacement of any of the organs, if permitted to continue, injures its symmetry and energy and leads to disorder and weakness" represented in brief the organizational ideal of so many of these early American professionals.[13] This professional aspiration, with its appeals to regularity, standardization, and a conception of military science grounded in the technical skills of engineering and artillery, would survive the deaths of Washington, Hamilton, and the Federalist Party. Their legacy lived on, because, whatever its flaws, only a regular army could defend the American nation-state. Indeed, in spite of their hostility toward standing armies, the Jeffersonians allowed a small regular army to survive their electoral triumph in 1800 and even authorized the establishment of a military academy at West Point in 1802.

Washington had commented in his "Sentiments on Peace Establishment" that a military academy was needed to preserve military and engineering expertise, "unless we intend to let the Science become extinct [in the new republic], and to depend entirely upon the Foreigners for their friendly aid, if ever we should again be involved in Hostility." The Continentals themselves had made a feeble start at military education during the Revolution. The garrison at the strategic post of West Point on the Hudson River had begun in 1778 as an informal military engineering school under the direction of French or French-trained officers, in conjunction with a Corps of Invalids (soldiers unfit for field service) responsible for training duties. Like so many of the other measures first proposed by Washington, and later championed by Hamilton, Congress proved unenthusiastic about military education even during the high tide of Federalist power. It did, however, authorize in effect a school for artillerists and engineers in 1794 at West Point as tensions with Europe increased.[14]

This shaky institution stumbled along in neglect and disorganization until Jefferson's authorizing legislation of 1802. The first superintendent of the new academy, Lt. Col. Jonathan Williams, was not another foreign-trained expert, but a noted American authority on science and engineering. However, he still set out to create an American version of the French "Officieurs du Génie" at the infant academy. It was left to Williams's students, especially Thayer, to put the academy on a solid footing after the War of 1812, but Williams himself had a not insignificant influence on the academy's later development. For better or for worse, he bequeathed the academy a conception of engineering far more grandiose than the highly technical set of skills we now associate with the subject; in his words, "The Science of an Engineer is applicable to almost every profession in Life; it is highly essential in some and injurious to none." Foreshadowing the scientific and Francophilic cast of mind that dominated West Point's curriculum until the Civil War, Williams wrote Maj. Decius Wadsworth: "Our guiding star . . . is not a little mathematical School, but a great national establishment to turn out characters which in the course of time shall equal any in Europe. To be merely an *Engineer*, an inventor, a maker or director of Engines is one thing, but to be an Officeur *du Genie* is another. I do not know how it happened but I cannot find any full English Idea to what the French give to the profession. We must always have it in view that our Officers are to be men of Science."[15]

And as befits men of science in this period, Williams even formed a scientific organization, the United States Military Philosophical Society, to go hand in hand with the military academy. Foreshadowing future tensions over the scientific cast of West Point's curriculum under the Thayer system, Timothy Pickering, an old Federalist supporter of military education in general, declined membership in Williams's society and instead called for more practical military training. Nevertheless, many serving officers saw the organization in a favorable light and hoped to become members during the society's heyday between 1805 and 1810 under Williams's personal tutelage. Although the group could never mobilize political support for a true national university as Williams had hoped, the society did conduct experiments to evaluate weapons technology; serve as a forum for the presentation of papers on military topics, usually of a technical sort; and give professional advice to the government on various proposals related to military engineering.[16] Later in the antebellum period, the various permutations of the Ordnance Department (staffed mostly by West Pointers) conducted practical testing and experimentation on a more regular basis, but West Point would remain a center of discussion for tactical reforms, with the battalion of cadets performing proposed drill movements for tactical review boards.

The hostility of Secretary of War William Eustis doomed Williams's attempts to establish the young academy on a firmer basis, however, and the War of 1812 proved an even more serious distraction. The ineptitude of the early American war effort dearly repaid the government for its general indifference and occasional hostility toward a competent American military establishment. In the campaigns of 1812 along the Canadian border, Brig. Gen. William Hull's expedition in the Northwest surrendered to the British at Detroit in mid-August 1812, the British repulsed Maj. Gen. Stephen Van Rensselaer's thrust against Queenston on the Niagara front in the late autumn, and Maj. Gen. Henry Dearborn's strike against Montreal also stalled. In both of the latter campaigns, militia forces had helped seal American defeats by refusing to cross the border. British forces captured Lt. Col. Winfield Scott, in fact, partly because of the citizen-soldiery's refusal to reinforce him during the Queenston campaign.[17] Worse yet, none of these miscues matched the rout of American forces defending Washington at Bladensburg and the capital's subsequent fall in 1814.

Scott and a clutch of aggressive young officers—including Maj. Gen. Jacob Brown, Bvt. Maj. Gen. Edmund P. Gaines, Bvt. Maj. Gen. Alexander Macomb, and Maj. Thomas S. Jesup—finally restored the country's military fortunes in 1814 and helped implement major professional reforms after the war's end. Jesup, himself a self-described student of French and British tactics, worked well under the like-minded Scott, who used European methods at a camp of instruction for Brown's Left Division in Buffalo during the spring of 1814. That training program laid the foundation for success at Chippewa and Lundy's Lane in 1814, which showed that properly trained American troops could match European regulars volley for volley in Old World fashion, and served afterward as a long-standing point of inspiration for the regulars.[18]

Not only did the new generation of professional regular army officers adopt the infantry tactics of their European counterparts, but it also imbibed the habits and customs of a European profession of arms still strongly rooted in aristocratic habits and traditions. Pretensions to gentility affected by the officers of the old army would only cause further friction with a republican America poised on the verge of the Jacksonian revolution. In contrast to his desertion by the militia while occupying hostile territory in Queenston in 1812, Scott fondly remembered his British captors and contrasted their gentlemanly treatment of him to what he remembered as the barbaric treachery of several Indian allies of the British. This preference for Western nation-state adversaries, as opposed to Indian fighting, would mark the regular army throughout the century. In another example of friendly relations with opposing British officers, Jesup and Phinias Riall, a British general, both recuperated from wounds received at Lundy's Lane in the same house in Buffalo, where Riall presented Jesup with his own sword to replace Jesup's damaged sidearm.[19]

After the War of 1812, the U.S. Army also began to send its officers to Europe to acquire professional military knowledge for use at home, although many American officers became increasingly resentful of any use of foreign-born officers that cast doubt on their own qualifications. Nevertheless, most still saw Europe as the seat of military science and continuously compared themselves to the professional standards of the Old World. Indeed, Simon Bernard, a Frenchman, played a major role in the construction of American seacoast fortifications after the War of 1812 until his return to France in 1830.[20]

In the spring of 1815, Chief Engineer Joseph G. Swift ordered two West Point graduates, Capt. Sylvanus Thayer and Lt. Col. William McRee, to travel to Europe for the purpose of "an 'examination of the military establishments,' 'Fortifications,' 'Schools,' 'Work-shops,' and Libraries in France, Germany & England—particularly the first and last named nations, — to collect Books, Maps and Instruments." Their selection for this mission represented a high privilege and responsibility; Thayer received both a brevet rank and extra compensation for the assignment. It was no coincidence that both of these officers were engineers, because the secretary of war's orders included special reference to seacoast fortifications. The books and military material the mission would acquire were slated for the library of the now more established if still internally riven military academy at West Point.[21]

Thayer spent much of his time visiting cultural sites that any well-bred gentleman should be familiar with. In a telling passage from his report to Swift on October 10, Thayer, reflecting both his long-standing admiration for Napoleon and his cultured gentility, spent as much time condemning the allies for their mistreatment of French cultural treasures as he did bemoaning the closure of French military institutions, which he could no longer visit. Swift, reflecting the aristocratic flavor of even the "scientific" corps of engineers, had also previously written Thayer that "you must have the means of travelling as a gentleman, & of seeing the best company." The international aristocracy Thayer traveled among gave an informal and personalized air to his professional mission. This allowed Thayer to confer with various French authorities on military engineering despite the allied closures of all military schools. Thayer also later learned from French officers in the spring of 1817, after the political situation had calmed and military schools reopened, that he and McRee could still visit various fortifications despite the government's refusal to give official permission.[22]

In a more strictly professional vein, Thayer also hoped to acquire models and plans giving specific instructions on how to build various objects, including but not limited to roofs, domes, and artillery pieces. The mission acquired around a thousand volumes of military writings, many of which were pamphlets bound together by workmen in Paris. Despite the impressive effort involved, both officers admitted that they may have made unnecessary purchases because they could not always remember what the academy library already possessed. The fact that neither held a simple list of what the library already owned hardly speaks well of the academy's institutional competence.[23]

Indeed, McRee frankly reported that "among the military books there must inevitably be found a considerable portion of trash. We were indeed too little acquainted with them to determine from our own knowledge their individual worth. Their general character or that of the author was, in most cases, the only rule by which we could regulate our choice." The two did seem to do well enough, though, and showed enough expertise to collect material on the eighteenth-century debates over artillery and tactics in the French army that had proved so important during the Napoleonic Wars and afterward. The two officers thus showed a healthy interest in nonengineering subjects, which was also reflected in the acquisition of large numbers of maps of European theaters of war. Going beyond the simple acquisition of material, Thayer even took up the study of German. McRee himself may have summed up the mission's competence best when he remarked that "upon the whole, we are too little pleased with our work to ask for it, entire approbation. — But, we have one consolation in common with all that have no excuse. . . . We *might* have done worse."

McRee also showed a healthy independence of mind with regard to French military prestige that not all his antebellum successors shared. He aimed to collect military writings "upon these subjects that had formerly excited great interest and continued to divide opinions" in order "to have all the evidence upon questions that concern us, and that *we shall have to decide on in our turn*." Indeed, McRee seemed less impressed with France after his visit, referring to his "Blunted Curiosity" for visiting military installations and making the pithy remark that "the pumpkins do not grow one whit bigger in France, than at home." It is unsurprising that McRee eventually resigned from the engineers in protest at the influence of the Frenchman Simon Bernard on the Fortifications Board.[24]

Nevertheless, McRee probably would not have made any substantive objection to Thayer's comment as superintendent that the French language "may be considered as the sole repository of Military science." And Thayer's admiration of the French would certainly have met no dissent from Capt. James Renwick of the Corps of Topographical Engineers, whom Swift sent to England in 1815 to acquire books and instruments for the academy.[25] Swift himself exhibited his Francophilia by ordering the translation into English of various texts produced and used at the École Polytechnique in 1816.

In the same year, Swift hired Claudius Crozet, an alumnus of the same distinguished French school, to teach engineering at West Point, and Crozet promised to use the same methods as his own teachers at the Polytechnique. He and three other Frenchmen sat on a faculty composed of seven members. Crozet clashed with Thayer's strong (some would say imperious) hand at the military academy and left in 1823, but he helped establish the engineering department that Dennis Hart Mahan would eventually convert into the premier academic department at the academy. The Frenchman later played an important role in the founding of the Virginia Military Institute, establishing one of many links between West Point and the most prominent state military school in the country.[26] In the immediate postwar period, military expertise traveled across the Atlantic in all forms—books, devices, and individuals.

That expertise also traveled informally, in addition to "official" missions like that of Thayer and McRee. Winfield Scott's time in Europe from 1815 to 1816 included most of the distinguishing characteristics of informal and unofficial visits by American officers to Europe during the antebellum period. Scott's trip was more akin to a genteel American's grand European tour (i.e., a vacation for the cultured) than Thayer's official mission. Scott had originally planned to go as far as Russia to visit its military establishment, and he did in fact review the various national armies of the Grand Alliance against Napoleon, report profitable professional contacts with Prussian colleagues to the War Department, and make other visits to consult with European officers and visit various military posts. Nevertheless, much of his European tour involved "dipping a little into society—French, Dutch, German, and Italian, as well as English and Scotch—when returning homeward;—visiting theaters and libraries; glancing at the wonders of architecture, sculpture, and painting;—seeing a little of the interior of Oxford and Cambridge, and paying devotion to many scenes of historic fame."[27] Jacksonians had a point when they equated professional officers with Old World aristocracy.

Scott, like Thayer, had a very negative view of the allied occupation, but Francophile officers could still appreciate the charged atmosphere of postwar Paris. Even Renwick, the aforementioned topographical engineer and admirer of French military science, found the prospect of visiting Paris under allied occupation a heady idea—describing the scene he hoped to find as "a spectacle in a military point of view which can never perhaps again be witnessed such noble armies with such complete equipment." Whatever their opinions of Napoleon the man, most American officers of the antebellum period held a certain awe for the epic sweep of the Napoleonic Wars and would have agreed with Renwick's observation: "How the terrific splendor of the wars of the last 15 years has paled the lustre of all former European battles."[28]

While in Europe, Scott acquired large numbers of European books on army administration, which he then used to help compile his *General Regulations* between 1818 and 1821. Scott claimed to have made a comprehensive review of European military books on the topic, and he cited the British and French regulations as major influences. Scott did not neglect previous American practice, either official or unofficial—for example, in his instructions on laying out the camp for a division of artillery, he followed the instructions given in an early West Point textbook—but the manual sought a new level of organizational regularity in the American army. To this end, Scott included regulations for all the staff bureaus and for the military academy in his volume. Scott also submitted the regulations to fellow officers for comment.[29]

American officers fully participated in a larger European profession of arms and drew on Old World practice for the New World army they were trying to create. The old army of the New World owed much of its organizational and bureaucratic patterns to British influence, while American tactical doctrine, the subject of the following chapter, modeled itself along French lines, with various changes to match American conditions. Not only did the French military model benefit from the reflected glories of Napoleon, but it could also call on the old Franco-American alliance from the Revolution.[30]

Although U.S. Army officers may have been part of an international fraternity of arms, they were still Americans. While in Paris, Scott arranged for a dinner to celebrate the anniversary of Jackson's victory at New Orleans in reply to a British celebration on the anniversary of Washington's capture during the late war. Scott also wrote home to Secretary of State James Monroe that "indeed it is in Europe, that a citizen of the U.S., learns, by comparison, to place the highest value on his own country & government." Renwick also expressed nationalist sentiments while overseas. He reported with pride from England in 1815 that the British "very kindly admit that we are worthy to descend from them" and that American naval exploits had supposedly gained renown in Europe. Renwick's comments about the army's performance during the War of 1812—"we certainly have every reason to be proud of many parts of our war however unadvisedly & without proper preparation it may have been begun"—reflected regular army officers' pride in their accomplishments on fields like Chippewa, their shame for disasters like Bladensburg, and their determination to prevent such catastrophes in the next war. A year later, while in London, he echoed Scott with the comment that "I find I have grown a much better American since I have been abroad than even the war made me" and declared high hopes of American achievements one day surpassing the stodgy Old World.[31]

COLONIALS, CONTINENTALS, AND FEDERALS

Nevertheless, Europe still stood as the primary frame of reference for many American professionals, and it is no surprise that Thayer consciously modeled West Point's instructional methods on the teaching methods used at the École Polytechnique. Reflecting both his own background as an engineer and the close association Washington and Hamilton had made between military education and the more technical branches of the military art, Thayer created a curriculum with a strong emphasis on science and engineering. He declared that "a knowledge of general history, ethics [&c.] can be equally well acquired after leaving the institution but the reverse is the case with Philosophy, Engineering, Topography [&c.] which require the aid of instruments, apparatus & instructors."[32]

Some officers, however, criticized the Thayer system for not devoting enough time to practical military training. In 1822 Alexander Macomb, future commanding general of the army, gently admonished Thayer that "you are aware that the character of the institution is Military and not philosophical, and while the several branches of the sciences, which are taught at the Academy are deemed highly important and essential in forming Scientific officers, the main object of the institution is to predominate over all others."[33] Thayer stuck by his guns and in the end outlasted his critics.

The Thayer regime went beyond book learning in math and science. It also inculcated certain habits of thought and action, modeled in many ways on Thayer's own conduct as a gentleman officer. The old army did not create a stereotypical social type to which we can reduce all West Pointers—the "fuss-and-feathers" finery of Winfield Scott contrasts sharply with Sylvanus Thayer's severe dignity, after all—but the icy austerity of the Thayer system left every graduate marked in some way, for better or for worse. Thayer's famed punctuality and aloof presence at the annual examinations represented his profession's devotion to rigid ideas of duty, but this went hand in hand with aristocratic gentility. When Thayer's pay was reduced to that of his substantive rank as captain, he complained to Swift that the salary was insufficient "unless he would consent to live in a style which would degrade the station which he holds."[34] Not only did old army officers see themselves as men of "military science"; they also saw themselves as "gentlemen." The contrast between this ethic of scientific aristocracy and a more popular egalitarian ethos would help cause great friction between regular army officers and the American societies they were obligated to serve.

Thayer's revitalized academy rapidly became the heart and soul of an old army determined to redeem itself from the early humiliations of the War of 1812. The older generation of officers who had earned its spurs in that war gave the academy's graduates its full support. Winfield Scott, a nongraduate, became something of a fixture at the academy during the summer, and his tomb stands in the post cemetery. Even after Thayer's resignation in 1833 to protest President Andrew Jackson's differing views on cadet discipline, his influence lived on in the form of his student successors, who continued to administer the academy in the spirit of the "Father of the Military Academy." Using one measure of West Point's importance to the old army, West Point graduates' proportion of commissions in the army went from 15 percent in 1817 to 64 percent in 1830. West Point, among other reforms, also increased the institutional solidity of the army as a whole. The median career length of officers rose to twenty-two years in 1830 from ten in 1797.[35]

The spirit of "military science" in the postwar army did not confine itself to West Point, however. Many civilians had also recognized the shortcomings of American military organization during the War of 1812 and hoped to prevent the same problems from recurring. Secretary of War William H. Crawford at the end of 1815 asked Congress to maintain the army's staff organization on a war footing, because "the experience of the two first campaigns of the last war . . . has incontestably established not only the expediency, but the necessity of giving to the military establishment, in time of peace, the organization which it must have to render it efficient in a state of war." Reflecting the early prominence of the scientific branches in the American service and the germination of Hamilton's idea of an expansible army, Crawford also proposed that the artillery, engineer, and ordnance branches be increased, "considering the qualifications of the officers of that corps, and the great utility which may be derived from transferring them into the line of the army, when a sudden augmentation of the military establishment should become necessary at the approach of war." The rush of demobilization obscured these proposals, however, until the forceful ability of new secretary of war John C. Calhoun brought some of them to pass. Under Calhoun's tenure, Thayer received enough authority to push through his institutional reforms at West Point, the expansible army plan was fully fleshed out in intellectual terms if still unfulfilled in practice, and army administration received a "method, order, and economy" it had not previously possessed.[36]

Connected to Calhoun's philosophy of "method, order, and economy" was Winfield Scott's creation of the Army Regulations of 1821. This important organizational document created a full and thorough manual of all sorts of standardized procedures, ranging from camp management to correct paperwork. The old Revolutionary War Blue Book of von Steuben had also included much practical guidance on operations in the field, but Scott's regulations went into far greater detail, while adding explicit bureaucratic forms and procedures nowhere to be found in the Blue Book. For example, Steuben did not include the exact format of preprinted forms. Scott provided copies of the standardized blanks the army was to use; most involved the staff departments, whose specific procedures received much treatment in the new regulations.

Scott's regulations systematically laid out in one convenient volume the procedures of the staff system put in place in the Army Bill of 1818. Indeed, Scott and Quartermaster General Thomas S. Jesup had corresponded with each other regarding the formulation of Scott's Army Regulations and Jesup's own new regulations for the Quartermaster Bureau. Calhoun's General Staff system used a system of independent staff bureaus with a chief based in Washington, and with each bureau's officers acting under the orders of his respective bureau chief as opposed to the line commander at his respective post. Although this system served the interests of administrative efficiency, it also led to resentments among line officers who believed that the independent staff bureaus usurped the authority of field commanders for the sake of trivial paperwork, and this would mar staff-line relations throughout the century.[37]

Among the different bureaus, the duties of the surgeon general, paymaster general, and chief engineer are self-explanatory enough. The Ordnance Department supervised the procurement and manufacture of military weapons and accoutrements, while the Commissary General handled other purchases, except for soldiers' rations, which was the special province of the Subsistence Department. The Quartermaster Department arranged for the transport and distribution of supplies, which included responsibility for the construction of military roads. The quartermasters also managed construction of buildings at inland posts. Under the guidance of the professionally minded Jesup, the Quartermaster Bureau became the most important of the supply departments, gradually absorbing more and more of the Commissary General department's responsibilities until its abolition in 1835. The Quartermaster Bureau would also frequently find itself tasked with duties outside of its original legal authorization during the antebellum period.[38]

Jesup's administrative acumen and prominence in the army—he held a field command in Florida during the Seminole War—helps explain the bureau's increasing importance. Jesup's new regulations in 1818 cited both European and American precedents along with his own experience to increase administrative efficiency and public accountability for private property. Indeed, Jesup served as quartermaster general for forty-two years until 1860, providing an institutional continuity that left an indelible stamp on army administration. In the words of the historian Mark Wilson, "Jesup built and ran a bureaucratic national organization during a time when such a thing was virtually unheard of in American government and business." This organization's relative insulation from the partisan imperatives of the Jacksonian party system and its administrative capacities, which proved capable of exponential expansion during the Civil War, had nothing preordained about it. Furthermore, in large part because the Quartermaster Bureau before the war "was already the best-qualified organization in America to handle complex procurement and logistical problems," old army men maintained a large measure of influence on Federal procurement, supply, and mobilization during the Civil War. Finally, both initial heads of the Confederate Quartermaster and Ordnance bureaus were also old army veterans from the same bureaus in the Federal service—Abraham C. Myers and Josiah Gorgas.[39]

The General Staff as a whole combined special strengths in logistics with a weak command structure, reflecting a mix of European and American practice. Both the Prussian and French armies had had to create institutions capable of handling the large size and complexity of Napoleonic-era military operations—structures built on the coterie of special military assistants who made the cumbersome wheels of the military machine mesh and turn in an era where no single commander could personally control armies that sometimes numbered in the hundreds of thousands.[40] These institutions focused on the process of planning and directing actual fighting, while the American General Staff focused on logistics, record keeping, and all the tasks that make military operations possible but do not determine them.

Up to the Civil War, American generals could still effectively use the far more personalized command systems of pre-Napoleonic Europe with great effect, and Calhoun's reforms not unreasonably made no provision for adopting either French or German reforms in staff work on the command level.[41] The sometimes barely company-sized actions of the Indian

COLONIALS, CONTINENTALS, AND FEDERALS

wars did not require the administrative machine of a Berthier or Scharn-
horst, while even American conflicts with foes organized along European
lines did not require the elaborate command systems of the continent.

The highly dispersed nature of the American military establishment, with outposts strung out along a vast continental frontier, and with
poor — if not downright wretched — means of communications, did require special logistical and administrative aptitude, which John C. Calhoun's bureau system did in fact provide. This American General Staff,
like everything else in the old army, represented a New World adaptation
of European models (Figures 1–3). Following the practice of old Albion,
the American service attached most of its logistical responsibilities to the
office of the quartermaster general. In contrast, German quartermaster
officers continued to exercise duties similar to those of their early modern forebears who had also handled reconnaissance and routes of march,
whereas the French service did not have a significant role for quartermaster officers after Richelieu's reforms in the middle of the seventeenth
century.[42] Indeed, the American General Staff looked very similar to an
organizational chart of Wellington's headquarters staff.

Note the similarity of terminology and names between the American and British charts — quartermaster general, adjutant general, paymaster general, commissary general — and the separation of artillery
and engineer troops under their own chiefs, which report directly to the
field commanders.[43] The special privileges and relative excellence of the
"scientific" arms of the American army — best exemplified by the engineering-heavy curriculum at West Point and the excellence of American
artillery during the Mexican War — would mark the American services'
character throughout the antebellum period.

We should not forget one important and glaring difference, however;
the American General Staff was a system of bureaus headed by chiefs located in Washington, whereas Wellington's staff managed an army in the
field. The American staff system focused almost entirely on questions of
administration that could and frequently should be handled from a centralized location in Washington, while the tactical control of armies was
left in the hands of individual commanders unassisted by the expert staff
assistants of European practice. Scott's regulations did mandate the ranks
of chiefs of staff for brigades, divisions, army corps, and armies proper in
the field, a "chain of subordination" among the different chiefs of staff
from brigade to division, and a requirement that a field army have representatives of each respective bureau at its headquarters. Nevertheless,

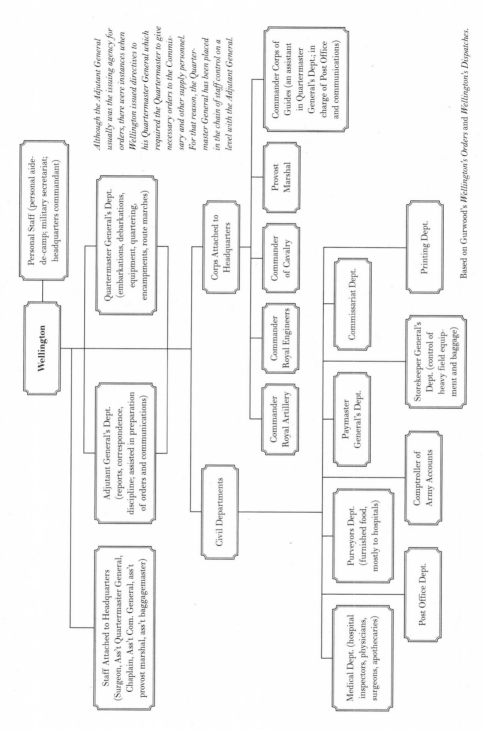

Wellington

Personal Staff (personal aide-de-camp; military secretariat; headquarters commandant)

Quartermaster General's Dept. (embarkations, debarkations, equipment, quartering, encampments, route marches)

Adjutant General's Dept. (reports, correspondence, discipline; assisted in preparation of orders and communications)

Staff Attached to Headquarters (Surgeon, Ass't Quartermaster General, Chaplain, Ass't Com. General, ass't provost marshal, ass't baggagemaster)

Corps Attached to Headquarters

Commander Royal Artillery

Commander Royal Engineers

Commander of Cavalry

Provost Marshal

Commander Corps of Guides (an assistant in Quartermaster General's Dept.; in charge of Post Office and communications)

Civil Departments

Medical Dept. (hospital inspectors, physicians, surgeons, apothecaries)

Purveyors Dept. (furnished food, mostly to hospitals)

Paymaster General's Dept.

Commissariat Dept.

Post Office Dept.

Comptroller of Army Accounts

Storekeeper General's Dept. (control of heavy field equipment and baggage)

Printing Dept.

Although the Adjutant General usually was the issuing agency for orders, there were instances when Wellington issued directives to his Quartermaster General which required the Quartermaster to give necessary orders to the Commissary and other supply personnel. For that reason, the Quartermaster General has been placed in the chain of staff control on a level with the Adjutant General.

Based on Gurwood's *Wellington's Orders* and *Wellington's Dispatches.*

FIGURE 1. Wellington's Headquarters Staff (from Hittle, *Military Staff*, 142)

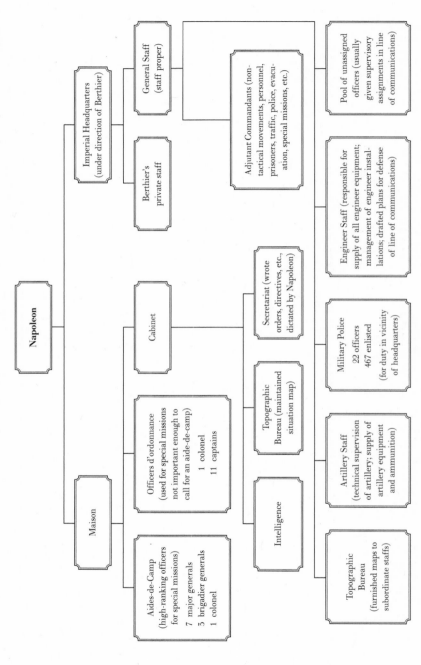

FIGURE 2. Napoleon's Headquarters Staff (from Hittle, *Military Staff*, 107)

Based upon Rene Tournès's *Le G. Q. G. de Napoleon I* and de Philip's *Etude sur le Service d'Etat-major Pendant les guerres du Premier Empire*.

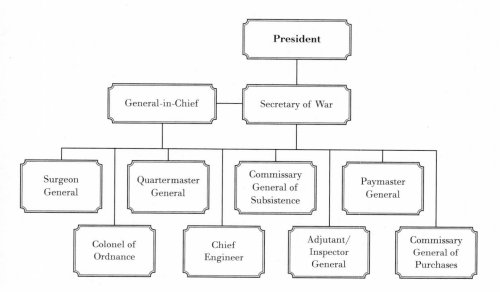

FIGURE 3. U.S. Army General Staff (1818). The diagram represents the General Staff organization for 1818. The 1821 reorganization more or less vindicated the principles established in 1818, with minor variations—the adjutant general lost his function as inspector of the army to two independently appointed inspectors, and the Ordnance Bureau was merged with the Artillery, although it would later become independent again in 1832. The Purchasing Department would eventually be abolished permanently, there would be a short-lived Clothing Department, and a Topographical Engineers Department would be added in 1831, but for the most part, this chart shows the basic outlines of American General Staff organization up until the Civil War. See Heitman, *Historical Register*, 1:37, 48, 43–44; Risch, *Quartermaster Support of the Army*, 201.

For some of the relevant legislation, see the following: United States, *Public Statutes*, March 3, 1813 (2:819); February 8, 1815 (3:203); April 24, 1816 (3:297); April 14, 1818 (3:426–27); March 2, 1821 (3:615). Note that although the 1818 legislation did not specifically refer to a new Subsistence Bureau (it only specified a commissary general, the same title held by the Purchasing Department chief), that was clearly the understood meaning—see, for example, U.S. Congress, *American State Papers*, Military Affairs, 1:848.

The anomalous and organizationally confused position of the general-in-chief on this simplified diagram reflects the failure of nineteenth-century American military policy to define the position adequately. See Skelton, "Commanding General and Problem of Command."

despite the copious amounts of detail he gave on many different questions of army administration, Scott gave no specific guidance on the proper tasks of staff officers who did not represent one of the General Staff bureaus beyond vague recommendations on the proper form of orders and a list of possible duties. Furthermore, even Hamilton's elaborate system of a fundamental school and specific schools of application for different combat arms, which achieved temporary fruition at various times during the antebellum period, did not include a specialized staff school that provided for higher-level training in operations, on the model of the Prussian Kriegsakademie or the French staff school at Rue de Grenelle.[44]

In contrast, Scott devoted 147 of 355 pages of his regulations to detailed procedures and sample forms for the governance of the various staff bureaus. The de facto independence of the staff bureaus, a consequence in part of the ambiguous status of the general in chief in Washington and the weakness of most civilian secretaries of war, corresponded with the administrative focus of the American staff system. The system of bureaus more closely matched French staff organization than British practice, but American staff practice in this period displayed no obvious influences from the French Etat-Major, despite the ready availability of an English translation of Paul Thiebault's influential Napoleonic-era staff manual. This manual had laid out the basic structure of French staff organization. Furthermore, the absence of a strong chief of staff in the American staff system to coordinate the bureaus in the field hardly testifies to any conscious American imitation of French practice.[45]

The American military establishment thus possessed an excellent administrative and logistical apparatus, which could virtually run on institutional autopilot under inexperienced secretaries of war.[46] This bureaucratic machinery could and did run an army dispersed across thousands of miles of frontier with reasonable aplomb and efficiency. What it could not do was effectively coordinate military operations on a national and strategic level, which hindered Union and Confederate war efforts during the Civil War. American strategic war planning relied on the efforts of the occasional secretary of war or officers who happened to give thought to the question, and it is a sign of the almost-relentless American emphasis on logistics that no permanent institutions for such planning existed until Elihu Root's reforms after the turn of the twentieth century.

Whatever its failings, by the end of Thayer's tenure at West Point, the old army could look at its organizational achievements with some pride. We should not take for granted the army's creation of a competent administrative apparatus. Even military historians too often forget the importance of the bureaucratic drudgery that keeps armies from degenerating into unorganized mobs. The most brilliant general wielding the most incisive strategic ideas can do nothing if his army cannot maintain a basic level of cohesion that requires regular feeding, clothing, transportation, and discipline. Morning reports and quartermaster returns represent more than red tape; they also provide the crucial bureaucratic grease that keeps the friction-prone gears of an army from stripping into dysfunction. The new West Point–officered army had its flaws, but it was far better prepared for the Mexican War than the pre–War of 1812 army had been for its own conflict. And without the regulars, the early Civil War armies would have been even more disorganized than they were, although which combatant this would have benefited more (if any) is an open question. But that war was far in the future.

CHAPTER TWO

Tactical Expertise and the U.S. Army before the War with Mexico

★ ★ ★

Wars do not win themselves; soldiers, generals, and armies must organize, train, equip, and finally fight their way to victory. The army of the United States did exactly that during the Mexican War, and it won the prize of Alta California with its fine harbors and increased the nation's territorial landmass by a third. Furthermore, the war also provided the conquered territory over which Free-Soil and proslavery forces would contend for the next decade and a half, leading eventually to the Civil War in 1861. An outright American defeat or a less stunning military victory might not have prevented some other form of sectional tension from leading to civil war, but the actual historical Civil War of 1861 to 1865 was made possible only by a conquering American army marching into Mexico City like Cortez and his conquistadors returned.

A host of factors lay behind American military victory — military, diplomatic, political, and cultural. One issue that historians have not examined as thoroughly as they might is the military effectiveness of the U.S. Army. Because of political imperatives born from Jacksonian ideology, which made Americans reluctant to spend large sums on war making, and a not inconsiderable amount of internal dissent in the United States, the administration of President James K. Polk could not fully deploy the country's superior material resources against Mexico. Furthermore, Mexican military abilities and national will, which the Polk administration consistently underestimated, were quite substantial. Manifest Destiny could become manifest only if certain concrete conditions found fulfillment, one being an American military competent enough to use limited resources to good effect.

That competence depended on the old army's creation of three distinct infantry, cavalry, and artillery branches with standardized weapons and tactics. The importance of establishing these three combat arms on a reasonably solid footing cannot be overstated. During the Mexican War, infantry formed the bedrock of an army as an all-purpose and cost-effective arm that could both defend and attack. Cavalry was of limited value in defending a position but possessed the mobility needed for reconnaissance and screening, while also (at least in theory) possessing sufficient shock and celerity to exploit decisive battlefield opportunities. Perhaps most important in the case of the Mexican War, artillery provided tremendous firepower, but lacked the solidity of a battalion of infantrymen standing fast with bayonets fixed.[1] All three arms had their own strengths and weaknesses and worked best as the complementary pieces of a larger whole.

The possession of these three combat arms along with a functioning staff system represented a bare minimum of organizational competence, which the United States had not possessed in 1812, despite having thirty years of peace after the Treaty of Paris to prepare for the War of 1812.[2] The United States, then fighting a war on its own soil, had found the time to recover with respect to Great Britain; however, fighting a war of conquest on foreign soil thirty years after the Treaty of Ghent, Polk could not have afforded the two years of bungling allowed to President James Madison. In short, there was nothing automatic about the creation of a competent regular army after 1815.

Indeed, the officers of the old army deserve much of the credit for the creation of the three combat arms. Two active and reformist secretaries of war, Calhoun and Joel R. Poinsett, provided crucial support in the political arena, but even they could not have done all the necessary spadework unaided. Professionally minded officers went to the time and trouble of translating foreign manuals, sitting on tactics boards, commenting on proposed tactical manuscripts, and even traveling to Europe to collect and adapt the professional expertise of the Old World. Without the completion of all of these sometimes-mundane tasks, the elaborate reforms of Calhoun and Poinsett would have gone for naught. Furthermore, these officers could not expect much public support from a polity still devoted to the citizen-soldier ideal. The old army persevered, however, and in 1846 the United States could boast of an army far better prepared for a European-style war at the commencement of hostilities than any other previous army in the history of the republic.

What makes this achievement of the regular army even more impressive is that it spent most of this period engaged in taxing frontier duties very different from its hard-won reformulation of Old World military institutions. Some historians have criticized the regular army for refusing to devote much professional thought or discussion to Indian fighting, but in the regulars' defense, no Indian force could replicate the British sack of Washington.[3] Hostile Indians could and did give the regular army much embarrassment and grief, but even the most successful native insurgents of this period, the Florida Seminoles, did not achieve final victory. Furthermore, the old army's almost-relentless focus on fighting a European-style war did prepare it for both the Mexican War and Civil War, which were conducted along more or less orthodox nation-state lines.

Nevertheless, despite all their professional pretensions, regular army officers had only mixed success before the Mexican War in achieving a level of expertise comparable to their European counterparts. Pressing constabulary needs on the frontier and the widely dispersed nature of the American service prevented either officers or enlisted men from gaining much experience comparable to what they would face during the Mexican War. The old army did succeed, however, in establishing a standardized set of tactical manuals and a core cadre of competent officers, whose younger members had acquired just enough training at West Point to make up for their lack of field service.[4] This cadre was able to convert frontier army regulars and citizen-soldier volunteers into relatively competent field armies capable of defeating their Mexican opponents. For all its flaws, the regular army had enough institutional solidity that in the hands of competent commanders, or the downright brilliant Winfield Scott, it could achieve the war aims of the Polk administration.

Because the Mexican War vindicated the institutional forms of the pre–Mexican War old army, both contending Civil War armies ended up inheriting the doctrinal and organizational legacies of the 1820s and 1830s. Two of the major combat arms, the artillery and infantry, would see major changes in equipment—the introduction of rifled cannon for the former and the rifle-musket for the latter—but those technological advances would be assimilated into patterns of tactical thought established before the Mexican War. Most forward-thinking regular army officers tended to view the introduction of the rifle-musket before the outbreak of the Civil War as an evolutionary development within the light infantry tradition of European and American practice. Furthermore, the old army's institutional focus on a small cadre of regulars proved ill suited for the special problems of scale created by the Civil War.

For all these reasons, both this chapter and the Mexican War chapters look forward to the Civil War in a manner that does some violence to the much more confused pace and progress of events during the actual period in question. For example, the thorough treatment of American light infantry tactics before the Mexican War does not mean to claim that old army officers themselves would have seen such ideas as the most significant issue in their professional lives but aims only to help explain post–Mexican War reactions to the introduction of the rifle-musket. Even with regard to the Mexican War, the chapter uses a deliberate foreshortening. The American artillery officers who put their branch on a solid footing in the decade before the Mexican War probably did not expect or fully anticipate the decisive role their arm would play in the battles of 1846 and 1847.

THE U.S. ARMY'S infantry had had no standard tactical manual at the outbreak of the War of 1812, and the cavalry and artillery branches would have no coherent systems of instruction until the early 1840s. Indeed, after the end of the War of 1812, the cavalry branch would not even exist until the authorization of the 1st Dragoon Regiment in 1833.[5] The artillery branch, the most effective and decisive of American combat arms during the Mexican War, would not even have a standardized system of equipment until 1841. After several decades of slow but sure persistence, the regular army on the eve of the Mexican War would have, in addition to the logistical apparatus created by Calhoun's General Staff reforms, enough trained officers to put three reasonably well-articulated and differentiated combat arms — infantry, cavalry, and artillery — into the field for a full-blown nation-state war.

The formulation of standardized tactics was as important as it was mundane. The nineteenth-century tactical manual served as the indispensable grammar of battlefield maneuver. There is nothing "natural" about lining up in long lines with one's fellows and tramping around a battlefield shooting at other groups of soldiers doing the same; furthermore, the inherent tendency toward chaos in war requires a special degree of regimentation. A manual could be better, or it could be worse; a general might choose the appropriate evolution at the appropriate time, or he might not; but without some system of standardized tactics, an army was only a disorganized body of individuals with weapons, incapable of the intense trials of strength in battle that nation-state wars demanded. Furthermore, a common manual would greatly facilitate the training of citizen-soldier volunteers by the regular army in wartime.

The first combat arm the old army put on a solid footing was also the oldest and most important—the infantry. The branch received a common tactical manual relatively early in 1815, although efforts before and during the War of 1812 to adopt standardized infantry instruction had failed because of a mix of army politics and field commanders' resistance to the tactical innovations of William Duane's official tactics. Scott had ignored Duane's congressionally mandated manual at his camp of instruction at Buffalo in the spring of 1814. Instead, he used his own copy of the 1791 French infantry regulations and the Lacroix edition of Macdonald's English translation of the French tactics,[6] which helped result in the relative success of Jacob Brown's command at Chippewa and Lundy's Lane.

The absence of a common manual of instruction was still sorely felt, however, and then congressmen Calhoun and others raised the issue in 1814. The army commissioned a tactics board in response, imitating a French practice that would persist in the American service through the rest of the century. That board, headed by Scott, adopted a revised and adapted version of the French infantry tactics of 1791 in early 1815.[7] Scott, for better or for worse, would be the army's primary infantry authority until the mid-1850s, and he would also supervise the promulgation of the 1825 and 1835 tactics. The 1835 tactics would continue to see service even during the Civil War, although Hardee's 1855 tactics constituted the standard manual for the Civil War armies.

In light of all the endemic structural problems with the regular army—scattered frontier posts with very little provision for large-unit training, underfunding, the dispersed nature of Indian warfare, and undermanning—we should not overestimate these manuals' influence in the peacetime constabulary army. The American service did, however, by 1815 have some kind of more or less accepted tactical manual ready for use in the event of a war against a European-style army, as opposed to none at all. And peacetime efforts to standardize tactical instruction probably had at least some effect: the 1825 tactics included a general order that attempted to prohibit the use of any other training regimen, while the Infantry School of Practice from 1826 to 1837 probably aimed to achieve a higher level of standardization. Scott also had made real efforts to disseminate the 1835 tactics throughout the army via the mails, proposing that all officers receive all three volumes, while sergeants and musicians receive only the first volume. All West Pointers also learned the standard tactics themselves as members of the battalion of cadets, and the increasing proportion of West Pointers in the regular army officer corps disseminated this sort of basic practical knowledge throughout the army.[8]

Historians have criticized the first 1815 board for making only a straight translation of the 1791 French tactics for the American service, but Scott's first board did make significant adaptations of the French original to American conditions and practice. It adopted the two-rank system as the "habitual order of formation," which the British regulars had used throughout the second half of the eighteenth century in North America, and which von Steuben had used in the Revolution's Blue Book. The French army, in contrast, finally moved to a partial adoption of the two-rank formation in its 1831 regulations.[9]

The 1815 tactics also followed the old Blue Book in using a quick time of 120 steps a minute, as opposed to the French regulation of 100 steps a minute. Perhaps reflecting a perceived American need to move faster and more flexibly on the broken terrain of American battlefields, the American common time of 90 steps a minute and double quick time of 140 steps a minute both exceeded French practice (76 and 120 steps a minute, respectively). Von Steuben's Blue Book and Smyth's little-used adaptation of the 1791 French tactics had prescribed a common time of 75 steps a minute (the English step rate), while Duane used 90 steps a minute for quick time.[10] The original source for the 1815 tactics' common time rate of 90 steps a minute may be Duane's abortive handbook. Close-order drill required soldiers to move in step at important and specified rates to maintain formation in battle, and the 1815 board increased the standard movement rates of American soldiers by a significant margin over accepted European practice. Nevertheless, outside of revisions and changes to conform to the more open and swifter order of American infantry practice, the tactics were more or less derivative of the French manual.

The 1825 infantry tactics continued the American practice of adapting Old World methods to New World practice. Scott, who supervised the 1824 tactical board, still overreached when he told his aide-de-camp that he expected to produce an infantry system "in advance of that of any other nation at this time." The board also may not have been as thorough as Scott claimed in taking into account post-1791 tactical developments in Europe. Nevertheless, its incorporation of a light infantry drill that Commandant of Cadets William Worth had used at West Point and its clear deviations from the 1791 French tactics do reveal considerable independence from Old World models in the American service. In another sensible reform, the board also tested its tactics with field trials among the cadets at West Point and the troops at the artillery school at Fortress Monroe.[11] A later tactics board used West Point cadets as guinea pigs during the formulation of Hardee's tactics in the mid-1850s.

The incorporation of Worth's light infantry system, whatever its faults, also forecast the increasing influence of systematized light infantry methods in the antebellum American service. In European practice, light infantry formations distinguished themselves from the line by the use of aimed fire at will by individual soldiers, dispersed formations, the use of terrain for cover, and an indifference to the precise alignments of close-order tactics. Light infantry usually served only as support units for line infantry in Europe: covering the flanks against surprise, harassing and slowing down an enemy to expedite a retreat or withdrawal, probing and feeling forward during an attack to force an enemy to reveal its positions, and serving as pickets or outposts.[12] Despite all these functions, line infantry still dominated as the primary combat arm, because only troops arrayed in close order and equipped with the bayonet had the special staying power and physical weight of mass so necessary in an era where the cavalry charge remained a serious threat.

In North America, both the difficult terrain — making set-piece European battles less common — and the fighting methods of the indigenous peoples made light infantry methods play a special role during the wars for empire. The British regulars adapted themselves to North American conditions by a more widespread use of light tactics, while the fighting methods of rifle-armed militiamen operating in dispersed order could sometimes be likened to the light infantry methods of European armies.[13] Nevertheless, militiamen still could not match the organizational staying power and versatility of regular troops trained in light infantry methods — that is, the regulars' ability to stay in the field for longer periods of time, their greater logistical capacity, and their ability to fight in orthodox fashion when necessary. The citizen-soldier ideal portrayed the regular army soldier as a tyrannized automaton capable of fighting only in the rigid formations of the Old World, a view that assumed an unnecessary relationship between civil liberty and military flexibility.

The greatest deficiency of American troops during the Revolution was an inability to fight in close order against British regulars, and the first American professionals in the Continental army devoted all their energies to rectifying that flaw. In the meantime, however, European soldiers began to increase the role of light infantry on the continent. In the eighteenth century, French military thinkers debated the proper role of light infantry methods, among other things, and set the stage for the increased use of those methods during the Revolutionary and Napoleonic eras. The 1791 French tactics did not include instructions for light infantry, but a provisional regulation of 1792 did give some guidance on the use of light troops. Outside official doctrine, the French armies of the French Revolution and of the Napoleonic period used large numbers of skirmishers in conjunction with line infantry deployed in close order, either column or three-rank line of battle, depending on the situation. The British army revived its old expertise in light infantry and combined it with a variation of ancien régime linear tactics that used the more flexible (if also more brittle) two-rank line of battle, but most continental armies chose to imitate the French.[14]

Continental European practice as a whole during the Napoleonic period emphasized the training of troops who could fight as both light and line infantry, and American practice followed that example out of either conscious imitation or organizational necessity. The American service was too small and dispersed to sustain a system of infantry specialization. Even the militia-scorning Continentals may have been influenced by light infantry methods—von Steuben's quick time of 120 steps per minute had exceeded the British quick time of 108 steps per minute, after all. With the regular army's ability to fight in close order finally vindicated at Chippewa and Lundy's Lane, some officers could and did comment shortly after the publication of the 1814 infantry tactics manual on the need for better light infantry instruction. Maj. C. K. Gardner, a regular army officer and former adjutant of one of the post–War of 1812 military divisions, published his own revision of the 1815 tactics in 1819 and included a section on light infantry instruction based on British practice.[15]

Gardner believed that the militia could be made militarily effective if trained and equipped as light infantry, but he still thought that Congress in wartime would need "to add to the regular regiments, just a sufficient number to constitute the heavy ranks, requisite for charges in particular cases, and to be a centre for the rallying and manœuvring of the forces called into the field." Furthermore, "from the variety of service to which United States soldiers are particularly liable, the light infantry instruction may be considered applicable to every infantry battalion." Gardner remained committed to the professional belief that training and regular discipline were necessary, even for light infantry, arguing that "men never can attain perfection as *light infantry*, without being thoroughly grounded, in the first place, in *slow movements* in *close order*."[16]

The 1825 infantry tactics filled the needs Gardner perceived by declaring it necessary to train all troops in light infantry tactics. The new light infantry section gave instructions on aimed fire, firing and loading while kneeling or lying down, moving into extended order, and utilizing supports and reserves. Furthermore, breaking even farther away from the French regulations of 1791, the 1825 tactics abolished the three-rank formation altogether. Forecasting later French practice, it also made quick time the standard pace for the "*interior* movements of the battalion." The manual did not conceive of light infantry acting on its own unsupported, however, and considered the extension of an entire battalion into skirmish order a rare occurrence. Indeed, the manual instructed light infantry under attack from cavalry in open terrain to close up and withdraw to the protection of the main body of infantry deployed in close order.[17] The vulnerability of dispersed light infantry, especially against heavy cavalry using shock tactics and the *arme blanche* ("cold steel," i.e. bayonet, saber, or lance), would be a constant concern among American professionals throughout the entire antebellum period.

Scott's 1835 revision of the American infantry regulations added no new significant changes to American light infantry tactics. This new edition was based on the French infantry tactics of 1831, which had altered the old French tactics of 1791 by incorporating the situational use of the two-rank line of battle and specific light infantry regulations. The new American manual followed its 1825 predecessor in stipulating the combined use of light and line infantry and measures to repel cavalry. Reflecting the broader trend in Western infantry tactics of using an increasingly open battlefield order, however, the 1835 tactics further dispersed the American skirmish order by stipulating a standard interval of ten paces between files, in contrast to the default six-pace intervals in the 1825 tactics. Furthermore, while the 1825 tactics gave a cap of twelve paces to the size of the interval no matter how disrupted the terrain might be, the 1835 tactics gave no such suggested limit.[18]

Scott's new 1835 regulations did, however, slow down the stipulated advance rates of American infantry in order to conform to French practice. The 1825 tactics prescribed a quick time with a pace of 120 steps a minute, while the 1835 tactics prescribed a quick time with a pace of only

110 steps a minute. Double quick time in the 1825 tactics moved at 160 steps a minute, whereas the 1835 tactics prescribed a pace of only 140 steps a minute. Furthermore, although the 1835 tactics did prescribe a run in situations of absolute urgency, which the 1825 tactics did not include, the older tactics prescribed double quick time for all movements conducted in extended order, whereas the 1835 regulations prescribed double quick time or the run only in "cases of absolute necessity." The 1825 tactics did, however, give officers discretion to slow movements down in order to prevent excessive fatigue, a fear that the 1835 regulations also expressed, and which would prove to be a problem with the even swifter movements of Hardee's tactics.[19]

The leading historian of Civil War minor tactics has made much of the increased movement rates found in Hardee's tactics, which he connects closely to the arrival of the rifle-musket: common time of 90 steps a minute with a 28-inch step, quick time of 110 steps per minute with the same stride length, and a double quick time with a 33-inch step at 165 steps per minute. The figures for Hardee's tactics do seem significant in comparison to the 1835 regulations (90 per minute, 110 per minute, 140 per minute, respectively, all at 28 inches), but they do not seem so striking when compared to the 1825 tactics (90 per minute, 120 per minute, and 160 per minute, respectively, all at 28 inches; also see Table 1).[20] American officers had considered the use of quicker infantry movements long before the arrival of the rifle-musket.

Indeed, the adoption of Scott's 1835 tactics also gave rise to a wide-ranging professional debate within the American military establishment over the merits of the new tactics. The biggest foe of Scott's 1835 tactics, the author "Clairfait" in the *Army and Navy Chronicle* (a short-lived professional journal), denounced Scott's tactics in April 1835 on the grounds that, although light infantry methods were especially well suited to the American service, the new 1835 tactics mandated an inferior light infantry system. Indeed, the *Army and Navy Chronicle* reprinted a piece in 1836 that saw the early disasters of the Seminole War as caused partly by the absence of a specialized light infantry corps in the American army. Clairfait was also not alone in believing the 1825 light infantry drill superior to the new tactics; "Young Fogram" backed his ideas in his own article in late August 1835. Furthermore, the debate over Scott's dropping of the original light infantry tactics had enough of an effect that Philip St. George Cooke, one of the army's prominent frontier cavalrymen, would twenty-two years

TABLE 1
Movement Rates in Infantry Tactics

Source	Common Time	Quick Time	Double Quick
Blue Book	24 in./75 pm	24 in./120 pm	
1791 French tactics	24 in./76 pm	24 in./100 pm	24 in./120 pm
Lacroix	24 in./76 pm	24 in./100 pm	24 in./120 pm
Smyth	24 in./75 pm	24 in./100 pm	
1792 U.K. tactics	30 in./75 pm	30 in./108 pm	30 in./120 pm
Duane, *Hand Book*	24 in./76 pm	24 in./90 pm	24 in./120 pm
Duane, *System*	24 in./76 pm	24 in./108 pm	24 in./120 pm
1815 U.S tactics	28 in./90 pm	28 in./120 pm	28 in./140 pm
1825 U.S. tactics	28 in./90 pm	28 in./120 pm	28 in./160 pm
1833 U.K. tactics	30 in./75 pm	30 in./108 pm	35 in./150 pm
1835 U.S. tactics	28 in./90 pm	28 in./110 pm	28 in./140 pm
1841 U.S. tactics (Dragoon)	28 in./90 pm	28 in./120 pm	
1845 French Chasseurs tactics	25.59 in/76 pm	25.59 in/110 pm	32.68 in/165 pm
Hardee	28 in./90 pm	28 in./110 pm	33 in./165 pm

Sources: Riling, *Von Steuben and His Regulations*, 13. *École du soldat, Réglement* [1791], 1:31 [20], 92–93 [206], 144 [108]. United States, War Department, *Rules and Regulations* [1808], 6 [S.6], 13 [S.16], 14 [S.17]. Lacroix, *Rules and Regulations for the Field Exercise, and Manoeuvres of the French Infantry*, 1:13, 101 [107–8]. Smyth, *Regulations for the Field Exercise*, 7, 20. [Great Britain], War Office, *Rules and Regulations* [1792], 6 [S. 6], 13 [S. 16], 14 [S. 17]. Duane, *Hand Book for Infantry*, 21. [William Duane], *The System of Infantry Discipline* [1814], 13 [53], 75 [65, 69–70]. Duane also sees quick time as "the common time of military camps" (ibid., 75 [69]). United States, War Department, *Rules and Regulations for the Field Exercise and Manœuvres of Infantry* [1815], 15 [20], 79–80 [105–6]. United States, War Department, *Infantry Tactics* [1825], 24 [132], 58 [351], 245 [1577]. Note that in the same edition of the 1825 tactical manual, there is a reference to the limited use of a pace of 150 steps per minute. This is not explicitly called double quick time, however. See ibid., 86 [545]. [Great Britain, War Office], *Field Exercise and Evolutions of the Army* [1833], 10 [6], 15 [15–16]. Winfield Scott, *Infantry Tactics* [1835], 1:29 [115], 82 [347], 132 [562], 2:89. United States, War Department, *Cavalry Tactics* [1841], 1:90, 95. *Ordonnance du roi* [1845], 18 [32], 21 [41–42]. Hardee, *Rifle and Light Infantry Tactics* [1855], 1:24–26.

Note: Movement rates are measured in steps per minute, with the individual steps measured in inches.

later comment on the change in tactics with the statement that "the old tactics (which being admirably suitable, and truly American, has been dropped)."[21]

Clairfait also criticized Scott's move to a three-rank formation, citing British success with the two-rank formation during the Napoleonic Wars, the nature of American terrain, and the supposed incompatibility of the three-rank formation with the expansible army concept. The 1835 tactics themselves prescribed a two-rank formation for the army in its non-expanded state, which meant that in wartime no part of the army would be familiar with the more difficult three-rank pattern.[22]

Clairfait's statements did not go unopposed. "Hindman" mounted a vigorous defense of the new tactics and rejected Clairfait's ideas about training pure light infantry with no background in close-order tactics. Hindman argued that light infantry tactics should be a "*supplement* to the schools of the company and battalion," as opposed to the practice of the 1825 tactics, which "gave a new and duplicate or parallel system of tactics" — what Clairfait had actually praised. In a later number that followed the same theme, Hindman asked, "Does any person desire to have in our army companies, or battalions of infantry or rifle, without the capacity of going through the exercises and manoeuvres *of the line* — that is, in *closed* files? Without such capacity, how even (when skirmishing) rally in column, square, or circle, to resist cavalry?" Hindman clearly wished to follow continental practice in training all-purpose infantry capable of fighting both in line and in extended skirmish order. Indeed, Hindman revealed an impressive knowledge of overseas developments, citing the new British regulations of 1833 and the elaborate process by which the French had created their 1831 infantry tactics in an attempt to refute Clairfait's defense of the 1825 tactics.[23]

In response to Clairfait's criticism of the three-rank formation, Hindman claimed that field commanders still had total discretion with regard to using two or three ranks, which may have been true on a practical level, but that seemed hardly compatible with a literal reading of the 1835 tactics. Clairfait's opponent made a reasonable point in asking why field commanders should not have the option of using the heftier and more durable three-rank formation in appropriate circumstances, but his dismissal of the greater difficulties of training three-rank formations seems strained. When firing in a three-rank line of battle, either the front rank kneels or the rear rank loads muskets to exchange with the center rank, and using the formation successfully required extra training that green American troops might not be able to afford in wartime. Hindman's glib assertion that American armies should simply wait until they were properly instructed reflects an unrealistic expectation of Old World proficiency. One wonders if Hindman also paid excessive deference to the French when he reports in one article that he, an American officer, had read a French translation of Sir William Napier's English-language *History of the War in the Peninsula*. Other officers recognized Hindman's Francophilia and criticized him for it — Philo-Clairfait sarcastically asked, "Because the French Commission did so and so, and adopted such a manoeuvre, does it make the manoeurvre correct? Are we to follow blindly the steps of individuals, which are evidently erroneous?"[24]

The opposition to Scott's reforms had some effect; for example, it forced a return to the two-rank formation.[25] Nevertheless, the tactics were still adopted, for better or for worse. Whatever the 1835 tactics' flaws, they still served well enough in Mexico. Furthermore, while Clairfait and Hindman almost certainly do not represent the average line officer on a frontier post, the very fact that such distinctive individuals existed in the first place helps explain the difference between the regular army's success in the first battles of the Mexican War and its failures in 1812. Hardee's tactical reforms of the 1850s and the infantry fighting methods of the Civil War would all build on the foundations that American professionals laid between 1815 and 1835.

Scott's 1835 tactics still reflected, however, the dangers of excessive Francophilia. Scott had altered perfectly reasonable American practices in order to conform with the most recent French revision, with only questionable benefits at best. Although technological advances in infantry weapons had not yet made themselves felt, frontier conditions and Indian fighting valued light infantry methods at a special New World premium, which many American officers had obviously recognized. Instead of creating new training and command structures that could cope with the corresponding loss of tactical control by officers in extended order, Scott's 1835 infantry tactics proposed to make the standard infantry formation more rigid by adding a third rank and slower in movement by reducing the prescribed pace of quick and double quick time.

In Scott's defense, he did not totally discard previous American practice — Scott preserved the swift common time of ninety paces a minute, and he did not affect the American practice of training soldiers to load and fire lying down, even though the French tactics of 1831 made no provision for this. Scott's new system also still ensured that light infantry training would be incorporated into common American practice. For example, Chief Engineer Joseph G. Totten saw fit in 1840 to propose legislation to specifically provide for an "Instructor of Infantry, Light-Infantry & Rifle drill, manoeuvres & Tactics" at West Point. Furthermore, the French infantry tactics of 1831 were the product of a mature and well-trained professional army, and they could and would still serve the U.S. Army well enough in the Mexican War and beyond.[26]

If the development of American infantry tactics does not mirror a straight and easy path of progress, American artillery had a more uniformly positive evolution during this period. By the outbreak of the Mexican War, American artillery was probably the combat arm most comparable to the best European armies, but even in Calhoun's day the red-legged regiments did not seem to have a very promising future. The reformist secretary of war had convened a board of ordnance and artillery officers to formulate a system of guns with standardized calibers, carriages, and functions in late 1818, but in an unfortunate act of excessive Francophilia, it approved the already-outdated Gribeauval carriage of Napoleonic France instead of the British army's more mobile stock trail carriage. The funding cuts in the army reduction bill of 1821 only made matters worse.[27]

The army adopted H. Lallemand's *Treatise on Artillery* as its standard manual in 1821, but it proved a poor textbook for practical instruction. Furthermore, the underfunded Artillery School of Practice at Fortress Monroe failed in its aim of producing a trained cadre of artillerists during the decade of its existence (1824–34). The school of practice did not even have a common tactical manual for instruction. Worse yet, even after several fact-finding trips by American officers to Europe and yet another board's deliberations in the early 1830s, the American service still had no standardized system of artillery equipment. It was not until Poinsett's tenure as secretary of war that a successful mission to Europe by American officers settled the question of bronze or iron for field artillery in favor of the former, and the regular army finally adopted a coherent system of artillery equipage in 1841. The 1839 Ordnance Board, a new institutional innovation, had established the basis of the new system and would supervise the development of American weapons technology throughout the 1840s and 1850s.[28]

While the Ordnance Board finally standardized the technical specifications of American artillery, three young West Point–trained artillery officers spearheaded the formulation of a standard tactical system in the late 1830s and early 1840s. Capt. Robert Anderson (USMA 1825), 1st Lt. Miner Knowlton (USMA 1829), and Bvt. Maj. Samuel Ringgold (USMA 1818) certainly did not agree on all points—Anderson preferred French practice, Ringgold had a strong preference for the British horse artillery regulations, while Knowlton seemed to take an intermediate position between the two—but that very disagreement originated in healthy intellectual debate. Both Knowlton and Anderson also served as artillery instructors at West Point for part of their careers, either before or during the formulation of Anderson's 1841 tactics.[29]

Ringgold did not lack professional credentials. In 1838 Secretary of

War Poinsett ordered him to organize a company of light artillery at Carlisle Barracks—which also served as the training depot for the dragoons—with men drawn from the 1st and 2nd Artillery Regiments. In 1839 Poinsett designated another three companies as field artillery, which represented a large advance in tactical mobility in an artillery establishment that had previously served as either "red-legged" infantry or static garrisons in coastal forts. These assignments solidified Ringgold's status as the army's leading practitioner and advocate of horse artillery, which was later vindicated by his excellent combat record in the Mexican War.[30]

Shortly before Ringgold began training his model company of horse artillery, Robert Anderson had submitted a translation of the French artillery tactics in May 1837 to the adjutant general for perusal and approval. Because he preferred the British horse artillery regulations, Ringgold contested Anderson's use of the French tactics. The War Department sought to settle the issue by establishing a tactics board to compare "the system of instruction for Field Artillery, prepared by Captain Anderson, with the code of instructions for the exercise and movements of the British Royal Artillery." The board proved less than entirely successful in settling the dispute. The War Department ended up adopting Anderson's manual on April 29, 1840, as the official tactics *except* for the sections on horse artillery in deference to Ringgold's opposition. There seems to have been at least some acrimony in the dispute between Ringgold and Anderson, with Knowlton caught somewhere in the middle. Anderson won a temporary victory when the War Department rescinded the addendum on horse artillery in General Orders No. 46 of 1841.[31] In the end, however, Ringgold did manage to incorporate the British horse artillery system into official American practice in the revised artillery tactics of 1845.

Anderson did not lack for support in advocating the French system—Winfield Scott, the old army's other great Francophile, threw his support behind his old aide-de-camp—but Ringgold was not the only officer who expressed misgivings about a heavy reliance on French practice. Bvt. Maj. Gen. Edmund P. Gaines, although quite a professional himself, decried officers "who have never seen the flash of an Enemy's Cannon—who have acquired distinction only in the mazes of French Books, with only that imperfect knowledge of the French Language which is better adapted to the Quackery of Charlatans, than the common-sense science of war." Even Knowlton, friendly with both Scott and Anderson, had doubts about the strong French influence in the American service. Writing on April 20,

1840, after the board adjourned, he declared himself undecided as to which system, British or French, was superior. He pointed out, however, that the American service had borrowed so much from French practice, even

> in the preparation of the materials of war, notwithstanding the superior reputation of the English in every thing relating to the mechanic arts. So that we are now in no very good condition to borrow from any nation but the French. A decided superiority alone would justify us in adopting any thing at variance with our general system. Even changes of form should be discouraged. Had our adoption of French tactics &c. been always the result of deliberate comparisons made between them and the systems of other nations, we might proceed perhaps without much danger to adopt the improvements of the French without giving ourselves the trouble of inquiry or comparison. But we all know that it has been a habit with our countrymen, since the revolutionary war, to refer to the French on all military matters, and to adopt from them as a matter of course, without much reference to the English or any other nation.[32]

Nevertheless, for all the old army's real faults, even Anderson's original tactics before the incorporation of the British horse artillery drill should not be seen as an unthinking translation of the French original. Brig. Gen. Abram Eustis did make efforts to use Anderson's tactics in training Poinsett's large concentration of troops at Camp Washington in 1839, and Anderson attempted to develop a set of commands compatible with Scott's infantry tactics. Indeed, his tactics stipulated that artillery soldiers learn the schools of the soldier and of the company in the infantry tactics *first*, and that officers be familiar with the tactics of all the branches. The 1845 artillery tactics also attempted to use infantry forms of command as much as possible and recommended that officers know the tactics of the other branches, although it did not require that artillerymen actually be drilled in the infantry tactics up to the school of the company. With the publication of a new set of cavalry tactics in 1841, however, the new artillery regulations mandated that mounted artillerymen look to the cavalry tactics for instruction in horsemanship.[33]

The connection between mandated procedure in a tactical manual and actual practice in the field is never self-evident, but in the case of the artillery regulations, we possess evidence that artillery officers received the new 1840 tactics with interest. Anderson's extant collection of papers includes several letters from officers asking for points of clarification with regard to the new tactics. Furthermore, Anderson almost immediately began work on a revised edition, which would better reconcile the different commands of the infantry, artillery, and cavalry branches. Anderson also sent out this new manuscript for testing in the field by his fellow officers. Some of the issues seem like mindless minutiae — for example, officers discussed the question of whether there should be a specific drill for mounting artillerymen on caissons — but the most important point for our purposes remains the fact that American artillery officers took the tactics seriously enough to deal with such questions in the first place. That seriousness may have sometimes been misplaced, but the drastically different fortunes of the professionally indifferent pre–War of 1812 officer corps and their professionally aware pre–Mexican War successors calls into question modern distaste for drill manual drudgery.[34]

The War Department set up another board to review Anderson's new manuscript in 1843, which included his old rival Ringgold, and the board proceeded to take more than a year to review the new tactics. At least one fellow officer not on the board sent comments to Anderson, and the army conducted several practical trials of the tactics. The new system, which included the adaptation of the British horse artillery regulations that Ringgold had so strongly advocated, was finally adopted by the War Department on March 6, 1845, in time for use during the Mexican War. Anderson himself understood the limits of American tactical development. Back in 1837 he had declared that if the War Department approved his translation of the tactics up to and including the school of the battery, the rough tactical equivalent to a company of infantry, then "it would be proper to have it extended to embrace the Evolutions of four batteries, and to render it complete another volume should be compiled to containing [sic] & one or two chapters on harnessing and on the school of the carriage, and *the exercises or manual[s] of the different kinds of guns — cannon howitzers & mortars.*"[35] Unfortunately, the 1845 tactics still extended only to the school of the battery, but American field artillery found its tactical system more than adequate during the Mexican War.

The old army officers who put the artillery arm on a solid basis during the decade or so before the Mexican War also made efforts to systematize its practical training and instruction in the field. In lieu of the none-too-successful Artillery School of Practice at Fort Monroe, which had closed in 1834, the War Department attempted after 1841 to use the one congressionally authorized company of light artillery in each artillery regiment to train the other batteries in turn. In 1842 it also issued General Orders No. 21, which mandated a set of comprehensive procedures to govern target practice for both fixed and field batteries in three designated months out of the year. The orders declared that "the general objects of this practice are—to give to officers and men the ready and effective use of batteries; to preserve on record the more important results for the benefit of the same or future commanders, and to ascertain the efficiency of guns and carriages." Furthermore, in a sign that bode well for the future of the horse artillery, eight extra blank cartridges per month were provided for "mounted" companies to drill with during the other nine months of the year. General Orders No. 65 of the same year stipulated that post commanders transmit to the adjutant general's office full reports of the target practice results. The program of target practice must have been implemented to at least some degree, because the adjutant general published the consolidated target practice results of all the artillery posts in General Orders No. 10 of 1844.[36]

Although the U.S. Army would never have a strong tradition of heavy cavalry armed with either saber or lance, the creation of a mounted combat arm to deal with the Plains Indians did help further develop the horse artillery. Ringgold's model battery had been trained at Carlisle Barracks, home to the Mounted School of Instruction after 1838. The formulation of a standard tactical system for the dragoons also bore much similarity to the contemporary process of tactical standardization in the artillery branch. The dragoons had received their first drill manual in 1834, but there were various problems with distribution, and the ever-present American problem of dispersal along the frontier helped lead to the establishment of the Mounted School of Instruction in the first place. In the fall of 1840, the ever-diligent Poinsett ordered 1st Lt. William Eustis and 2nd Lt. Henry S. Turner to translate the French cavalry tactics for the American service. Yet another tactics board met in late 1840 and early 1841 to review the translation.[37]

The cavalry arm of the American service even went as far as to send officers to the French cavalry school at Saumur for training. American ordnance officers had gone to Europe in search of models and ideas with regard to equipment, and some artillery officers had also observed European practice firsthand, but only the cavalry arm systematically sent officers to a foreign school for instruction. Along with Eustis and Turner, 1st Lt. Philip Kearny, a future Civil War major general, went overseas in 1839–1840. In the first mission, Poinsett ordered Eustis and Turner to finish a compressed form of the Saumur course of instruction in one year, while Kearny was to leave the school early to observe regiments in the field. Kearny's assignment focused more on reporting "the differences that exist in the organization, in the maneuvres, in the police, in the administration, and in all the internal regulations of the French Cavalry & our own" than on tactical issues. Kearny even managed to spend some time observing French regiments in the field in Algeria.[38]

The following year, Poinsett sent Capt. Lloyd Beall, 1st Lt. William J. Hardee (the same Hardee of the 1850s tactical manual), and 1st Lt. W. I. Newton to Saumur on a similar mission. The American officers were greeted as fellow officers in the international profession of arms, and the French commandant of the school even sent certificates of good conduct to the American minister in Paris on behalf of Newton and Hardee. The first year's worth of officers had also reported a very hospitable reception. The second class of American officers, who clearly reveled in the Old World's martial aristocracy, even went as far as to request a larger pay allowance. In their view, as representatives of the American service, they should return the civilities of their French hosts, "which if they did not would subject them to the imputation of meanness." The effectiveness of the missions should not be exaggerated. Kearny, for example, had such poor French-language skills that he had to have a letter translated into English to explain the purpose of his mission to French officers, and the American officers received nothing more than the beginning course of instruction for a cavalry officer.[39] Nevertheless, if far from perfect, the direct transfer of expertise from Europe did at least put the American cavalry arm on a stronger footing, and Hardee would go on to head the infantry tactics revision of the 1850s.

Poinsett also managed to institute some large-scale if limited combined arms training in 1839 at Camp Washington near Trenton. The War Department also revived the Infantry School of Practice at Jefferson Barracks in 1843 when the 3rd and 4th Infantry were able to reconcentrate, which proved especially useful when those units were sent to Mexico. Nevertheless, Camp Washington proved to be a one-time experiment, and American tactical manuals continued to give very little guidance on where and when to use individual tactical movements, leaving those decisions to the discretion of field commanders. The declaration in the 1845 artillery tactics that with respect to combined operations of artillery, cavalry, and infantry — "No rules can be laid down for conducting batteries to the positions they are to occupy; for the order, gait, and direction of each battery, are modified by the configuration of the ground to be passed over, as well as by the march of the infantry and cavalry" — could be applied to American theory and practice as a whole.[40]

Indeed, we should not overestimate the effects of all these efforts. For the entire antebellum period, there was some truth to future Confederate Lt. Gen. Richard S. Ewell's jibe that on the frontier he had "learned all about commanding fifty United States dragoons, and forgotten everything else."[41] Nevertheless, despite all the challenges of institutional weakness and frontier service, enough American officers maintained sufficient professional pride to build for their service a strong foundation in European military tactics. The simple presence of even some sophisticated debate over such tactics impresses us all the more, especially when compared to the state of the army before the War of 1812. But in the end, beyond the most elementary of military skills, American soldiers of this era would still have to learn their craft through experience above all else, and experience they would receive aplenty in Mexico.

CHAPTER THREE

The Old Army's Vindication

The Mexican War

★ ★ ★

One historian has called the Mexican War a "rehearsal for conflict" — a sort-of dry run for the larger conflict that occurred thirteen years later.[1] Many future West Point generals learned their trade in the field during the Mexican War, whose lessons and legacies would prove both problematic and indispensable for the later fratricidal conflict. Many of the earlier war's distinguishing characteristics foretold to some extent the later clash of arms: conflicts between professionals and citizen-soldiers, civil-military tensions at the highest levels of war making, domestic political disagreements with battlefield implications, and a contentious debate over slavery's future in the republic. Nevertheless, the Mexican War's actual combatants possessed no such foresight, and our own knowledge of the Civil War can be as much hindrance as blessing in understanding the Mexican War on its own terms.

One important underlying cause of the Civil War — the political dispute over the fate of slavery in territory acquired after the Mexican War — required a decisive American victory in Mexico. Unfortunately, any study that looks back on the Mexican War from the later sectional conflict can fall prey to glibly assuming the existence of that decisive victory. Much of the war's far-from-preordained results stemmed from the deliberate creation of a reasonably competent professional military establishment in the United States after the end of the War of 1812. Furthermore, the outcome of individual battles and campaigns frequently hung in the balance, depending on the vagaries of individual command decisions and the capricious fortunes of war.[2]

Nevertheless, American military professionals interpreted the war in a straightforward fashion. Indeed, the war vindicated their faith in professional military expertise, and the stunning success of American arms cannot gainsay that belief. After two years of active campaigning, the United States in effect conquered 529,017 square miles of territory, including the valuable and future state of California. In terms of both blood and treasure, approximately 12,876 American soldiers lost their lives while the monetary costs broke down to forty-eight cents an acre.[3] These costs were far from trivial, but they remain astonishingly low. Whatever its morality or lack thereof, when seen in purely military terms, we must declare the Mexican War a glorious triumph for American arms.

In retrospect, that triumph was all the more impressive in light of its less than entirely expected nature. Both Mexican and British observers had a reasonably fair understanding of the deep flaws in the vaunted militia system, an understanding far more plausible than most contemporary Americans' ideologically jaundiced view of the subject. Mexican scorn for the small regular army, which stood 3,300 men short of its authorized strength of 8,613, had much truth to it. The laborious reforms of the War of 1812 generals and their pupils at West Point had not yet met any test in battle. The Mexicans also knew of the decidedly mixed record of American arms during the previous war with England. The *Times* of London in April 1845 declared that "neither of the belligerents possesses an army at all proportioned to the vast extent of the operations necessary to accomplish any practical result." Poinsett himself expressed great admiration for the irregular Mexican cavalry while serving as the American minister to Mexico, while the British, Spanish, and Prussian ministers at Washington would later predict failure for Winfield Scott's Vera Cruz campaign.[4]

Moving beyond questions of tactical competence, Mexico also seemed to have serious advantages. Mexico had many similarities to the rebellious colonies of the American Revolution and the United States during the War of 1812 — it possessed a vast territory with primitive transportation infrastructure, great strategic depth, a population at least somewhat hostile to the invader, and all the advantages of defensive warfare. The United States had won both of those earlier wars despite much bungling and misdirection with military forces that possessed as many flaws as the problem-ridden Mexican army.

Rugged and unforgiving terrain marked northern Mexico, along with a climate difficult for any army and its accompanying logistics. The region also afforded the Mexicans a good deal of strategic depth, or, to use the words of Charles Elliot, British minister in Texas, "I believe that it would require very little skill and scarcely any exposure of the defending force to draw the invading columns well forward beyond all means of support from their own bases and depots into situations of almost inextricable difficulty." Indeed, the Mexican republic was no stranger to foreign invasion. It had, after all, thrown back a seaborne expeditionary force of Spanish regulars in 1829.[5] Any amphibious strike against the Mexican heartland would also require the negotiation of the dreaded yellow fever–plagued lowlands along the Gulf coast.

Partisan controversy in the United States even echoed, in a less severe form, Mexico's greatest weakness — chronic political instability. Furthermore, the same republicanism-based political culture that helped make the American polity more stable and effective as a whole had some of its own peculiar disadvantages in the military sphere. The continued American faith in the irresistible martial powers of the citizen-soldier would cause frictions between the regular army officers managing the expeditionary armies and much of their personnel. The Polk administration's loyalties to Jacksonian democracy — few West Pointers would have forgotten that it was Jackson himself who had ended Thayer's rule at West Point — only increased civil-military tensions. The Whig affiliations of the two major American field commanders, Bvt. Brig. Gen. Zachary Taylor and Winfield Scott, added further fuel to the fire. Compared to Mexico, the United States was a political and economic juggernaut, but the Union's socioeconomic advantages did not necessarily translate into military power.

Luckily for Polk, a professionally competent regular army, excellent leadership on the battlefield, and a fair amount of simple good fortune converted American social advantages into practical military power. The administration also benefited from Taylor's opportunity to concentrate and train his field army before hostilities commenced. In order to increase the pressure on the Mexicans to negotiate a settlement that would yield him California, Polk had dispatched Taylor in the summer of 1845 to command an "Army of Observation" at Corpus Christi, Texas. By mid-October, Taylor had concentrated almost four thousand officers and men — most of the regular army. The concentration allowed both officers and enlisted men to drill and train in the large-unit maneuvers of a proper European-style army, which the widely dispersed state of the old army in its Indian campaigns usually prevented. The period of training clearly did Taylor much good, although its benefits should not be exaggerated.[6]

On February 3, Taylor received an order from Secretary of War William Marcy to advance to the Rio Grande (see Map 1). The Army of Observation began its 150-mile march on March 8; after reaching the river, Taylor and the Mexican garrison at Matamoros on opposite sides of the

Rio Grande eyed each other warily. The overall Mexican commander, Maj. Gen. Mariano Arista, formally announced the opening of hostilities to Taylor shortly after the former's arrival at Matamoros on April 24. Arista began to cross the Rio Grande, and Taylor proceeded to reinforce Fort Texas, a work planned and begun earlier by Capt. Joseph K. F. Mansfield, a West Point–trained engineer and future Union major general. Complaints about an excessive emphasis in the West Point curriculum aside, the presence of trained engineer officers in Taylor's army proved especially useful, because it allowed Taylor to march most of his army to his supply base at Port Isabel while leaving only a five-hundred-man garrison to hold Fort Texas.[7]

Arista responded by leaving a force under Maj. Gen. Pedro de Ampudia to lay Fort Texas under siege on May 3. The engineers' walls proved stout enough to withstand the Mexicans' light artillery, and the garrison held out while the primary mobile field armies maneuvered and dueled. On May 7, after receiving recruits at Fort Isabel, Taylor marched down to relieve Fort Texas. Arista recalled Ampudia from the siege lines around Fort Texas and sought to block Taylor's advance at a water hole named Palo Alto. The two forces collided with one another on May 8, where Taylor won a tactical victory, by virtue of holding the field, but not a strategic one, because the road to Matamoras remained obstructed.

Superior American artillery at Palo Alto compensated for a Mexican superiority in numbers: of 2,288 soldiers under Taylor, 9 were killed, 44 wounded, and 2 missing, while of around 3,270 Mexicans, 102 were killed, 129 wounded, and 26 were missing. The battlefield was reasonably open, allowing the excellent American field artillery to work at its full potential. Some reports claimed that small-arms fire killed no more than a dozen Mexicans. On the American left, the artillery proved absolutely crucial, with Col. James Duncan's battery doing the most to win the day. The laborious reforms of Ringgold, who fell mortally wounded during the battle at the head of a battery, and his fellow artillerymen during the late 1830s and early 1840s had already reaped tremendous benefits.[8]

On the next day, May 9, Arista withdrew his troops to a strong defensive position called Resaca de la Palma by the Americans and Resaca de la Guerrero by the Mexicans. Chaparral, a sort of thick brush, dominated the field, which drastically reduced the effectiveness of artillery. Nevertheless, its potency the previous day continued to have a profound effect on Mexican morale. That bruising experience had weakened the rank and file's trust in Arista, which Ampudia's conspiratorial whispers of treason

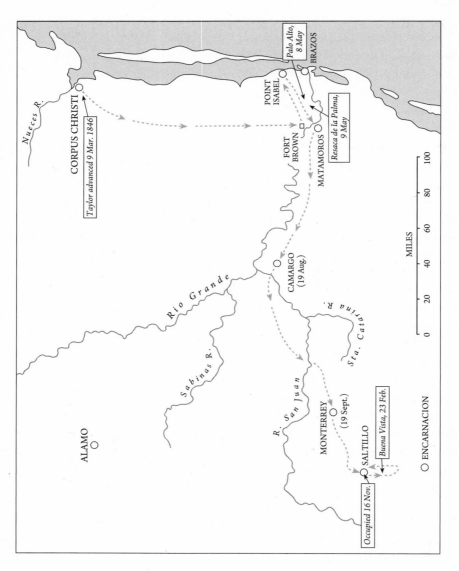

MAP 1. The Mexican War: Zachary Taylor's Campaign

Taylor advanced 9 Mar. 1846

Palo Alto, 8 May

Resaca de la Palma, 9 May

Occupied 16 Nov.

Buena Vista, 23 Feb.

CORPUS CHRISTI

POINT ISABEL

BRAZOS

FORT BROWN

MATAMOROS

CAMARGO (19 Aug.)

MONTERREY (19 Sept.)

SALTILLO

ENCARNACION

ALAMO

Nueces R.

Rio Grande

Sabinas R.

R. San Juan

Sta. Catarina R.

MILES

0   20   40   60   80   100

only exacerbated. To add insult to injury, many of the Mexican troops had had no opportunity to eat for a full day. Nor did Arista himself recognize the threat Taylor presented until it was too late.[9]

When Taylor's advance guard made contact, he threw Ringgold's old battery, now commanded by 1st Lt. Randolph Ridgely, forward on the road while the infantry was deployed in "open order" into the chaparral. The fighting was confused and chaotic, which made overall command and control difficult, if not impossible. This confusion played, however, to American strengths in small-unit leadership, stemming in part from the old army's new cohorts of West Point–trained junior officers. Taylor was not known for his dexterity in grand tactics, and his exposed place at the front of the line in the American center suited him just as well. In their highly dispersed state, and with no opportunity to use conventional shock tactics, most of the American infantry fought in effect as light infantry, except for the fact that the crowded chaos of the chaparral must have made aimed fire essentially irrelevant. A small party of American troops discovered a path that allowed the Mexican left to be turned, and the Mexican army broke. The Mexicans eventually retreated to Linares, where by the end of May barely 2,638 men could be mustered. U.S. forces now possessed the crucial moral advantage of victory in the war's first battles, an advantage that would never be relinquished for the duration of the conflict. One British general rightly claimed that "victories gained . . . early in a war engender that feeling of self-confidence which is, in fact, the twin brother of success."[10]

The old army as a corporate institution deserved almost all the credit for these early victories. Other factors do not suffice as explanations. Taylor's generalship had left much to be desired: although his indomitable courage profoundly inspired the troops in his immediate presence, "Old Zach" proved entirely unable to restrain infighting among his own senior officers during the army's encampment at Corpus Christi and had left most command decisions on both battlefields to his more professional subordinates. American arms proved fortunate that neither battle required much tactical cunning on his part. The Mexicans had not represented a hopeless cause: Arista was hardly a brilliant general, but he was not cowardly or inept; Ampudia's destructive scheming was matched by Taylor's loss of Bvt. Brig. Gen. William J. Worth's services for the sake of a petty spat over the vagaries of brevet versus lineal rank. The average Mexican soldier was a dissatisfied and abused conscript, but the old army also struggled with desertion and relied on some of the most desperate members of

THE OLD ARMY'S VINDICATION

American society to fill its ranks. Furthermore, many Mexican troops had fought bravely and well.[11]

The Mexican forces suffered from crucial disadvantages in professional expertise and small-unit leadership, as seen both in American artillery superiority and in the chaotic small-unit engagements at Resaca de la Palma. Resaca de la Palma showed that the dispersed frontier army did not have the purely deleterious influence on American military effectiveness that old army reformers had so often bewailed. The battle's decentralized small-unit engagements, with company-grade and noncommissioned officers providing most of the leadership, had many similarities with the scouts and skirmishes that marked so many of the Indian wars. Duty on a frontier post inculcated a certain independence of spirit and self-reliance among even the most junior of officers. In broken and rugged terrain, or in an urban setting such as the later battle at Monterrey, individual initiative on the part of company-grade officers could prove far more useful than "scientific" expertise in artillery or fortification. Indeed, the old army's campaigns of pacification against hostile Indian peoples would also prove similar to later clashes with Mexican guerrillas.

Nevertheless, it was still the decidedly unprofessional Zachary Taylor who captured the American imagination more than anyone else during the war. The almost immediate idolization of Taylor after Palo Alto and Resaca de la Palma, which eventually catapulted "Old Rough and Ready" to the presidency, revealed the strength of preexisting martial ideals in the United States. Taylor — with his plain frock coat, self-mended britches, bluff courage in battle, and suspicion of the newfangled military science — corresponded almost perfectly to the American ideal of a republican general. In contrast, Scott, a far abler commander, had the misfortune of being called "Old Fuss and Feathers" for good reason. Even the triumphs of Vera Cruz could not make up for his aristocratic hauteur and marked egotism.[12]

Polk himself had a negative view of Scott, believing him a pompous pedant, and ignored much of his wise military advice early in the war. Scott had advised the administration in the summer of 1846 that the volunteers should not enter Mexico until September in order to avoid the problematic rainy season on the Rio Grande and use the time to properly train the new volunteer regiments. The Polk administration, strongly committed to the Anglo-American militia tradition and deeply suspicious of Scott's previous sallies into Whig politics, saw all this as unnecessary delay. The American citizen-soldier had no need for Old World training, with its drill and regimentation—manly republican virtue would be more than enough. Scott did not help matters when several notes were published—one seeming to claim the mantle of martyrdom for being so busy that he could have only "a hasty plate of soup" for lunch and another complaining about having to take the field with a fire on his rear, presumably from the Polk administration. All these factors prevented Scott from taking any field command in the summer of 1846.[13]

Taylor's rising political star would also cause further frictions with the Polk administration, eventually leading to a triangle of mutual suspicion and antipathy among and between the head of the American state and his two senior army commanders. Although American political culture denigrated standing armies and aristocratic generals, it also placed great value on military achievement in candidates for political office, as long as those former soldiers seemed properly republican. The humble Taylor fit the bill perfectly after his early victories on the Rio Grande, and Secretary of War William Marcy commented on Taylor's presidential potential shortly after receiving word of Palo Alto and Resaca de la Palma. Unfortunately for the Polk administration, Taylor turned out to be a Whig. Furthermore, the administration had a better idea than did the public of Taylor's failings as a field commander. It became increasingly suspicious of Taylor's political ambitions and military capacities, which caused Taylor in turn to become increasingly suspicious of the administration.[14]

While new regiments of these volunteers drilled and concentrated on the Rio Grande, Taylor prepared a full-scale invasion of the northern provinces of Mexico (see Map 1). On September 20, Taylor ordered Worth (who had returned to the army) to send his division to the north and west of the strategic city of Monterrey to cut off the Mexicans' communications with Saltillo. Ampudia commanded the Mexican garrison of 7,303 men opposing Taylor's invasion force of 6,000. Worth's troops performed well on September 21 and 22, but the remaining forces under Taylor's direct command bungled their assaults on Mexican positions to the east. On September 23, Brig. Gen. John A. Quitman moved into the city from the east. Worth, who had received no orders from Taylor, assaulted the Mexicans from the west on his own initiative to support Quitman's advance. American forces made progress at driving into the city, but resistance was fierce enough that Taylor lost confidence and ordered a withdrawal during the afternoon in order to avoid night fighting in the city. Luckily for Taylor, Ampudia then asked for terms. The Mexicans surrendered the city, and the two parties even concluded an armistice. Nevertheless, in historian

THE OLD ARMY'S VINDICATION

Justin Smith's harsh words, "nothing saved Taylor from a disaster that would have meant the ruin of his army but the poltroonery of one man, Ampudia." However messy, the American victory at Monterrey only further strengthened the image of American invincibility; after Ampudia's withdrawal to San Luis Potosí, Mexican officers forbade further talk of American military excellence.[15]

The Polk administration repudiated Taylor's armistice, which the increasingly paranoid general interpreted, not unreasonably, as a rebuke. The political situation had become increasingly complicated in Washington, where David A. Wilmot, a northern Democratic representative from Pennsylvania, had pushed through the House a provision that aimed to prohibit slavery from any territory acquired from Mexico. This triggered yet another sectional controversy. War weariness gradually worsened and opponents of the war became increasingly vocal as prospects for a short and decisive conflict receded. Civil-military tensions became increasingly tense in the fall of 1846, when the Polk administration realized that a campaign against Mexico City itself would be needed to fulfill its war aims. The administration reluctantly chose Scott as the expedition's commander, because neither Taylor nor the potential Democratic candidates for the command had the military capacity for such a complex operation.[16]

Increasing tensions among Scott, Taylor, and Polk would lead to Taylor's last and unnecessary military triumph at Buena Vista. Taylor, aware of the Polk administration's suspicions, misinterpreted Scott's assignment to the Vera Cruz campaign as one part of a dastardly conspiracy to undermine his own position. Taylor even broke with Scott, who had always tried to sustain his subordinate's authority against the machinations of the increasingly hostile Polk. Scott and the administration left Taylor enough forces to defend his position at Monterrey, while they assigned Taylor's seasoned regulars to Scott's Vera Cruz force. Nevertheless, in an act of extraordinary pique, Taylor disregarded his orders to stand on the defensive and moved his forces to an advanced and more vulnerable position in the vicinity of Saltillo.[17]

With the political situation in Mexico demanding a victory to redeem the nation's arms, Santa Anna marched his army north from San Luis Potosí to face a weakened and exposed Taylor. Even after a difficult march, Santa Anna still arrived at La Encarnación, roughly thirty-five miles from Taylor's position at Agua Nueva, in mid-February 1847 with 15,000 men. Recognizing the danger, Taylor rapidly withdrew to a strong defensive position chosen by Brig. Gen. John E. Wool, a doughty professional, at Buena

THE OLD ARMY'S VINDICATION

Vista. Taylor would fight the coming battle with a little more than 4,500 officers and men, almost all of them volunteers with the exception of three batteries of regular army artillery and a few hundred dragoons.[18]

The inherent strength of the American position, the excellence of American field artillery, the inspiring example of Taylor's indomitable courage, and a fair amount of luck saved American arms from a crushing defeat. Santa Anna himself recognized the strength of the position and later likened the field to Thermopylae, but his provisions were running short and he decided to commit to battle. Like all closely fought battles, not much separated victory and defeat. A more vigorously conducted lancer charge against the stand of Mississippians and Indianans here, a sudden assault by the Mexican vanguard against the still unprepared Americans there, and the battle might have turned out very differently.[19]

Nevertheless, armies make their own luck much of the time, and the American artillery arm proved its worth again. Wool declared in his report that "without our artillery we could not have maintained our position a single hour." When Mexican lancers threatened to fall on the American supply train at the hacienda of Buena Vista, the batteries of Capt. Thomas W. Sherman and Bvt. Maj. Braxton Bragg (the future commander of the Confederate Army of Tennessee) helped an Indianan brigade and the 1st Mississippi—the latter unit commanded by Col. Jefferson Davis, a West Point graduate and future president of the Confederacy—repulse the Mexican horse. Later, when the American center was about to break, the same batteries of Sherman and Bragg just barely held off surging Mexican troops, despite the absence of proper infantry support.[20]

Taylor may have brought on the battle through his own stubborn folly, but his unflappable demeanor helped retrieve the situation. When Taylor's able aide, Maj. William W. S. Bliss, declared the day lost at one point, Taylor replied, "I know it, but the volunteers don't know it. Let them alone, we'll see what they do."[21] Taylor personified in his battlefield bearing that crucial but indefinable quality of martial presence under fire that every successful general needed. However much the corps of engineers dominated West Point and presided as a demigod over the old army, war was not truly a "science." The admiration of the volunteers for Old Zach was as much a product of ideological preconceptions and newspaper humbug as a representation of reality, but if enough individuals believe in a myth and misrepresentation, the idea can take on a life of its own. Furthermore, Taylor's unflappable courage did in point of fact have real battlefield benefits. Brilliance bereft of a certain steadiness of spirit does

THE OLD ARMY'S VINDICATION

63
★

no good in war; courage can even make up for a distinctly subpar mind. Looking forward to the Civil War, the organizational and institutional weakness of both contending armies would make the peculiar personal qualities of individual commanders even more profoundly important.

Winfield Scott may not have had Taylor's bluff indifference toward hostile fire, but he was no shrinking violet and, like Taylor, he had a distinguished service record dating back to the War of 1812. Furthermore, Scott had many of the martial talents that Taylor lacked — sound strategic sense, organizational acumen, and reasonably effective control over subordinates in battles. Those qualities, combined with regular army efficiency, a generally strong performance by the volunteers, and Mexican missteps would all help make the Vera Cruz campaign of 1847 one of the greatest achievements in the history of American arms.

Not only did the final decisive strike against Mexico City require a commander of greater strategic capacity than Old Zach; it also demanded a higher level of institutional sophistication than did the previous American campaigns. Taylor's battles had relied on excellent small-unit leadership for infantry, a competent artillery arm, and just enough administrative support from the staff bureaus, especially with regards to logistics. The western expeditions in New Mexico and California involved impressive marches and great independence of initiative on the part of American commanders, but those small-scale expeditions looked more like enlarged versions of Indian-fighting expeditions than nation-state warfare.[22] In contrast, Scott's campaign would require a high level of cooperation with the navy, a full-scale amphibious assault, a siege train, and far more extended lines of communication than those faced by Taylor. The Polk administration had hoped — erroneously, as it turned out — that the occupation of Mexico's northern provinces would force its government to the negotiating table. American military policy now demanded the more ambitious and risky venture of landing troops on a hostile coast and marching on the Mexican capital.

Scott's assault troops landed on March 9, 1847, at Collado, roughly two and a half miles from Vera Cruz proper, in specially designed surfboats (see Map 2). The local Mexican commander, Brig. Gen. Juan Morales, overestimated American strength and allowed the operation to proceed uncontested. By evening, the entire assault force — a little more than 8,600 men — was ashore without a single casualty. On March 18, the American forces began building formal siege works. The engineering expertise of Scott's staff, including Capt. Robert E. Lee, served him well,

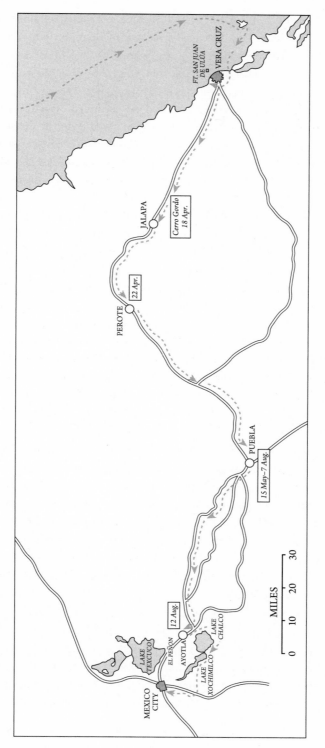

MAP 2. The Mexican War: Winfield Scott's Campaign, Overview

as did the army's ordnance branch. Scott's excellent relations with the navy also proved crucial, because a battery of heavy naval guns brought shoreside contributed to the siege. Siege craft was the most "scientific" of contemporary military operations, and one that did actually require the technical education provided at West Point. Whether every regular army officer needed to know how to man and place a mortar is a different issue, but the American armies of the War of 1812 would not have been able to conduct a similar operation. After a four-day bombardment that threw 463,000 pounds of hot iron into the city, and the deaths of several hundred Mexican civilians and troops, the garrison surrendered both the city and the covering fortress of San Juan de Ulúa.[23]

It was then imperative that the expeditionary force move inland before the onset of the yellow fever season. The advance guard started the march inland on April 2 with the rest of the army following shortly thereafter. The route of the American march was predetermined by its heavy artillery train, which could be supported only by the national highway that led to Mexico City. By April 12, the divisions of Bvt. Maj. Gen. David E. Twiggs and Maj. Gen. Robert Patterson reached a strong set of Mexican fortifications at Cerro Gordo. The position possessed great inherent strength, but a shortage of water, widespread illness, and the intimidating record of American arms hurt Mexican morale. The engineers again proved their worth when Lee located a path that allowed Scott to turn the Mexican left — a potential gambit that a talented Mexican engineer, Lt. Col. Manuel M. Robles Pezuala, had warned Santa Anna of to no avail. Sappers made the route practicable for infantry and artillery on the sixteenth and on the following day Twiggs's division captured the important hill of Atalaya. With covering fire from artillery dragged up to the summit of Atalaya, a direct assault by portions of Twiggs's division took the important hill of El Telégrafo on April 18, while another force cut off the Mexican escape route. Brig. Gen. Gideon J. Pillow, a political appointee, mishandled a supporting attack on three detached Mexican batteries, but the error was retrieved when the Mexicans surrendered after realizing that their communications were cut. The complete rout of the Mexican forces, at a cost of 63 killed and 368 wounded out of 8,500 men engaged, essentially dissolved the Mexican army for the time being.[24]

Scott continued to move American forces farther into the valley of Mexico, but he decided to send home his twelve-month volunteers before the onset of the dreaded yellow fever season. The volunteers refused to reenlist despite Scott's exhortations and the obviously exposed situation of the American expeditionary force. The whole episode may have reminded Scott of the battle of Queenston during the War of 1812 where militiamen had refused to cross the border in his support, which helped lead to his eventual capture. The departure of the volunteers only further darkened the old army's opinion of citizen-soldiers, who seemed in this case more concerned with their rights than what the regulars saw as their patriotic duty. Scott's army now numbered barely 7,113 men.[25]

In the meantime, Scott concentrated his remaining forces at Puebla where he lived off the surrounding countryside and awaited the arrival of reinforcements. Nicholas P. Trist, head clerk of the State Department and a fluent Spanish-speaker, arrived at Vera Cruz on May 6 to serve as the Polk administration's diplomatic representative. Scott, perhaps suffering from the ennui of waiting for the new volunteer regiments to arrive, misconstrued Trist's mission as an attempt by the Polk administration to undermine his authority and treated the envoy accordingly. Fortunately for all parties involved, the two figures eventually managed to reconcile. Scott and Trist attempted to reach a diplomatic settlement with what passed for a Mexican government at the time but failed. Eventually, the new regiments of volunteers arrived, and on August 7 Scott resumed the advance toward the enemy capital. He now had a mighty host numbering all of 10,738 officers and men — four "divisions" under Twiggs, Worth, Quitman, and Pillow — to conquer Mexico City.[26]

Santa Anna, a master at extemporizing armies, had around 20,000 to 25,000 troops available to defend the capital and made no real attempt at hindering the early portions of Scott's advance. The Mexican forces were extremely raw, but they were at least drawn from families of a higher social class than the impoverished peasants who had manned most of the previous Mexican armies. The remaining residents of Mexico City had recovered to some degree from the disaster at Cerro Gordo and were ready to help Santa Anna repulse the foreign invaders. Furthermore, wetlands surrounded the city, which restricted American forces to a network of raised roadways that the Mexicans could easily defend and fortify. From the American position at Ayotla, roughly fifteen miles east of Mexico City, the invading expeditionary force had only four practicable lines of advance, all known to the Mexicans (see Map 3). The Americans could not stay at Puebla forever — their numbers were scarce; like all premodern armies in camp, disease was an ever-present scourge; and the yellow fever cut off their escape. Scott needed victories, and he needed them soon; the Duke of Wellington himself claimed that Scott's expedition was doomed.[27]

THE OLD ARMY'S VINDICATION

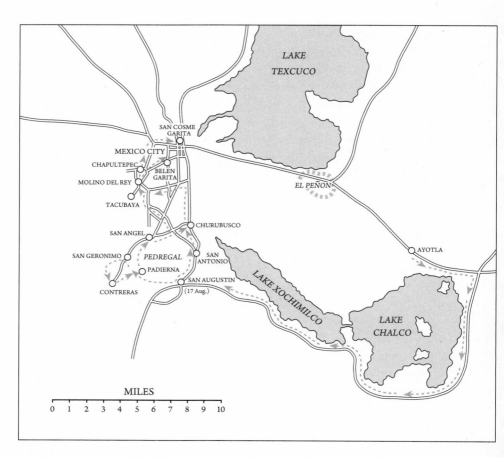

MAP 3. The Mexican War: Winfield Scott's Campaign, Mexico City

Scott once again put his engineers to good use by having them recon-
noiter the different lines of advance. In the end, Scott chose the south-
ernmost route, which allowed him to bypass the most powerful Mexican
works. Scott succeeded in turning those fortifications east of the city, but
now he faced another set of Mexican defenses and a rocky and treacherous
lava field. The lava field, roughly two and a half miles across, stood between the troops of Maj. Gen. Gabriel Valencia at a promontory overlook-
ing the Padierna farm and the strong Mexican position at San Antonio on
the east side of the field. Once again, the engineers proved their worth.
Lee and 1st Lt. P. G. T. Beauregard managed to find an improvable path
through the difficult lava field to Padierna. On the morning of August
19, Lee supervised the improvement of this trail by work parties drawn

from Pillow's division. Scott hoped to use this path to turn the San Antonio position from the east. The commanding general did not expect a general engagement, but when Pillow found Valencia's command before him, he ordered under his own authority an immediate attack that was promptly repulsed. The Mexicans even managed to bloody the usually superior American artillery.[28]

American forces eventually managed to turn Valencia when troops under Brig. Gen. Persifor F. Smith discovered a small path that allowed them to storm the strong Mexican position from the rear, while Twiggs conducted a diversionary attack to their front. Lee had provided crucial services as a guide and messenger in the coordination of this decisive assault. Smith's attack was a classic example of the power of shock tactics; his assault force fired one volley and then let loose a bayonet charge. Valencia's force disintegrated, with 700 fatalities and 843 captured, at an American cost of only 60 men killed and wounded. Santa Anna then withdrew to Churubusco and rallied his forces in a well-situated convent and a fortified bridgehead.

Scott smelled blood and ordered Twiggs to unleash an immediate attack on the convent in an effort to smash the withdrawing Mexican forces. Twiggs's troops made disjointed and disorganized assaults on the position to no avail. American artillery found itself bested again. After that effort petered out, Worth reached the bridgehead and began another headlong assault, with no engineering reconnaissance of the enemy position. The Mexicans repulsed the initial attack, but Scott ordered a turning movement by Brig. Gen. James Shields's and Brig. Gen. Franklin Pierce's brigades to cut off the Mexican line of retreat behind Churubusco. This drew off some of the troops at the bridgehead. A portion of Worth's command also managed to flank the Mexican left and threatened to cut off its line of retreat. The Mexicans lost heart, and units from the 8th and 5th Infantry Regiments finally managed to storm the works.[29]

The elimination of the bridgehead allowed U.S. forces to bring dominating artillery fire on the convent and weaken its defenses. The convent's garrison fought fiercely, partly because of the presence of the San Patricios, a unit composed of American deserters. The garrison finally fell after an assault by the 3rd Infantry, yielding 1,259 prisoners. In the meantime, the brigades of Pierce and Shields charged the Mexican reserves stationed on the road north of the river and drove them from the field. Santa Anna estimated that he had lost more than a third of his men, while Scott saw 12 percent of 8,497 men engaged shot down.[30]

Churubusco was not a model victory, but neither was it a near disaster like Monterrey. American commanders had at times proved far too aggressive, even to the point of reckless arrogance. Historians have criticized Scott for not maintaining complete control of his forces during the entire engagement, but Scott still emerged victorious. While Cerro Gordo and Contreras had depended in part on excellent reconnaissance by the engineers and dexterous turning movements, Churubusco relied more on the stubborn stolidity of American infantry. Like Buena Vista, the battle was won as much by American élan as by tactical skill. The American invaders had acquired that crucial measure of self-confidence that comes only with a consistent and constant stream of victory.

The historian K. Jack Bauer has argued that the Mexican forces were now beaten, and that Scott could have taken the city with a vigorous pursuit. Instead, Scott decided to allow his troops to take a breather and even went as far as to sign an armistice with the Mexican government, believing it a preliminary to peace. Scott, like the Polk administration, hoped for a negotiated settlement rather than the complete subjugation of Mexico. When Santa Anna disregarded several provisions of the truce and Scott realized that he had misjudged the Mexican political situation, the American commander resumed active operations on September 6. Upon receiving erroneous word of a cannon foundry at El Molino del Rey, a complex of fortified buildings southwest of the city, Scott ordered Worth's division to take the position by storm on September 8. Although ultimately successful, the attack proved to be a costly and essentially pointless victory. Worth lost a quarter of his division, and the Americans might have fared even worse if the Mexican cavalry commander, Maj. Gen. Juan Alvarez, had pressed home a counterattack that may have been hindered by his fear of the American artillery.[31]

Scott now had to choose between two different lines of attack — the causeways leading to the southern gates or the western approaches to the city. Scott overrode most of his engineers' advice and chose the western approaches. The western approaches would require the American forces to reduce the garrison at Chapultepec, the fortified citadel that normally housed Mexico's military academy, but that avenue of advance stood on firmer ground than the marshes in front of the fortified southern gates. On September 11 Quitman's division mounted a demonstration to the south of the city, and on September 12 U.S. forces hurled two thousand artillery rounds against Chapultepec, causing considerable damage. Quitman's demonstration had confused Santa Anna, and he attempted to shift forces to the focus of Scott's attack only on the day of the artillery bombardment when it was already too late. During the same evening, Scott readied his forces for an assault on September 13. He had stripped his right nearly bare for the sake of his turning movement.[32] It was vintage Scott—avoid the strongest points of enemy resistance through maneuver and deception in order to strike at his vulnerabilities.

Scott ordered the volunteer divisions of Pillow and Quitman to form the bulk of the strike force, but he attached to both units special storming parties of regulars drawn from the divisions of Twiggs and Worth. Capt. Silas Casey, a future authority on infantry tactics in the old army and Civil War major general, commanded the regulars attached to Quitman. Around 160 Marines also provided another picked force. The Mexican position was impressive but undermanned. The initial American assaults were unsuccessful, but continued pounding—some of it coming from reinforcements provided by one of Worth's regular army brigades—finally broke the defenders. On a tactical level, the assaults do not impress the impartial observer. One of the storming parties reached its objective only to find its scaling ladders missing, which ground its effort to a halt. Pillow's and Quitman's initial assaults became disjointed and confused. American artillery did at least play an important role in softening the position. Nevertheless, the attack's eventual success owed more than anything else to Scott's successful strategic deception, rather than any special tactical dexterity with regard to the assault itself.[33]

After Chapultepec's fall, Mexico City's fate was essentially decided, and both Quitman and Worth took the Belén and San Cosmé gates. Santa Anna still had available roughly 5,000 men and eighteen guns at the city's citadel, and another 7,000 in reserve. American losses had also been significant, although not crippling: 130 killed, 703 wounded, and 29 missing. Furthermore, the battered American forces could no longer support one another directly. Nevertheless, many important civilian leaders in the city feared the destruction and chaos of urban fighting. The Mexican troops still had numbers, but they were also severely demoralized. Ever since Taylor's first battles on the Rio Grande, the Mexican army had been defeated time after time. When the Stars and Stripes went up over Chapultepec, Santa Anna had snarled, "I believe if we were to plant our batteries in Hell the damned Yankees would take them from us." Or, to use the resigned words of another ill-fated defender of Mexico, "God is a Yankee." Santa Anna declared his duty to the demands of honor done, and civic leaders surrendered the city to the triumphant *gringos*.[34]

THE OLD ARMY'S VINDICATION

The war was not quite over yet, however, and some American forces remained in Mexico until September 6, 1848. Both armies agreed to an armistice on March 6, 1848, after Trist managed to finally extract a treaty out of the Mexican government, despite his official recall by the Polk administration. Mexican guerrillas vexed U.S. forces until the signing of the armistice, long after Scott's capture of the Mexican capital. Anderson, the highly professional artilleryman, had worried about Santa Anna resorting to an irregular strategy as early as November 1846, describing such a conflict as "the most dangerous of all kinds of war." Nevertheless, while U.S. forces took losses, Polk's successful acquisition of all his initial war aims do not speak well of the insurgents' success. Harmony also proved elusive within the American high command. The administration unceremoniously relieved Scott in January 1848 because of an embarrassing dispute between Scott, Worth, and Pillow.[35] The whole affair smeared the reputations of all parties involved, both the generals in Mexico City and the Polk administration, but the spat was in the end more petty than harmful.

The political conflagration over slavery's fate in America's new conquests was anything but petty. After many twists and turns, this political dispute would finally result in the election of Abraham Lincoln and the outbreak of war. The political legacies of the Mexican War did not stand alone, however. The experience the old army acquired in Mexico, both as individuals and as a corporate institution, could not help but have a substantial influence on the conduct of the Civil War, because the regular army fought no other nation-state wars in the interval between the two conflicts.

On the level of corporate organization, the war vindicated the regular army's faith in all the laborious reforms enacted after the War of 1812 to professionalize the American military establishment. For all of their mishaps, every Mexican War battle was at least a tactical victory for the American forces. Taylor's highly professional subordinates made up for his limitations as a field commander, and their technical excellence in such diverse areas as artillery and logistics made Taylor's very victories possible. Although many regulars understated the quality and contributions of the volunteers, the fact remains that the old army formed the core of the most successful American field armies.[36] Even at Buena Vista, where the American infantry was all volunteer, regulars had officered and manned the important artillery batteries.

While these tensions did not harm the war effort in any substantive way, real frictions arose between the regulars and volunteers during the war. The regulars saw the volunteers, enlisted men and officers alike, as inefficient, incompetent, undisciplined, and even barbaric in their conduct toward Mexican civilians. The volunteers, in turn, saw the regulars as arrogant, pedantic, rigid, and jealous of the volunteers' rights and merits. One regular, 2nd Lt. George B. McClellan, wrote his mother that "the volunteers carry on in a most shameful and disgraceful manner; they think nothing of robbing and killing the Mexicans." Even Taylor continuously complained about the depredations of the volunteers, which outraged regular army professionals in general. Regular army men, in contrast, demanded a higher standard of conduct from their own men for both ethical and military reasons. They hoped to avoid inciting the Mexican population into supporting guerrilla violence against American forces. Many of these old army officers would carry these attitudes into the Civil War — the most important being McClellan, who would become the most prominent Federal military advocate of a conciliatory policy toward Confederate civilians.[37] This would help lead to frictions between conciliatory old army officers in the Union high command and Radical Republican advocates of "hard war" policies against secessionists — the most important being the use of emancipation to attack the Confederate social system.

Nevertheless, while the regulars saw the war as a vindication of their faith in professionalism, and although their achievements did inspire a higher public opinion of West Point, that did not mean that most Americans had forsaken their traditional faith in the citizen-soldier. Historian Robert W. Johannsen points out that "in the general praise that was directed toward the military achievements in Mexico the distinction between [volunteers and regulars] was often blurred." The fallen Ringgold could be praised as both romantic hero and well-trained professional at the same time.[38] The war's victorious conclusion did not indicate any real need to increase dramatically the size of the peacetime regular army, while the use of volunteer regiments seemed to solve any lingering concerns about the collapse of the traditional militia system.

Citizen-soldier enthusiasts were not the only individuals who inherited a legacy of mild complacency from the war's successes. The American artillery had proved itself tremendously effective in suitable terrain, and American infantry tactics also seemed more than adequate, with shock tactics and the bayonet retaining their effectiveness. Furthermore, light infantry tactics and skirmishers retained the important, but not predominant, role that they had held in Napoleonic practice. For example, Capt. C. F. Smith, a future Civil War major general, commanded a light infantry battalion during the war. During the Mexican War, light infantry and sharpshooters performed traditional roles, such as the securing of a line of march and reconnaissance. Although Americans had a tendency to exaggerate the military efficacy of their supposed prowess with the rifle, the Mexican War also did see the use of skirmishers and even some sniping. For the most part, the Mexican War confirmed the old army's faith in the Napoleonic-era tactical system it developed in the interval between the War of 1812 and Palo Alto.[39]

The old army had plausible enough reasons for its complacency, however. The prospect of future problems during the Civil War, mostly involving the sheer size of that conflict's volunteer armies, only appears clear with hindsight. Finally, although the war vindicated the regulars' faith in professionalism, there remained a powerful impulse toward further professional development and reform, and the service adopted new rifle-muskets, French light infantry tactics, and artillery equipage in the interval between the Mexican War and the Civil War. In sum, the old army, for better or for worse, saw its sterling performance in Mexico as proof of its ability to master and guide further military change in the United States.

CHAPTER FOUR

Tactical Continuity in the Decade
before the Civil War

✷ ✷ ✷

Although it by no means rested on its laurels, the regular army did not depart from its comfortable professional tracks in the interlude between the Mexican Cession and the Civil War. Professional soldiers supervised gradual changes in weapons and tactics, while Jefferson Davis's reformist tenure as secretary of war (1853–57) looked much like Poinsett's steward-ship of the War Department in the late-1830s. Both Poinsett and Davis built on and further elaborated Calhoun's legacy, rather than institute any drastic change in American military policy. Two different wars and more than a generation's worth of experience had supported a military policy built on the foundation of a small but reasonably well-trained force of regulars. In times of "peace," the regulars guarded the restive Indian frontier in dispersed posts; in "war," they served as the veteran core of a mixed regular and volunteer army capable of defeating whatever modest nation-state army the United States might face from either European or hemispheric rivals. The striking military success of the Mexican War vin-dicated this system, and its basic premises would structure the old army's activities throughout the 1850s.

American policymakers had never intended the old army to serve as a training cadre for volunteer citizen-soldier armies numbering in the hundreds of thousands. Nevertheless, with the militia system in decrepit disrepair, both the Union and Confederate armies in 1861 possessed no alternative models of organization. Furthermore, the regulars needed no apologies for adopting the training-intensive military system that had proved so useful in Mexico. In any conflict with a European power, the old army would face an expeditionary force severely constrained in size by distance, while the less than overwhelming size of Mexican field armies during the previous war showed that no hemispheric power could swamp the small regular army with sheer numbers. Furthermore, even if old army officers had predicted the size and scale of the Civil War, few American officers and administrators would ever have countenanced a military establishment explicitly designed to crush a sectional rebellion. Indeed, sharp controversies in the North over the military's role in civil government during both the Civil War and Reconstruction showed that the strong Anglo-American animus against military intervention in civil affairs went far beyond specific debates over the fate of slavery as a social institution.[1]

During the interregnum between the Mexican War and the Civil War, the old army's officer corps proved active and vibrant, but even its most reformist officers continued to operate within a professional context that Calhoun would have recognized. The regular army developed and manufactured a new rifle-musket in line with contemporary trends in small-arms technology; it adopted a tactical system derived from the French chasseurs to correspond with the new weapons; it extended the course of instruction at West Point to increase the quality of military education; it continued to adapt and adjust the already excellent American artillery arm to match the European state of the art; it sent an observer mission to Europe to learn lessons from the Crimean War; and it even constituted true cavalry regiments, which better fit European practice. Every one of these reforms reflected the regular army's emphasis on training, discipline, and European-style professionalism, which it then bequeathed to the Union and Confederate armies.

The high level of professionalism demanded by the chasseurs' methods reflected well on the old army's desire to improve its service, while the regular army's reaction to the new rifle-musket also reflected a healthy willingness to blend the new with the old. American professionals had long experience with light infantry tactics and methods before the Mexican War, and they naturally saw the equipping of all infantry formations with the new rifle-musket as a natural extension of the Napoleonic practice of giving all infantry units training in light infantry tactics. Instead of only receiving some training in skirmishing and target practice, now line infantry would also be equipped with rifled weapons as opposed to smoothbore arms.

The old army did realize that the invention of the minié ball had accelerated the pace of change in infantry tactics to some extent, and American professionals, in response, moved to adopt the methods of the French Chasseurs à Pied. The chasseurs, an elite light infantry force, emphasized skirmishing, greater celerity in movement, intensified target practice, special training in bayonet fencing, and high levels of physical conditioning. Following Napoleonic practice, they did not totally discard shock tactics with the bayonet. The chasseurs' experience during French colonial campaigns in North Africa made their tactics even more appealing to American officers who had their own irregular wars against indigenous insurgents.[2] The Napoleonic Wars had seen a movement away from the cumbersome linear tactics of Frederick the Great to a more flexible articulation of small attack columns screened by clouds of dispersed skirmishers. American professionals simply carried that progression a step further by envisioning an even more dispersed and swift-moving battlefield that included riflemen carrying the new rifle-muskets moving at double quick time.

It was also the regular army's own Ordnance Department that tested, developed, and manufactured the new rifle-musket. The bureau has received some criticism from historians, who have argued that overly conservative regular army officers stifled weapons innovation during the Civil War, especially with regards to the adoption of breechloaders. Unfortunately, Allan Nevins's and Robert V. Bruce's portrayal of an Ordnance Department filled with excessively conservative officers ignores American officers' close examination of overseas developments in relation to small arms. In 1856 the bureau published for distribution throughout the regular army and the militia a collection of excerpts from both its own tests of rifle-muskets and experiments conducted by the British and the French. Ordnance officers may have made misjudgments both before and during the Civil War, but reasonable errors of judgment differ from overly conservative obstructionism.[3]

How exactly did new technological improvements affect infantry arms? To put it simply, the rifle-musket allowed infantrymen increased accuracy at longer ranges with no degradation in rate of fire. Rifling added a set of grooves along the interior of a barrel that imparted spin to a bullet, which stabilized it in flight. Before the invention of the minié ball by a French officer of the same name, however, rifled arms were beset by problems — the most important being acquiring a tight-enough fit between bullet and barrel to allow the grooves to impart the necessary spin. Early rifles sometimes even required the use of a mallet to pound a ball into the barrel for loading, which drastically increased the time needed to load a weapon. One could argue that rate of fire is even more important in military settings than range and accuracy, and the lethargic firing rates of conventional rifles prevented their use from spreading beyond specialized units.

In the 1840s, French officers experimented with various expedients and innovations, eventually resulting in the minié ball that used a conical bullet with a hollowed-out base containing a wooden plug. American ordnance officers adapted the French invention by doing away with the plug, which made the bullet easier to manufacture. The new "Burton bullet" could be easily dropped into a rifle-musket's barrel, because now the explosive force of the powder expanded the bullet's base and created a tight fit for the barrel's grooves. The bullet's conical tip also allowed for a more aerodynamic flight. The larger bullet resulted in reduced muzzle velocity, but the rifle-musket still had enough raw carrying power to be lethal at long ranges. In Ordnance Department tests, the new rifle-musket could penetrate three-and-a-quarter white pine planks (each plank being one-inch thick) at a range of a thousand yards.[4]

More importantly, the rifle-musket was far more accurate than previous smoothbore weapons. One modern authority, Jac Weller, found that he could "hit a 72 [inch] square target with at least three out of 15 shots at 400 yds. Nothing but sheer luck would put a spherical slug from a round ball rifle into a target of this size at this range." True smoothbore muskets were even worse — Weller commented that "if I could get five consecutive shots into a group less than 36″ across at 100 yds., I reckoned it mostly luck." In contrast, the Model 1855 Springfield group size was 11.5 inches at the same distance.[5]

While the Ordnance Department handled technical issues of design and production, Secretary of War Davis assigned Bvt. Lt. Col. William J. Hardee the task of developing a new tactical manual to go with the new weapon. Hardee had acquired an excellent Mexican War record after returning from the French cavalry school at Saumur. He chose the manual of the Chasseurs à Pied as his model, which he adjusted somewhat to fit American conditions. Hardee added instructions on loading and firing while kneeling and prone (a characteristic light infantry method), which were not present in the French original, and he gave somewhat more detailed instructions for a number of the commands. Hardee also had at least some contact with other officers while preparing his translation of the chasseur tactics. For example, he asked Bvt. Col. Edwin V. Sumner, a future Civil War major general, if there was a third volume of the chasseur tactics covering the "Evolutions of the Line" (drill for formations larger than a single battalion) and for clarification with regards to some fine points of drill. In late July 1854 the adjutant general requested a tactical board to convene at West Point to review Hardee's work, where it would have access to the school's excellent military library.[6]

The review board assembled in mid-August at West Point where it
used the corps of cadets and the engineer company stationed at the post as raw material for field trials. It issued its official report in December. The board's report provides a rare and underutilized window into professional opinion on Hardee's tactics, which in manual form give very little information on the background behind their creation. The report's stated purpose — "to present concisely, a view of this system and its general harmony with the existing drill for heavy Infantry" — is interesting in and of itself. In their original formulation, Hardee's tactics were never supposed to be a complete replacement for Scott's 1835 infantry tactics; the old army instead intended Hardee's contribution to be a light infantry supplement to the tactics of traditional "heavy infantry," that is, line infantry fighting in close order. Davis's original order of March 29, 1855, authorizing the manual explicitly declared the new tactics "adopted for the instruction of the troops when acting as Light Infantry or Riflemen," implying of course that Scott's tactics would be used when they were *not* acting as such units. As late as 1863, 1st Lt. George L. Willard — an old army authority on target practice — would argue for the continued use of smoothbore weapons among line infantry units, while specialist skirmisher units used the new rifled arms.[7]

The review board's report also made the point that "a battalion instructed in this system can take its place in a line of battle composed of heavy Infantry, and perform all the movements required in the evolutions of the line, as prescribed by our present system." It should be remembered that Hardee's manual — like the original French manual — only went as far as the school of the battalion and gave no instruction in larger-unit maneuvers, which were still left to Scott's 1835 manual. In a private letter to Davis, Capt. Silas Casey, the president of the board, also called for a separate revision of the heavy infantry tactics. Even when the War Department finally ordered all foot soldiers to be regularly exercised in Hardee's tactics in 1857, the declared reason was because they were "usually employed as light troops," not because heavy line infantry would be done away with entirely.[8]

The Ordnance Department program of arms manufacture also reflected the old army's continued commitment to at least a formal distinction between heavy and light infantry. The Model 1855 Rifle-Musket was not the only new small arm issued; the bureau also produced a Model 1855 Rifle at the Harpers Ferry armory, which replaced the Model 1841 Rifle. The new minié rifle was the same .58 caliber as the more famous Springfield rifle-musket, but it was 6.6 inches shorter in overall length (49.4 inches versus the line infantry musket's length of 56 inches). Light infantry arms had traditionally been more compact to facilitate greater celerity of movement, but—unlike the Model 1841 Rifle—the new Model 1855 Rifle added a saber bayonet attachment, which showed the influence of new French ideas on bayonet fencing. Indeed, Hardee's tactics implicitly assumed that the troops using his manual would be equipped with true rifles (as opposed to rifle-muskets), because it made reference only to saber bayonets. The line infantry used socket bayonets. As with the chasseurs, however, the addition of a bayonet did not indicate any lesser commitment to the virtues of aimed fire, because the 1857–58 versions of the rifle even added special crosshair front sights that were never used in American rifle-muskets.[9]

Hardee himself did not see his manual as a total replacement for Scott's tactics. When West Point considered abandoning the new five-year course at the academy instituted in the late 1850s, Hardee's proposed four-year curriculum based most of its "theoretical instruction" in tactics on his own translation of the chasseurs manual, but he retained some of the material from Scott's tactics. Indeed, the first lesson of the tactical recitations covered among other things the much-maligned oblique march included in Scott's manual, which was absent from Hardee's light infantry tactics. Furthermore, Hardee also requested that cadets obtain instruction in the "Evolutions of the Line" contained in Scott's third volume—large unit maneuvers above the battalion level, which Hardee's own manual did not cover.[10]

This is not to say that the tactics board did not see Hardee's drill as a real improvement over Scott's tactics. It praised various changes in forming line of battle and paid special attention to the new drill's provisions for skirmishers. Even the new skirmish drill showed continuities with the past, however. Reflecting an unwillingness to break totally with Napoleonic shock tactics, the board praised the new skirmish drill's provisions for rallying in case of a cavalry assault by using four-man "comrades in battle," which "prevents that individual isolation, which is to be avoided, when skirmishing with the enemy." Although the report did comment on the increased speed of Hardee's drill, with all maneuvers performed in at least quick time, nowhere did it indicate that this measure was taken in response to the increased firepower of the rifle-musket, contrary to the arguments of the leading historians of Civil War minor tactics, Perry D. Jamieson and Grady McWhiney. Both have argued that "the rifle gave defenders greater range and accuracy of fire than the musket, and Hardee tried to compensate attackers for this by allowing them to advance more rapidly than Scott had permitted." Such intentions are mentioned nowhere in official discussions *contemporary* to the formulation and adoption of Hardee's drill manual.[11]

Reflecting previous Anglo-American ideas about the suitability of light infantry methods to frontier warfare in North America, the board also believed Hardee's tactics "might be most advantageously employed in the contests which so frequently occur with the Indian tribes on our frontier." Reflecting Americans' self-image as a people too free and valiant for Old World discipline and rigidity, the board even made the pious declaration that "from the nature of our country and the character of our people, it is peculiarly expedient to substitute for immobility in the ranks and machine like movements, intelligence, rapidity of motion, and accuracy of fire." Casey, the board's president, took a much more critical stance in a private letter he wrote separately to Davis, however. Raising the issue of whether Hardee's tactics should be exclusively adopted for infantry instruction, he argued that "should it become necessary in our country to call out large bodies of troops, a very considerable portion of them would not be equal to the effectual performance of it, and not one half of our Army as at present constituted, could do it justice."[12] American officers' professional aspirations had to contend with the realities of a widely dispersed constabulary with little opportunity for extensive European-style training.

In the small and close-knit regular army, knowledge of the new tactical reforms and their purpose spread quickly, even to the cadets at West Point, whom the review board used as guinea pigs. In a family letter, George William Cushing described "the new French drill": it "was called by the cadets 'Shanghai drill.['] The Sec. of War, was here last week, and we had a grand review &c . . . it [the drill] is much different from the old system of tactics, instead of marching about like so many animated pokers, the men carry their pieces at a trail or right shoulder shift, and run at a kind of trot, keeping dressed, though, and it is a very pretty drill to look at." Cushing even made reference to the distinction between heavy and light infantry in a letter he wrote less than a week later. George D. Bayard also mentioned the tactical experiments in letters sent home, showing an awareness of the tactical board's mission: "They are now drilling the Battalion by squads at a new system of Tactics, which has just by [sic] translated from the French by Col. Hardee, & which it is proposed to substitute for the system at present employed by skirmishers or Light Infantry. The object is to make the movements much more rapid."[13]

Furthermore, the regular army did not simply adopt the translated version of a French drill manual; it also officially adopted the other key elements of the chasseur system—bayonet fencing, intensified target practice, and improved physical conditioning, all of which were designed to build confidence and morale among troops. French military thought in this period put a strong emphasis on the role of élan in battle. It emphasized intense training regimens as much to teach practical skills as to inspire confidence in soldiers who had to face combat. As usual, American officers followed the French lead. For example, Bvt. Capt. George B. McClellan translated a French bayonet practice manual in the early 1850s. Most significantly, McClellan would attempt to incorporate these training methods into his own organization of the Army of the Potomac in the winter of 1861–62. Furthermore, while the regular army had instituted target practice at West Point as early as 1817, it issued new manuals and regulations in the 1850s. McClellan himself had earlier drilled the sapper company at West Point in bayonet fencing and target practice with musketoons—a shortened version of the infantry musket—shortly after the Mexican War.[14]

In his report on the Delafield Commission's visit to the Crimean War, McClellan covered all the elements of the French system—bayonet fencing, gymnastics, and marksmanship training. This observer mission continued the pre–Mexican War tradition of sending officers across the Atlantic to find and bring back European military expertise. In addition to a reference to bayonet fencing, McClellan gave special praise to a noncommissioned officers' course at Vincennes that included "gymnastics, scaling walls, swimming, fencing with the bayonet, singing, dancing, reading, writing, &c." The young captain and future major general declared that "the efficiency of the French infantry is in no small degree attributable to the great attention paid to these points throughout the army." He grumbled that "some essential parts of the French instruction have been omitted in our own, such as the system of gymnastics, natation, &c." The post libraries and night schools established in the 1840s and 1850s at some American installations may very well owe something to the French gymnastic school's coverage of nonmilitary subjects. Right after his high praise

82
★

TACTICAL CONTINUITY

of the French system of gymnastics, McClellan also covered marksmanship training in the French army. It is also telling that McClellan, a de-
fensively minded engineer, made no comments on any perceived increase
in defensive firepower created by the rifle-musket's increased accuracy.[15]

In line with McClellan's emphasis on the importance of a holistic
system of infantry training that integrated physical conditioning, target practice, and bayonet fencing, 1st Lt. John C. Kelton, an instructor at
West Point, proposed curriculum reforms for the West Point Department
of Small Arms in the late 1850s that included instruction in calisthen-
ics, gymnastics, swimming, and various forms of fencing with the foil,
rapier, sword, and bayonet. Kelton combined these measures with target
practice for both muskets and pistols. Cadets would be instructed to hit a
four-inch-square target four out of five times at a range of 100 yards, to
hit a fifteen-inch-square target three out of five times at 250 yards, and to
estimate distances ranging from 100 to 600 yards.[16]

Kelton was not alone in closely linking target practice to bayonet fencing. Mid-nineteenth-century French and American professionals believed
in the importance of both the bayonet and firepower. Even the 1858 target
practice manual included a section on bayonet fencing, declaring that "a
soldier thoroughly drilled in firing would still be wanting in an essential element of defence if he had not been instructed in fencing with
the bayonet. With skirmishers, particularly, the skilful handling of their
muskets, both in firing, and fencing, add both to the efficiency of attack,
and vigor of defense. As there seems to be a connection in that way between target practice and bayonet exercise, the following instructions for
individual defence by infantry against cavalry are added to the system of
target practice."[17]

The manual respected cavalry's fighting power to such an extent that it
spent six pages on instructions to infantrymen for facing down horsemen.
It was a reasonable concern — heavy cavalry armed with saber or lance
had always been most deadly when attacking disorganized infantry fleeing in retreat. The traditional Napoleonic tactic to cope with cavalry was
to form a stolid square bristling with bayonets. The increased dispersal
of Hardee's tactics seemed to make infantrymen more vulnerable toward
horsemen; skirmishers in extended order lacked both the physical and
psychological stolidity of a square. Hardee's tactics responded to this problem with sections on rallying that make ample references to squares and
cavalry.[18] The whole issue proved irrelevant during the Civil War, where
heavy cavalry charges never received a fair trial, and where the somewhat

weak cavalry traditions of both armies had their hands full with mastering reconnaissance and raiding functions. However, old army officers did not have such a window into the future, and they had had to fight off vaunted Mexican lancers during the preceding war.

Professional soldiers had good reason to fret over the confidence or lack thereof soldiers held when deployed in relative isolation as skirmishers, because shock tactics had always relied more on psychological effect than on physical damage. Successful cavalry charges in Napoleon's day never made much hand-to-hand contact with organized infantry in battle order—either the infantry broke and ran before the horsemen actually collided with them, making themselves extremely vulnerable to cold steel, or the cavalrymen's charge sheepishly petered out in the face of both musketry and an uncowed row of bayonets. American officers hoped that bayonet fencing would give an infantryman enough skill with the arm to fend off a horseman, but it was also designed to provide an isolated skirmisher enough confidence to stand and fight cavalry unassisted in the first place. The manual therefore declared that "infantry soldiers may feel full confidence that the combat, in most cases, will end to their advantage, and if they are skilful with the bayonet it will last but a short time."[19]

Shortly before the Civil War, 1st Lt. Cadmus M. Wilcox, an old army officer and future Confederate major general, wrote a treatise on rifles that displayed at a high intellectual level the mix of change and continuity found in American tactical thought during this period. On the one hand, Wilcox's work reflected the new emphasis on firepower and light infantry methods, declaring that "these experiments [at Vincennes] proved that the fire of skirmishers was more effective than that of file, and that the latter was more so than that of company: which seems to be attributable to the fact that the skirmisher is not annoyed by the smoke, his comrades, or the commands of his officer; while in the fire by file, the smoke and the file on either side derange constantly his aim and position; and in the fire by company the necessity of obeying the command of the officer does not permit a deliberate aiming, and forces the soldier to pull the trigger suddenly and with a jerk."[20]

Wilcox also saw new challenges on the battlefield resulting from the rifle-induced dispersion of armies and hoped to deal with the problem by giving subordinate commanders more initiative: "Fields of battle having a greater extent in [the] future, more instruction, quickness, and accuracy of observation, will be required on the part of the battalion commanders, and greater latitude should be given them by tactics, with the view of enabling them to take advantage of all the exigencies of the field." He wrote that "the great desire to prescribe by rule, and with mathematical precision, different tactical formations for battle will probably cease; for every field there are tactical manoeuvres peculiar and well suited to it, which the talent of the general, from his knowledge of its configuration, the physical and moral condition of his own and the opposing force, will know how to apply." In line with these ideas, Wilcox advocated the use of the more limber two-rank line of battle and proposed a smaller battalion size of six companies of one hundred men each, as opposed to the standard configuration of ten companies, in order to facilitate greater rapidity in movements and reduce the amount of frontage exposed to fire when in column.[21]

Even as progressive an officer as Wilcox, however, did not totally discard past precedent. For example, Wilcox argued in favor of small columns because of their perceived ability to concentrate more fire against cavalry when deployed in squares. Wilcox also praised Hardee's tactics for, among other things, improvements in the deployment of such squares. Furthermore, the future Confederate general also did not entirely discard the bayonet. In *Rifles and Rifle Practice*, he declared, "It may, however, be observed, that the ability to use the bayonet may under many circumstances be of great importance, and a course of instruction and drills with this view will furnish the soldier with a means of defense, when exposed in single combat with an enemy, or when engaged in siege operations, that may often save his life." Indeed, Wilcox praised the French saber bayonet used for the carbines of the zouaves and chasseurs — and also adopted by the ordnance bureau for its *minié* rifles — as a "formidable weapon in hand-to-hand contests." Wilcox's own comments to Davis on Hardee's tactics also criticized the new drill's practice of placing taller men in the first rank, partly on the grounds that "in an attack with the bayonet it would be better to have the taller men in the rear rank."[22]

Although Wilcox advocated a smaller battalion size, he also hoped to retain the traditional European practice of designating special elite light infantry units. One of four battalions in each of Wilcox's regiments (what in American practice would be normally called brigades) would be composed of men who "excel others in the use of the rifle, and have greater aptitude for the duties of light troops." Wilcox did not just see these battalions as highly specialized skirmishers, however; they would sometimes be held in reserve as shock troops, "to be launched at critical periods of battle in mass, moving with the *accelerated pace* against the almost victorious adversary." Wilcox cited several Crimean War examples to illustrate his point. He probably believed that troops on a contemporary battlefield swept by rifle-musket fire would now need to cover ground more quickly, but Wilcox certainly did not emphasize this point to the same degree as Jamieson and McWhiney. Indeed, in his comments on Hardee's proposed tactics, Wilcox had only praised double quick time for enabling "us to form and present in the speediest possible manner line of battle faced in any given direction." Wilcox makes no mention of actually advancing forward at the double quick to counter the increased *defensive* firepower of the rifle-musket.[23]

Wilcox did, however, perceive the reduced effectiveness of the cavalry and artillery arms. He argued that "cavalry, in the hands of a skillful general, must ever be a formidable arm; but at present it becomes more difficult to manoeuvre it properly on fields of battle; its charges against infantry will be made with more danger and loss to itself, and with less probabilities of success." Wilcox also observed that "it is clear that field artillery, with its present range, cannot with any chance of success remain in action in front of infantry; its comparative efficacy is lessened and even by extending the range by increase of calibre, or by a successful application of the principle of rifling, cannot restore it to its former comparative condition [in relation to infantry]."[24]

In sum, the future major general argued that "the new rifle clearly gives to infantry, in all secondary operations of war, and in the defence of positions, an element of force that it did not possess formerly." Wilcox envisioned a larger and more extended battlefield, with more long-range engagements by infantrymen armed with rifles and trained in light infantry tactics to compensate for new command problems and to better deploy the rifle-musket's superior firepower. Nevertheless, even though Wilcox maintained that the newfound firepower of infantry could now suppress artillery fire to make way for a cavalry charge, "*in its legitimate sphere of action in removing obstacles, in the attack and defence of forts and fortresses, artillery remains intact, as well as in the grand tactics of battles.*"[25]

In line with French thinking, Wilcox also emphasized the morale-boosting effects of equipping infantrymen with the most technically advanced weapons. Wilcox declared that the average foot soldier "will be inspired with more confidence, knowing the range and accuracy of his arm . . . he will fire with the utmost coolness, and with a certainty that the smooth-bore and round ball never could inspire." He speculated that "it may be that the infantry soldier, occupied with the care of aiming and adjusting his sight, will have his mind diverted from thoughts of danger, and be in the moral condition attributed to cannoneers, whose proverbial *sang froid* in the presence of the enemy is said to be due to the occupation that the pointing or aiming of the piece gives."[26]

This emphasis on the morale-boosting effects of new weapons, and the regular army's emphasis on training in general, indicated that the old army remained anything but a technological determinist. For example, most regulars agreed on the necessity of target practice of some sort and would have agreed with Wilcox's declaration that "a rifle, whatever may be its range and accuracy, in the hands of a soldier unskilled in its use, loses much of its value; hence the necessity of giving the most detailed and thorough practical instruction as to the means of preserving the piece, and of attaining the greatest possible precision of fire." Furthermore, regulars also feared ammunition wastage, which explains much of the old army's animus against breechloaders. Nineteenth-century armies generally had to carry their ammunition with them, and any exponential increase in ammunition expenditure required a corresponding increase in logistical capacity—no small problem in the wide expanses of North America. The 1858 target practice manual argued that, "so far from urging soldiers to fire rapidly, they ought to be urgently cautioned *against it*; the instruction should endeavor to habituate the soldiers to coolness and deliberation. One shot well aimed is worth ten fired at random." Indeed, Wilcox reported that the French had deliberately left off an elevating sight on the rifle muskets of their line infantry to dissuade soldiers from firing at excessive range, although the carabiniers of the zouaves and chasseurs did include long-range sights.[27]

Historians can and do frequently confuse high-level discussions of doctrine with actual practice in the field, but during the 1850s there is some evidence that ideas about the latest French tactics filtered down into the army as a whole. For example, Capt. W. S. Ketchum of the 6th Infantry, stationed a continent-width away from West Point at "New San Diego" in California, found the time between 1859 and 1860 to forward to the adjutant general two lengthy and unsolicited commentaries on Hardee's tactics and Heth's target practice manual. Furthermore, enough knowledge about the new French tactical system filtered down through the officer corps that many officers did attempt to put their volunteers through target practice and bayonet drill during the Civil War.[28] These efforts had at best mixed success, but they do indicate at least some antebellum exposure to the new methods expounded by Hardee and Kelton.

TACTICAL CONTINUITY

In addition to the training-intensive tactical system of the 1850s, American ambitions for a highly trained professional force helped push through the extension of the West Point curriculum to five years from four in 1854. The army adopted the five-year program in part to rectify long-standing complaints that cadets did not receive enough practical military training. The first five-year course proposed in 1845 had allotted more time to practical military training, and the academic board that year heartily endorsed reforms "to correct what is felt as an evil, particularly as upon no point is public censure found to bear more heavily and with a less disposition to excuse its errors, than upon that of professional ignorance." However, that academic board still maintained that nothing should be taken away from technical instruction. Even future Civil War corps commander Capt. Erasmus D. Keyes, who had voted against the first five-year plan on the grounds that he thought it excessively taxing, agreed with the scientific premises of the board, declaring that "it has been settled that scientific acquirements are the basis of military knowledge." The actual five-year program adopted in 1854 roughly matched the earlier proposals, with extra time allotted to the humanities, practical military training, and Mahan's capstone course in military science, in addition to the usual Thayerite emphasis on mathematics, engineering, and the physical sciences.[29]

During the debates surrounding these curricular reforms, Secretary of War John B. Floyd reflected this reformed Thayerite status quo when he criticized Maj. Alfred Mordecai's proposal to reduce the amount of scientific training given to cadets. The object of the academy, in Floyd's view, "is not merely to supply material suitable for the different parts of a fixed military establishment; but to create in the country a competent knowledge in the highest branches of military science, in anticipation of emergencies altogether beyond the scope of our habitual military force. The education should, therefore, be of the same general character and the minimum standard of proficiency should be high." In his instructions to the curricular review board, Floyd emphasized that "the great mission of the Academy is to engraft on the mind of the cadet the principles of a thorough scientific military education, and considering the time requisite for this object, it is doubtless impracticable to bestow as much attention upon practical instruction as would be required to turn out perfect adepts in every branch." Indeed, with the regular army's improved standing after the Mexican War, many militia officers paid great deference to the regulars in military matters.[30]

Despite the respect given them by the officers of volunteer companies,

American military professionals were fully cognizant of the West Point curriculum's limited function. Since Thayer's tenure at the academy, its curriculum was the beginning of training for professional officers, as opposed to its end, whether that further training came in the form of the short-lived branch schools of practice or in the less institutionalized system of sending officers overseas. Or, to put it another way, Superintendent Richard Delafield later praised the readopted four-year curriculum's instruction in fortification for, among other things, "unfolding to the cadet a course of study for the future that will enable him to apply his knowledge to localities when called upon to practice his profession." With respect to the instruction in infantry tactics, Delafield, in a similar vein, commented that it "suffices as a basis for any officer who may desire to improve himself after leaving here." Mahan followed a similar line of thought when he commented during a curricular review in 1860 that, although the academy can lay "a good foundation of mental training in professional studies, the rest must be left to the efforts of the individual, who, if he estimates at its just importance his position as an officer, will neglect no opportunity to supply what he will feel as deficiencies. . . . As it is, we do little more, and can do no more, than lead the graduate to the threshold of scientific and professional knowledge, by furnishing him with the first elements. With these he will be able to penetrate and see his way clearly." Indeed, the academic board eventually turned against the five-year course, partly out of the belief that overtaxed and intellectually exhausted graduates would be unwilling to continue the pursuit of professional knowledge after they left the confines of the academy.[31] The exigencies of the Civil War put an end to any further discussion or experimentation with a five-year curriculum at West Point.

The adoption of the rifle-musket, the introduction of bayonet fencing, the creation of a target practice manual, experimentation with a five-year program at West Point, the reestablishment of the Artillery School of Practice in 1860, and the Delafield observer mission to Europe for the Crimean War — all these reforms and measures represented the regular army's continuing confidence in the benefits of professionalism. Although the most vibrant intellectual activity centered on infantry tactics, old army artillery and cavalry officers continued to adapt and evolve. Artillerists experimented with new rifled weapons and the twelve-pounder gun-howitzer that would become the backbone of Civil War batteries, while continuing to train and prepare for the next war. The horse soldiers even managed to acquire two true cavalry regiments, as opposed to dragoons, although the regular army would never be able to constitute true heavy cavalry in the European sense of the term.[32] All in all, the old army continued to adapt and change within the broad confines of a general commitment to professionalism that had served it well in the Mexican War, and which probably would have served just as well in a war against either a European power or a less-distant nation-state rival.

CHAPTER FIVE

The Beginning of the End

The Old Army on the Precipice

★ ★ ★

The old army, even with its much-improved post–Mexican War reputation, returned to its usual status of social isolation, as it dispersed itself
throughout the United States' newly conquered possessions. The army's
ethic of professionalism soldiered on, but officers continued to complain
of Congress's penurious budgets and the army's scattered condition in
company-sized outposts. Far more dangerous threats to the old army's existence loomed on the horizon, however, and even the regular army officer
corps could not escape the gathering sectional tensions of the 1850s.

The sectional crisis eroded an important part of the old army's fiber —
its ethic of national service to the U.S. government. Of the 487 graduates
of West Point with some kind of affiliation with a slave state — either as
their birthplace or as their place of residence at the time of their appointment to the academy — 173 stayed loyal to the Federal colors, while 251
supported the new Confederacy (Table 2). Ten officers still in the service
resigned their commissions during the secession winter and seem to have
played no active role in the war, while 57 mostly older officers who had
resigned before the war stayed out of the fratricidal conflict. Of the 300
graduates affiliated with states that officially seceded, 60 stayed with the
Union, 200 rallied around the Confederate colors, 5 serving officers resigned, and 36 stayed out of the conflict. Clearly, most southerners chose
the new Confederate nation over the old Union, but a sizable minority
drew their swords against their native states.[1] For most southerners, the
bonds of region and section proved stronger than the associations cultivated in the regular army.

In the decade before Lincoln's election, sectional feelings had become
an increasing problem within the fellowship of the old army. Even at West
Point, the old army's citadel of nationalism, where the faculty had banned

TABLE 2

West Pointers' Affiliation or Behavior in the Secession Winter

Residence	Union	Confederate	Resigned	Stayed Out	Total
All slave states	173 (36%)	251 (52%)	10 (2%)	57 (12%)	487
Upper South	159 (43%)	162 (44%)	9 (2%)	40 (11%)	66
Lower South	14 (12%)	89 (74%)	1 (1%)	17 (14%)	121
Unionist state	113 (60%)	51 (27%)	5 (3%)	21 (11%)	187
Confederate state	60 (20%)	200 (67%)	5 (2%)	36 (12%)	300

Sources: The primary source for these statistical data is Cullum, *Biographical Register*. I went through every West Point class from 1802 to 1860 to find every graduate born, appointed from, or possessing a place of residence at time of admission in a slave state (including Washington, D.C.) still living in April 1861. For the sake of the database, all such cadets were considered "southerners." I also reviewed cadets with northern birth states and at-large appointments to see if their place of residence at admission was a southern state, with the caveat that I excluded those cadets who seemed obviously "northern" — that is, they received northern volunteer commissions (Civil War volunteer commissions below the rank of general were handled by the states) or retired to a northern state. States of residence for at-large appointed cadets can be found in Cadet Cards Arranged by State, United States Military Academy Archives.

Note: Upper South is defined as Arkansas, Delaware, Kentucky, Maryland, Missouri, North Carolina, Tennessee, Virginia, and Washington, D.C. Lower South is defined as Alabama, Florida, Georgia, Louisiana, Mississippi, South Carolina, and Texas. Union is defined as those slave states (including the District of Columbia) that stayed in the Union: Delaware, Kentucky, Maryland, Missouri, and Washington, D.C. Confederate is defined as those slave states that joined the Confederacy: Alabama, Arkansas, Florida, Georgia, Louisiana, Mississippi, North Carolina, South Carolina, Tennessee, Texas, and Virginia. Also note that not all the numbers add up because several graduates served with the Union army for a time and then later resigned to join the Confederacy.

student debate on nullification in the early 1840s, sectionalism began to divide the battalion of cadets. Perhaps the most spectacular example of sectional tension at the academy in the 1850s was the famous fight in 1859 between Wade Hampton Gibbes, a South Carolinian, and Emory Upton, one of the few bona fide abolitionist cadets at the academy. Gibbes accused Upton of having had sexual relations with African American students during his time at Oberlin, and when Upton heard of the remarks, he demanded satisfaction. The fight was remembered by many long after the war as a premonition of future hostilities. Even Morris Schaff, in his generally reconciliationist memoir of West Point, remembered with pride how Upton's roommate, John Rodgers, faced down a "mob" of southern cadets shouting "maledictions" after the fight's conclusion. Less spectacular, but perhaps more significant, was the division of companies in the battalion of cadets along sectional lines by the late-1850s, which would have been unimaginable to previous generations of cadets. On the frontier, officers began to discuss political questions more frequently, and in Bleeding Kansas, the old army would have to deal directly with sectional tensions.[2]

Nevertheless, the relatively high level of Unionism in the regular army among southerners, as opposed to other forms of federal office holding, testifies to the regular army's uniquely nationalist character. Vast numbers of high-level elected officials and even lower-level officials, such as customs collectors and postmasters, felt no compunctions about waging war against the previous owner of their allegiance; in contrast, a sizable number of officers proved willing to do violence against even their own family members. In one especially spectacular example, Col. Philip St. George Cooke of Virginia, who famously declared "I owe my country much, my state little," saw both of his sons and one of two daughters estranged for his loyalty to the old Union. His son-in-law, Capt. James Ewell Brown Stuart, who went on to become the Confederacy's most famous cavalry commander, even went so far as to change his son's name in retribution.

Not only did the sectional crisis rend the fabric of the old army on the personal level of friends, classmates, and even families; it also shattered the regulars' antebellum consensus of complete obedience to civilian authority. The regular army for most of the antebellum period was not a "political" institution by contemporary uses of the term. Or, to put it another way, the old army was political, but not partisan — generals on occasion ran for president, officers used connections in Congress to further their careers, and most certainly held opinions on political decisions of the day — but regular officers had no real institutional influence on those issues.[3] The relatively minuscule regular army labored under too many suspicions for it to ever have a political influence commensurate with its European contemporaries on the continent. It instead saw itself as an institution too dignified to involve itself in the rough-and-tumble world of Jacksonian democracy and contented itself with a self-image of selfless obedience to whatever political leadership happened to hold the levers of power.

Regular army officers could and did enact policies they disagreed with. Many of them had not looked kindly on the Mexican War, but those objections obviously did not hinder their battlefield performance. Others had harsh criticism for American Indian policies, but that criticism did not prevent them from acting as the federal government's mailed fist on the frontier. Old army officers followed orders for a variety of reasons: ingrained obedience to authority found in any military, personal ambition, a strong sense of duty, or moral indifference, but the American tradition of civilian control also loomed large. From at least the Newburgh Conspiracy on, American governments had aimed to separate political decisions from military agents out of a fear of military usurpation. Secession scrambled the certainties of complete obedience toward civilian political leaders. Southern officers, faced with two competing claimants to the mantle of civilian control, now had to choose between them; some stayed with the national colors, while others became revolutionaries.

Most importantly, however, while sectionalism divided the political loyalties of the old army's officer corps, it did not affect many of these officers' other basic assumptions about their profession's proper place in society. Almost all old army men, Union and Confederate, remained committed to the conventions of organized nation-state war waged by soldiers in uniform, subject to military discipline. Although some Confederate commanders with regular army backgrounds would tolerate the assistance of Confederate guerrillas behind Federal lines, the primary military instrument of both sections remained the uniformed soldier. Even the most revolutionary wartime measure, the Union arming of slaves, remained within these broad parameters. Even though Confederates refused to recognize them as such, United States Colored Troops fought in uniformed units subject to military discipline, as opposed to irregular organizations akin to the Indian scouts later used by the U.S. Army on the frontier. The presence of old army men at the heads of both contending armies, with their notions of order and discipline, helped keep the violence of the American Civil War confined within the ritualized boundaries of European nation-state warfare, with its uniforms, pitched battles, and formal surrenders.

The old army's own experience as a constabulary force dealing with antebellum sectional tensions showed the other possible forms of violence the Civil War could have taken—everything from the aborted slave insurrection of a John Brown to the low-level guerrilla warfare of Bleeding Kansas. Indeed, Winfield Scott himself had commanded federal troops in Charleston during the nullification crisis of 1832–33, where they engaged in nonviolent policing. Long before Kansas-Nebraska, the Wilmot Proviso, and the Mexican War, and even before Texas annexation, President Andrew Jackson had ordered Scott to Charleston in November 1832 to keep a discrete watch on the restive city. The army as an institution tended to resent these nonmilitary missions, which it saw as beneath its proper role as a regular nation-state army built along European lines, even when it successfully conducted these operations.

Scott conducted his mission to Charleston with marked diplomacy and restraint, traits common to the general practice of antebellum regulars in difficult law-and-order situations. One of Scott's protégés, Maj. Robert Anderson, acted in much the same way during his ill-fated tenure as commander of the Federal garrison at Fort Sumter in 1861. Both officers subscribed to an abstracted conception of national authority that saw itself as elevated above parochial concerns, whether strictly sectional or simply partisan. While in Charleston, Scott had quietly readied the garrison for an attack during the earlier crisis but made no overtly hostile gestures. Instead, he exhorted South Carolinians to stay in the Union and invoked standard nationalist arguments, telling one citizen that, even if South Carolina peaceably left the Union, "when one member shall withdraw, the whole arch of the Union will tumble in," leaving three confederacies in North America hostile toward one another. Events in Washington eventually defused the incipient sectional crisis, but Scott deserved credit for being able to work in harness under Jackson — a not inconsiderable achievement in light of their difficult personal history — and for not provoking any unintended hostilities during the crisis.[4]

Even proslavery filibustering, the main sectional problem for the regular army aside from Bleeding Kansas, had precedents before the Mexican War. The filibustering of the 1850s was proslavery and southern, but extralegal adventurism in foreign possessions was by no means an activity exclusive to slaveholders. In 1837 a rebellion in Canada inspired widespread — and sometimes violently active — support from sympathetic Americans living close to the border. Washington had no desire to spark a war with Great Britain over the issue and found itself faced with the need to maintain American neutrality. At first, local authorities tried unsuccessfully to stop unauthorized excursions by overzealous Americans, but when a British officer crossed to the American side of the border to destroy a steamer ferrying supplies to Canadian rebels and killed an American citizen in the process, the situation threatened to explode.

President Martin Van Buren responded to the emergency by dispatching Scott to the northern border in January 1838. Scott, hampered by a scarcity of regulars caused by the demands of the Second Seminole War in Florida, used mostly rhetoric and exhortation, along with small forces of whatever reliable militia and regulars were available, to defuse tensions and persuade Americans on the border to refrain from extralegal violations of neutrality. The government dispatched extra regulars by the summer of 1838 under the command of then general-in-chief Alexander Macomb to help maintain American neutrality, but Scott remained in the region intermittently until 1841 to deal with various small crises until the border troubles finally died down. Even with Macomb's reinforcements, Washington had only two thousand regulars to guard the border, and the ability of the federal government to compel obedience to American neutrality laws should not be overestimated.[5] In all of its pacification missions during the antebellum period, the regular army struggled with scarce resources.

The old army may have had many different kinds of constabulary problems throughout the antebellum period, but sectionalism was the most pressing issue of the 1850s. Nevertheless, sectionalism did not totally compromise the regular army's reputation for nationalist impartiality, even in as contested a region as Kansas. The center flexed and stretched against the pressure, but before South Carolina left the Union in December 1860, it still held. Many of those southern-born officers who rallied around the Confederacy's banner became sectional only after their home states forced the question. Before the reality of secession, they willingly subsumed their own opinions and beliefs to national authority. For example, Col. Albert Sidney Johnston, the primary Confederate field commander in the West before his death at Shiloh, also served as a nationalist commander of the Mormon expedition and conducted himself as the typical regular army officer — irritable but judicious and generally restrained. Johnston had no sympathy for the Mormons, and he openly clashed with the conciliatory Alfred Cumming, the territorial governor appointed by President James Buchanan, but the colonel did make sincere attempts to prevent unnecessary clashes with the Latter-Day Saints. He also respected the administration's final decision to sustain Cumming in his policy of conciliation.[6]

Old army customs and strictures did not hem in only future Confederates' personal inclinations and instincts. Free-Soil officers also sometimes found themselves ordered to carry out the will of southern-leaning administrations, and most bit their tongues and followed orders. For example, Col. Edwin V. Sumner, known during the Civil War as a "Republican" general and a member of Lincoln's personal bodyguard during his inaugural trip to Washington, willingly obeyed orders he disagreed with in Kansas. On Independence Day, 1856, Sumner dispersed the Free-Soil Kansas state legislature elected in defiance of the proslavery territorial government sponsored by the administration of President Franklin Pierce. A mournful Sumner declared to the assembly, "Gentlemen, I am called upon this day to perform the most painful duty of my life." To add insult upon injury, the antislavery press vilified Sumner, and Secretary of War Jefferson Davis made a show of rebuking Sumner for supposedly exceeding his instructions. "Old Bull" Sumner, the doughty regular who later hoped to deal with a suspected assassination plot against Lincoln with the cold steel of drawn cavalry sabers, even had to face accusations of disloyalty from Republican congressman during the secession winter.[7]

Northern-born officers did not stand alone as the only disinterested guardians of Federal authority in Kansas. Philip St. George Cooke of Virginia hesitated to involve the regular army in police actions, reflecting the country-party antimilitarism that even the regulars had absorbed into their very bones. When Cooke arrived in Lecompton in 1856 at the territorial governor's request with 134 men (one indication of his scanty resources), he suggested that the governor call the district court into session instead of using a military force "legally so powerless under the usual circumstances." The already-old soldier simply did not agree with the governor that the situation was all that serious, declaring that because of his familiarity to Missourians from long frontier service, "I had a strong conviction that, by reserving myself from the petty embroilments of armed constabulary duty, I should be able, in a real crisis, to exercise a very beneficial moral influence."[8]

Cooke's reluctance to act did not reflect any marked bias toward either faction in Kansas. He believed that the disorders in Kansas stemmed from motives more criminal than ideological, an attitude shared by many of his fellow officers, and during the "August War" crisis of that year Cooke refused to accede to the proslavery acting governor's demand that Cooke invest and capture the free-state town of Topeka. Cooke claimed he had no authority to do such a thing and declared that "if the Army be useless in the present unhappy crisis, it is because in our constitution and law civil war was not foreseen, nor the contingency [of] a systematic resistance by the people to governments of their own creation, and which, at short intervals, they may either correct or change."[9] Cooke's unconditional Unionism during the Civil War shows that he rooted this belief more in old army caution and restraint than in any deep sympathy for secessionist arguments about states' rights.

Both Cooke and his new commander, Bvt. Maj. Gen. Persifor F. Smith, became increasingly irritated with Territorial Secretary Daniel P. Woodson's aggressively proslavery policies. Ironically enough, the Pierce administration had appointed Smith for his southern sympathies and Democratic politics in order to replace Sumner, whom it not unreasonably suspected of Free-Soil sympathies. On August 31, Cooke complained of his suspicion that "that my presence emboldens the militia and *others* to these outrages [against Free-Soilers]." In another incident, when Cooke sent a free-state leader to Lecompton to see Woodson in late August, the governor promptly arrested him, much to the mortification of Cooke, who saw this as a violation of a flag of truce and his own military honor. In the meantime, incensed Free-Soil forces mustered 800 men and threatened to attack Lecompton. Cooke confronted the Free-Soil force with his own troops, and after much negotiation, he arranged for a Free-Soil withdrawal and an exchange of prisoners that returned the free-state leader.[10]

Cooke emphasized the peaceful outcome of his confrontation with the Free-Soilers, for he "had stayed the madness of the hour, and prevented, on almost any terms, the fratricidal onslaught of countrymen and fellow citizens." Looking back on the experience ten years after Appomattox, Cooke reminisced on that prelude to later events: "It was part of the education of both parties that they still respected national authority. There was one flag yet! At Lecompton I rode alone — leaving my forces far behind — in front of an army of thousands, which, with cannon-matches lighted, were about to attack the territorial capitol, and ordered them to retire, and the nation's representative was obeyed!"[11]

When Cooke declared himself "the nation's representative," he did not see himself as a mere federal employee, which would have made him a simple mercenary or, worse yet, some partisan beneficiary of the Jacksonian spoils system. In a volume of memoirs published in 1857, Cooke gave an almost mystical description of his calling to the colors as a young officer; he recalled that, as he stood on a flatboat, "the scabbard of my sword (fastened to the belt by a ring) unaccountably became detached, and fell into the river and disappeared, leaving the blade still more strangely suspended: it was an omen. Thenceforth I was devoted to the service of the Republic."[12] Other regulars would not have shared Cooke's romantic sensibility, but most would have agreed on a collective self-image as the disinterested guardians of national authority.

Embellished as Cooke's account was, both parties in Kansas did generally respect the regular army uniform enough to forbear from resisting it directly, as opposed to surreptitious evasion.[13] In light of the small federal forces deployed, this respect testified to the ability of regular army officers to maintain some degree of national authority in very trying circumstances. Indeed, the old army's scarce resources and deeply held American suspicions about standing armies intervening in civil affairs may have helped inculcate habits of impartiality and restraint. With very few coercive resources, old army officers had to appeal to a tenuous moral authority to perform their constabulary tasks. During the Civil War, most Unionist old army men tried to treat Confederate civilians with the same restraint, adopting in many ways the methods of their previous constabulary experience. The changed circumstances of the war would doom these conciliatory policies, however.

In the antebellum period, however, the constabulary status quo remained, and most regular army officers, especially those in high positions of responsibility, went as far as to discipline their own soldiers for excessively aggressive behavior in civil contexts. For example, when Capt. George T. Anderson, a Georgian and future Confederate brigade commander, tried, in one historian's words, to "shoot up" a band of partisans in southeast Kansas in April 1858, Brig. Gen. William S. Harney promptly replaced him. Not only had Anderson violated the old army principle of restraint, but his precipitate actions with only limited resources had resulted in a humiliating repulse. The regular army sought to use its forbearance to help prevent the embarrassing situation Anderson found himself in. Rumors of Anderson's prejudice against Free-Soil settlers exacerbated matters, and he subsequently left the service.[14]

The Pierce administration did not appreciate the regular army's relative evenhandedness in Kansas. Not only did the administration have to contend with politically unreliable regular army officers, but its civil appointees also took actions at variance with proslavery forces. Pierce's newly appointed territorial governor, John W. Geary, arrived at Leavenworth on September 9, 1856, and embarked on a policy of impartial conciliation. Both he and Persifor Smith, an officer originally appointed by Pierce for his supposedly southern sensibilities, decided to disband and reorganize the old proslavery territorial militia and rely more heavily on the better-disciplined and relatively impartial regulars. Geary also reenacted Sumner's former policy of dispersing *all* armed bands in Kansas, whatever their political allegiance. When a small army of proslavery partisans prepared to attack Lawrence, where Free-Soilers armed themselves to repel the assault, Geary called on Cooke for aid.[15]

With a little more than 400 men at Lawrence, Cooke faced about 2,500 proslavery militia. Cooke exhorted the militia to disband, appealing, as he put it in his official report, "to these militia officers as an old resident of Kansas and friend to the Missourians to submit to the patriotic demand that they should retire, assuring them of my perfect confidence in the inflexible justice of the governor, and that it would become my painful duty to sustain him at the cannon's mouth. Authority prevailed, and the militia honorably submitted to march off to be disbanded at their place of rendezvous." Another small force of troops under Capt. Thomas J. Wood in the meantime disarmed a large band of free-state freebooters. With various other measures, including the interdiction of free-state partisans coming from the North and the stationing of troops at polling places to reassure free-staters, Geary restored relative order to most of Kansas by November 1856.[16]

Kansas's political problems required political solutions, however, and the regular army could not restore peace to the territory with purely military means. Proslavery forces in Kansas and Washington drove Geary out of his office in March 1857, while Smith conceded defeat to political pressure and withheld his support from the governor. The incoming Buchanan administration hoped to save the principle of popular sovereignty and appointed Robert J. Walker to the governor's post. Walker, committed to making popular sovereignty work as intended, demanded and received from Washington substantial formal authority to use regulars to enforce his will, but problems with the Mormons and the Indians on the frontier stripped the Kansas garrisons of much of their strength. Walker did manage to keep most of the territory reasonably quiet in 1857 with a fairly impartial course that ended up supporting free-state forces, but his evenhandedness cost him his post when Buchanan decided to cast his lot with the proslavery Lecompton constitution. After Walker's departure, the always-troublesome southeastern section of Kansas flared up again in 1858. The Buchanan administration's unwillingness to commit resources to the region doomed all attempts at pacification, and southeastern Kansas would be troubled until the Civil War when problems in Kansas merged with the guerrilla war in Missouri.[17]

Despite the old army's relative impartiality, certain officers' actions still revealed the increasingly sectionalized state of the officer corps. In the summer of 1856, Maj. John Sedgwick, a Connecticut native and future Federal corps commander, allowed Free-Soil forces to reduce a proslavery post unmolested. Sedgwick's own cavalrymen still policed Free-Soil mobs, however, during the contentious constitutional convention in Lecompton in the fall of 1857. Before the presidential campaign of 1860, even Capt.

Nathaniel Lyon, who later became a staunch Republican, proved willing to use force against antislavery forces. Lyon had some success in suppressing antislavery Jayhawkers in southeast Kansas during the summer of 1858, although violence flared again when the regulars were withdrawn. Lyon's conduct after Lincoln's election only two years later shows how much the secession winter changed matters. Lyon, then an ardent Republican, illegally subverted his orders by giving intelligence to Jayhawkers, and he even violated the Fugitive Slave Law by loaning federal horses to the Underground Railroad.[18]

Nevertheless, the broad continuities of the old army's experience in the 1850s also help explain the confused and indecisive conduct of many southern-born regular army officers during the sectional crisis. Southern fire-eaters in the regular army and northern-born officers lost no sleep over their loyalties when secession broke out; both groups could act swiftly and decisively for obvious reasons. Unionist officers from the Upper South, in contrast, frequently had to wrestle with their consciences, and the struggle often took so much time that they opened themselves to the charge of moral vacillation and weakness. Neither trait seemed compatible with the old army's ideas about honor and duty, but the deceptive solidity of the status quo during the 1850s helps explain why so many Upper South officers found themselves caught unawares when secession exploded on the landscape.

The most extreme examples of conflicted loyalties were the four West Pointers who first served the Union army and then went Confederate — William T. Magruder of Maryland (USMA 1850), Donald C. Stith of Maryland (USMA 1850), Richard K. Meade of Virginia (USMA 1857), and Manning M. Kimmel of Missouri (USMA 1857). Future Confederates were not the only officers who reversed themselves; William H. Emory of Maryland, a close friend of Jefferson Davis and lieutenant colonel of the 1st Cavalry, had deposited a letter of resignation with his family in Maryland while stationed on the frontier. John Emory forwarded the letter to the War Department unbeknownst to William when the 6th Massachusetts fired on rioters in Baltimore on April 19. Lincoln accepted the resignation but brought William back to the service when the colonel learned of his brother's premature decision.[19]

Most officers proved more decisive. They made an active choice to support one side or the other, rather than only resigning their commissions or staying out of the war if they had already left the service. W. T. H. Brooks commented on the social pressures arrayed against resignation when he wrote shortly after Sumter that if he resigned, "to settle in the north any place would be subjecting myself to all kinds of contumely insult &c."[20] Nevertheless, a few officers took that course, including Maj. Alfred Mordecai, the prominent ordnance officer who had done so much for the artillery branch. Mordecai resigned his commission and stayed out of the sectional fight.[21] Taken as a whole, only ten slave-state West Pointers (2 percent) resigned their old army commissions at the outbreak of war and did not join the Confederacy, while only another fifty-seven graduates (12 percent) already out of the service made no known commitment to either contending government.

Even those slave-state graduates who stayed out of the conflict seem to have been able to cite age as a reasonable and honorable excuse. Of the 57 who stayed out of the service, 27 (47 percent) were graduates of West Point classes of 1830 or earlier; in contrast, of the 487 slave-state West Pointers living at the outbreak of secession, only 90 of 522 (17 percent) graduated in either the class of 1830 or earlier. Mordecai himself graduated in 1823. A graduate from the class of 1830 would have already been in his early fifties at the outbreak of secession, well past the prime age for the rigors of nineteenth-century field service.[22]

Age also played some role in determining a slave-state officer's loyalties. Of 90 West Point graduates of the class of 1830 and before, 27 (30 percent) joined the Confederacy, while 224 of 397 graduates (56 percent) of the classes of 1831 to 1860 did the same. More important than simple age, however, was length of time and achievement in the service, as measured by rank. The lower the rank an officer acquired in the old army, the less tightly he was bound to the regular army uniform. Although all three slave-state West Pointers with generals' stars joined the Confederacy, 10 of 13 full colonels stayed loyal to the Union, while only 3 joined the Confederacy. Forty-three of 85 (51 percent) field-grade officers (colonels, lieutenant colonels, and majors) stayed loyal, while 34 (40 percent) joined the Confederacy. In contrast, of the slave-state West Pointers who left the army, either before or during the secession crisis, at the lowest commissioned rank of second lieutenant, 100 of 167 (60 percent) seceded, while 34 (20 percent) served the Federal colors.[23]

Raw statistics tell only part of the story, but other evidence fleshes out the numbers. Officers from the Upper South states who seceded provide the best test cases for examining questions of loyalty during the secession winter. The examples of Maj. George H. Thomas, Col. Philip St. George Cooke, and Bvt. Lt. Gen. Winfield Scott, all Unionists, can be fruitfully contrasted with Col. Robert E. Lee's decision to join the Confederate cause. All still wore the Federal uniform at Lincoln's election; all could boast of distinguished service records; all opposed secession; but all did not make the same choice about their ultimate loyalties.

Thomas, like Lee, showed some hesitation during the secession winter, but he chose the federal Union over the Old Dominion. Like Lee, Thomas had a distinguished career in the Mexican War, earning two brevet promotions to captain and major for gallantry at Monterrey and Buena Vista. In the fall of 1860, he served in Texas with Lee, where Thomas — himself a slaveholder — probably expressed pro-southern sentiments in the wake of John Brown's failed raid and the upcoming presidential election. He left Texas for a leave of absence that began on November 12, and on his way east he severely injured his back in a train accident.[24]

While convalescing from his back injury, and when Virginia's fate regarding the Union seemed doubtful, Thomas contemplated resignation from the army and applied for an instructor's position at the Virginia Military Institute. In March, with Thomas's back improving, Governor John Letcher of Virginia offered Thomas the position of chief of ordnance for Virginia. The commonwealth had not yet seceded, and Thomas refused the appointment, writing "that it is not my wish to leave the service of the United States as long as it is honorable for me to remain in it, and, therefore, as long as my native state remains in the union, it is my purpose to remain in the army, unless required to perform duties alike repulsive to honor and humanity." Thomas's statement was hardly an affirmation of unconditional Unionism, and at this point he seems to have left his options open.[25]

Nevertheless, when Thomas found himself faced with the painful prospect of irrevocable decision, he chose the old Union over the new Confederacy. On April 4 Virginia still affirmed its opposition to secession, and on April 6 Thomas willingly returned to active service long before his leave's original date of expiration and despite continued problems with his back. On the way to Carlisle Barracks in Pennsylvania to meet his regiment, Thomas received word of the firing on Sumter. In Carlisle, he voluntarily reaffirmed his oath of allegiance to the United States before a magistrate. After the Virginia convention passed an ordinance of secession, Thomas also sent word to his wife and sisters of his decision to stay with the Union.[26] He cast his die and never seems to have regretted it in either word or deed.

Indeed, after the war, the biographer Thomas B. Van Horne recorded a conversation in which Thomas "said there was no excuse whatever in a United States officer claiming the right of secession, and the only excuse for their deserting the government was what none of them admitted, having engaged in—a revolution against a tyranny, because the tyranny did not exist, and they well knew it." Van Horne also plausibly claims that Thomas "believed that there was a moral and legal obligation that forbade resignation, with a view to take up arms against the Government," and even "condemned the National authorities for accepting the resignation of officers, when aware that it was their intention to join the rebellion as soon as they were in this way freed from the obligation of their oath of allegiance." For whatever reason, Thomas never uttered these words in public, and his only public reference to his decision referred to the gratitude he felt to the federal government for a free West Point education. Nevertheless, toward the end of the war in March 1865, he wrote these harsh words on the Confederacy as a whole: "Their cause was cursed in the beginning but their infatuation has led them on in their suicidal course until they now see nothing before them but disgrace & infamy. God grant that our land may be henceforth freed from the likes of them."[27]

Thomas was no Republican, however. After the war, George L. Hartsuff, a West Pointer from New York and future Union major general who conversed with Thomas in late 1860, claimed that "General Thomas was strong and bitter in his denunciations against all parties North and South that seemed to him responsible for the condition of affairs. . . . But while he reprobated very strongly, certain men and parties North, in that respect going as far as any of those who afterward joined the rebels, he never in my hearing, agreed with them respecting the necessity of going with their States; but he denounced the idea, and denied the necessity of dividing the country, or destroying the Government." Such sentiments square well with the characteristically conservative Unionism of most regular army officers.[28]

Furthermore, Thomas did not totally renounce his southern identity during the war. Even toward the end of the war, he still spoke fondly of his service in the Lower South. In a letter to a fellow Unionist, he wrote: "I often think of the pleasant time we had at New Orleans Bks where I was always so cordially welcomed at your house, also of Fort Moultrie where the who[le] garrison lived on as cordial and friendly terms as the members of a family, and where we also had so many sincere friends as I thought among the inhabitants of Charleston and [the] neighboring country. I often wonder what has become of them." Thomas even waxed nostalgic with that other notorious southern sympathizer, William Tecumseh Sherman, and reported that he and Sherman "have frequently talked over our pleasant and happy tour of service on Sullivan's Island & I find he looks back to those happy days with as much pleasure as I do." Both Sherman and Thomas, Ohioan and Virginian, were political conservatives; both had southern sympathies; and both had acquired an absolutely inflexible Unionism in the antebellum regular army.[29]

Thomas's decision to stay with the Union also went beyond questions of ideology. He had, after all, married a northern woman he had met while serving as an instructor at West Point in the early 1850s. Although Frances Kellogg Thomas claimed after the war that her husband had independently chosen Union over state, her northern background must have had some effect. Because of his regular army obligations, moreover, Thomas had spent fewer than eighteen months in Southampton County the quarter century before the Civil War. This probably loosened whatever affective bonds that may have once connected him to his native state and county.[30]

Thomas still had much family in Virginia, however, and the residents of Southampton County still saw Thomas as one of their own when they presented him a ceremonial sword in 1848 for his service in the Mexican War. The harsh reaction of Thomas's sisters in Southampton to their brother's Unionism in 1861 certainly implies an expectation among his kinfolk that he would follow the Old Dominion. Southampton legend contains many stories of familial wrath: the demand that Thomas change his name; the symbolic rebuke of turning the errant brother's portrait to the wall in the ancestral home; the refusal of his sisters to acknowledge Thomas's existence when Union officers brought them aid out of courtesy to their comrade-in-arms; and a few other colorful if sad anecdotes. Thomas's brothers eventually reconciled, but his sisters never forgave him. Many former Confederate officers also revealed an earlier expectation that Thomas would secede when they claimed after the war that he had openly declared his intention to join the Confederate cause before he reversed himself.[31]

Other anecdotal evidence supports the assertion that regular army Virginians who stayed with the Union incurred real personal costs. 1st Lt. William Rufus Terrill, West Point Class of 1853 and a brigade commander killed at the battle of Perryville in Kentucky, saw his brother James Barbour join the Confederate service. Family tradition has it that William discussed the issue with his father and resolved to stay with the

Union as long as he did not have to serve in Virginia, and Terrill did spend most of his career in the western theater. His father declared, however, "Do so, and your name shall be stricken from the family record, and only remembered in connection with your treachery to the country that gave you birth." Some sort of conflict must also have existed in John Gibbon's family. Gibbon, raised in North Carolina and the future commander of the famous Iron Brigade in the Army of the Potomac, saw three brothers serve the Confederacy while he served the Union. During the war, Gibbon explained his decision to his wife by writing that "You must reconcile yourself to the idea that I am bound to go into a fight if for no other reason to give the lie to my enemies and prove my loyalty to the gold old stars and stripes."[32]

Philip St. George Cooke, the antebellum regular army's leading authority on cavalry, may have carried a burden of familial estrangement even more severe than Thomas's and Terrill's. James Ewell Brown Stuart, husband of the elder Cooke's daughter, Flora, took such offense at his father-in-law's Unionism that he changed the name of his son, Philip St. George Cooke Stuart, to James Ewell Brown Stuart Jr. Stuart wrote his wife, "Be consoled . . . by the reflection that your husband & brothers will atone for the father's conduct." Stuart referred to the fact that 1st Lt. John Rogers Cooke, Philip St. George Cooke's son and a regular army officer (although not a West Pointer), had joined the Confederate cause along with both of Cooke's sons-in-law (Stuart himself and Charles Brewer, a former regular army surgeon). Only one of the Cooke children, Julia Turner Cooke, did not become estranged; she married Jacob Sharpe, an officer in a New York volunteer regiment during the war. The war's conclusion did not end the estrangement; only Cooke's nephew, John Esten Cooke, a novelist and writer of some note, proved willing to reconcile himself to the old soldier.[33]

Cooke, unlike Thomas and Lee, never wavered during the sectional crisis. He had been stationed in Utah during the secession winter, and he changed the name of his post from Camp Floyd (named after the ardently prosecession secretary of war John B. Floyd) to Fort Crittenden, in honor of the old Kentucky senator who was trying to iron out a sectional compromise. When he heard of the resignations of his son and two sons-in-law in Missouri, Cooke is reported to have exclaimed, "Those mad boys! If I only had been here!" When he found his own loyalty questioned, Cooke mournfully wrote to his superiors in Washington on June 17, 1861: "Instead of sympathizing with the unhappiness of my family disunion, they taunt and impute it as a crime! The Department, I doubt not, knew of the acts of my far distant, long absent, unhappy sons . . . But I dismiss the subject—with loathing."[34] Eleven days earlier, Cooke had also written a public letter to the *National Intelligencer* in Washington declaring his true loyalties.

Indeed, Cooke even disclaimed any strong bonds to Virginia in that letter: "At fourteen years of age I was severed from Virginia; the National Government adopted me as its pupil and future defender; it gave me education and a profession, and I then made a solemn oath to bear true allegiance to the United States of America, and to 'serve them honestly and faithfully against all their enemies or opposers whatsoever.' This oath and honor alike forbid me to abandon their standard at the first hour of danger." Cooke claimed he was now a man of the West, unsurprising in light of his decades' worth of service on the frontier. Taking a conservative Unionist position, Cooke wrathfully denounced the conduct of southern extremists, with special invective against South Carolina. He also chided northern actions, though with much less heat, and did not totally disavow his bonds with Virginia. Cooke admitted that "if I had been on the ground I might have felt tempted to shoulder a musket in defence of the mother of *dead* statesmen, 'right or wrong,'" but he finally declared, "I owe Virginia little, my country much."[35]

Winfield Scott, another old soldier from Virginia, also believed that the Union colors deserved compulsory obedience. Like Cooke, he mixed unconditional Unionism with a conservative political attitude that emphasized the orderly and nonviolent resolution of sectional conflicts. In the fall of 1860 Scott called for a policy of measured restraint. He wrote Secretary of War Floyd a letter in October where he affirmed the right of a state to secede *and* the right of the federal government to force it back into the Union. Scott also seemed to assume the loyalty of the federal military, believing that that loyalty combined with a firm but moderate administration policy would head off secession.[36] Scott tried to steer a middle course, but, as events would show, his loyalties to the Union remained preeminent.

When Scott heard rumors that southerners would try to disrupt the Electoral College balloting on February 13, 1861, he declared that anyone interfering "should be lashed to the muzzle of a twelve-pounder gun and fired out of a window of the capitol. . . . It is my duty to suppress insurrection—*my duty!*" Scott throughout the secession winter strengthened some federal posts in the South, took various other precautions, and in

March carefully guarded Lincoln's inauguration. He cited Jackson's reinforcement of the Charleston garrison during the nullification crisis in 1833 to try to persuade Buchanan to reinforce Fort Moultrie in December 1860. Scott also heartily approved of Robert Anderson's bold withdrawal of his Charleston garrison to the more secure Fort Sumter in late December 1860.[37]

Scott's conservative attitudes toward secession could be summed up by what he claimed in his memoirs (written during the Civil War) to have told his soldiers during the nullification crisis: "These nullifiers have, no doubt, become exceedingly wrong-headed, and are in the road to treason; but still they are our countrymen, and may be saved from that great crime by respect and kindness on our part. We must keep our bosoms open to receive them back as brothers in the Union."[38] He advised Lincoln in late March 1861 to abandon both Fort Sumter in Charleston and Fort Pickens in Florida as a sign of conciliation toward the South.

Lincoln resolved instead to reinforce Sumter in April after word reached Washington that Fort Pickens's reinforcement had miscarried because of a garbled order, leaving Sumter as the only remaining Federal post that could be reinforced. Scott acquiesced to his commander in chief's policy and participated in early Union war planning. When Lee refused the Federal field command, Scott told Lee that "you have made the greatest mistake of your life; but I feared it would be so." The loyal Virginian held his position as general-in-chief until a brief power struggle with George B. McClellan forced him to resign on October 31 at the age of seventy-five, ending a military career that had begun before the War of 1812.[39]

Cooke, Thomas, and Scott stood in stark contrast to and even waged war against Robert E. Lee. Like those Virginians who stayed with the Federal service, Lee strongly opposed secession. On January 23, 1861, he wrote, "The framers of our Constitution never exhausted so much labor, wisdom, and forbearance in its formation, and surrounded it with so many guards and securities, if it was intended to be broken by every member of the Confederacy at will. . . . It is idle to talk of secession. Anarchy would have been established, and not a government, by Washington, Hamilton, Jefferson, Madison, and the other patriots of the Revolution." Unlike his former comrades-in-arms, however, there were limits to Lee's Unionism; on the previous day, in a letter to Martha Custis Williams, he wrote that "there is no sacrifice I am not ready to make for the preservation of the

Union save that of honour."[40] For Robert E. Lee, honor demanded that he stay with the Old Dominion above all else.

But what of Philip St. George Cooke's honor? Cooke had cited both his oath to the people of the United States to "serve them honestly and faithfully against all their enemies or opposers whatsoever" and his honor as the touchstones of his decision to stay with the Union. The historian Alan Nolan has pointed out that Lee had taken the same oath, which makes no provision for states' rights or loyalties to the Old Dominion, no matter how strongly felt.[41] George Thomas, like Lee, had also qualified his loyalties with a reference to honor, but he clearly decided that suppression of the rebellion did not fall under his own escape clause. The aged Scott had declared it his "duty" to put down the rebellion, which Lee himself believed to have no legal justification.

Furthermore, Lee's resignation from the U.S. Army leaves open many questions. Southern-born officers believed that the resignation of their commissions released them from their oaths to combat the enemies of the government of the United States, and even during the Civil War, American officers in both sections could resign their commissions. All officers agreed, however, that resignation remained honorable only under certain conditions. For example, no self-respecting regular would have looked well on a colleague who resigned his commission right after being ordered to lead an assault. In a less extreme example, the historian Douglas Southall Freeman argues that Lee could not have resigned his commission "under orders" without bringing disgrace to himself. Freeman also admits that Lee may have stood with the Union if he had not been replaced by David Twiggs as department commander of Texas, because he would have been honor-bound to defend his post when secessionist Texans demanded its surrender before Virginia's own secession. Regular army officers, Unionist and secessionist, agreed that Twiggs's surrender of his department involved an unconscionable breach of faith, and most Confederate West Pointers made sure to resign their commissions before they joined the Confederate army.[42] More vexatious, however, is the question of whether Thomas's contention was correct — that resigning with the intent to take up arms against the United States could not possibly be seen as honorable.

Finally, if Lee could not bear coercing his home state back into the Union, he could have simply resigned and joined neither the Union nor Confederate war efforts. Even within Lee's own family, opinion remained divided on secession. As distinguished a regular army officer as Alfred

THE BEGINNING OF THE END

Mordecai of North Carolina, perhaps the leading ordnance specialist of the antebellum period, chose that path, and considering Lee's advanced age and political opinions, that option may have been the most compatible with both his regional ties and his obligations toward the U.S. government.[43]

Indeed, in some ways Lee's age, length of service, and Upper South background better fit the profile of a Unionist officer. Lee was one of only three full slave-state colonels to serve the Confederacy — ten of his fellow colonels chose the Union instead. Even when we look only at Virginians, the statistics continue to point to Lee staying with the Union. While nine of twenty-seven (33 percent) Virginian graduates of West Point classes up to and including the class of 1830 went Confederate, a higher percentage of older graduates stayed with the Union: thirteen of twenty-seven (48 percent). Lee's behavior better fit the profile of a younger West Pointer from Virginia. Of 99 Virginian graduates of the classes of 1831 to 1860, 61 (62 percent) went Confederate, whereas 31 of 99 (31 percent) stayed with the Union.

In a testament to the powerful nationalizing effects of the old army on its officer corps, even some Lower South officers remained loyal to the Federal service.[44] For example, 2nd Lt. William P. Sanders, who had moved to Mississippi at the age of seven from his birth state of Kentucky, possessed strong southern credentials but remained with the Union. Jefferson Davis himself had interceded for him while a cadet at West Point and prevented his dismissal for academic failings. 2nd Lt. Edward Porter Alexander, a future Confederate artilleryman from Georgia, served with him on the West Coast and later described him as "intensely Southern in all his views of it [secession], more so I think than any other Southern officer in the army with whom I met during the whole period of the initiation of hostilities. His family were from Kentucky & Mississippi, & he frequently claimed connection or relationship with Jefferson Davis." When Alexander left to join Confederate forces, he fully expected Sanders would be a future comrade; Sanders instead rose to the rank of brigadier general of volunteers in the Federal service and would be killed in action while fighting troops under Alexander's own command at Knoxville in November 1863. Sanders must have strained relations with his family over his Unionism, because three of his brothers served in Mississippi cavalry regiments.[45]

The creation of a viable Confederate government made all these questions of proper loyalties moot, however, and now old army veterans prepared for war. They had all chosen their political loyalties, right or wrong, and now only battle could decide the physical fact of states' rights and secession. These political differences of opinion still retained within them certain important shared values among old army officers—ideas of honor and oath keeping, along with obedience to some kind of lawful authority, however that might be defined. Lee himself declared after the war that "obedience to lawful authority is the foundation of manly character."[46] These shared ideas, most importantly, reflected the basic presumption that legitimate military force required organization, hierarchy, and discipline, all modeled on the old army's institutional patterns. Commissioned officers as gentlemen of honor kept their oaths and obeyed their proper superiors. This fundamental attitude helped set broad limits to Civil War violence, preventing both a systematic use of guerrilla and partisan warfare by Confederate commanders and Federal commanders' complete dissolution of the distinction between Confederate combatant and noncombatant. The war would thus be fought out for the most part on the battlefield, between uniformed armies, organized along roughly comparable lines. The old army, in this sense, lived on in both armies, regardless of the sectional crisis.

CHAPTER SIX

War in Earnest

The First Battles of 1861

★ ★ ★

The political aspirations of both contending sections to govern proper nation-states, recognized by their Western peers in both Europe and the New World, produced the environment in which the old army could establish an early institutional predominance in the war's management. Although both the Union and the Confederacy believed in the martial valor of the citizen-soldier volunteer, neither questioned the inherent legitimacy of uniformed forces under some form of military discipline, even if those notions of discipline frequently clashed with citizen-soldier ideals. Furthermore, both sections subscribed to ideas about social stability and political authority that made the Confederate use of a strategy based on guerrillas or insurgents all but impossible. The violence and chaos of guerrilla-infested Missouri showed why most Confederates had no desire to shatter their social order, including slavery and other forms of race control, for the sake of making the South ungovernable in the usual American sense of the term. Guerrillas did become a significant influence on the war, and a problem Federal forces eventually had to contain to win the war, but they never became a major part of Confederate military strategy.[1]

Eugene A. Carr displayed a typical Old Army distaste for irregular methods, condemning Free-Soil radical James Lane on January 28, 1862, as downright "wicked" and "without religion, honor, principle, or human feeling." Instead, he appealed to "the laws of civilized warfare" as the best guide for Federal action in a "cause which is just and holy and should be supported by honest means."[2] Unlike Sherman, who later embraced property destruction as a legitimate war measure, Carr as late as the Vicksburg campaign retained his preference for the restrained methods of a McClellan or Maj. Gen. Don Carlos Buell. Writing during that campaign as a division commander, Carr fretted over what he saw as wanton and unnecessary Federal destruction of private property, fearing that Union forces "will meet with some signal disaster as a punishment." Carr held these views, despite his wholesale commitment to the war's prosecution, declaring in the same letter that "everybody now ought to encourage the draft and let us beat them by main strength and awkwardness if we can not find any generals." Such anxieties about property destruction had stronger support in the Army of the Potomac, where Brig. Gen. Alfred Sully had described Fredericksburg's sack after its capture in December 1862 as a "frightful scene" driven by alcohol. Indeed, Sully expressed the common regular army distaste for constabulary duties as early as June 1861, where he complained of being ordered to "go to peoples houses by night seize the leading secessionists from their families & march them off as prisoners just like a police-man apprehending a thief. . . . The most disgusting business I ever had to do."[3]

Confederate leaders also regarded irregular warfare with deep unease. On April 1, 1864, Lee bluntly wrote that "experience has convinced me that it is almost impossible, under the best officers even, to have discipline in these bands of Partisan Rangers [officially sanctioned Confederate ir- regulars], or to prevent them from becoming an injury instead of a ben- efit to the service, and even where this is accomplished the system gives license to many deserters & marauders, who assume to belong to these authorized companies & commit depredations on friend & foe alike." Lee also feared the demoralizing affects of these troops on his regular units. Even Porter Alexander, who later contemplated guerrilla war against the Union as a last resort, wrote in the spring of 1862 that "our soldiers are committing many shameful outrages which are a disgrace to the country & some ought to & I hope will be, shot, as examples. The Yankees could be no worse than many of them are."[4] Alexander distrusted ill-disciplined troops as much as Lee, and his commander appealed to those fears at the end of the war to discourage his subordinate from pursuing guerrilla war against Federal forces.

Both sections' political leaders, having committed themselves to nation- state war, then in turn bound themselves to the only group of men who had the background and knowledge for managing such a conflict—the officer corps of the antebellum U.S. Army. This caused some inherent problems in the war efforts of both nations. Political and military leaders had in the antebellum period structured the old army to fight brush-fire Indian wars and moderately sized nation-state wars roughly comparable to the War of 1812 and the Mexican War. They had never imagined putting

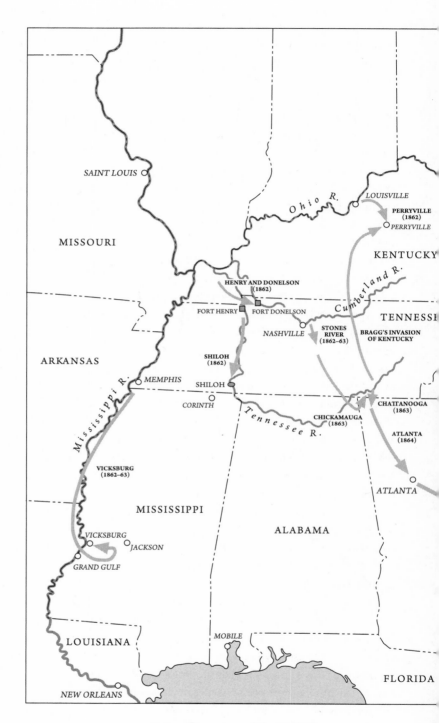

MAP 4. Campaigns of the Civil War

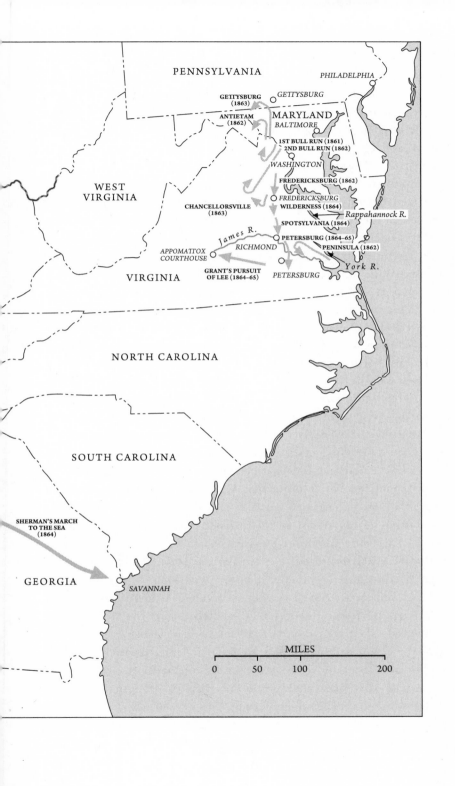

PENNSYLVANIA

PHILADELPHIA

**GETTYSBURG
(1863)** ○ *GETTYSBURG*

MARYLAND

**ANTIETAM
(1862)** *BALTIMORE*

**1ST BULL RUN (1861)
2ND BULL RUN (1862)**

WASHINGTON

WEST
VIRGINIA

FREDERICKSBURG (1862)

○ *FREDERICKSBURG*

**CHANCELLORSVILLE
(1863)** **WILDERNESS (1864)**

Rappahannock R.

SPOTSYLVANIA (1864)

James R.

PETERSBURG (1864–65)

APPOMATTOX
COURTHOUSE *RICHMOND* **PENINSULA (1862)**

York R.

VIRGINIA **GRANT'S PURSUIT
OF LEE (1864–65)** *PETERSBURG*

NORTH CAROLINA

SOUTH CAROLINA

**SHERMAN'S MARCH
TO THE SEA
(1864)**

GEORGIA ○ *SAVANNAH*

MILES

0   50   100   200

millions of men under arms. Many of the old army's tactical ideas worked best with well-drilled troops comparable to the hard-bitten regulars who had formed the core of the armies during the preceding war in Mexico. The regular army's leadership in the field also lacked any real command experience comparable to the sheer size of a Civil War field army.[5] Nevertheless, the regular army officer corps would play a crucial role in the creation, command, training, and fighting of Civil War armies.

Unfortunately for both sections, the scarce numbers of available old army men, the impatience of a public opinion that forced immediate military action, the rawness of the volunteers, and political disorganization in both sections produced armies of dubious military competence at the war's first important battles. These early forces show that we cannot take for granted the military machinery of an effective army; someone must give troops at least some basic level of training, discipline them properly, feed them, clothe them, equip them, pay them, and even lead them into battle. For all the regular army officer corps's obvious shortcomings, they possessed more of this indispensable expertise than any other group of Americans, North or South.

These early battles had a special importance, especially First Bull Run fought in northern Virginia in July 1861. Winfield Scott had early on seen the dangers of any early Confederate victory. He warned Maj. Gen. Robert Patterson on June 8 that "we must sustain no reverse . . . a check or a drawn battle would be a victory to the enemy, filling his heart with joy, his ranks with men, and his magazines with voluntary contributions." The Federal commander at Bull Run, Brig. Gen. Irwin McDowell himself had recognized how important the battle's outcome would be, "establishing the prestige in this contest on the one side or the other."[6] Confederate defeat at this battle might well have proved fatal to the cause of secession, while a Federal defeat decisive enough to lead to the fall of Washington might have doomed any attempt to restore the Union.

The Confederates gained a signal victory that ensured secession would be far more significant than the Whiskey Rebellion or the Mormon War, but the Federal army survived to fight another day. This inability to annihilate the Union army at one blow stemmed in large part from the rough equilibrium in training, cohesion, and leadership that existed between the two armies. This rough equilibrium in competence continued throughout the war, sustained by roughly equivalent rates of learning in armies led by similar old army–dominated command structures and manned by comparable citizen-soldiers. This made the annihilation of a Civil War field army in a set-piece battle — the great Napoleonic dream of Civil War commanders — a supremely difficult task.

The roughly comparable abilities of both contending armies intensified the importance of individual leadership and even random luck in battlefield decisions. A few different decisions here and there at Bull Run could have shifted the fortunes of war either way. The "battles and leaders" approach to Civil War military history thus remains anything but obsolete. While some military history can and should focus on questions of organization — training, minor tactics, doctrine, and the like — it cannot ignore the actual ebb and flow of battles and campaigns, driven in part by command decisions. Furthermore, historians must also take into account cultural, political, and social factors when analyzing Civil War military operations.

The continued strength of the citizen-soldier ideal in the American military imagination produced the most militarily significant cultural and political pressures on early Civil War military operations. These citizen-soldier ideals pushed early Civil War armies into seeking a quick decision on the battlefield and downplayed the importance of training and preparation. After the initial surge of enthusiasm in the Lower South for the war, Governor Thomas Moore of Louisiana informed Richmond on July 6, 1861, that "Enlistments for the war, especially when they know they are to go into a camp of instruction, will be very slow." Both armies believed the coming conflict to be a lark that would be quickly settled in favor of their own more virtuous and glorious arms. The variegated collection of uniforms present at First Manassas — including but not limited to imitations of French Zouave garb, coonskin caps, headgear modeled on the equipage of Italian *bersaglieri* in honor of Garibaldi, and plain civilian dress — all displayed Americans' romantic vision of war. Unfortunately, whether they liked it or not, the more fanciful elements of antebellum military culture had to give way to battlefield reality, but the citizen-soldier ideal never entirely disappeared. For example, even after the Confederate introduction of conscription in the spring of 1862, a war measure necessary for national existence, Confederate officers still struggled against popular prejudices with regards to conscripts. Indeed, the historian Alice Fahs has shown that as the war dragged on, Civil War literary culture emphasized the individualistic and sentimentalized soldier suffering on the battlefield and in the hospital, as opposed to Sherman's Old Army view that "an army is not a popular organization, but an animated machine, an instrument in the hands of the Executive for enforcing the law."[7]

Nothing comes without its price in war, and the same ideological commitment that allowed both the Union and the Confederacy to build vast armies from scratch also produced pressures on the respective army leaderships to act as quickly as possible. Nevertheless, the wave of volunteerism did in a sense vindicate the popular belief that a substantial standing army was unnecessary, because large numbers of citizen-soldiers had actually rallied to the colors in a time of crisis. The problem would be how long it would take to make the new volunteer armies proficient in the art of war, and how long those troops would be willing to serve under the colors.

Early in the war, the initial wave of martial enthusiasm obscured such practical problems. Confederate general and former Virginia governor Henry Wise declared to J. B. Jones, a Confederate War Department clerk, on April 12 "that it was not the improved *arm*, but the improved *man*, which would win the day. Let brave men advance with flint locks and old-fashioned bayonets, on the popinjays of the Northern cities — advance on, and on, under the fire, reckless of the slain, and he would answer for it with his life, that the Yankees would break and run." On June 12, Jones wrote that "a vast majority of our people are for 'carrying the war into Africa' without a moment's delay." As early as April 27, the *Richmond Enquirer* boasted that the Confederacy's preexisting martial prowess would make up for its lack of training. Even the cautionary warning by the *Charleston Mercury* that the Union would fight well was not actually all that cautionary. It might declare that "the North will open the ball with hard fighting," but it also foresaw southern triumph after only "a few effective victories."[8]

In the North, heavy public pressure, led by Horace Greeley's *New York Tribune*, demanded that the Lincoln administration take decisive military action. The well-known *Times* of London correspondent, William Howard Russell, commented on June 22 that "the absurdities I have seen in the New York papers about military matters are enough to drive a soldier mad." In a well-meaning if profoundly ill-considered gesture, the *Tribune* printed as its motto in early July: "THE NATION'S WAR CRY! *Forward to Richmond! Forward to Richmond! The Rebel Congress must not be allowed to meet there on the 20th of July!* BY THAT DATE THE PLACE MUST BE HELD BY THE NATIONAL ARMY." In a dark foreboding of the future pall of suspicion that would cloud relations between some Republicans and the Union's military leadership, Greeley even questioned Scott's true loyalties when he seemed too sluggish. He dismissed Scott's defenders' appeals to strategic problems as the obfuscation of a mercenary caste. On July 7, Russell reported to his diary a Republican senator's unhappiness with the regulars at a breakfast meeting. Even after the Union catastrophe at Bull Run, when the *Tribune* was put on the defensive and disclaimed responsibility for McDowell's premature assault, Greeley could still faintly sneer at "putting down a rebellion by forming 'camps of instruction.'"[9]

Some experienced military leaders in both sections knew that the war would be no lark, but they were the exceptions that proved the rule. Lee himself had hoped that from the war's outbreak enlistments would be for the duration and was irritated by overconfident southerners who saw a need for only short terms of enlistment. He wrote as early as April 30, 1861, that the war might last ten years. Lafayette McLaws, a future Confederate major general and old army veteran, reported in late June 1861 with some dry (if skeptical) amusement that "I heard several grown men to day, about an hour since, say that there was no need of so many troops from the South as the Yankees would not fight." In contrast to such general sentiment, Lee, acutely conscious of Confederate weaknesses in war material and supply, cautioned Col. Thomas J. Jackson stationed at Harpers Ferry on May 12 that "you know our limited resources, & must abstain from all provocation for attack as long as possible." In Washington, Scott's original war planning in May called for an expedition of sixty thousand men to receive four and a half months of training before setting out to retake the Mississippi River.[10]

Current and former regular army officers frequently served as counselors of caution in both sections. Sherman wrote on May 23 that "I have seen enough of War not to be caught by its first glittering bait, and when I engage in this, it must be with a full consciousness of its real character." He criticized Lincoln for calling out far too few troops in his first proclamation for volunteers. On June 12, he wrote his wife that "in war all is uncertainty & chance." He reported a conversation with Scott where the old general fretted that public clamor for action, "Genl. Impatience," would precipitate reckless and unwarranted military movements. After the early Federal victory at Rich Mountain shortly before First Bull Run, future Union major general William Rosecrans cautioned his wife not to overstate the Federal success, because "while trying to get my troops in proper position I could not help thinking if the enemy had disciplined troops and any enterprize how they would have stirred us up." Indeed, McDowell admitted in his original plan for First Bull Run that "for the most part our regiments are exceedingly raw and the best of them, with few exceptions, not over steady in line." He still believed in "every chance of success" with good leadership, but McDowell knew how green his forces were.[11]

The American public did not completely ignore these cautions. The Washington correspondent of the *New York Times* argued that "important distributing posts [for volunteers] should be under the command either of officers of the regular army, or of civilians of more than usual military sagacity and executive ability." The same correspondent also recommended that West Point cadets due to graduate soon, "young men who have made military science their careful study, and arms their profession," be used as drillmasters for the new volunteers, while decrying the appointment of officers for purely political considerations. After the war, one volunteer recalled that he and his comrades had at first believed regular officers to be "superior beings" shortly before Bull Run. In the Confederacy, Lee's long service in the regular army hardly stymied the near-universal enthusiasm with which Virginia hailed his initial appointment as commander in chief of the state's military forces. The *Richmond Enquirer* took tremendous pride in the services provided by former old army officers. Nevertheless, as early as June 1861, J. B. Jones commented on the rift between citizen-soldier generals and West Pointers.[12] That division between the citizen-soldier ideal and old army professionals had real effects in both sections, but we should not view it as an unbridgeable chasm.

At least some early volunteers realized that they needed training and drilling. Henry Warren Howe, then a private in a Massachusetts artillery company, declined the extra pay of staffing a military post office, writing a week before Bull Run that "[I] should lose my drill; the latter is important should I go into action." One Confederate volunteer from South Carolina, Capt. John Bratton, talked in a letter to his wife in the spring of 1861 about the need to prepare for the next day's drill the night before, because "an officer so new and green cannot take too many precautions against embarrassing positions, besides it is as much my duty to be a good officer as it was in the first instance to be a volunteer." Even Sterling Price, who had no love for West Pointers, recognized the importance of drill and had a former regular army officer, Alexander Early Steen, serve as drillmaster for the Missouri state guard troops concentrating at Cowskin Prairie in the summer of 1861.[13]

The Federal high command sent many of the newly graduated members of the West Point Class of 1861 to Washington to serve as drillmasters for the volunteers. At Harpers Ferry, Joe Johnston and Thomas J. Jackson worked their men hard on the parade ground. The first regiments raised by Virginia after Lincoln's proclamation for volunteers benefited from the Virginia Military Institute cadets turned into drillmasters at the Virginian camps of instruction. Western units also associated drill with soldiering. The Missouri state guard even engaged in some target practice in camp. The best historian of the Confederate Army of Tennessee, Andrew Haughton, estimates that "most volunteers in the western armies received from three weeks to two months of training at a camp of instruction, before moving north to the Confederate front line in Kentucky." In the Confederacy, current and former students at various military academies — VMI being the most important — provided much assistance in the early training of the armies.[14]

Bisectional Zouave-mania reflected in one sense the willingness of volunteers to train, if that training could also be made compatible with their romantic enthusiasm. Thomas Reade Rootes Cobb praised a volunteer militia unit present at Jefferson Davis's inauguration in February 1861 for both its brilliant uniforms and its skillfulness in the "Zouave Tactics." But it was a northerner, Elmer Ellsworth, who represented the most spectacular manifestation of the Zouave *rage militaire*. Ellsworth combined romantic enthusiasm for the outlandish costumes, quick movements, and vaguely oriental origins of the Zouaves with a hearty disdain for incompetent militia officers. Ellsworth had before the war won fame as the commander of a volunteer militia company in Chicago that claimed to specialize in the French Zouave drill. He and his company toured twenty different northern cities in the summer of 1860.[15]

Ellsworth's ideas did reflect the influence of the new chasseur drill. Like French and American regulars, he emphasized bayonet practice and an infantry drill less dependent on close order. These similarities proved superficial, however. The portions of Ellsworth's manual that covered skirmishing represented only a shortened version of Hardee's tactics. Ellsworth simply removed some of the explanatory instructions Hardee included on skirmishers, along with the references to battalion-sized units. For example, while sections 15–20 of the skirmisher drill in Hardee's tactics and 1–6 of the skirmisher drill in Ellsworth's manual were identical in their coverage of the principles of deployments, Ellsworth removed Hardee's introductory comments on battalion fronts in section 21 and, most importantly, Hardee's practical commentary on the reduced emphasis on alignments, the function of skirmishers as a screening force, the importance of reserves, and the necessity for officers to maintain strong control

WAR IN EARNEST

over their men while skirmishing. Indeed, when Ellsworth visited West Point with his company during its summer tour, Hardee had grumbled that the outsized movements of these volunteers were for the most part impractical.[16]

Ellsworth's changes deemphasized the regular army's focus on training, discipline, and the military chain of command, which reflected the frictions between him and the old army men at the West Point review. He excised the section in Hardee that declared, "Officers should watch with the greatest possible vigilance over a line of skirmishers. . . . In all the firings, they, as well as the sergeants, should see that order and silence are preserved, and that the skirmishers do not wander imprudently; they should especially caution them to be calm and collected; not to fire until they distinctly perceive the objects at which they aim, and are sure those objects are within proper range."[17] While Ellsworth's open-order tactics drew off of romantic notions of aggressive military valor, the skirmishing of actual veterans later in the war shows the care and caution skirmishing required to be militarily effective.

For example, one veteran later described an advance of skirmishers during the Appomattox campaign with the following: "Hunters of big game in the backwoods can understand the nervous excitement which thrills one in advancing upon an enemy, whether a wild beast or an armed soldier, through thick woods where only occasional glimpses would enable you to see but a few rods in advance." This comment could be seen as simply a vindication of the myth of the American rifleman, advancing through the woods like a seasoned hunter, as opposed to being ambushed like the doomed Maj. Gen. Edward Braddock during the Seven Years' War. But the rest of the passage moves away from that tradition, "Still our lines advanced, not rapidly but cautiously—very cautiously, every man for himself in a sense—on the alert and watchful. . . . when the woods became more open, a longer view could be obtained, and at last through the openings we could see what looked like fresh earthworks of considerable magnitude. Then greater caution was observed—each skirmisher advanced from tree to tree—jumping, creeping, crawling—observing the general alignment, and at the same time keeping the keenest watch in front." Note the combination of individual initiative ("every man for himself") and larger-unit discipline ("observing the general alignment"), combined with due military caution, as opposed to impetuousness.[18]

It would be the absence of larger-unit discipline that would so badly plague the early Civil War armies, which was reflected in Ellsworth's

own unit's notorious lack of discipline both on and off the battlefield.[19]
These problems shared the same wellspring in the myth of the untutored
citizen-soldier who did not require drill, discipline, and training. Even the
best-drilled of the volunteer units, who were somewhat familiar with the
chasseur system imported by the regulars in the 1850s, could not escape
this subterranean source of American martial culture.

The national preoccupation with the bowie knife also reflected some
of these ideals. The bowie knife, or "Arkansas toothpick," actually had a
fairly intimidating reputation early in the war. Wise had advocated the
use of such knives rather than long-range rifle fire, and he claimed that
the saber bayonet was "inferior to the *knife*. Our men would require long
drilling to become expert with the former, like the French Zouaves; but
they instinctively knew how to wield the bowie-knife." Western Unionists
also laid claim to the weapon, with one writer claiming after the war that
two Civil War volunteers from Iowa and Michigan had used the weapons
effectively.[20]

While some Americans saw the bowie knife as a distinctly American
weapon born of the rough-and-tumble frontier, a vocal minority of Confederates called for the use of guerrilla methods, which they saw as distinctly southern. Such calls began early; Brig. Gen. Philip St. George
Cocke, the first Confederate commander at Manassas, hoped to use the region's heavily wooded terrain as cover for guerrilla operations by riflemen.
Cocke, not to be confused with Col. Cooke of the Federal Dragoons, had
graduated from West Point, but he had served in the Old Army for only
two years before dedicating his life to progressive farming methods and
the Virginia Military Institute. Indeed, although the old army in general
opposed the tactics of insurgency, it did have plenty of experience with
partisan methods both in Mexico and on the frontier. Robert Anderson
himself, a veteran of the Seminole War, had described guerrilla warfare
as "the most dangerous of all kinds of war" while serving in Mexico.[21]

George Fitzhugh, one of the old South's premier intellectuals, also
called for guerrilla methods. He declared in July 1861, "We deem it a
happy circumstance that the officers of our army will be generally composed of young men, who will not be martinets, adopting on all occasions
the tactics of the schools, but ready on proper opportunities to pursue that
desultory partisan method of warfare before which invading armies gradually melt away." Fitzhugh did not dispute the necessity of regular army
methods; he praised Lee and recognized the militia's inability to mount
offensive operations, but he remained wedded to partisan methods. He

acknowledged that "no doubt [we] are about to horrify our distinguished experienced officers, late of the federal army, when we say that for defensive war, militia, in some localities and under some circumstances, are superior to regulars." In Fitzhugh's view, southern terrain, and most importantly, southern social characteristics, made the Confederacy impregnable to invasion, because the invading Federals would be faced with invincible southern partisans.[22]

The *Charleston Mercury* also cited the rough and broken nature of most Confederate terrain as an ideal theater of operations for guerrillas, which in its view would be better armed with deer guns than military arms. The *Mercury* even advocated the use of cold steel with partisan infantry: bowie knives or spears, if long muskets and saber bayonets could not be acquired. Other Confederate nonprofessionals before First Bull Run expressed doubts about the role of "scientific" officers who had come out of West Point's engineering-heavy curriculum. Governor Francis W. Pickens of South Carolina privately wrote Brig. Gen. Milledge L. Bonham, a volunteer general with some military experience in the Seminole Wars, that Brig. Gen. P. G. T. Beauregard's "very science makes him hesitate to make a dash." Pickens did not realize that the old army had also been fully aware of the romantic and aggressive heritage of Napoleon. In fact, Beauregard himself proved to have overly aggressive inclinations before First Bull Run.[23]

Such dissenting ideas could not prevent old army men from dominating the Confederate high command. Even Fitzhugh's reasonably well-developed arguments contained a host of problems, and his historical analogies were at best debatable. Nonmiltary issues gathered the most interest from Fitzhugh, in line with his antebellum defense of slavery: the relationship between commercial power and civilization, the beneficial purging that could come with war, and the general superiority of southern life and manners versus their northern adversaries.[24] Whatever the intellectual merits of Fitzhugh's broad-brush ideas as political and social thought, they had very little relevance to the nuts-and-bolts necessities of building, operating, and fighting actual armies.

Fitzhugh's inconsistent comments later in the fall in *De Bow's Review* only highlight the limited usefulness of his military recommendations. Fitzhugh now criticized Confederates who favored more aggressive operations during the fall and winter after First Manassas, only months after he had denigrated the value of professional military expertise. He sounded like an arch professional when he declared, "We all implicitly trust to our doctor and our lawyer within the line of their profession; and it is equally natural and right to trust to our experienced and educated officers, whether educated in camp or at military schools, in war matters." Fitzhugh even cited the northern advance before Bull Run as a vindication of caution by claiming that the Lincoln administration's inability to defy public impatience played a major role in the Federal defeat.[25]

Another article in *De Bow's Review* showed how southern chauvinism, the cult of the citizen-soldier, and professionalism could all mix with one another in sometimes curious combinations. This author quoted Cadmus Wilcox's treatise on rifles at much length to show the importance of new infantry firearms, but added the nonprofessional assertion that "the common rifle of the [southern] country, in the hands of its woodsmen, will be found to equal the Maynard or the Colt in less experienced hands." The rest of the article was an almost verbatim quotation of Wilcox's work, except for the old sectional claim of special southern marksmanship. This opinion was limited not only to citizen-soldiers; Confederate Gen. Joseph E. Johnston referred to the same ideas in his post–First Manassas report.[26] Different military traditions, professional and amateur, could and did frequently mix together, but what set Johnston's recommendations apart was his practical knowledge of tactics, logistics, and army administration. It was those qualities that put Johnston and his old army comrades in positions of high responsibility in both sections' armies, not the unstable mix of citizen-soldier, sectional, and professional military cultures that existed in the war's early phase.

The volunteers needed to learn basic field maneuvers through drill, be equipped with appropriate military weapons, learn how to properly handle those weapons, gain sufficient march discipline, become proficient in basic administration, and acquire enough faith in both their officers and their comrades to fight effectively. The old professional controversy between the adherents of firepower and shock had no relevance to armies that could not march for a few days without disintegrating into a mob of stragglers. The importance and value of the professional West Pointers to the contending armies centered precisely on their possession of basic military skills from the very beginning of the war, not their familiarity with complicated doctrinal questions that even some of their own number were either ignorant of or found uninteresting and altogether pointless. A West Point education might not teach the wisdom and moral courage required for positions of high responsibility, but a graduate of the academy could at least be counted on to be a real soldier in the most rudimentary sense of the term. Not until the volunteers acquired this fundamental level of military proficiency, which they did in an astonishingly short period of time considering the circumstances, would professional debates over

shock, firepower, and field entrenchment became more than academic.

This basic level of military competence also included the building of an effective administrative and logistical apparatus in both armies. One staff officer in the Federal Army of the Cumberland put it well when he wrote on the responsibilities of an army quartermaster that, "with the commissary and the ordnance officers, he has to administer the affairs of, and provide for, a city, as it were; but upon him alone falls the duty of transporting the supplies and stores of the other two." A Confederate quartermaster officer also described his onerous but important duties well when he recalled in his memoirs that "no persons connected with the Confederate armies received so much abuse as the quartermasters, whilst but few, if any, officers performed more arduous and constant duties than did those of the Q.M. Department, especially when engaged in field service. Let forage be plenty or scarce, let the roads be good or bad, let the sun shine or the rain fall, subsistence had to be procured, provisions transported, and the army material moved." Luckily for both armies, the old army's main strength had been in its logistical and administrative bureaus, and although obvious problems of scale now presented themselves, both adversaries benefited from old army experience in these areas.[27]

Ready or not, civilian leaders pressured Federal generals to act, and McDowell complied with political realities in July 1861. McDowell focused his efforts on the important rail junction at Manassas in northern Virginia, thirty miles from Washington and ninety miles from Richmond. Two Confederate field armies stood in opposition: Joseph Johnston's eleven thousand men in the Shenandoah Valley and Beauregard's eighteen thousand men at Manassas Junction proper. McDowell aimed to fall upon Beauregard in isolation with his own army of thirty-five thousand, while Patterson's force of eighteen thousand men kept Johnston occupied in the Valley. McDowell initially hoped to turn Beauregard's right, but further reconnaissance and an unintended engagement at Blackburn's Ford by Union Brig. Gen. Daniel Tyler's division forced McDowell to attempt to turn the Confederate left instead.[28] McDowell's battle plan was sound, but Patterson would prove unable to prevent Johnston's junction with Beauregard.

The junction did not necessarily compensate for Beauregard's inadequacies as a field commander. One modern authority has mocked with an almost incredulous derision Beauregard's muddled orders on the eve of the battle at Bull Run. Pickens had been right to see hidden flaws in P. G. T. Beauregard's professionalism and real knowledge of military science, but the flaws were of an altogether different character from what he supposed. The problem was not the Creole's lack of aggressive initiative, which his fantastic military schemes in 1861 showed aplenty, but the absence of the practical experience and simple common sense that would have directed his real military learning into more useful channels.[29] While military science and book learning in most cases had real advantages, neither was it a panacea.

On the Federal side, McDowell's battle plan almost immediately miscarried because of various delays in getting the divisions of Cols. David Hunter and Samuel P. Heintzelman across Bull Run Creek because of the poor conditions of the roads, mistakes by guides, and the Federals' generally inadequate knowledge of the terrain. Once across the river, the brigades of Cols. Ambrose Burnside and Andrew Porter made a series of poorly coordinated and disjointed attacks at Matthews Hill against a small Confederate brigade under Col. Nathan G. Evans. Beauregard finally realized his left was about to be turned and began to dispatch reinforcements to the threatened portion of his line. Evans bought the Confederates crucial time, and the brigades of Col. Francis S. Bartow and Brig. Gen. Bernard E. Bee brought the Confederate forces to a little less than half of the Federal strength in that sector of the field. Aggressive Confederate leadership made up for the lack of numbers, however, and bought more time for reinforcements to arrive. The appearance of Heintzelman's division and then Col. William T. Sherman's brigade from Tyler's division finally overwhelmed the Confederates on Matthews Hill, but the fighting there had taken away three precious hours from McDowell. This allowed Beauregard and Johnston to continue to shuttle reinforcements to their left.

Even with Matthews Hill taken, McDowell still had to either neutralize or take by assault the Confederate batteries on Henry Hill, slightly to the southeast of the previous position. Jackson arrived there with his brigade and earned the sobriquet of Stonewall that would mark him throughout the English-speaking world. Beauregard and Johnston then managed to piece together a new Confederate line around Jackson's fresh brigade. McDowell moved forward the regular army batteries of Capts. Charles Griffin and J. B. Ricketts to serve as the center of the Federal attack. Local Federal infantry units provided poor support for the batteries, which helped lead to their capture. It did not help that a case of mistaken identity allowed a battalion of Confederate infantry to let loose an unopposed volley against a section of Griffin's pieces. Fear of fratricide vexed both sides at this stage of the war, because uniforms had yet to be standardized. The initial Confederate capture of the Federal batteries was the turning point of the battle, although both armies continued to struggle for a time over the hill. As the fight went on, however, Confederate reinforcements continued to arrive, and the last Federal attempt to turn the Confederate flank via Chinn Ridge to the west of Henry Hill failed. Federal forces managed a reasonably orderly retreat until a small force of pursuing Confederates created a panic by shelling a bridge across Cub Run. Ignominy then pursued the Federals from there to Washington. The Confederate troops, battered and disorganized by victory, allowed the Federals to escape unmolested.

Both armies unsurprisingly fought Bull Run, the first significant engagement of the war, with the tactical methods of the antebellum period. Light infantry was used as a vanguard to cover columns on the march; skirmishers probed positions to determine the enemy's whereabouts; but both armies relied primarily on close-order tactics. In addition to the aimed fire of skirmishers, both forces used controlled volley fire by infantry in line of battle. Short-range volleys, such as that of the 33rd Virginia against the 11th New York and 1st Minnesota, also still had a tremendous effect, even if they did little real damage.[30]

True cold steel also had not disappeared. Hunter tried to carry Matthews Hill with a bayonet charge by the 2nd Rhode Island, but the regiment was far too bloodied at that point for the effort. A charge by the 1st Louisiana battalion, later called the Louisiana Tigers, that included the use of the vaunted bowie knife was a slightly more successful example of shock tactics, because it did buy the Confederates much-needed time. Two of Jackson's regiments did conduct a bayonet charge successful enough to do the same during the fight for Henry Hill. There was even an effective cavalry charge by Stuart against the 11th New York and 1st Minnesota, although it benefited from the initial disorganization caused by the short-range volley of the 33rd Virginia.[31]

Unfortunately for both armies, shock tactics required high levels of training far beyond either Union or Confederate troops' abilities. Brig. Gen. James Longstreet's advance across Blackburn's Ford during his skirmish with Tyler displayed the rawness of Confederate drill, because the narrowness of the crossing proved difficult for his green troops to negotiate. Another example of inexperience during the last desultory Confederate movement across Blackburn's Ford was a short-range volley that went high and had no effect on a Federal battery commanded by Capt. Henry Jackson Hunt, who would eventually become the artillery chief of the Army of the Potomac. The 33rd Virginia's first volley against the 1st Minnesota and 11th New York at Henry Hill also went high, with the muskets raised at a forty-five-degree angle that was worse than useless.[32]

Federal troops also showed extremely poor fire discipline. Even some of the regulars under Maj. George Sykes could not help but fire high. Pvt. Josiah Marshall Favill of the 71st New York complained of rear-rank troops firing blindly at the risk of hitting their front-rank comrades. Sherman grumbled early in the campaign that "on the Slightest provocation [the volunteers] bang away — the danger from this desultory firing is greater than from the Enemy as they are always so close whilst the latter keep a respectful distance." Col. William B. Franklin, a brigade commander under Heintzelman, declared in his report on Bull Run that "it is my firm belief that a great deal of the misfortune of the day at Bull Run is due to the fact that the troops knew very little of the principles and practice of firing. In every case I believe that the firing of the rebels was better than ours. At any rate I am sure that ours was very bad, the rear files sometimes firing into and killing the front ones."[33]

On a higher level of command and organization, brigade commanders and above had an unfortunate habit of committing their units in piecemeal. For example, the Federal assault on Matthews Hill had been in the end successful with Sherman's timely appearance, but it had been originally mishandled with uncoordinated attacks made by single regiments, as opposed to whole brigades bringing their weight on a position in unison.[34] As the attacking force, Federal commanders bore a heavier burden of coordination in their deployments, as opposed to the Confederates who only needed to shuttle reinforcements to threatened sections of their line. The Union army's problems with coordination would have been irrelevant if its attacks had begun on time, but Federal unfamiliarity with the area's road map as a result of defective staff work delayed the assaults.

Whatever their faults, the Federal brigade commanders at Bull Run did attempt to use terrain to their advantage, which was a reasonably good sign of battlefield competence. Col. Erasmus D. Keyes ordered two regiments during the late afternoon assault across Stone Bridge to first load their muskets lying down in a slight declivity before mounting a charge against a battery. Union Brig. Gen. Robert C. Schenck also covered his brigade's advance with terrain features, such as a hollow masked by a ridge and woods. Sherman's brigade masked itself in the sunken roadbed of the Warrenton road as shelter before its assaults on Henry Hill. At a lower level of command, Sykes's battalion of regulars also used terrain features to cover its own retreat after the Federal rout.[35]

The Confederates also took advantage of terrain features. Their ability to use cover during the battle impressed Maj. William F. Barry, McDowell's chief of artillery. Confederate marksmen concealed themselves in the second-growth forest on the eastern and southern fringes of the Henry Hill plateau, while the Confederate batteries also exploited terrain features to their advantage. Confederate Col. Arnold Elzey used the woods on Bald Hill as cover for his infantry during the latter portions of the battle. Col. J. B. Kershaw of the 2nd South Carolina, a volunteer with Mexican War experience, also had enough sense to take advantage of a roadbed for cover. Col. Eppa Hunton of the 8th Virginia, a former militia general who would go on to a distinguished Confederate military career, exploited a ravine for the same purpose during a lull in his unit's action. Finally, Jackson himself sited an excellent set of defensive dispositions during his crucial engagement on Henry Hill. Soldiers also sometimes spontaneously headed to cover for shelter without orders.[36]

Neither army could benefit from a strong core of well-drilled regulars, such as Tyler's at Palo Alto and Resaca de la Palma. Federal forces during the Bull Run campaign also inherited some of the same problems with expiring enlistments that had affected American armies during the Mexican War, and which would plague Union forces throughout the entire Civil War. Most of Patterson's three-month volunteers refused to serve beyond the official expiration of their enlistments in July, and he used their refusal "to stand by the country for a week or ten days" as his excuse for failing to prevent Johnston's reinforcement of Beauregard at Manassas. The pressure of those enlistments expiring had also played a role in compelling McDowell to strike at the Confederates in July.[37]

But the most instructive point of distinction between the contending American armies at Bull Run and U.S. forces in Mexico centered less on the military proficiency of the armies in absolute terms than on the relative competence of the various armies in relation to one another. American troops in the Mexican War had a superiority in training, cohesion, and leadership sufficient to overcome Mexican advantages in numbers and the inherent difficulties of operating as an army of conquest in enemy territory. At Bull Run, no such basic superiority existed; even that great

Mexican War standby of U.S. superiority in artillery did not exist at Manassas. The regular army batteries were probably of a higher quality than the Confederate arm, but they faced far more effective counterbattery fire from the Confederates than their predecessors had in Mexico.[38] Furthermore, the higher quality of Confederate troops allowed them to face Federal batteries far more staunchly than Mexican troops had during the earlier war.

The inability of the regular army batteries at First Bull Run to obtain successes comparable to those of Palo Alto also serves as a useful case study in the most important deciding factors of a Civil War battle: morale, unit cohesion, and the unpredictable vagaries of battlefield fortune. Some historians have in contrast emphasized the supposedly outdated Napoleonic tactics of the regular Federal artillery to explain its failure at Henry Hill and the subsequent turn of the battle against McDowell. W. Glenn Robertson even specifically cites the rifle-musket as the primary cause for the failure of Mexican War artillery tactics at First Bull Run, despite the large prevalence of smoothbore muskets among both armies' troops at this point in the war.[39] These historians argue that the unsupported advance of both Griffin's and Rickett's batteries stemmed from a conscious and outdated use of Napoleonic tactics that demanded artillery aim for a decisive blow by aggressively unlimbering within short canister range of enemy infantry.

John Hennessy even goes so far as to argue that McDowell actually intended to advance Griffin's and Rickett's batteries without infantry support, but the sources he cites do not support this assertion. In fact, Griffin bluntly declared after the battle that he believed McDowell's order to move the batteries assumed infantry support. The artillerymen may have thought their supports woefully inadequate, but Barry did in fact attempt to provide them. As for any cultural prejudice in favor of the use of unsupported artillery, little evidence exists that the old army expected artillery to fight in a stand-alone fashion. Griffin testified before congress that Braxton Bragg's experience at Buena Vista was an extreme example of sacrificing a battery to save an army that just happened to succeed against the odds. Even during the Mexican War, it is not clear that the American batteries ever intended to fight without infantry supports. Bragg had asked Taylor for those supports during the crucial final engagement at Buena Vista, and Taylor's response, "Major Bliss and I will support you," would have hardly been so legendary if it was normal practice for artillery to fight alone.[40]

Griffin also declared in his congressional testimony that without infantry support, artillery "is helpless by itself — perfectly helpless." Capt. John Gibbon, the first commander of the famed Iron Brigade and a future Union major general, hardly endorsed the unsupported use of artillery in the most important Civil War–era American artillery treatise, *The Artillerist's Manual.* He wrote before the war that "artillery cannot defend itself when hard pressed, and should always be sustained by either infantry or cavalry." As for wheeling one's artillery up to within three hundred yards of the enemy and blasting away with canister, Gibbon called the occasions for such tactics "very rare" and that the batteries that do such a thing "require much tact and resolution to know how to profit by them." Gibbon cited Palo Alto as one appropriate example of aggressive close-in artillery tactics, but there was no consensus within the American artillery arm that closing with canister should be standard practice when fighting infantry. Confederate military thinking also did not advocate the use of unsupported artillery. *De Bow's Review* approvingly quoted a French military work (Viele's "Hand Book of Active Service") warning that, "if not well supported by infantry, it [artillery] falls readily into the enemy's hands."[41]

Questions of doctrine aside, unsupported artillery at Bull Run was able to fend off poorly organized infantry attacks. Hunt's battery at Blackburn's Ford did exactly that during one of the battle's last engagements when the charging Confederates misaimed their short-range volley. That mistimed volley highlights the importance of a unit's concrete fighting abilities, as opposed to abstractions concerning the fate of "Napoleonic" warfare. Hunt was supposed to be supported by infantry, but in this case, his supports were disorganized by poor deployments, and his artillery fire was so hot that their assistance was simply not needed. Finally, Griffin himself believed that he could have shredded the Confederate battalion that mauled a section of his pieces with an unopposed volley if he had not been prevented from doing so by Barry's misplaced concerns about fratricide, although he of course would have preferred to have adequate infantry supporting him.[42]

In addition to simple misfortune, problems with morale and cohesion doomed the Federal batteries on Henry Hill more than the assumed obsolescence of Napoleonic artillery tactics. Griffin himself had been skeptical of the ability of the Fire Zouaves to support his batteries, because he "had seen them on the field in a state of disorganization, and I did not think they had the moral courage to fight." Porter, Griffin's brigade commander, believed "there was enough to support it [Ricketts and Griffin] if the troops had been steady." In response to the congressional query, "Were not Griffin's and Ricketts' batteries moved too far forward to be supported by infantry" [Griffin had believed his original position to be far superior], Porter replied, "Not with good infantry." The effectiveness of Confederate counterbattery fire against the Federals also played a role in the defeat of Griffin's and Ricketts' batteries.[43] The inability of regular army artillery to attain the same successes it had achieved during the Mexican War had nothing to do with the rifle-musket, and everything to do with the presence of reasonably competent Confederate artillery, some bad luck with regards to mistaken identity, and the disreputable performance of one regiment of raw volunteers.

The same equilibrium of competence that prevented a few batteries of well-trained artillery from deciding the battle in favor of the Federals also prevented Confederate forces from fully exploiting their victory. Although the Federal retreat did become a rout, Confederate troops proved too battered and disorganized for an aggressive pursuit. A shortage of cavalry compounded the problem. Johnston and Beauregard had won by a razor-thin margin, which did not stem from the sort of demonstrable military superiority that would have allowed them to follow up their victory with a march on Washington. For most of the Civil War, Union and Confederate armies would be locked in this relative state of organizational parity as both sets of troops made their gains in military skill at roughly comparable rates. It was not until the end of the war that Confederate forces had been so severely weakened in material terms that Federal forces could actually destroy opposing field armies.

In the interim, much of an individual battle's outcome depended instead on the generals in command of the respective armies. Command decisions became one of the crucial variables in deciding a contest between armies that stood on a roughly level playing field when it came to military skill.[44] For example, in the crucial eastern theater, the average regiment in the Army of the Potomac fought as hard and as well as its Confederate counterpart using the same drill manual as their opponents, but the Confederates benefited from far superior brigade, division, corps, and army commanders. Two men, Robert E. Lee and George B. McClellan, were largely responsible for creating this state of affairs, and the following chapter centers around the legacies they bequeathed to the opposing armies, which they, more than anyone else, created and defined.

CHAPTER SEVEN

The Peninsula

Lee and McClellan Leave Their Legacies

★ ★ ★

The Confederate victory at First Manassas had chastened, even humiliated, Union pretensions to military prowess, but the northern war effort only girded itself for further and much more impressive efforts. Confederate activity in contrast stagnated during the following winter, leading to a series of catastrophes during the early campaigns of 1862. The fledgling nation saw most of Tennessee fall into Federal hands, a Confederate counterstrike in the western theater shattered at Shiloh in April, and New Orleans fall later that month. In Virginia, George B. McClellan, the first commander of what was now known as the Army of the Potomac, stood at the gates of Richmond by the summer of 1862. After the Seven Days, a series of battles between June 25 and July 1, Lee's own newly christened Army of Northern Virginia relieved Richmond from imminent investment and collapse. McClellan's strategic repulse gave rise to and anticipated many of the war's most important general characteristics in the eastern theater: a dysfunctional Federal military and civilian high command marked by mutual distrust and infighting; the overwhelming prominence of Lee's Army of Northern Virginia at the very core of Confederate nationhood; and the establishment of an aggressive culture of command among Lee's officers and men that would bring its more cautious Federal counterpart to grief more times than not throughout the remainder of the war.

Lee successfully expelled McClellan from his near stranglehold on Richmond despite the latter's reliance on earthworks and the larger number of rifled infantry arms among McClellan's troops. Although, on a tactical level, the Peninsula campaign foreshadowed many of the elements that mark the Overland campaign's supposed similarity to the western front of World War I, Lee acquired decisive strategic results. He launched assault after assault on entrenchments — most resulting in grievous losses for the Confederates. Yet, by the end of the campaign, Lee had clearly gained the upper hand. Grant did the same during the Overland campaign with far less telling results, although from a military perspective he did manage to force Lee into a slow demise by siege. These different outcomes had less to do with battlefield technology than with the decided superiority in combat leadership and morale that the Army of Northern Virginia had acquired and maintained over its opponent in the intervening two years.

That military superiority originated for the most part in the character of two men: Robert E. Lee and George B. McClellan. The decisions of generals have profound consequences on the battlefield, such that, in the words of one Federal officer, "the personal character of a general officer in moments of difficulty has a powerful influence upon the result."[1] Lee won the strategic and psychological victory during the Seven Days that began the process by which the Army of Northern Virginia would acquire its famed élan and offensive spirit. That victory resulted in large part from McClellan's cautious temperament, which put him at a severe disadvantage to the aggressive Lee. For all the numerous organizational problems that bedeviled the Confederate armies, along with its substantial losses, McClellan's withdrawal to the James made it possible for Lee to begin the process of stamping the Army of Northern Virginia with his distinctive command style and temperament. This fortuitous development for the Confederacy overrode the strength of McClellan's position and the grievous causalities he inflicted on Lee's troops while fighting on the defensive and utilizing entrenchments.

The overall weakness of army organization among both Federals and Confederates in all theaters between First Bull Run and the Seven Days allowed Lee and McClellan to preside over the crucial formative moments of their armies' respective martial cultures. Every army struggled to find its organizational footing during this period, which made its early commanders all the more important. By 1864 Lee's army could still maintain its advantages in leadership and competence despite grievous attrition among its original core of commanders, while even Grant's personal presence could not totally overcome the Army of the Potomac's ingrained culture of caution. In the western theater, however, Federal troops benefited from generals far superior to their Confederate counterparts. Anglo-American antimilitarism had created a situation where the Union and Confederacy had to build field armies out of whole cloth, and old army men — with all their individual virtues and vices — wove that uniform cloth's warp and woof for better or for worse. Their efforts would spin forth armies of increasing competence, but many problems would remain for both Union and Confederate forces.

The Union defeat at First Bull Run awakened in the North the realization that training and organizing an army required substantial time and energy, which strengthened McClellan's status as the Army of the Potomac's master organizer. Many northerners believed that the *Tribune* and its ilk had advocated a counsel of folly that helped lead to Bull Run, and Horace Greeley indecorously retreated in the face of criticism. For example, the *New York Times*, whose more sympathetic attitudes toward "military science" preexisted Bull Run, had something of a field day with Greeley's perceived rebuke on the battlefield. McClellan would have more time than did his predecessor to prepare for what most northerners saw as the final death-grapple with the rebellion. By January 1862 the Union states even — with some reluctance — ceded to the West Point–dominated Quartermaster Bureau most of their procurement responsibilities for volunteer regiments.[2] This allowed the old army's strongest bureaucratic branches — its supply bureaus — to manage large parts of the Union's mobilization of war matériel.

At the front, volunteer officers also recognized the benefits of training and preparation. Maj. Wilder Dwight of the 2nd Massachusetts argued in a letter written on September 7, 1861, that "To-day our army is crippled by the ideas of equality and independence which have colored the whole life of our people. Men elect their officers, and then expect them *to behave themselves!* Obedience is permissive, not compelled, and the radical basis is wrong." Dwight, who had attended a private military school in his youth, even declared that "it is only necessary to appreciate the fact that, in war, *one will* must act through all the others, to see that American soldiers with all their presumed intelligence and skill, have *the one lesson* yet to learn." Josiah Marshall Favill, who became a second lieutenant in the 57th New York after fighting at Bull Run in the 71st New York as a private, wrote in his diary shortly after Bull Run that "we shall go home and refit for a long period, organize and discipline an army, and when officers and men have learned to adjust themselves to their new positions, and know each other and their duties thoroughly, then commence afresh, and go on to victory, or sustain defeat with dignity." Favill counted his blessings that "we were especially fortunate in having many officers thoroughly well up in tactics, and having in the ranks over a hundred old soldiers, who had served in the regular army of either the United States or Great Britain. All who know anything of the service will appreciate the advantage of having these old soldiers to instruct the recruits in the many details that can never be learned theoretically."[3]

Former regulars in the Federal service certainly did not mind the new emphasis on training and organization. Many regulars had cited a failure of discipline above all else as the cause of the Bull Run rout. Capt. Daniel P. Woodbury of the Engineers in his official report argued that the volunteers had not acquired "the instinct of discipline which keeps every man in his place [in the ranks]." He did not see the southern troops as actually superior in discipline but believed that their position on the defensive saved them from disorganization. Russell, the British correspondent, proved less charitable when he attributed the stinging Federal defeat "first to deficient morale of officers, & want of discipline of men — ie. inferiority to their opponents." Brig. Gen. William F. Barry, McDowell's former artillery chief, cited the "uninstructed state" of the Federal forces, but also believed the negligence of "indolent" regimental and company officers an important failing. Brig. Gen. James B. Ricketts, another artilleryman at Bull Run, argued that "many of the officers were inferior to the men themselves. The men were of as good material as any in the world, and they fought well until they became confused on account of their officers not knowing what to do." Brig. Gen. Andrew Porter, a brigade commander at First Manassas, also blamed the officers more than the men. Eminently justified perceptions of rank incompetence and worse in the officer corps helped inspire the use of examination boards to dismiss inefficient officers from the service.[4]

First Manassas, for obvious reasons, did not have the same chastening effect in the Confederacy as it had in the Union. Looking back on the battle in the midst of the fights swirling around Richmond during the Seven Days, Mary Chesnut recorded in her diary that First Manassas "did nothing but send us off into a fool's paradise of conceit. And it roused the manhood of the Northern people." The Prussian observer Justus Scheibert later recalled much of the same thing. The Confederacy's impressive victory at the war's first major battle helped breed among Confederates an initial post-Manassas attitude of self-satisfied overconfidence. This delayed necessary measures of national mobilization, such as conscription, until the following spring when the Union stood almost on the verge of victory. Barely three days after the battle, the *Richmond Examiner* could thunder that "Ohio and Pennsylvania ought to feel, in less than four weeks, the terrors which agitate the cowardly and guilty when retributive vengeance is at hand. . . . In four weeks our generals should be levying contributions in money and property from their own towns and villages." On July 22, J. B. Jones wrote that "every one believed our banners would wave in the streets of Washington in a few days."[5]

Such underlying aggressiveness showed that the Confederate public's complacency stemmed more from self-satisfaction than laziness. And that complacency did not completely interfere with the processes by which the Confederate armies slowly learned their trade in the field. Nevertheless, many Confederates continued to thirst for offensive action throughout the fall and winter after First Manassas. In late September, the frustrated *Examiner* rebutted counsels of caution that cited northerners' precipitate demands for a quick advance as the root cause of the Federal defeat at Bull Run; it believed that the Confederate victory at Manassas "demonstrated, at once and forever, the superiority of the Southern soldier." The editorial repudiated any argument based on military expertise, preferring to trust to the "hard common sense" of "the people." Indeed, old fears of military usurpation survived in wartime Richmond; the following February, the *Examiner* blamed a "few officers from the old army" for starting an effort to muzzle the Confederate free press.[6]

In October, the *Examiner*, although still willing to defer to Lee's antebellum reputation, declared in relation to operations in western Virginia that "the General, we doubt not, now feels the necessity of a more adventurous policy, and he is quite capable, we hope, of adapting his plans to the exigency." They would have not been pleased, if they could have seen Lee's comments to his wife four days earlier: "I am sorry, as you say, that the movements of the armies cannot keep pace with the expectations of the editors of papers. I know they can regulate matters satisfactorily to themselves on paper. I wish they could do so in the field."[7]

The *Examiner* continued to complain of the lack of offensive Confederate action in early January, now arguing that too many Confederate troops were wasting away from disease in camp rather than taking the fight to the Yankees. Now it no longer made excuses for Lee, whom the press mocked for pedantic book learning. Lee's less than stellar performance in the fall of 1861 led to a new sobriquet among disgruntled Confederates: "Granny Lee." Others called him "*old-stick-in-the-mud.*" The criticism had some merit; Lee's plan of attack at Cheat Mountain in his first Civil War campaign called for no less than five converging columns acting in concert. Such a high standard of efficiency proved far beyond the abilities of his raw volunteers. Furthermore, a strong argument can be made that Confederate forces were, in fact, far too passive after the unavoidable initial disorganization that beset the Confederate army after First Manassas; who knows how a smashing victory in early 1862 might have affected northern morale or the Confederacy's chances of interna- tional recognition? The soldiers themselves certainly wanted a quick decision to the war.[8]

Grumbling about the old army and West Point continued to increase, which reflected public impatience with the flagging war effort. Success silences critics and strengthens national unity in wartime, but defeats only breed dissension. And the defeats eventually came for the Confederacy in the winter and spring of 1862. West Pointers would become a natural scapegoat for a culture so strongly committed to the citizen-soldier ideal. For example, the prominent South Carolina fire-eater James Henry Hammond wrote in a March letter to William W. Boyce, a Confederate congressman, that "West Point is death to us." Boyce also had no affection for West Pointers, citing Davis's "West Point red tape" as a cause for the Confederacy's overly "languid" military policy, as opposed to "advancing boldly." In April 1862 the *Examiner* characterized West Pointers as lethargic engineers overly addicted to siege operations.[9]

In early June, Mary Chesnut recorded comments from another elite Confederate woman, Louisa Susannah McCord, that "God does not deign to send us a general worthy of [Confederate soldiers]. I do not mean drill sergeants or military old maids who will not fight until everything is just so. The real ammunition of our war is faith in ourselves and enthusiasm in our cause. West Point sits down on enthusiasm—laughs it to scorn. It wants discipline." McCord revealed herself to possess as little military knowledge as her nation's men folk when she declared that "the great Napoleon knew all about the *business* of war. He left nothing to chance and worthless understaffers. He knew every regiment, its exact numbers. Its officers, down to the least sergeant and corporal." Recent scholarship has in fact shown that Napoleon's command system, by necessity, left much to the discretion of his corps commanders, who were hardly "worthless understaffers." Wade Hampton, who later went on to become one of the finest citizen-soldier generals of the war, made a more judicious criticism to Mary Chesnut on June 16, that "if we mean to play at war as we play a game of chess—West Point tactics prevailing—we are sure to lose the game. They have every advantage. They can lose pawns ad infinitum—to the end of time—and never feel it."[10]

Edward A. Pollard, the associate editor of the *Richmond Examiner,* also castigated West Point in an early history of the war's first year published in 1862. Praising the anti–West Point Sterling Price, Pollard described him as "something better than a pupil of West Point—he was a general by nature, a beloved commander, a man who illustrated the Roman simplicity of character in the nineteenth century." Like many of those hostile to West Point, Pollard believed in what he saw as hard fighting, with partisans if necessary, as opposed to the enervating book learning of the scientific regulars. Pollard's verdict on Lee's performance in western Virginia in 1861 dripped with contempt, describing him as "a general who had never fought a battle, who had a pious horror of guerillas, and whose extreme tenderness of blood induced him to depend exclusively upon the resources of strategy." Pollard's eulogy for Brig. Gen. Benjamin McCulloch's fall at Pea Ridge on March 7, 1862, focused on his experience as a partisan commander of the Texas Rangers during the Mexican War rather than on his later evolution into an aspiring regular. Even when he praised West Point–graduate Stonewall Jackson, he declared: "But Gen. Jackson had been brought up in a severer school of practical experience than West Point . . . an iron will and stern courage, which he had from *nature*, made him peculiarly fitted to command" (emphasis added).[11]

Regardless of its rhetorical excess, Pollard's *Richmond Examiner* did have a point with its editorial of June 10 that "if [Richmond's] fate depends on a game in which '*spades are trumps*,' played by two eminent hands of the old army, each knowing everything that the other knows, there is no doubt but that the Confederate government will, sooner or later, be spaded out of Richmond." If Lee truly personified the deliberate lethargic engineer, then Richmond would indeed have fallen under the shot and shell of the Young Napoleon's fire-belching siege train. Nevertheless, the *Examiner* erred in charging either Davis or Lee with a passive commitment to defensive warfare. Davis himself had hoped for an offensive in the fall of 1861, but the poor condition of Confederate forces in Virginia and his generals' reluctance caused him to accept a defensive posture.[12] Lee's aggressive instincts would appear in short order.

Finally, Lee's rejoinder to mutterings in and out of the army about spadework and entrenchments had much merit, belying some historians' portrayal of him as overly pugnacious and indifferent to the value of fieldworks: "Our people are opposed to work. Our troops, officers, community & press. All ridicule & resist it. It is the very means by which McClellan has & is advancing. Why should we leave to him the whole advantage of labour. Combined with valour, fortitude & boldness, of which we have our fair proportion, it should lead us to success. What carried the Roman soldiers into all countries, but this happy combination. The evidences of their labour last to this day. There is nothing so military as labour, & nothing so important to an army as to save the lives of its solders."[13]

Nevertheless, as late as October 1862, Joseph Brown, the governor of Georgia, could still issue paeans to the cult of the citizen-soldier volunteer, even as it became increasingly clear the Confederacy needed conscription to keep its armies in the field. After another expansion of the draft, Brown declared, "The volunteer enters the service of his own free will; he regards the war as much his own as the Government's war, and is ready, if need be, to offer his life a willing sacrifice upon his country's altar; hence it is that our volunteer armies have been invincible when contending against vastly superior numbers with every advantage which the best equipments and supplies can afford. Not so with the conscript." Brown even continued to claim a constitutional right for men to elect officers. And while Sherman bemoaned the Federal practice of not refilling veteran regiments depleted by casualties with conscripts that benefited from the preexisting organization's experience and expertise, Brown condemned the practice as a violation of the volunteer's rights of association.[14]

Confederate commitment to the citizen-soldier ideal died hard, and in late 1861 a new and possibly decisive Confederate offensive after First Manassas would have required a comprehensive mobilization of Confederate resources that simply did not occur in the interim between First Manassas and the spring of 1862, when Union military success pushed Confederate nationhood to the brink. The historian Emory Thomas described this period in his history of the Confederacy with an appropriate chapter title, "Confederate Nationality Confounded."[15] Focusing on the presumably inherent martial superiority of Confederate soldiers—worse yet, trusting to that supposed fact for victory—did nothing to mass the manpower, material, and organizational resources that would be needed to defeat the gathering forces of the Union.

Successful military operations in the field depended far more on basic proficiency in army administration and training than on vague claims of inherent martial prowess. Unfortunately, neither Federal nor Confederate forces possessed a comprehensive and standardized system of training; the quality of drill an individual soldier received tended to depend on the initiative of regimental commanders. One soldier in the Army of Northern Virginia who had enlisted in the Confederate service in May 1861 did not experience his first drill until as late as May 1862.[16] The newly formed

Army of the Potomac under McClellan probably had the most thorough and systematic training received by any Civil War field army, but this exception proved the rule. Furthermore, that army's decidedly mixed combat record showed that training and drill did not obviate the need for strong leadership at the head of the army.

Civil War–era close-order drill had its disadvantages; the available troop manuals had a necessarily abstract quality, and even such advanced (and far from standard) training as target practice and bayonet fencing could not duplicate battlefield conditions. Furthermore, the era's drill manuals, following French practice, did not specify under what circumstance an individual set of tactical evolutions and formations should be used. A Prussian observer who visited Lee's army in 1863 when it achieved veteran status extolled the benefits of experience over training, noting that "units in combat become independent; tactics, autonomous," and "seldom used in battle [is] the rigmarole of peacetime and the drill field." This assumption gave experienced officers in veteran armies tremendous discretion and flexibility, but greenhorn volunteers needed far more guidance. Nonetheless, flawed and problematic training remained far superior to no training at all, and excellent officers used drill as one of the primary methods to create and encourage the martial spirit and cohesion so vital to effective military organization. Furthermore, drill did frequently provide a steadying effect on troops engaged in combat. One Federal officer at Fredericksburg reported with pride his regiment's ability to execute drill ground maneuvers under fire and scorned "talk about it being impossible to drill under fire — our regiment did it at Fredericksburg."[17]

In the Army of the Potomac, McClellan, a talented drillmaster, began the process of organizing and training what became the primary Federal field army in the eastern theater. Little Mac faced various challenges, including the failure to use the regular army properly, which helped nullify an institutional advantage the Union possessed over the Confederacy. McClellan rightly preferred either that the regulars be kept intact and recruited to full strength to serve as a crack reserve, akin in many ways to the Guards regiments of Europe, or that the organization be entirely broken up in order to distribute to every volunteer regiment a bare leavening of professional expertise. Instead, following "a middle course . . . resulted less favorably than either of the plans indicated," where the regular army as a formal organization remained intact, but with many of its officers leaving it for the volunteer service. In Grant's view, the regular army should have been disbanded, arguing, and overstating the case to some degree, that the absence of a preexisting Confederate standing army meant that "military education and training was distributed throughout their whole army. The whole loaf was leavened." McClellan did still put the regulars to good use as members of a Provost Guard tasked with enforcing discipline. Some regular commissioned and noncommissioned officers also served as drillmasters to the volunteers. McClellan also established a system of provisional brigades that trained incoming volunteer regiments before they took posts with brigades in the field.[18]

The Confederate victors of First Manassas also continued to drill and train, despite the general tone of smug self-satisfaction that marked Confederate public opinion. In spite of all the logistical difficulties, Johnston's troops continued to acclimate themselves to field service, and the Confederate commissariat would eventually assemble enough supplies—in fact, huge stocks of stores had to be destroyed during the spring 1862 evacuation of the Rappahannock line. Furthermore, although Joe Johnston did not possess Little Mac's organizational acumen, Confederate forces in Virginia benefited from a deep stock of reasonably well-trained officers drawn from both West Point and the Virginia Military Institute. While the Union kept its regular army intact because of bureaucratic inertia and fears of continued trouble on the Indian frontier, the Confederate forces in the East did a better job of evenly distributing professional military expertise.

Even the *Examiner* recognized the value of training. It still had little respect for the northern volunteer, denouncing the massing Federal armies as composed of brutalized peasants transformed into deadly regulars by harsh discipline, but it did call for conscription to meet the new threat. It even acknowledged that new calls for Confederate volunteers would produce an army "incapable of answering to all the calls of war, when opposed to an army under the iron rule of enforced enlistment and regular discipline."[19]

In the West, both contending forces also continued to drill to prepare for battle. However, the western armies of the Confederacy had special challenges in training not shared by either the Confederate forces in Virginia or Federal forces in both theaters. The eastern army in Virginia possessed a far greater proportion of West Pointers than did the western armies, which was further supplemented by the large numbers of VMI alumni in what later became the Army of Northern Virginia. In one concrete example, Lt. Col. Daniel Beltzhoover, commander of a battery at Belmont in Polk's western army and an officer who had provoked complaints about "rough and unfeeling treatment," grumbled that "I don't meet a man once a month who knows anything about [the] military. I have not seen a field officer who can drill a regiment, or a General who can review a brigade but McCown, who is an old artillery captain." The Confederate garrison at Fort Donelson did not receive an efficient heavy-artillery drill-master until January 1862. In contrast, many of Grant's troops benefited from excellent instruction at Camp Defiance in Cairo, Illinois.[20]

Early in the war, officers frequently had no better knowledge of their duties than did their enlisted men, which could only hinder regimental training and organization. For example, in the 31st Illinois, future major general John Logan's original regiment, a private instructed officers in the company drill by virtue of his previous service in the Mexican War. In a Confederate regiment in Polk's opposing army, officers clashed with each other over differing interpretations of proper orders on the parade ground. Officers in all the various armies, Union and Confederate, had to go to recitations, or classes, to learn the tactics and regulations. McClellan put it well in his memoirs when he remarked that volunteer officers "were instructed *pari passu* as they instructed their men." Such episodes and methods could hardly inspire confidence in the abilities of a regiment's officers among the rank and file; one Union cavalry veteran put it more succinctly by remarking that "the blind led the blind, and often both fell into the ditch, though not always at the same time."[21]

The officers of both armies did gradually improve over time. Shortly after First Bull Run, the Federal Congress enacted a program of examinations that helped weed out incompetent officers, especially in the junior grades below colonel. By March 1862 the examination boards expelled 310 officers from the service. Offenses included such dubious behavior as chronic drunkenness and disability resulting from syphilis. The Confederate Army also used officer review boards to weed out the inefficient. Hard experience in the field also helped to increase discipline, cohesion, and leadership in the armies. After viewing the Confederate armies in 1863, a Prussian observer later wrote that, because they emphasized battlefield practicality, "consequently the Confederates, iron in march-discipline anyway, formed battle lines with incredible speed, and complete even to skirmishers out front."[22] The same could have been said of veteran Federal troops.

But in an environment of almost overwhelming ignorance, West Point–trained professionals could and did dominate the command echelons of both armies at the early stages of the war. As battlefield experience brought to the fore highly qualified citizen-soldiers, this old army monopoly on both armies' senior ranks had mixed effects. The Civil War armies of both the Union and the Confederacy inherited the antebellum U.S. Army's profound respect for seniority, and this limited the pool of officers eligible for corps and army command at the end of the war. Even distinctly mediocre commanders such as Ambrose Burnside and John Pemberton could retain positions of responsibility through the sheer force of inertia established by their early general officer commissions. Furthermore, many regular army men had an inherent mistrust of even the best citizen-soldier generals, for reasons that went beyond questions of strict professional merit.[23]

For example, in his memoirs, Sherman wrote regarding both John Logan and Francis P. Blair that "both were men of great courage and talent, but were politicians by nature and experience, and it may be that for this reason they were mistrusted by regular officers like Generals Schofield, Thomas, and myself." That mistrust, and because "it was all-important that there should exist a perfect understanding among the army commanders," led to Sherman's selection of Howard over Logan for command of the Army of the Tennessee in 1864. Or, as Sherman put it in a wartime letter on a different issue, "we must deal with men as we find them and it is not Logans fault that he was a Citizen only three years ago, and looks at all questions from another view than a professional soldier."[24]

McClellan's influence on the Army of the Potomac's command echelons throughout the entire Civil War stemmed from his early influence on the appointment of all general officers in the army. His authority had not been unlimited, but during the army's most formative months, he could ensure the advancement of such close friends as Baldy Smith, Fitz John Porter, and William B. Franklin to positions of high command and prominence. Furthermore, it was McClellan who organized the brigades and divisions that became the primary building blocks of the army,[25] and whose commanders would be eligible for positions of higher responsibility later on during the war as a result of the army's iron-clad respect for seniority.

Indeed, Stephen Taaffe, the leading historian of the Army of the Potomac's corps commanders, classifies roughly half of them as McClellan loyalists. This includes individuals who held positions of great responsibility long after McClellan's relief in the fall of 1862. Examples include George Meade, Winfield Scott Hancock, John Gibbon, Ambrose Burnside, George Stoneman, John Sedgwick, and William "Baldy" Smith. All held major general commissions. In Taaffe's taxonomy of corps commanders, those composing the most significant group of corps commanders in the Federal eastern army were the McClellanites, as opposed to those generals directly beholden to the Lincoln administration, whom Taaffe characterizes as scheming opportunists (Joseph Hooker being the best example), and the small minority of officers who reached corps command primarily through battlefield excellence. While some of the McClellanite generals proved competent leaders — Meade and Hancock being perhaps the best examples — many proved decidedly mediocre and overly cautious. Lt. Col. Alexander S. Webb, although he would not have attributed the origin of the problem to McClellan's temperament, still described the problem well when after the battle of Chancellorsville he condemned most of the Army of the Potomac's leaders as "cautious stupid & without any dash they delay 20,000 men at times in order to skirmish with 20 or 30 cav^{ly} & one piece of arty. They all think the enemy wiser & braver & quicker than themselves & such men should *not* command."[26] Grant would face similar problems in 1864 during the Overland campaign.

McClellan's training program for the Army of the Potomac also reflected the premises of the old army's tactical reforms in the 1850s. He drilled his troops in bayonet fencing, target practice, and basic close-order drill. If the competent and West Point–trained William B. Hazen is any indication, some bayonet drill also probably occurred in western units with especially conscientious West Pointers at their helm, although the Army of the Potomac had probably the most comprehensive training program. The division headquarters of Brig. Gen. Fitz John Porter, McClellan's most prized subordinate, exemplified the foundations of the old army's chasseur-based tactical system when it declared on February 9, 1862, that "instruction in bayonet exercise will not be slackened but in each branch instruction must be equally progressive. The success of each regiment may depend upon the perfection in these Branches of instruction and the General Commanding wishes to be certain that when a regiment is called upon to use the Bayonet it will be done promptly skillfully and successfully every Regiment may expect to reap its honor in this way but to win them and give confidence it must be instructed." In the same order, Porter's division headquarters also mandated detailed instructions regarding target practice, including exercises in estimating distances. Vermont volunteer Wilbur Fisk also endorsed bayonet exercise, because "proficiency in this [bayonet] drill must give one great confidence in a bayonet charge."[27] The antebellum concern with giving soldiers the confidence and élan necessary for wielding the bayonet coexisted with target practice and aimed fire.

McClellan even attempted to train his troops in larger unit exercises. These included sham battles where soldiers fired blanks. McClellan's program of large reviews also helped to give his army a special élan that for the most part had a positive effect throughout the war. These reviews also had more practical benefits, akin to those of brigade drills and sham battles, in acclimating the men to large-scale maneuvers. The famous review on November 20, 1861, at Bailey's Cross-Roads involved ninety regiments of infantry, nine regiments of cavalry, and twenty batteries, in sum, around fifty thousand to sixty thousand men. Some units in the review benefited from marching sizable distances with full marching loads. Indeed, the Army of the Potomac also did some drilling with knapsacks for conditioning purposes, and McClellan hoped to give his men basic field experience before committing them to pitched battle. Nevertheless, the success of the training program between the 1861 and 1862 campaigning seasons should not be overestimated. For example, even some of the regulars in Sykes's division at the battle of Gaines's Mill on June 27, 1862, had not yet mastered the manual of arms,[28] never mind all the problems that would be seen at Shiloh and the Peninsula.

Indeed, although critics of West Point painted a portrait of the academy's products as paper pedants, many old army officers themselves emphasized the benefits of practical field service. Sherman wrote his brother John before First Bull Run that Lincoln should look to the old army's frontier veterans for officer appointments; "McDowells promotion as Brigadier will not give satisfaction for the reason his service has been too much in cities, and too little on exposed Frontiers. In the war on which we are now embarking paper soldiers wont do." In another letter, Sherman wrote that "there are in the old army, on the Frontiers, far from Washington many clever and intelligent officers, familiar with the 'common life of a soldier,' whose habits are worth half a life of Book study." Sherman even brushed off his brother's high opinion of his military abilities by lamenting his lack of "a previous schooling with large masses of troops in the field, one which I lost in the Mexican War by going to California." Sherman, nevertheless, had no inherent hostility to professional book learning; he praised McClellan's appointment to the command of Ohio's forces, appreciating both McClellan's professional credentials as a member of the Delafield Commission and his creditable combat record in Mexico.[29]

It would also take some time before most troops became properly equipped, even in the North with its substantial industrial plant and easier access to European arms. Col. John Logan in the western Union army complained that at Belmont in 1861 "many of the guns of my command choked and burst while in battle, though the boys soon had better ones in their hands," presumably through capture of Confederate weapons. Throughout 1862 and beyond, both Union and Confederate troops would exchange older weapons for newer models captured in battle.[30] Although at least some Confederate units in the western theater possessed quality weapons, proper arms proved a special problem for Confederate troops in the isolated Trans-Mississippi.

Despite these continued problems, the first significant action of 1862, Grant's Forts Henry and Donelson campaign, displayed some of the fruits of improving combat proficiency. Brig. Gen. C. F. Smith even managed to lead a successful bayonet charge on a selected point of the Confederate line at Fort Donelson by ordering his troops to take the caps off their muskets. A Civil War muzzle-loading musket used a percussion cap fitted to a firing pin to ignite the powder loaded into the weapon's barrel. Smith sought to prevent his troops from halting prematurely and engaging the enemy in a pointless close-range fire fight before they gained their objectives by ordering them to disable their weapons for the duration of the charge. One Federal officer's wise comments on the fatal halt of Confederate troops at a stone wall during Maj. Gen. George E. Pickett's doomed attack at Gettysburg applied to all frontal assaults on prepared positions: "That halt at the wall was the ruin of the enemy, as such halts almost always are; yet so natural is it for men to seek cover that it is almost impossible to get them to pass it under such circumstances." Smith's own inspired leadership also played a crucial role in his charge's success. Furthermore, only a slight force of Confederates armed with shotguns held the works under attack. The works remained inherently strong, however, with thick abatis — obstructions fashioned from felled trees with their sharpened branches pointing outward — covering them, and we must give Smith's storybook charge some credit for the Federal success. One historian has described the assault as "a fatal rupture in Confederate defenses," which helped lead to the disastrous Confederate surrender.[31]

Smith's successful bayonet charge showed that shock tactics could still be effective with highly motivated troops and some degree of foresight on the part of commanders. Furthermore, there was no inherent contradiction in the use of skirmishers to cover an assault by the bayonet. In Smith's report, he recounted that "on the receipt of the order the artillery was ordered to open heavily and the brigade commanders to press forward with large numbers of skirmishers, and make a dash at any available opening, whilst the Second Iowa . . . was ordered to lead the assault. The regiment was ordered to rely on the bayonet and not to fire a shot until the enemy's ranks were broken."[32] This had essentially been one of the premises of the old army's tactical system of the 1850s — that cold steel and aimed fire could go hand in hand. Smith himself had commanded light infantry during the Mexican War.

The battle at Gaines's Mill during the Seven Days on June 27 had an even more spectacular example of shock tactics. The Federals held a strong position here on a plateau, with successive and lightly entrenched lines of infantry above Boatswain's Creek at the plateau's base, and artillery supports on the crest. On the Confederate side of the creek stood a gentle slope with another ridgeline behind it, all exposed to Federal fire. Brig. Gen. William H. C. Whiting's division made the decisive attack on the position with the brigades of Brig. Gen. John Bell Hood and Col. Evander M. Law. In one example of deliberate use of shock tactics, Hood, a brigade commander, took charge of his original regiment, the 4th Texas, and gave specific orders that his troops were not to fire until ordered to when they were within extremely close range of the enemy. One participant, Decimus Barziza, recorded the dangers of pausing to fire, writing that "they who had gone in at this point before us, and had been repulsed, stopped on this hill to fire [the ridgeline on the Confederate side], and were mowed down like grass."

Nevertheless, the lieutenant colonel of the 4th was unable to maintain fire discipline and the regiment let loose a volley where the previous assault lines had stalled. Worse yet, across the whole division's front, demoralized pieces of previous assaults clogged the lines and even discouraged the fresh troops from further exertions. Some of these troops huddled behind the crest of the ridgeline whose cover the previous assaulting troops had been unable to resist. In the end, however, Hood regained control of his men and continued the charge, with the 4th Texas now showing better fire discipline by firing a volley into the backs of fleeing Federals, who seem to have been completely demoralized by the charge's vigor. The 4th's success inspired the rest of the division, which swept the defending Federals from the hill. The historian Robert Krick has argued that this charge of the 4th Texas and the supporting 18th Georgia was the turning point of the battle. At the very least, Hood showed that sheer momentum could take a strong defensive position.[33]

Nicholas A. Davis, chaplain of the 4th, later attributed the assault's success to Hood's order to restart the charge at the top of the rise where previous attacks had stalled, "instead of halting and making the fight, as others had done and been driven back." Hood himself wrote after the war that "I knew full well that if the men were allowed to fire, they would halt to load, break the alignment, and, very likely, never reach the breastworks." Or, as another participant later wrote, "we understood why Gen. Hood wanted us to go to the enemy without firing; for in piles all around us were other Confederates, who stopped to load their guns, lay dead and dying." Hood strove to keep the 4th's advance as disciplined as possible, telling them "'Steady.' 'Steady' I don't want you to run." The commanders of the 18th Georgia also strove to maintain order in their assault, the major and adjutant "coolly commanding, 'close up,' 'Dress to the right' or 'left,' while every other officer exerted himself to preserve the line unbroken." The commander of the 4th Alabama in Law's brigade, Lt. Col. O. K. McLemore, a West Pointer known for his focus on drill and discipline, used similar measures to regulate his regiment's assault, amid the broken remnants of previous assaults. Robert T. Coles, the regimental adjutant, later recalled that the colonel "called out as coolly as on drill, 'Guide centre; keep the step—one, two, three, four; one, two, three, four,' and continued calling out the step until we passed over the Virginians, and then he gave the order to charge." Although there is no report of an order to the troops to hold their fire, the regiment managed to keep its momentum, and it did not pause until it reached the first line of Federal works.[34]

Like Smith's assault at Donelson, these attacking troops managed to maintain their crucial forward momentum. In contrast, most Civil War assaults became short-range fire fights; the historian Paddy Griffith has pointed out that in these sorts of engagements, the attacking force suffers a terrible disadvantage because of its exposed position.[35] Hood had less success than Smith in maintaining fire discipline among his troops, but his injunctions and demeanor had impressed on them the importance of maintaining their offensive momentum. That in turn allowed him to carry the Federal position. Smith's and Hood's attempts to push their troops forward and avoid a possibly fatal loss of momentum during a charge were neither the first nor the only attempts at thinking through shock tactics during the war. However, such attempts proved few and far between in both armies.

This should not be terribly surprising, because what passed for old

THE PENINSULA

army doctrine had been almost entirely formulated by ad hoc methods involving the occasional tactical review board, individual translations of foreign works, and officers' overseas visits. These methods sufficed only for the development of a set of competently produced basic tactical manuals, and the exigencies of the war prevented either army from developing the institutional devices by which tactical methods could be evaluated, developed, and disseminated.[36] Although assault tactics would reach higher levels of sophistication later in the war, even the most successful forays proved far too dependent on the abilities of individual officers and bereft of the organizational support that might have made the war's later operations far more tactically decisive.

For all the professionals' deficiencies, senior civilian political leaders could and did make far worse military judgments. Shortly after the stunning Union victories at Forts Henry and Donelson, Secretary of War Edwin M. Stanton showed that excessive faith in the military power of moral righteousness did not limit itself to complacent Confederates. He declared "that battles are to be won now and by us in the same and only manner that they were ever won by any people or in any age, since the days of Joshua, by boldly pursuing and striking the foe." Understandably frustrated by McClellan's self-serving appeals to military science as an excuse for simple lethargy, Stanton went so far as to condemn "military combinations" — McClellan's strategy or military science — as a product of "infidel France" during its revolution. Stanton instead claimed that "patriotic spirit, with resolute courage in officers and men, is a military combination that never failed."[37]

While Stanton focused on the moral righteousness of a general, the antiadministration *New York Herald* cited abstract social theory as an explanation for military competence. The *Herald* argued that northern-born West Pointers benefited from the North's commercial society, because "Southern officers have remained in the army, doing nothing ever since. The consequence is they know nothing but more army routine. The Northern officers not content with so inactive a life, have embarked in business pursuits, which have sharpened their wits and enlarged their capacity for generalship." Reflecting a mix of whiggish distaste for standing armies, northern enthusiasm for industrial society, and the Democratic Party's unbounded faith in George B. McClellan, the *Herald* naturally cited Little Mac's railroad experience as an "immense advantage" compared to Confederate officers who wasted their lives in the parasitic world of a standing army.[38] Both the *Herald* and Stanton disagreed on many

151

THE PENINSULA

things, but like the southerner George Fitzhugh, their ideas on military competence had more to do with social theory and ethics than with strictly military issues. As it turned out, McClellan's railroad background did not guarantee battlefield success any more than did Maj. Gen. Benjamin F. Butler's supposed moral rectitude as a Radical Republican.

The ferocious battle at Shiloh on April 6–7, almost a full year after the outbreak of hostilities, showed once again that basic problems of organizational competence remained more important than abstract questions of strategy or social organization. The troops at Shiloh had obvious deficiencies in equipment, organization, and training, despite the fact that a full year had passed since the outbreak of hostilities. For example, the 15th and 16th Iowa had not even mastered the manual of arms. One Confederate battery had not yet fired a shot. What little training the Confederate artillery had it owed — unsurprisingly — to a West Pointer, Maj. Francis A. Shoup. It was not until after the Shiloh campaign at the Confederate encampment in Tupelo that the Army of Tennessee's artillery would receive extensive training to supplement the inadequate preparations of the previous fall. Despite the presence of some Enfields, much of the Confederate army was equipped with a hodgepodge of squirrel guns, shotguns, and outdated smoothbore muskets. The Federals, however, did not have any noticeable superiority in their own small arms. Before the battle, Maj. Gen. Braxton Bragg had bluntly described his six brigades as "the mob we have, miscalled soldiers." Ironically enough, Bragg's troops may have been the best drilled in a raw army about to go on the offensive.[39]

Extremely poor fire discipline remained a continuing problem with green troops. Soldiers frequently saw firing as a form of emotional release from the extreme strain of battle; for example, one Iowan at Shiloh, Warren Olney, reported his unit firing smoothbore volleys without orders at a totally ineffective range of three hundred to four hundred yards: "But though our action was absurd, it was a relief to us to do something." Drill was supposed to help with the problem; to wit, the colonel of the 32nd Indiana had to use the expedient of ordering his troops to go through the manual of arms in order to steady them after they prematurely opened fire at too great a distance. Brig. Gen. John Logan, one of the best Union officers drawn from civil life, sounded almost like a regular in his constant exhortations to his men to fire only under orders and to make sure to aim their fire at an actual Confederate.[40]

Nevertheless, one soldier at Shiloh, commenting on some of his comrades, remembered that "we were ordered to fire, and as soon as I let go of Ned's gun, he stuck it up in the air, shut both his eyes, and fired at the tree tops, and Schnider did the same. But Schnider was in rear rank behind Curly and he cut a lock of Curly's hair off just above his ear, and burned his neck." The same soldier's later comment that "it is very trying to one's nerves to lay under fire and not be able to do anything in return" serves as good an explanation as any for the emotional release some men found in discharging their weapons. One Confederate officer bluntly complained that "stragglers would fall from their own lines and, retiring under cover of another line, fire recklessly to the front." The historian Andrew Haughton even cites a report of actual fratricides from rear-rank men in the Confederate army. Civil War armies would struggle for years with the problem of soldiers continually loading their weapons without actually firing them.[41]

Basic problems with discipline also included a propensity to pillage. Initial success demoralized many of the Confederate troops at Shiloh in the same way Grant's troops had lost discipline at the battle of Belmont the previous November; they simply could not resist the opportunity to pillage the captured Federal camp. One Confederate officer had harsh words for the short-term Confederate volunteers, declaring that "the disorders resulting from want of proper discipline were numberless; the most fatal to the consummation of a success so gallantly begun being the lawless spirit of plunder and pillage so recklessly indulged in."[42] Even veteran troops would have been subject to the simple exhaustion and inevitable disorganization that the first day of fighting produced in the Confederate army, but breaking ranks to pillage enemy camps before the day was truly won represented a level of demoralization over and above being fought out.

Both army commands also had their own defects. Grant and Sherman at the very least could have prepared themselves better for the attack, although in their defense, Grant's rationale against entrenching so that the raw troops could focus on drill had a certain plausibility to it. Furthermore, the ever-pugnacious C. F. Smith, reflecting the same aggressive school of thought that had made his bayonet charge at Donelson successful, believed that entrenchments would enervate the troops. Indeed, even after the war, John Bell Hood argued that "a soldier cannot fight for a period of one or two months constantly behind breastworks . . . and then be expected to engage in pitched battle and prove as intrepid and impetuous as his brother who has been taught to rely solely upon his own valor." On the Confederate side, Johnston and Beauregard have received some critical appraisals by modern scholars for their battlefield performance. The Creole has drawn fire for a muddled battle plan, and historians have criticized Johnston for neglecting his overall responsibilities as army commander. In fact, Beauregard learned nothing from First Manassas, because his plans at Shiloh were also far too complicated and "Napoleonic" for their own good. Confederate staff work for the march on Pittsburgh's Landing also proved of dubious quality.[43]

Nevertheless, some officers knew and understood tactics well enough to even use assault columns by division — columns with a two-company front commonly used in Napoleonic practice. The 32nd Indiana managed to make a charge while in column by division and then take advantage of its breaking foes by deploying into line and opening fire on the fleeing Confederates. Later in the day, it deployed four companies as skirmishers as opposed to the usual two but retained the column, in an interesting mix of firepower and shock. This early use of light-infantry methods at Shiloh also showed that such tactics did not require the universal use of the rifle-musket, which was not possible at this stage in the indifferently armed armies of the western theater. On occasion, whole regiments deployed as skirmishers. Sharpshooters even picked off artillerists with aimed fire. The commander of the sharpshooters from the second brigade of Union Maj. Gen. Lew Wallace's division used a swell in the ground to snipe at an artillery battery during one assault. Furthermore, Shiloh also saw at least some deliberate sniping at field officers.[44] Although it did not replace the primacy of the battle line, sharpshooting seemed to have had at least some effect on the battle.

From the Union's perspective, the bloodbath at Pittsburgh's Landing gave some support to McClellan's lethargic pace on the Peninsula, which he had moved his army to in mid-March. Little Mac also continued to benefit from the stinging memory of McDowell's ill-fated and ill-prepared army at First Bull Run. Even the *New York Tribune* gave Little Mac the benefit of the doubt during his laborious preparations in front of Richmond.[45] Nevertheless, a growing chorus of voices in the North, especially among Radical Republicans suspicious of McClellan's openly Democratic politics, pressed for their Young Napoleon to make a decisive move on Richmond.

Richmond's fall would have been yet another blow to Confederate morale in a miserable spring, and going beyond political effects, the city also possessed much of the new nation's limited industrial capacity. To take Richmond, however, one must first deal with the Confederate army that defended it. Some historians overemphasize Lincoln's later dictum that the Confederate field army, as opposed to Richmond, should have been the proper objective point of the Union forces.[46] After Lee's Army of Northern Virginia became a living embodiment of the Confederacy, that doctrine gained more merit, but Joe Johnston's army before Richmond had no such significance in the spring of 1862. Even if a substantial Confederate field army in Virginia survived Richmond's fall that spring, the Confederate cause would still have suffered a perhaps fatal blow after the litany of catastrophes in the West.

Richmond's strategic importance in both military and political terms made it a plausible objective for McClellan's campaign, and his overall strategy proved in many ways sound. McClellan first hoped to turn Johnston out of his Rappahannock line with an amphibious movement to Urbanna; when Johnston foreclosed that maneuver by withdrawing to Richmond, the Young Napoleon then moved his troops to the Peninsula between the York and James Rivers southeast of Richmond. Although he professed some hope for taking the city in a *coup de main*, Little Mac did not act with that sort of speed and resolution. He contented himself with slowly working his way up to Richmond from Fortress Monroe in order to invest the city with siege works and heavy artillery. With secure seaborne lines of communication, and a marked superiority in artillery, McClellan had time on his side, if he could assure the Lincoln administration of Washington's safety from any potential spoiling attack by the Confederates.[47]

Lee, an accomplished engineer, knew as much about siege craft as McClellan, and he had no intention of allowing the campaign to become a regular siege. Shortly after taking command of what became the Army of Northern Virginia, he wrote Davis in early June that "it will require 100,000 men to resist the regular siege of Richmond, which perhaps would only prolong not save it." Furthermore, Lee also feared an investment, because any breakout attempt would require the storming of strong works by raw Confederate troops, which Lee described as "extremely hazardous." There were distinct limits to the general's audacity. In sum, Lee perceived and feared McClellan's overwhelming superiority in logistics and heavy ordnance, which would prove fatal to the city during an investment. Even the far-more cautious Johnston agreed on that point and had hoped to strike McClellan's army at a vulnerable point rather than wait for a doomed siege.[48] Lee fought all of the battles of the Seven Days to prevent that outcome.

THE PENINSULA

Nevertheless, shortly after he took command on June 1 after Johnston's disabling wound at Seven Pines, Lee proceeded to dig in to buy time and allow a repositioning of his troops to strike Little Mac's right flank. His men complained about digging entrenchments, grumbling that earth moving was work fit only for slaves, but martial discipline made only so many concessions to cultural preference. Mary Chesnut, like many others, complained in her diary entry of June 16 that "Lee is king of spades. . . . Our chiefs contrive to dampen and destroy the enthusiasm of all who go near them. So much entrenching and falling back destroys the morale of any army."[49] Lee shared with Confederate public opinion and his own soldiery a fondness for aggressive and decisive action, but a fine eye for detail and military practicality set him apart from the impatient public. Lee's bloody campaign during the Seven Days between June 26 and July 1, including the aforementioned Gaines's Mill, did not give him the battle of annihilation he hoped for, but it did expel the Federals from the very gates of Richmond.

Despite real problems with Confederate military organization, Lee's army and campaign saved Richmond from a doom that seemed inevitable. If McClellan had been more aggressive, he could have broken the Army of Northern Virginia on the Peninsula with his superior numbers and position, but the opportunity had dissipated into the hot summer air of the Peninsula. Instead, Lee's pugnacious approach made him a hero to a Confederate public that craved successful and aggressive generalship, even though his attacks on McClellan rested more on his own military judgment than on any desire to placate newspaper editorialists.[50] The Confederate public had finally found a general capable of translating its desire for pugnacious methods into practical military measures, while Lee saw his army benefit from the rising morale on the home front produced by its own victories.

While the Peninsula Campaign left a powerful legacy in favor of Confederate independence, the Union received a bitter cup of woe. On the Union home front, Little Mac's performance on the battlefield became a contentious political issue, with only Democrats accepting the Young Napoleon's explanation that he had been insufficiently supported by the Lincoln administration. McClellan did not help matters by making it no secret that he favored a conciliatory policy toward the seceded states that would leave slavery untouched. Although Lincoln proved almost Job-like in his patience, large portions of the Republican Party saw McClellan as politically unsound, perhaps even treasonous, and completely incompetent. Unfortunately, as the army's molder, founder, and first chieftain, McClellan left an imprint that long survived his relief, especially with regards to the army's officers. Many shared his conservative Democratic politics, especially the veterans of the old army who carried their institution's general political conservatism into the Civil War armies. They, along with many others, saw Republican attempts to make the army a willing instrument of a more aggressive war policy as partisan meddling.

The politicization of military policy also infected public debate in the Union. As one historian has pointed out, debates in the northern press over military leadership did not center on military merits but, "in the final analysis, amounted to a struggle between those who anticipated emancipation as the ultimate goal of the war and those who would refrain from meddling in any manner with the institution of slavery."[51] The politicization of military questions—inevitable in any circumstance but driven to special extremes by the North's party-orientated political structure—introduced potentially catastrophic conflicts in the upper reaches of the Union's military and political leadership. Frustrated, for eminently justifiable reasons, by McClellan's mixture of conservative politics and military lethargy, the most ardently antislavery segments of the ruling northern political party began to make correct political ideas a proxy for military competence, leading them to support such dubious marshals as Maj. Gen. John Pope and Ben Butler. McClellan's old army allies hardly helped matters by using "military science" as a partisan club to pound Radical Republicans in open political combat. Mundane but crucial questions of military practicality became lost in the public controversies over the war's proper aims and its relationship to moral rectitude.

CHAPTER EIGHT

Morale, Cohesion, and Competence from Second Bull Run to Missionary Ridge

✶ ✶ ✶

Military historians have tended to draw a straight line between Lee's repulse at Malvern Hill, the last battle of the Seven Days, and the tactical stalemate of the Overland campaign in the summer of 1864. In the intervening period, each significant battle becomes a further proof of the superiority of the tactical defensive, especially in conjunction with fieldworks: the bloody repulse of attacking Federal troops at Fredericksburg in December 1862, the defeat of attacking Confederates at Gettysburg the following July, and George Meade's refusal to make a suicidal attack on Confederate entrenchments at Mine Run. Successful offensive victories such as Second Manassas and Chancellorsville become Pyrrhic triumphs of no strategic significance, while Lee's setback at Antietam is chalked up in many ways to Lee's failure to entrench. All these campaigns did lead in at least a chronological sense to tactical stalemate during the Overland campaign, but that important campaign should not represent a culminating point in Civil War military history through which all previous events must be distended and distorted.[1]

The minié bullet and the trench certainly had a profound effect on battlefield conditions during this period, but all those effects had to be channeled through a military machinery grounded as much in flesh and blood as in lead and cordite. That mediation made questions of cohesion, morale, and competence far more important than the technical qualities of the rifle-musket taken in isolation. The rifle-musket's increased accuracy did play a role in Civil War battles, but an individual army's morale and general military competence remained of prime importance. The success or failure of frontal assaults depended on a variety of factors that included the morale of the troops in question, the quality of their respective leaders, and the degree of preparation an assault received, in addition to the technical qualities of the infantry arms in play. Taken as a whole, the outcomes of specific battles depended not so much on technology as on the characteristics of each army's individual leaders, its organizational virtues and vices, the force of circumstance, and the fighting qualities of the line troops involved. This complex constellation of factors tended to configure itself differently at different times and places throughout the war.

In order to achieve the annihilation of an enemy army in the field, one army had to have a marked superiority in leadership, organization, and morale. Some Civil War armies were better organized or better led than others, but the differences were not usually marked enough to allow for the complete destruction of its opponent on any given battlefield. In contrast, the U.S. Army had a decisive advantage in leadership, morale, and organization throughout the entire Mexican War, and that persistent advantage led to its spectacular military successes in the previous conflict. Armies do not operate in isolation, and measuring their competence requires comparison to their adversaries on the battlefield. The general equilibrium of competence among Civil War armies more than anything else contributed to the climate of military indecision that predominated until the spring of 1865.

By the end of the Seven Days, both Union and Confederate forces had achieved a reasonable level of tactical competence at the brigade and regimental levels, adequate march discipline, and reasonably good unit cohesion. Even the much-maligned Federal retreat after Second Bull Run, one of the Union's more disgraceful defeats, remained reasonably orderly; there would be no Federal repeat of the dreadful rout after First Bull Run. The coherent coordination of different units at the division and corps levels, however, tended to tax the leadership ranks of Civil War armies so severely that even victorious armies usually could not obliterate their opponents in an open-field battle.[2] On the tactical level, a few individual commanders continued to attempt to think through the problem of assault tactics, as opposed to simply hurling troops against an enemy line, but neither army ever systematized these efforts on a larger organizational level. Recurrent problems with coordinating larger units also frequently squandered whatever local tactical success an especially talented regimental or brigade commander might achieve.

Taken as a whole, the campaigns between Second Bull Run and Missionary Ridge continued the same process of halting improvement in military competence among both contending armies that had begun in

1861. Because both sets of troops improved at roughly comparable rates, neither gained much of an advantage over the other on an organizational level. Union troops did benefit from superior material resources, but defects in Federal manpower policy and the inherent difficulties of conquering hostile territory counterbalanced that advantage. Divisions in the Federal high command only exacerbated these structural problems. Pope's short-lived appointment as primary Federal army commander in the east inspired widespread hostility and obstructionism among both McClellan and his loyalists, which, along with Pope's own failings, helped lead to the catastrophe at Second Bull Run in August 1862. Col. Hermann Haupt proved prescient for writing in July that the western general's controversial proclamation to his new command that "I have come to you from the West, where we have always seen the backs of our enemies" was "a virtual declaration of war between him and McClellan destroying all harmony of action."[3] However, although the Army of the Potomac found itself consistently outmatched in Virginia, it had enough inherent organizational strength and élan to prevent its Confederate opponents from annihilating it in the field.

And even in the Army of Northern Virginia, problems with large-unit coordination remained. For example, at the smashing Confederate victory of Second Manassas in August 1862, Stonewall Jackson still could not properly deploy his overwhelming strength against a Federal force of one division during the fighting on August 28 near Groveton. Two days later, he also failed to give timely support to Longstreet's attack, which may have saved the Federals from total annihilation. On the corps and divisional levels, Civil War armies would gradually improve in this respect. That improvement already displayed itself at Second Bull Run in Longstreet's reasonably well-coordinated assault on August 30, launched with an entire corps over a front extending more than a mile and executed within forty-five minutes.[4] Nevertheless, the natural chaos attendant to any battle, the heavily broken nature of American terrain, and the primitive state of battlefield communications (i.e., mounted orderlies riding to-and-fro) would be inhibiting factors that would never be entirely overcome.

In the case of the Army of the Potomac, continued command problems—due in large part to McClellan's own overly cautious temperament—prevented the force from taking full advantage of its opportunities during the Antietam campaign of September 1862. On that climactic battlefield, the rifle-musket and the flexibility of Napoleonic-era infantry formations remained less important than continuing Federal problems with coordinating assaults. For example, all three brigades of Brig. Gen. James B. Rickett's division in the 1st Corps intended to attack the famous Cornfield on the northern part of the battlefield in unison; instead, one brigade first went in unsupported, followed by another, again without support, and the last brigade saw its original commander suffer a mental collapse and was never really fully engaged until Confederate Brig. Gen. John B. Hood's division in Longstreet's corps made its counterattack.[5]

The Confederates proved too weak in numbers to hope for anything other than a defensive victory at Antietam, while the Federal assaults, ill coordinated and mistimed, could not obtain a decisive tactical decision on the first day. Like the Peninsula campaign, however, the most elementary amount of strategic decisiveness on McClellan's part would have made this tactical indecisiveness irrelevant. McClellan's many faults and missed opportunities have been listed ad nauseum by historians, so there is no need to rehash the issue in full. Suffice to say the Young Napoleon had twenty thousand fresh troops who could have obliterated the bloodied remnants of the Army of Northern Virginia on September 18 when Lee refused to immediately leave the field.

Worse yet, the Army of the Potomac suffered from the various failures of Federal manpower policy. Because of the Lincoln administration's premature closure of recruiting offices during the spring, new calls for raw recruits had to be made in July and August. These new recruits composed almost one-quarter of McClellan's infantry, around twenty thousand men. To compound the problem, political considerations caused the Federal government to raise most of these new troops in entire regiments, as opposed to using them as replacements in veteran units. This allowed state governors further opportunities for political patronage, but at much cost to the army's efficiency. Sherman described the policy of raising new regiments as opposed to refilling veteran ones as "the greatest mistake made in our civil war." This problem existed throughout the war; for example, there was even resistance in one regiment late in 1864 to dispersing a new company of recruits throughout a regiment, as opposed to keeping it intact. At the battle of Perryville, less than a month after Antietam and during the ill-fated Confederate invasion of Kentucky, Federal forces would also struggle with raw, sometimes-ill-armed troops. Despite some political opposition to the refilling of old regiments with new conscripts, the Confederacy did not rely to the same degree on raw and newly formed regiments.[6]

The absence of a rational replacement system hounded Federal arms throughout the war, but at Antietam, the cause of Union arms had the special misfortune of finding one raw regiment of nine-month men, the 16th Connecticut, on a crucial part of Maj. Gen. Ambrose E. Burnside's 9th Corps flank during the Army of the Potomac's final opportunity for a decisive victory on September 17. The regiment had all of three weeks' experience in the army and had loaded its weapons for the first time the day before. The unit "had never had a battalion-drill, and only one dress-parade, and hardly knew how to form in line of battle." Not surprisingly, the Connecticut men broke when attacked, losing forty-two men killed and 143 wounded in an engagement where Brig. Gen. Maxcy Gregg's South Carolina brigade inflicted casualties at a ratio of eight or nine to one. The rout also managed to carry away the veteran 4th Rhode Island, which in turn exposed the 9th Corps's flank and forced its withdrawal. Who knows how the battle might have turned if the flank regiments had held and the 9th Corps could have maintained its offensive impetus toward Sharpsburg. Regardless, it is at least certain that such a sad performance showed that whatever the flaws of Civil War close-order drill, it was still better than no training at all.[7]

Although even a high-quality regiment like the 6th Alabama had problems with firing too high during the engagement at South Mountain, the Army of Northern Virginia did not have to worry about breaking in entire regiments of greenhorn troops. Indeed, the remaining Confederate forces that made it to the battlefield at Antietam and had not been lost to the army through straggling represented the cream of what was already a veteran army. Furthermore, *every* one of Lee's 184 infantry regiments had been bled before in battle, and there was strong continuity in the army's brigade- and division-level leadership.[8]

In the arena of administrative aptitude, the Army of Northern Virginia had more serious problems. Lee had more success in purging the army's higher ranks of lackluster commanders than in improving the army's basic administrative apparatus. For the entire Antietam campaign, Lee himself had no clear idea of how many fit-for-duty soldiers he possessed, because of faulty record keeping on the company and regimental levels. The most critical issue, however, centered on logistics. Not all of this can be laid at the feet of organizational mismanagement; the loss of Tennessee and a drought had deprived the Confederate commissariat of resources. Nevertheless, the improved performance of the supply bureaus after a series of reforms instituted after the campaign show that there was much room for improvement. At Antietam itself, however, the wretched state of Confederate logistics caused much of the army's straggling. Lee as a consequence lost more than 20 percent of his strength by the time of the battle, leaving him with fewer than thirty-five thousand men to begin the fighting.[9]

The Army of Northern Virginia's organizational difficulties helped contribute to Lee's strategic defeat at Antietam. Although Lee won a limited tactical victory in terms of raw casualties — 12,401 Federal wounded, killed, and missing versus 10,318 Confederates — Maryland still had not risen up in revolt, and the Army of the Potomac was put out of action only for the moment. Lee had been able to draw on provisions in the lower Shenandoah Valley for some time, but he had not been able to lurk in Maryland and southern Pennsylvania for the entire autumn as he had originally hoped. Worse yet, the marginal Federal victory allowed Lincoln to issue the Preliminary Emancipation Proclamation, which proved to be one of the Confederacy's death knells. Historians have frequently used this long-term view of Antietam to assign it a pivotal role in the Confederacy's final defeat.[10]

Nevertheless, McClellan's failure to seize his opportunity to destroy the most important Confederate army in open-field battle combined with Lee's offensive posture during the campaign allowed Confederate confidence in the Army of Northern Virginia to continue to rise.[11] The strategic repulse at Antietam also did nothing to prevent Lee from stringing together two more victories at Fredericksburg and Chancellorsville, along with various tactical successes as late as the Overland campaign in 1864. Emancipation became a part of the Union's final and victorious grand strategy for the war, but that war measure proved more than a little controversial in the North at its inception. The Democratic Party made significant gains during the 1862 midterm elections, partly because of tensions in the Union over the nature and extent of Federal war aims. Furthermore, Antietam only served to further exacerbate civil-military tensions in the Federal high command in the East. McClellan's failure to follow-up his victory all but forced Lincoln to relieve him after the November elections, but he had created that army in his image, and the general's shade would haunt Republicans for years to come.

McClellan's partisans, influential in the Army of the Potomac until the end of the war, never forgave Radical Republicans not only for removing their beloved chief but also for the persecutions of Maj. Gen. Fitz John Porter, commander of the 5th Corps, and Brig. Gen. Charles P. Stone. The

Congressional Joint Committee on the Conduct of the War, dominated by Radical Republicans, disgraced both of these generals for vague accusations of treason based for the most part on their conservative Democratic politics. The increasingly vitriolic attacks on West Point by some congressional Republicans and their allies only further exacerbated the civil-military divide. Regular army men did frequently express a certain pessimism regarding the prospects for Federal victory — one McClellanite officer had commented shortly after Fort Sumter that "I can't believe we will ever again be a united people. A few battles will sicken both sides & they will be glad to come to terms" — but this was hardly treason. Radicals also confused the aristocratic conservatism of many regular army men with criminal sympathy for the Confederacy. Although more old army officers than not, including McClellan, had little or no fondness for emancipation, or for any form of revolutionary violence, frank disagreement over war aims still differed from treason in many profound ways.[12]

Antebellum regular army officers had long overridden their personal consciences to do the bidding of their civilian superiors; suspicious Republican politicians should have realized that if officers could fight Indians and Mexicans in wars they considered morally dubious, they could do the same for another cause whose worth they doubted, emancipation. Furthermore, Pope's dismal performance should have shown Stanton and his congressional allies that ideological soundness did not automatically translate into military competence. Even some moderate and conservative Republicans had some sense of the risks involved in removing McClellan at this late stage of the campaigning season with no obvious successor waiting in the wings.[13]

Considering McClellan's failings, one can hardly blame Lincoln for relieving the Young Napoleon of his command. Lincoln had a good sense of what was and was not possible, and he had recognized the need to bring McClellan back to command after the catastrophe at Second Bull Run. As he put it to his secretary John Hay, "He has acted badly in this matter [Second Bull Run], but we must use what tools we have." Lincoln had also given McClellan more time to redeem his lost opportunity at Antietam, but the Young Napoleon failed to recognize the urgency of the situation. Lincoln, however, erred in choosing a man who did not believe himself qualified for the task of leading the Army of the Potomac.[14] Maj. Gen. Ambrose E. Burnside — a West Pointer who had performed reasonably well at the head of the 9th Corps in North Carolina in early 1862 but less successfully at Antietam — replaced Little Mac. Burnside faced, in addition to Lee and his army, intense political pressure and controversy at his rear and a leadership corps notorious for its infighting and backbiting.

Burnside, as even the most casual student of the war knows, suffered a grievous defeat during his first and only battle as commander of the Army of the Potomac. Historians have generally interpreted the battle of Fredericksburg in mid-December 1862 as a vindication of the superiority of the tactical defensive. However, modern historians oversimplify matters when they interpret the battle as a straightforward lesson in the superiority of the rifle-musket. Even historians like Edward C. Hagerman who focus on the Civil War's "modernity" admit Fredericksburg to be a transitional battle in many ways. While Lee had proved more than willing to dig siege lines outside Richmond, there was no substantial use of field fortifications by the Army of Northern Virginia at either Antietam or Second Manassas. Confederate troops did take advantage of terrain features such as swells in the ground and preexisting man-made features—the sunken road and the railroad cut being the two most famous respectively—but troops went no farther than impromptu measures such as piling up fence rails for improvised breastworks. At Fredericksburg, Longstreet's corps made more substantial preparations, including improvements to the famous stone wall on Marye's Heights, well-sited artillery emplacements, and Wilcox's works on Taylor's Hill. Nevertheless, in comparison to later campaigns, Longstreet's chief of staff admitted in retrospect that he was surprised by how few works the troops used, but Confederates did more digging here than at Antietam or Second Manassas.[15]

The reluctance of the Army of Northern Virginia to resort to the use of fieldworks probably had some relationship to a long-standing, if not especially well-articulated, fear among many old army officers that excessive use of entrenchments would enervate troops. Maj. Gen. Edwin V. Sumner, a West Pointer from Massachusetts, had opposed the use of works on the Peninsula, because "they have a tendency to make the men timid, and do more harm than good; and I think the most of the older officers of the army think so." Even McClellan did not entrench at Antietam. Sherman tried to justify his and Grant's failure to entrench at Shiloh by citing the fear of demoralization. The ever-aggressive John Bell Hood in 1864 would express the same misgivings about entrenchments shortly after his relief of Joe Johnston at the head of the Army of Tennessee in 1864.[16]

Although the Marye's Heights position proved extremely strong and probably impregnable to direct frontal assault, that obvious fact should not transform the Federal assaults into a simple testament to Burnside's inadequacies or the supposed indecisiveness of Civil War battles. Many of Burnside's problems rested not so much on the rifle-musket but on poor command and control on the part of the Army of the Potomac. For example, General-in-Chief Henry W. Halleck and the Union high command failed to ensure the prompt arrival of Burnside's pontoon train, which gave the Army of Northern Virginia the opportunity to concentrate at Fredericksburg in the first place. Furthermore, there was actually much merit to Burnside's actual battle plan, which involved a holding attack on Marye's Heights paired with a turning movement around Lee's right designed to cut the Confederate army's lines of communication. Unfortunately, Burnside failed to issue clear orders, and his subordinate on the Federal left, Maj. Gen. William Buell Franklin, lacked the initiative and self-direction to mount a coordinated assault against Jackson's corps on Lee's right. Franklin misinterpreted his commander's intentions and mounted only a limited demonstration on Jackson's front. Only two divisions under Brig. Gen. John Gibbon and Maj. Gen. George G. Meade attacked the Confederate right, but both were well led and had substantial success. Without adequate support, however, their efforts went for naught. Burnside had no business commanding the Army of the Potomac, but neither has he deserved some historians' aspersions.[17]

Finally, even the failed assaults on Marye's Heights bear a historical significance that goes beyond a sad tale of heroic failure or simple stupidity. As was the case at Donelson and Gaines's Mill, one commander on the battlefield—in this case, old army veteran Brig. Gen. A. A. Humphreys, a commander of a division of nine-month Pennsylvania men, future chief of staff of the Army of the Potomac, and commander of the 2nd Corps at the end of the war—showed some facility with organizing and leading a charge that relied on shock tactics. Hooker also attempted to support the attack with a preparatory bombardment by massed artillery. The artillery fire had "no apparent effect," and, unlike Smith's and Hood's attempts, Humphreys's bayonet charge failed because of the inherent strength of the Confederate lines, the quality of the troops who manned those lines, and the raw character of the Pennsylvania militiamen in his command. The enhanced technical qualities of the rifle-musket combined with fieldworks were at best only one of many factors.[18]

Humphreys did his best; he ordered the brigade's muskets unloaded and "rung"—dropping ramrods down barrels to check if the guns were truly unloaded—to prevent his troops from prematurely opening fire, and during the assault he also recklessly exposed himself to inspire his troops. He put himself at the front of Col. Peter H. Allabach's brigade for the first attempt at the wall. The troops stalled at the swale roughly two hundred yards in front of the Confederate line, however, where the previous wave of 2nd Corps troops had also gone to cover. Furthermore, at least some of them defied orders and prematurely fired their muskets. Many of the 2nd Corps troops trapped at the swale also demoralized the nine-month men—a situation reminiscent of the Confederates who had tried to persuade Hood's Texans to give up their charge at Gaines's Mill—by calling on them to stop, and some even used physical force to prevent the new troops from moving forward. Humphreys later complained that "one of the greatest obstacles to my success was the mass of troops lying on our front line. They ought to have been withdrawn before mine advanced. . . . Finding them lying there, the men of Allabach's Brigade, who had never before been in battle, instinctively followed their example." By almost sheer force of will, Humphreys and the brigade's officers restarted the charge from the swale. The Confederate position proved too strong however, and the assault broke. Humphreys tried again with his other brigade, led by Brig. Gen. Erastus B. Tyler, but that assault failed under similar circumstances.[19]

Another brigade commander at Fredericksburg and a West Pointer, Col. Norman J. Hall, also realized how difficult it could be for an advancing unit to resume a charge after it had given in to the temptation to open fire. He remarked in his official report that "the firing having commenced in my line, it was impossible to restrain it, so that an effective charge was not expected." At least one other commander, Col. Edward E. Cross of the 5th New Hampshire, issued orders to his troops to hold their fire until they breached the Confederate lines, but there seems to have been little thought or preparation given to the necessary assault tactics at higher levels of command.[20]

Burnside recognized to some degree the importance of maintaining offensive momentum in his own later aborted orders to the 9th Corps to attack the Confederate line in a column of regiments on December 15. He hoped that the Union troops, "by coming quickly up after each other, would be able to carry the stone wall and the batteries in front, forcing the enemy into their next line, and by going in with them they would not be able to fire upon us to any great extent."[21] The commanding general, however, made no mention of taking practical measures to maintain the necessary momentum similar to Humphreys's efforts to unload his division's muskets, and it seems that most if not all of the Federal assaults

MORALE, COHESION, AND COMPETENCE

earlier in the day made even fewer efforts to think through the shock tactics necessary to carry such a difficult position.

Indeed, even Humphreys's performance remained far from flawless. The division commander failed to attack with both of his brigades at the same time. When he tried to move Tyler's second-wave assault alongside Allabach's spent men on the swell for a renewed attack by both brigades, he succeeded only in moving the former brigade into the same confused position held by Allabach's survivors and the remnants of the 2nd Corps's previous assaults. Nevertheless, modern historians have been too hard on Humphreys for his "outdated infatuation for glory" and "his romantic, outmoded notions of warfare."[22] Indeed, Humphreys would go on to be a fine chief of staff to Meade and an excellent administrator. Although the former topographical engineer deserved criticism for not properly coordinating his two brigades, he still had a better understanding of both shock tactics and their necessity than many of his colleagues.

Humphreys correctly judged the strength of the Confederate lines, which meant "that our fire could have but little effect upon him, and that only mode of attacking him successfully was with the bayonet." The shattered remnants of countless 2nd Corps units huddled along the swale, and maintaining a desultory fire to no effect on the stone wall testified to that fact. Nevertheless, because Longstreet's veterans held the Confederate line, even the best troops using well-thought-out shock tactics probably could not have achieved a decisive breakthrough.

Finally, if better-organized Federal assaults had been joined to a vigorous action on the Confederate right by Franklin's wing of the army, who knows how the battle might have turned out. Commenting on the deleterious dissensions among the generals of the Army of the Potomac and its associated commands, J. Watts de Peyster wrote shortly after the war, "Had the Commander of the Left Grand Division [Franklin] supported Burnside, as Lee's Lieutenants always supported him, the successor of McClellan would have gained a glorious victory. It must not be forgotten, when considering this case, how Pope had experienced a similar treatment with equally unhappy results, disastrous to the Union cause."[23]

The battle at Perryville also had some examples of the importance of training and morale in deciding the outcome of assaults using shock tactics. Like Humphreys, Confederate Brig. Gen. George Maney realized the importance of offensive momentum. When his brigade made an assault on the Open Knob, in the words of one of his regimental commanders, "it came to a high fence at the edge of the wood, at which time it seemed impossible for humanity to go farther, such was the havoc and destruction that had taken place in their ranks. A temporary halt was the inevitable result. Here, at this critical juncture, Gen. Maney passed along the line from the right of the Georgia regiment to the left of the Ninth Tennessee, ordering and encouraging us to still press forward, as it was our last and only chance of safety and success." Like so many other Civil War assaults, a fence or other obstruction proved to be almost irresistible cover for attacking troops. Maney's aide then ordered the regiments to hold their fire in the new assault. After another stall in the attack, and the arrival of another regiment, the Confederates finally managed to take the position.

They were aided in large part by the raw state of the Federal defenders, and poor leadership on the part of Brig. Gen. William R. Terrill. Terrill fruitlessly ordered several of his raw and badly trained regiments to make bayonet charges they were incapable of executing, while they faced Shiloh veterans under Maney. Furthermore, the defenders had been fatigued by previous marching. Indeed, the historian Kenneth Noe marks the abortive bayonet charges of Terrill as the turning points in the assault, because they deprived the Federals of the strength of their terrain.[24] Shock tactics could work only under certain circumstances with well-trained and motivated troops. They proved fruitless when these conditions did not exist. Furthermore, these conditions grounded themselves in the competence and morale of the troops involved, not on the technical characteristics of their shoulder arms.

Although a strategic defeat for the Confederacy, Perryville hardly stood as an unalloyed triumph of the Union. It was better than yet another defeat, but it could not compensate for the later fiasco at Fredericksburg. Among that better-known eastern battle's many dismal results for the Union cause was increasing dissatisfaction in the Army of the Potomac. Many men yearned for Little Mac's return, which was not an entirely unreasonable desire if the only alternatives Washington could give them were the likes of Pope and Burnside. Historians do not think much of McClellan for good reason, but the fact remains that the soldiers of the Army of the Potomac still had great affection for their former chief after the battle of Fredericksburg. Shortly after McClellan's relief, Brig. Gen. Alfred Sully glumly wrote, "Whatever the world may say of him he certainly had the hearts of the old army of the Potomac with him & they would have willingly followed him wherever he might direct but as a soldier of course I must obey orders and shall act as I have always, do my duty & try not to grumble." Another officer, Capt. Thomas Fry Tobey, lacking

Sully's old army habit of ingrained obedience to civilian authority, went as far as to declare after the embittering battle of Fredericksburg that "if the President continues to show his Bourbon spirit of learning nothing from experience, the Grand Army *may* call on their General (for he is still *our* General, if he has been taken from us) to come back to them once more and let them place him where no man living shall have power to dictate to him." Tobey could make such threats even though he had no sympathies for the Democratic Party. Unsurprisingly, a strongly anti-emancipation soldier in Allabach's brigade would write shortly after the battle, "One day we fight for the Restoration of the Union: but the next, if proper authority can be learned in the acts of our rulers, we are striving for the predominence of some Abolitionist Scheme. . . . we are nothing (us poor soldiers) but food for sharks. . . . we will find in the termination that we have been aiding the ambitious predelections of *individuals*, and not the *supremacy of the laws*; the pretext which induced our enlistment."[25]

Lincoln compounded his mistake of appointing Burnside to his command by failing to sustain his subordinate in the face of factional scheming with the army. Lincoln unnecessarily compromised Burnside's position at the head of the Army of the Potomac by allowing Brig. Gen. John Newton, a division commander in the 6th Corps, and Brig. Gen. John Cochrane, one of Newton's brigade commanders, to undermine their chief after Fredericksburg, which only further strengthened the culture of conspiratorial backbiting that already marked the Army of the Potomac's leadership corps. Lincoln learned his lesson and began to clamp down afterward on this sort of insubordination, but this intervention compromised a possibly promising plan of campaign immediately after the battle, while the army remained in reasonably good spirits. This earlier campaign's cancellation led in turn to the infamous "Mud March" of January 1863, which horrid weather sabotaged. That dismal movement along with Burnside's own shortcomings as a logistician and administrator shattered morale in the Army of the Potomac far more severely than did the battle of Fredericksburg.[26]

In an extraordinary testament to organizational immaturity, even the materially well-endowed Union had problems during the Job-like winter of 1862–63 with the most basic tasks of army administration—the feeding, clothing, and paying of soldiers, along with medical treatment for an army's sick list. The fact that Federal logistics still depended in so many ways on the administrative talents of individual commanders certainly did not reflect well on the organization's overall strength. As it turned out,

Burnside's replacement, Joseph Hooker — originally known more for his hard fighting, mastery of army politics, and dubious morality — emerged as an accomplished administrator and logistician.[27]

The Army of Northern Virginia had its own logistical problems, stemming from defects in both transportation and organization. Adequate foodstuffs existed farther south, but the single-track railroad that served Lee's positions along the Rappahannock proved wholly inadequate. Furthermore, the Unionist and northern-born director of the railroad may have deliberately hindered Confederate supply operations. The difficult supply situation contributed to Lee's decision to post Longstreet and two of his corps's divisions, a quarter of his army, to supply-rich southside Virginia and eastern North Carolina, 130 miles away.[28] This gave Hooker a strategic opening to strike at Lee's dispersed army in the spring of 1863.

Despite its distinct logistical inferiority, however, the Army of Northern Virginia benefited from a higher level of strictly military ability than did its Federal opponent. Hooker had to contend with the usual defects of Federal manpower policy. In his case, 37,200 of his 114,442 infantrymen had terms of enlistment due to expire in April, May, and June. The imminent end of the enlistments caused all sorts of problems with discipline and morale. On June 7, roughly a month after the battle, one Federal soldier in the hard-luck 11th Corps complained that "our force here has been considerably weakened by the return home of reg'ts whose term of enlistment had expired." In contrast, Confederate manpower policy distributed conscripts among veteran units, and Lee had stocked his divisions and corps with leaders far superior to Hooker's officer corps. While Hooker possessed such mediocre, or simply awful, corps commanders as Maj. Gen. O. O. Howard or Maj. Gen. John Sedgwick, Lee still had Jackson by his side for this battle. Furthermore, while we can consider Hooker as something of a modernizer with regards to his use of a telegraph for battlefield communications, observation balloons, and a competent intelligence branch, his attitude toward artillery proved neither "modern" nor effective. Hooker reversed the previous tendency in the Army of the Potomac toward artillery concentration and thus deprived himself of adequate artillery coordination by the competent Brig. Gen. Henry Jackson Hunt. In contrast, the Army of Northern Virginia had a far more centralized, effective, and "modern" system of artillery concentration.[29]

Lee also proved more than willing to dig entrenchments. At Chancellorsville, Lee ordered one division commander to build fieldworks, which, in one historian's words, "was the first time, in open operations, that Lee had ordered the construction of field fortifications." This development should not be hailed as somehow revolutionary — Lee had once been called the "King of Spades," and he had always been willing to use entrenchments to maximize the troops available for offensive operations in another sector of the battlefield. Fredericksburg, however, seems to have especially impressed the usefulness of works on both eastern armies. Shortly after that battle, Lee had constructed strong works all along the Rappahannock, and the trend only continued at Chancellorsville. Hooker actually used a more extensive set of fieldworks, which followed Federal practice on the Peninsula and its own hard experience at Fredericksburg. Fieldworks and artillery concentration proved less important in the end, however, than Joe Hooker's catastrophic loss of confidence, the failures of his subordinate commanders, and the Army of Northern Virginia's ever-aggressive élan. The modernity of Hooker's command arrangements proved useless in the face of his physical and moral incapacitation.[30]

Chancellorsville involved few major frontal assaults on earthworks, aside from the special case of Second Fredericksburg, so the battle neither confirms nor refutes the rifle-musket school. Burnside's doomed charges at Fredericksburg showed that a poorly prepared and coordinated assault against well-led troops would fail, but a mid-May engagement during Grant's Vicksburg campaign showed that such circumstances did not always apply. The Federal assault on the strongly fortified Confederate bridgehead at Big Black Bridge on May 17 showed how strong works could be carried, if the attacking troops took adequate preparations and had an edge in morale. The Federals prepared their attack well, including a careful reconnaissance by Col. John J. Mudd, cavalry chief for Maj. Gen. John A. McClernand's 13th Corps. Brig. Gen. Michael K. Lawler used information gained from Mudd's reconnaissance to move his brigade into a meander scar close to the enemy lines that allowed him to shield the brigade from Confederate fire. The subsequent Federal assault benefited from both proper coordination and forethought. For example, Lawler later commented in his report that when asked by one of his colonels if he could storm the position, "Foreseeing that a charge by a single regiment, unsustained by the whole line, against fortifications as formidable as those in his front, could hardly be successful, at the same time I gave my consent to his daring proposition I determined that there should be a simultaneous movement on the part of my whole command."[31]

Two Hoosier regiments in a supporting position deployed skirmishers to distract the Confederate defenders while the assault brigade made its preparations, which included the movement of artillery into supporting positions. Lawler massed his own four regiments into a compact column with a two-regiment front and ordered his men to not open fire until they were virtually at the parapet. The Indianans followed in support from covering woods in the rear. The Federals opened fire somewhat prematurely at the abatis, but like Hood's Texans at Gaines's Mill, they did not allow the volley to compromise their crucial momentum. Fortunately for the Federals, demoralized east Tennessee conscripts stood on the opposite ends of their bayonet points and promptly broke. The litany of Confederate defeats during the Vicksburg campaign preceding this action had also disheartened the bridgehead's other defenders, and the entire Confederate position promptly collapsed. Lawler later commented in his report that "more men were captured by my brigade than I had men in the charge." His division commander, Eugene A. Carr, could later boast with pride that "the charge of Lawler's brigade is one of the most brilliant if not the most brilliant thing of the war."[32]

Grant's army had not yet truly cracked the nut of attacking fieldworks, however. The brilliance of the mobile portions of Grant's Vicksburg campaign deceived him as to how badly demoralized the Confederate troops were in Vicksburg proper. On May 19 he ordered a full-blown assault by all three of his corps with little preparation. Most of the assaulting Federals did not even bother to equip themselves with scaling ladders. The attack failed, and the Confederate garrison continued to rebuild its confidence within the confines of its strong works. Union commanders better prepared the second Federal assault on May 22, but that also proved futile. For this attack, Grant had now moved his troops into position within three hundred to four hundred yards of the Confederate works along with a large amount of supporting artillery. His instructions ordered his troops to hold their fire until they had taken the first line of works. In one positive sign of organizational competence, the army's pioneer troops made sure to provide themselves with the necessary ladders.[33]

Sherman also gave specific instructions to his divisional commanders. He ordered the formation of small storming parties equipped with planks and ladders for bridging and scaling the Confederate works and the use of columns by regiment to try to close on the Confederate position as quickly as possible. Sherman also ordered skirmishers to prepare entrenchments within one hundred yards of the enemy works in order to lay down a covering fire against Confederate artillery and infantry. The 21st Iowa in McClernand's corps also attempted to use suppressive fire from skirmishers to cover its assault. The general assault even used synchronized watches instead of the usual signal cannon, which finally avoided the old problem of acoustic shadows masking aural signals. In one of the more interesting attacks, Brig. Gen. John D. Stevenson of Maj. Gen. James B. McPherson's corps also ordered his troops to hold their fire until they were within the enemy works. The troops actually ended up losing their momentum, but the pause allowed Federal artillery to give them supporting fire. After the bombardment ceased, the troops reinitiated a charge, but in another sign of the still helter-skelter character of Civil War–era staff work, the storming regiment of Irishmen found their scaling ladders too short for their task.[34]

All in all, the Federal assaults proved a dreadful failure, despite the marginal improvements in planning. First of all, Grant struggled to co-ordinate large corps-sized assaults. The brilliant success at the Big Black bridgehead had been due in part to the fact that only two brigades and a few artillery pieces conducted the decisive attack, aided by the demoralization of the Confederates in the threatened sector. Despite Sherman's obvious attempts to think through the later assault, the historian Edwin C. Bearss bluntly calls the performance "pathetic," because Sherman committed only two regiments and a 150-man storming party for the morning attack. He deployed the rest of his troops in three different attacks during that afternoon, which allowed the Confederates to parry each one in detail. McPherson performed no better.[35] It is telling that almost two full years into the war, the finest Federal army of the period commanded by the Union's best generals still could not mount a truly coordinated frontal assault on entrenchments with more than one corps. It was far easier for regular army men to build and train armies to hold strong entrenchments than to take them.

A few months after Grant's failed assaults on the Vicksburg lines, the Army of Northern Virginia would show it suffered from the same sort of organizational weaknesses. Earl Hess, the leading modern authority on Pickett's charge at Gettysburg, has pointed out that this assault was better planned than Lee's Seven Days battles, but less thoroughly organized than Lee's last doomed attack on Fort Stedman during the siege of Petersburg. On the positive side of the ledger, Lee and his commanders attempted to compensate for the strength of the Federal position by using a massive artillery bombardment. Unfortunately, much of the Confederate ordnance overshot the Federal positions, and the inherent limits of

Civil War–era ordnance at long ranges due to problems with fuses and fire control made it of limited use as an offensive arm. Various defects in staff work reminiscent of but not quite equal to the failures of Malvern Hill during the close of the Seven Days did not help matters.[36] Most important, the Federal troops manning Cemetery Ridge possessed strong leadership and élan. Because the Confederates had no advantage in numbers, competence, or cohesion, the advantage naturally went to the defender fighting from a strong position, which made any attack — no matter how well organized — probably doomed.

Nevertheless, there was at least some awareness in the Confederate army, as in their Federal counterpart, that assaults needed to be prepared. Pickett's charge had seen some of those preparations, and the later feud between Longstreet and McLaws over the latter's conduct at Knoxville in November 1863 also shows some recognition of the need to prepare attacks properly. Longstreet accused McLaws of not preparing his assaults at Knoxville with sharpshooters, of neglecting to use picked men in the assault columns, and of not making provisions to either use scaling ladders or strike where such devices were not needed.[37] These were all reasonably high measures of proficiency, which at least some commanders recognized.

Even as late as 1863, however, we should not take for granted the rudimentary level of competence and cohesion displayed in McLaws's and Longstreet's feud. The most important Confederate field army in the western theater, the Army of Tennessee, found that out on November 25, 1863, when Federal troops successfully conducted a frontal assault on a powerful position at Missionary Ridge in Tennessee. What is most striking about the attack's success is its essentially unplanned nature, and how much of it was made possible by the sheer incompetence of the Confederate army's commanders. The Army of Tennessee's engineering staff placed its artillery on the geographic crest of the ridge, which created a large dead zone in front of the defensive line; demoralized local defenders dispersed themselves too widely; and commanders gave confusing orders. Grant, the overall Union commander, made no special tactical provisions to take the position and had ordered a demonstration by George Thomas's Army of the Cumberland to go no farther than the Confederate rifle pits at the base of the ridge. The attack became a general and fantastically successful assault on the position because of genuine confusion over the orders and spontaneous decision making from the assaulting troops, who

MORALE, COHESION, AND COMPETENCE

saw the need to move past the pits, because, in the words of one regimental commander, "they were found insufficient and altogether untenable, to have stopped here would have been annihilation."[38]

For the purposes of historical hindsight, the historian Edward Hagerman rightly emphasizes Sherman's use at Chattanooga of offensive fieldworks designed to allow attacking troops to retain the limited gains of a failed assault, which did foreshadow much of the war's future course. However, the crucial part of the battle occurred not on Sherman's front but at Missionary Ridge, where the rifle-musket and entrenchments did not make the tactical defensive automatically superior. Much of a position's actual strength still depended on questions of morale, cohesion, and competence. The Confederates holding the Missionary Ridge line lacked all three and suffered for it, despite the decidedly helter-skelter nature of the Federal assault. While Hagerman may declare Sherman "as perhaps the most advanced tactical thinker on the use of field fortifications in the Civil War armies" for his various innovations in offensive fieldworks, and may make much of improved Union command and control at the battle, the fact of the matter is that Sherman's and Hooker's more "modern" flanking attacks on Tunnel Hill and Lookout Mountain had far less success than the disorganized and impulsive charge of Thomas's much-maligned Army of the Cumberland.[39] More goes into war than the technical qualities of arms and ordnance — much still depends on the uncontrollable vagaries of Fortune, the ill-defined courage of the contending men-at-arms, and the basic competence of the leaders on hand.

CHAPTER NINE

Decisions East and West

The End of the Civil War

★ ★ ★

The Union armies finally brought the Civil War to a close during the 1864 and 1865 campaigning seasons, when Federal forces found a way to break the general military equilibrium between themselves and Confederate field forces. Even now, the Army of the Potomac continued to struggle to match its Confederate opponent, but Grant's entrapment of Lee in a siege made the matter moot. Historians have made much of Federal war planning for these last campaigns, seeing in them a "strategy of exhaustion" as the key to Federal victory, but the actual campaigns do not quite fit such broad-brush strokes.

The historians Herman Hattaway and Archer Jones have described Grant's strategic planning during the winter of 1863–64 as designed to defeat the Confederacy through attacks on vital logistical infrastructure, especially railroads and centers of munitions manufacture. Their treatment of Federal strategic planning that winter deserves much commendation, but like so many treatments of Civil War "strategy," it overstates the level of intellectual abstraction at which actual policymakers operated. Indeed, both historians admit that Grant made no explicit reference to a strategy of exhaustion in his war planning, but their commitment to abstract concepts like turning movements and the tactical superiority of the entrenched defensive allows them to read into Grant's plans ideas that he did not necessarily share.[1]

In the first place, Hattaway and Jones exaggerate Grant's belief in the powers of the tactical defensive. To use one example, they argue that, with regard to Sherman's Meridian expedition in February 1864, Grant, "confident of the power of the defense, felt no alarm, for 'with a man like Sherman to command[,] he is in no great danger' from a superior concentration." The cited document in the *Official Records* simply does not support the statement that the confidence Grant expressed here stemmed from his belief in the power of the tactical defensive. It sustains only the portion of Grant's letter the two authors quote, which expresses a confidence in Sherman's command abilities. Grant was not expressing confidence in the supposed invulnerability of Civil War armies when fighting on the defensive; instead, he was referring to his good friend Sherman's competence.[2]

Hagerman also assumes the superiority and significance of the tactical defensive, but unlike Hattaway and Jones, he argues that Grant's Overland campaign had at its base a strategy of attrition designed to overcome the problem of the entrenched defensive by gradually bleeding the Army of Northern Virginia to death. This interpretation ignores the fact that Grant throughout the entire campaign constantly attempted to turn Lee's army, rather than simply throw troops against entrenched Confederates in frontal assaults. Furthermore, Grant's own reference to attrition in his summary report on operations from 1865, "to hammer continuously against the armed force of the enemy and his resources, until by mere attrition, if in no other way," saw attrition as a method of last resort, as opposed to Grant's preferred technique. Hagerman struck closer to the mark when he surmised that "Grant did not have a systematic tactical outlook, but rather acted according to an appraisal of each situation as it arose, blending an erratic mixture of common sense about the new conditions of warfare with a predisposition to traditional tactics." Unfortunately, Hagerman makes an unsupported leap from this eminently sensible analysis of Grant's conduct of the Overland campaign to the idea that Grant had an implicit strategy of attrition.[3]

Both interpretations of Grant's strategic attitude understate the importance of Grant's tactical flexibility. Grant had no problem in principle with frontal assaults, but the Vicksburg campaign showed no special adherence to a strategy of attrition. Hattaway and Jones also make the reasonable point that Grant's overall strategic planning for the entire campaign never assumed that he would have to destroy Lee's army in battle without significant assistance from other Federal field armies. Nevertheless, Grant stood ready to bludgeon to death his opponent if he believed that he could derive a positive end from it. Both historians point out that Grant preferred a raiding strategy in Virginia, but it is also clear that Grant could abandon those methods if necessary.[4]

Furthermore, with regard to the whole issue of the tactical defensive, Grant never revealed any special interest in tactical questions. In his memoirs, the Union's greatest general described Hardee's tactics — the linchpin of the whole old army tactical system adopted in the 1850s after so much effort—as "nothing more than common sense and the progress of the age applied to Scott's system. The commands were abbreviated and the movement expedited." He was decidedly unimpressed with the new regulations, dryly commentating that while drilling his regiment on a town common, "if I attempted to follow the lesson I had studied I would have to clear away some of the houses and garden fences to make room." He more or less ignored the manual, adopting only its more fluid practice of giving commands, which was adequate to fulfill the basic tactical task of taking "my regiment where I wanted it to go and carry it around all obstacles." In an almost magnificent statement of Grant's indifference to book learning, and why historians should not overstate its importance, Grant concluded his discussion of Hardee's tactics with the statement that "I do not believe that the officers of the regiment ever discovered that I had never studied the tactics that I used."[5]

Indeed, as an army commander, Grant no longer held a position of any tactical responsibility. Focusing on Grant's nonexistent respect for the tactical defensive, leading to a "strategy of exhaustion," obscures the simplicity that helped make Grant such an effective planner. Grant's original strategy for Virginia clearly showed a preference for attacking Confederate logistics through a raid into southeastern Virginia, but the general was less interested in avoiding fighting per se than forcing a fight on ground of his choosing, as opposed to the usual confines of northern Virginia. Historians might better emphasize Grant's stated desire that winter to maintain the strategic initiative. Arguing for his original raiding strategy, he wrote, "It would draw the enemy from campaigns of their own choosing, and for which they are prepared, to new lines of operations never expected to become necessary." While contemplating circumstances in East Tennessee before he became general-in-chief, Grant declared to Halleck that he wanted "to be able to select my own campaign in the spring instead of having the enemy dictate it for me." Focusing on Grant's almost single-minded concern with the strategic initiative also helps tie together the diverse methods he used during the last year of campaigning in Virginia, which included frontal assaults, flanking maneuvers, cavalry raids, an unorthodox mine, and regular siege tactics.[6]

Although Grant may not have generally concerned himself with implementing a deliberate "strategy of attrition," the issue did have some play during the Civil War. William O. Stoddard, one of Lincoln's secretaries, reported after Fredericksburg that "we lost fifty per cent more men

179

★

than did the enemy, and yet there is sense in the awful arithmetic propounded by Mr. Lincoln. He says that if the same battle were to be fought over again, every day, through a week of days, with the same relative result, the army under Lee would be wiped out to its last man, the Army of the Potomac would still be a mighty host, the war would be over, the Confederacy gone. . . . No general yet found can face the arithmetic, but the end of the war will be at hand when he shall be discovered." Grant himself cited attrition as one post facto justification for his campaign's heavy losses in his official report at the end of the war.[7]

Historians have tended to overemphasize this after-the-fact justification, ignoring the crucial qualifier "if in no other way" that pointed to Grant's use of multiple Federal armies and maneuver even during the Overland campaign itself. Nevertheless, Grant's comments do at least show that the concept of attrition had its roots in wartime discussions. Indeed, there were also Confederate references to the idea; one Confederate officer during the Overland campaign believed that a strategy of attrition would be fatal to the Army of Northern Virginia, because "if it required the loss of twenty-five thousand to rob us of six thousand [Grant] was doing a wise thing for we yield our loss from an irreplaceable penury, he from super-abundance."[8]

Although Grant himself did not seem to have a real intellectual commitment to these sorts of strategic abstractions, he did have a very practical knowledge of politics, which did heavily influence his strategic plans. He proved willing to accommodate Lincoln's political needs when appointing commanders to important posts of responsibility.[9] Furthermore, as with every other campaign in the crucial Virginia theater, questions of strategy and leadership became wrapped up in partisan controversy.

While Republicans had called for more aggressive action and decisive victories during McClellan's tenure in command, many now called for patience with regards to Grant. Previously cautious Democratic papers now demanded the Lincoln administration prove itself with a swift victory in a presidential election year. The debates, however, should not be reduced entirely to questions of partisanship. One historian, Brooks D. Simpson, cites partisanship as the primary motivation behind Democratic concerns that the Lincoln administration would micromanage the new lieutenant general's campaign, but the Democratic press did display some nonpartisan consistency on this point.[10]

Even the extraordinarily pro-McClellan *New York World* made no attempt to cast aspersion on Grant's leadership during the worst moments of the Overland campaign. In August, after the Crater disaster, the *World* accused Radical Republicans and the Lincoln administration of trying "to make him [Grant] the scapegoat of the negro arming policy of the administration, and the imbecility of LINCOLN." Grant, because of his generally apolitical manner, reaped some political benefits by earning the respect of administration opponents, who saw him as the same sort of apolitical professional they adored in McClellan, as opposed to a transparently political general such as Maj. Gen. Nathaniel P. Banks or Maj. Gen. Benjamin F. Butler. Indeed, Grant had good relations with James Gordon Bennett's generally antiadministration and anti-Radical, but also anti-Copperhead *New York Herald*. Grant, who gave the Radicals the aggressive war they had so desired, also later became a target of some of the Radicals' ire. In February 1865 the Joint Committee called him to testify before it during an investigation into Butler's bungled military operations the previous December against Fort Fisher, which guarded the Confederacy's last port at Wilmington. George Julian was so dissatisfied with Grant's criticism of Butler that he even suspected him of being drunk during his testimony. It was an extraordinary accusation to make, even in a private diary.[11]

Nevertheless, Grant's unwillingness to involve himself in the same sort of political meddling as McClellan also earned him some points of respect among the Radicals. Some Radicals actually preferred a Grant presidency in August 1864 rather than another term for Lincoln, whom they blamed more than anyone else for the war's grinding stalemate. Bennett, from an entirely different political perspective, had called for a Grant presidency beginning in December 1863. Grant would have none of this speculation, thankfully, and wrote a letter to Elihu Washburne on August 16, 1864, in which he declared his support for the current commander in chief.[12] Grant's actions compared well to McClellan's open politicking in opposition to the administration while he wore the uniform. Furthermore, unlike the Democratic candidate for the presidency, Grant never presumed to lecture his civilian superiors on political questions.

Grant's unwillingness to scheme for political advantage like so many of his colleagues, especially those who had served in the politically charged atmosphere of the Army of the Potomac, may have shielded him from wartime criticism, but it did little to help manage the unreasonable expectations of the northern public. For all its partisan differences and bickering, the northern press shared a profound optimism at the beginning of the summer campaigns. When actual events dashed quick expectations of victory, the Lincoln administration came under heavy fire from all sectors of the political spectrum — Republican and Democratic.

It was irrelevant, if ironic, that Grant still had the upper hand in military terms, even after the beginning of the grinding siege of Petersburg in late June 1864. Lee himself had some idea of his desperate situation. Earlier that month he had told Lt. Gen. Jubal Early, "We must destroy this army of Grant's before he gets to [the] James River. If he gets there, it will become a siege, and then it will be a mere question of time." On June 21, after the siege of Petersburg had begun, Lee lamented to Davis that "I hope your Exc^y will put no reliance in what I can do individually, for I feel that will be very little. The enemy has a strong position, & is able to deal us more injury than from any other point he has ever taken. Still, we must try & defeat them. I fear he will not attack us but advance by regular approaches. He is so situated that I cannot attack him."[13]

Indeed, the historian Brooks Simpson, in a vigorous defense of Grant's conduct, has held northern public opinion responsible for its own near collapse of morale during the summer of 1864, on the grounds that its own inflated expectations could not possibly be fulfilled. Hattaway and Jones also write that "public opinion forced Grant into more of a frontal combat with Lee than he desired. . . . The battles resulted in disillusionment, for the victories cost so many lives that they lost their glamour and, apparently, produced little effect in winning the war. When the public and its leaders no longer demanded battles and victories, they had at last, to a degree, learned what their generals had known all along."[14] Professional military historians are right to criticize northern public opinion for simple ignorance.

Even regular army officers without Democratic sympathies had consistently criticized public ignorance of military affairs. Maj. Gen. Samuel R. Curtis in the western theater, who became something of a radical during his time in Missouri between September 1862 and May 1863, could bitterly reproach on September 4, 1862, the abuse unfairly heaped on generals in his view: "Our press everywhere seems to dote on detraction. Our Generals are much embarrassed and I think the army is much impaired by the violence and vindictive style manifested towards them. Every accident or oversight every delay or check is charged on some General who is greedily devoured by craven cowardly scriblers [sic]. Confidence and courage are shaken or destroyed. It is Mexican style. Whenever they were unfortunate some General was shot to satisfy a foolish sensibility." Commenting on the early portions of Grant's siege of Vicksburg, Curtis grumbled that "the public expectation is always far ahead of reason and reality. The hope of miracles seems still prevalent." Curtis, a West Pointer who had left the old army after only a year of service in 1832, made these comments, while at the same time denouncing regular army prejudice against volunteers.[15]

Indeed, in a scholarly field so marked by adherence to democratic pieties, a frank criticism of even "democratic" public opinion can be profoundly refreshing. Nevertheless, creating a sharp conflict between ignorant politicians wedded to anachronistic notions of decisive battle and modern generals dedicated to a complicated "strategy of exhaustion" obscures the fact that Grant's excellent strategic plans could have — indeed, *should* have — led to a *decisive* victory in the eastern theater by the end of the summer. A series of entirely avoidable organizational failures in the Army of the Potomac, along with some plain bad luck, transformed the Overland campaign into an indecisive war of posts, as opposed to irreversible forces rooted in the rifle-musket, easily articulated tactical formations, and fieldworks.

On the tactical and strategic levels, various missed opportunities for success during the campaign call into question the systemic indecisiveness of Civil War combat during this period. For example, at the battle of the Wilderness, Maj. Gen. Philip H. Sheridan and Brig. Gen. James Harrison Wilson ill-served Grant's larger campaign by mismanaging the Army of the Potomac's cavalry force. That failure caused Hancock to retain a portion of his corps as a reserve to foil a Confederate surprise on his flank — a nonexistent threat that he could have ignored if the cavalry had more effectively conducted its screening and reconnaissance duties. The Union cavalry would be even more derelict at Spotsylvania, although Grant is partly to blame for these problems.[16] As a whole, Grant allowed his cavalry during the Overland campaign to neglect its screening and reconnaissance functions. That organizational decision mostly stemmed from Grant's loyalties to Sheridan, and Meade's animosity toward the latter, as opposed to the rifle-musket and entrenchments.

A more spectacular failure at Spotsylvania, however, was Col. Emory Upton's unsupported breakthrough of the Confederate lines at Doles's Salient. Upton was in many ways the quintessential West Point professional, a staunch disciplinarian described by one of his men as "deeply impressed with the seriousness of warfare," and one who "had mastered its science." Given a brigade's worth (around five thousand men) of picked troops, he used a special assault formation where only the lead regiments capped their muskets. He made sure to impress upon his men "not to fire a shot, cheer or yell, until we struck their works." Furthermore, Upton gave each regiment in the formation a specific task to complete during the attack, whether it be enfilading fire on the flanks, capturing a Confederate battery, or acting as reserves. He also ensured that his subordinates knew their tasks and that the regimental commanders knew the ground. The point of attack had also been chosen with care; woods and a ravine allowed Upton's force to mass unmolested within a relatively short distance of the Confederate works. A preparatory artillery bombardment also supported the attack, and Federal skirmishers had driven out Confederate pickets from the woods to mask Upton's preparations.[17]

Upton also deployed the regiments in four successive lines of three regiments each. He probably hoped to compensate for the natural disintegrating effects of most linear assaults during the Civil War. The Prussian army observer, Justus Scheibert, had a useful description of this process, writing after the war that "skirmishers' fire prepared the attack. The nearer to the enemy, the more faulty the lines and the more ragged the first until it crumbled and mixed with the skirmishers. Forward went this muddle leading the wavy rest. Finally the mass obtruded upon the point of attack. . . . In sum it had been a division neatly drawn up. Now its units, anything but neat, vaguely coherent, resembled a swarm of skirmishers. . . . Of course, however brilliant the success, they could seldom follow through. Such a mass can be but badly led."[18] Scheibert also emphasized how the scarcity of Confederate numbers hindered exploitation of local successes, but Federal superiority on that score went to naught if the surplus troops were not immediately available to support engaged units.

Not everything in the assault went according to plan. Upton had ordered the men to even refrain from shouting during the attack, probably in an effort to maintain discipline during the march, just as Confederate officers at Gaines's Mill had tried to make their charge in a controlled cadence. The men of the 121st New York could not restrain themselves from yelling as they charged, and some even broke fire discipline. Also, the fourth reserve line proved unable to wait and joined in the charge prematurely.[19] However, just as at Gaines's Mill, these minor lapses in discipline had no real significance; the attack scored a spectacular local success, not because everything went according to plan (an impossible occurrence in battle), but because responsible commanders had planned *enough* to obtain success.

Unfortunately, poor staff work and general confusion prevented the supporting division from exploiting Upton's breakthrough. In a tragi-comedy of errors, the young colonel's supports in Brig. Gen. Gershom Mott's division were not told of a change in the time of attack, but even if they had been properly informed, the army high command had given muddled and confusing orders to Mott. Upton, with good planning, a well-considered use of shock tactics, and only a single brigade, had broken for a moment the supposedly ironclad tactical stalemate created by the rifle-musket and fieldworks, but his efforts went to naught because of organi-zational failures at the division, corps, and army levels of command.

Indeed, the same sorts of problems would afflict the more famous as-sault of the 2nd Corps on the whole Mule Shoe Salient two days later, which had been inspired by Upton's efforts. In the words of one 6th Corps veteran, Upton's attack "was a better planned and better executed assault than that of the Second Corps on May 12th." That later attack, while ini-tially successful, also floundered on failures in larger unit coordination and exploitation. After the war, Brig Gen. Francis Barlow, a 2nd Corps division commander, claimed that he had so little information on the Con-federate position the evening before the attack that he exclaimed to one staff officer, "For Heaven's sake, at least, face us in the right direction, so that we shall not march away from the enemy, and have to go round the world and come up in their rear." Using hindsight, Barlow also wrote that the Federal assault should also have made plans for units to sweep down the Confederate left flank after the initial breakthrough had been made. Instead, the Federal attack became disordered by a chaotic introduction of fresh troops in a constrained space with limited planning and fore-thought.[20] The superior planning and preparation behind Upton's attack stemmed in large part from its much smaller size and scope, which could be managed by a single talented officer.

Indeed, the historian Gordon Rhea has argued that even Grant's much-criticized attacks at Cold Harbor should be primarily criticized for errors in execution, as opposed to their larger strategic rationale. Grant had good reasons for attacking—his plausible judgment that Lee's army had lost much of its panache from the severe losses of the campaign, intel-ligence about Lee's poor health, and the political costs of accepting a stale-mate. But instead of finding a weak point and focusing the attack on that point, with proper preparations like those used in Upton's effort at Doles's Salient, Grant ordered an attack along the entire Federal front—in the words of one contemporary critic, "to charge along the whole length of the lines, some seven miles or more in length, hit or miss." Such a wide-front assault only invited the problems of large-unit coordination that bedeviled Civil War military operations.[21]

We should not confuse these examples of missed opportunities for decisive Union victory during the Overland campaign with some historians' counterfactual speculations about the Army of Northern Virginia — whether it be Lt. Gen. Richard S. Ewell's failure to take Cemetery Hill on the first day at Gettysburg, missed Confederate opportunities at the Wilderness, the loss of Lee's movement orders during the Antietam campaign, Jackson's lethargy during the Seven Days, or various other moments where historians have created scenarios for final Confederate victory. These counterfactuals have varying degrees of plausibility, but the fact remains that the Army of Northern Virginia's weaker material position usually made it more vulnerable to the inherent confusion and uncertainties of war. In other words, the Confederacy needed many more contingent factors to align in its favor to achieve an annihilation of the Army of the Potomac than the other way around.[22]

The Army of the Potomac did not need such dramatic good fortune to make the most of its own opportunities. All McClellan and Hooker had to do during the Seven Days and Chancellorsville, respectively, was hold their ground to deprive Lee of great victories, while McClellan could have and should have obliterated the Army of Northern Virginia at Antietam by simply launching an attack with his reserves on September 18. The Army of the Potomac's advantages in numbers and logistical support, combined with the more than adequate fighting power of its rank and file, gave it opportunities for victory unavailable to the Army of Northern Virginia. This material superiority was even more marked by the spring of 1864, with Lee's army maintaining much of its characteristic élan but its logistical situation further deteriorating.

Unfortunately, despite its material endowments, the Army of the Potomac lacked a strong cadre of corps, division, and brigade commanders of comparable talent to Lee's famous lieutenants. Even as talented an army commander as Grant needed a strong cohort of subordinate commanders to be successful. Although the presence of fieldworks did exponentially increase the power of the tactical defensive during the Overland campaign, the Army of the Potomac had the numbers and material support necessary to overcome that defensive advantage, if properly commanded and led. The dreadful losses during the campaign among the Federal rank and file (fifty-five thousand casualties) show more than enough fighting spirit among the army's humblest ranks, while Grant's performance at the army's top, though far from perfect, surpassed every one of his predecessors and proved equal to Lee's leadership. Unfortunately, the leadership ranks of the Federal eastern army continued to compare poorly to the Army of Northern Virginia. There is a grim significance for the army in the historian Stephen Taaffe's assessment that only a small minority of corps commanders in the Army of the Potomac attained their posts through meritorious service on the battlefield.[23]

As an organization, the Army of the Potomac had inherited from its original founder and organizer an undue caution and respect for the Army of Northern Virginia, strengthened by a long string of miserable defeats and close victories. The historian John Hennessy has commented that "most of the generals left to lead the Army of the Potomac in 1864 possessed little personal flair and only moderate combat records." Another historian, Stephen Sears, has remarked that "George McClellan, as it were, fathered the Army of the Potomac, and while his command of it ceased before the war reached its halfway point, his influence on its high command, for good or ill, lasted through to Appomattox." McClellan's powerful and long-standing legacy of caution and fractious contention also created an almost parochial sense of esprit de corps that hindered Grant's command and control of the eastern army. Even a West Point–trained professional such as Grant had to face the same sort of resentment Pope (another West Pointer) had received after his notorious references to western military success.[24] This sense of exclusive identity made it difficult for Grant to make the Army of the Potomac as effective an instrument of his will as the western armies he had commanded.

This absence of a strong cohort of corps and division commanders in the Army of the Potomac contributed as much to the Overland campaign's stalemate as did the increasing power of fieldworks. An unwieldy command structure where Grant had to be both the field commander of the Army of the Potomac and general-in-chief at the same time compounded problems. The initial dual-command relationship for the Army of the Potomac, with Grant as general-in-chief and Meade still in nominal command of the field army, caused problems during the Overland campaign and inhibited the unity of command and decision so vital to military efficiency.[25] Grant's ability to coordinate the entire Federal war effort while managing the Army of the Potomac at the same time testifies as much to his abilities as it does to Federal organizational failings.

Larger Federal strategic failures during the spring and summer of 1864 cast even more doubt on the modernity school's belief in the almost insuperable significance of field fortifications. All the command defects of the Army of the Potomac and all the earthworks of the Overland campaign would have become irrelevant if the Union had simply placed competent commanders at the heads of all the major Federal expeditions Grant had laid out in his larger strategy. As it turned out, only Sherman pulled his own weight on his avenue of advance, which put unplanned and unnecessary pressure on these two army commanders to bring the war to an end on their own. Butler botched his opportunity to take Richmond that summer, while Banks had deprived Sherman of a supporting expedition on Mobile by wasting his army in a badly handled sideshow on the Red River in Louisiana and Arkansas during the late spring. Maj. Gen. Franz Sigel and Maj. Gen. David Hunter also failed to press the Confederates in the Valley.

Even the grinding siege of Petersburg and Richmond, after the end of mobile warfare in Virginia, had one brilliant and ultimately squandered opportunity for relatively speedy success. At 4:46 a.m. on July 30, a massive mine dug by a regiment of Pennsylvania coal miners exploded under a section of the Confederate works manned by a regiment of South Carolinians. The explosion rent a huge hole in the Confederate line, which presented an opportunity the Army of the Potomac's high command promptly botched. For our own purposes, determining personal responsibility for the attack's failure is less important than listing the large systemic problems it revealed in the Army of the Potomac.[26]

Meade had become so suspicious of political criticism of his conduct that fears of a political backlash in the case of failure led him in part to alter Burnside's original plan of using Brig. Gen. Edward Ferraro's division of black troops as the lead assault unit. Both Meade and Grant feared that they would be accused of callous indifference to the slaughter of African American troops if the attack miscarried. Unfortunately, Ferraro's fresh African American division had more chances for success than the spent white units in the 9th Corps. Furthermore, the new lead division commander, Brig. Gen. James H. Ledlie, proved wholly incompetent, while friction between Meade and Burnside precluded proper coordination of Burnside's 9th Corps with the neighboring 5th and 18th Corps.[27]

The Army of the Potomac also still suffered from the chronic civil-military dysfunction of McClellan's tenure in command. Civil-military tensions between Little Mac's former command and Radical Republican politicians had long helped nurture a sense of alienated martyrdom in much of the eastern army's officer corps. By the winter of 1863 and 1864, the most outspoken conservative generals had been purged. Remaining Democrats such as Meade and Hancock, a shadow of his former self as commander of the 2nd Corps because of a serious Gettysburg wound, survived by virtue of their silence, but lingering resentments would never entirely disappear. Even with the relatively apolitical Meade in command, tensions remained, with much of the blame falling on civilian politicians. For example, even after Meade's victory at Gettysburg, many Radicals hoped to restore Hooker to his former command. Whatever opportunities Meade may or may not have had after the battle, it is at least safe to say that McClellan's failure to deal a decisive blow to Lee at Antietam should not be compared to Meade's much more difficult and uncertain situation after Gettysburg.[28]

The civil-military rift among the rank and file in the Army of the Potomac proved less severe, especially with the acquiescence of white troops to both emancipation and the enrollment of African Americans into the Union armies. Indeed, even during the bitter winter of 1862–63, when emancipation faced much higher levels of hostility, the army had directed its animus as much at politicians in general as at the Radical Republicans so ferociously disliked by the McClellanite officer corps. This sort of general contempt for a home front perceived as unsupportive and even treasonous led to fiercely hostile attitudes toward any hint of Copperhead sentiment in the North.[29] However, even though the Army of the Potomac's intense hostility toward northern peace Democrats eased tensions with Radical Republicans, it still revealed a worrisome gap between the opinions of the northern public and its most important field army. It did not help matters that the old army had nurtured this sort of disaffection during the entire antebellum period and that the Continental army back during the Revolution had harbored similar feelings of alienation.

Furthermore, clashes between the Union army's generals and politicians did not confine themselves to the eastern theater. In the West, Grant had had to struggle with the political ambition of John A. McClernand, who commanded the 13th Corps and vexed Grant throughout most of the Vicksburg campaign until his relief in late May, while Sherman showed himself at best indifferent and at worst contemptuous of the supposedly sacred principle of civilian control. Nevertheless, civil-military tensions in the western armies never matched the Army of the Potomac's level of dysfunction.[30]

In the Confederacy, Lee's titanic reputation immunized him from political pressure, but the Army of the Tennessee had its own problems with generals scheming for political advantage and influence. As a whole, however, Confederate civil-military relations caused fewer problems for its war effort, especially after Lee's rise to prominence after the Seven Days.[31]

Lee's record of battlefield success, combined with his strong working relationship with Jefferson Davis, gave the Confederate war effort in its most important theater a unity of purpose at the highest levels of political and military leadership. Despite the presence of an antiadministration faction that advocated allocating resources to the western theater, the Confederacy for the most part did not have the same sharp divisions over basic war aims that so afflicted the Union cause. Most Confederates desired some form of independence, a goal that was reasonably clear to all parties concerned, and Davis never had to compromise military ends for the sake of political coalition building to the same degree as Lincoln.

Lincoln, in a much more difficult political situation than Davis, had such a negative experience with the almost-inveterate caution of McClellan that he sometimes moved to the opposite extreme of excessive aggressiveness.[32] He, along with much of the rest of his administration, reacted very badly to Meade's supposed "failure" to destroy Lee after Gettysburg. His musings on a strategy of attrition after Fredericksburg do little credit to his usually formidable intellect — the Union certainly had more men to lose, but northern supplies of manpower and political will were hardly unlimited. Most importantly, Lincoln's desire for a quick and decisive end to the war, while juggling various politically motivated compromises on military policy, helped sustain the unfortunate Federal practice of raising new regiments instead of refilling existing ones, a relatively porous draft (as compared to Confederate conscription), and continued support of political generals in posts of responsibility. Despite Lincoln's own Job-like patience and willingness to trust and sustain generals like Grant, who had enough sense to respect Lincoln's political authority, the commander in chief bears some responsibility for the impatient political environment that nearly compromised even Grant's substantial military abilities.

Grant had suffered McClernand's difficult presence and had adopted a high-risk strategy at Vicksburg for political appearances, but it was during his planning for the 1864 campaigns that he was fully exposed to the political pressures of the eastern theater. When he realized the political importance of defeating Lee in open battle, he scrapped his original plan for a raid on Confederate logistics in southeastern Virginia and North Carolina. He acquiesced to the appointment of political generals of questionable competence to important commands in his larger strategy of coordinated military movements, although Grant himself deserves some blame for misjudging Butler's abilities. In bowing to public desire for a decisive end to the war, Grant used methods that ended up prolonging the war even further and endangered the Lincoln administration's chances for reelection. The administration's insistence that Lee's army be the objective point of any campaign in Virginia helped prevent Grant from exploiting Richmond's logistical and political importance to defeat Lee through maneuver and guile rather than hard fighting.[33]

War may be a preeminently political phenomenon, but politics is a question of means as well as ends. Politics distended military means to such an extent during the winter and spring of 1864 that military failure came perilously close to triggering political defeat for the Lincoln administration. The Union high command sacrificed military efficiency for short-term political gains, instead of incurring short-term political costs for the sake of a surer prospect for victory. Carr had been terribly prophetic after the battle of Wilson's Creek in 1861 when, with regards to Franz Sigel, the commander who failed Grant in the Valley, he wrote that the "adm[inistration] makes a terrible mistake in appointing its generals."[34] Or, to use another example, if Lincoln had replaced Banks with a more competent but less well-connected officer to conduct a simultaneous expedition against Mobile, Sherman might have taken Atlanta long before September and given northern morale a crucial boost during the grinding Overland campaign. The political costs of an earlier relief of Banks would have far more important dividends in actual military results. Although individual political and military leaders made these missteps, the northern polity as a whole still deserves much of the blame. Grant and Lincoln gave the "people" what they wanted during the Overland campaign — aggressive battles and generals respectful of political prerogatives. We can hardly blame post facto buyers' remorse entirely on solicitous Federal leaders.

Fortunately for the Union, although certainly not for the Confederacy, Sherman redeemed the stalemate in Virginia by a well-conducted and ultimately successful campaign against Atlanta. At the very least, this saved the Lincoln administration's prospects,[35] although an incoming McClellan administration might actually have seen the war through, especially because Grant's siege of Petersburg and Richmond looked much like what he himself had planned on the Peninsula. Nevertheless, a McClellan administration, combined with Democratic majorities in Congress, at the very least would have drastically altered the terms of Reconstruction, and perhaps even have threatened the finality of emancipation.

Regardless of the political consequences, Sherman's elaborate duel with Johnston, whereby both armies used heavy field entrenchments and avoided decisive battle for the most part, corresponds most closely to the modernization school's heavy emphasis on the indecisiveness of Civil War battle. Sherman had displayed his tactical creativity during the early assaults at Vicksburg, and his campaign against Johnston was far more tactically consistent than Grant's fluid and improvised methods during the Overland campaign. Aside from the isolated assault at Kennesaw Mountain, Sherman relied almost entirely on flanking maneuvers to advance on Atlanta. Johnston's characteristic caution abetted this strategy and led to his replacement by John Bell Hood, who failed in his efforts to use offensive attacks to relieve Atlanta. The Atlanta campaign and the scythe of destruction Sherman subsequently wielded during his famous marches through Georgia and the Carolinas, with their open attacks on southern society as a whole, correspond far more closely to the basic tenets of the modernization school than any other set of campaigns during the Civil War. Nevertheless, not too much should be made of the "modernity" of the March to the Sea. Armies had long lived off the land, and many had previously targeted civilian society. Despite the ruthlessness of his rhetoric, recent scholarship has shown that Sherman's methods should not be compared with the completely unrestrained attacks on civilians associated with "Total War." Sherman's famous expeditions through Georgia and the Carolinas may not even have had the profoundly depressing effect on southern civilians' morale he intended.[36]

We cannot, however, overstate the military significance of Sherman's logistical apparatus during and after the Atlanta campaign, which allowed Sherman to respond to Hood's attempt to cut his communications with Tennessee by simply mounting an expedition through Georgia. Sherman's supply system proved able to stockpile the necessary military stores in Atlanta that Federal troops could not acquire through foraging, including such important supplies as clothing, specialized equipage, and ordnance. This sort-of stockpiling had previously required secure waterborne lines of communication, which were not available at Atlanta, but Sherman's railroad crews managed to attain a high-enough level of proficiency with regard to protecting, repairing, and maintaining Sherman's one-track railway that they no longer required a secure waterway. That same railway had also sustained Sherman's original march on Atlanta. The Army of the Potomac's perfection of its own supply situation during the winter of 1863 and 1864 impresses us less because of the shorter distances involved, but compared to Burnside's mismanagement of the issue the previous winter, the eastern army had clearly made great strides in its administrative and logistical efficiency.[37]

In addition to the logistical damage wreaked by Sherman, Grant's reasonably conventional siege methods also deserve credit for the final Federal victory. Lee's own siege lines could only grow increasingly thin as Grant gradually spread his lines of investment westward toward the railway lines that kept Lee's army provisioned. Both the Union and Confederate armies in the siege lines became increasingly worn down, although the Confederates suffered more grievously from their increasingly desperate logistical situation, caused in part by a collapse of the Confederate railway system. Even among the far better provisioned Federals, however, Humphreys wrote in a letter dated September 6, 1864 that, "at the beginning of this campaign, the command of the Second, Fifth, or Sixth Corps was something to desire; each was a splendid corps. It is not so any longer; their losses have stripped them of their best officers and best men and the additions made to them are of very, very inferior quality. The effect of such continuous fighting and such excessive fatigue is everywhere visible in depressing the spirit of the men."[38] Grant continued to make various attempts at breaking the Confederate lines, while Lee managed to parry each blow until the final campaigns of the following spring.

All Grant really needed was enough competence and persistence to push the siege to its natural conclusion. Both contending armies during the siege mastered the art of static warfare — harassing and wearing down one another with constant sniping, picket forays, and artillery bombardments. This represented a culmination of the constant entrenching and skirmishing of the Overland campaign. The rifle-musket's increased accuracy became especially useful in these sorts of operations. Indeed, even during more mobile operations, specialist sharpshooter units were a feature of Civil War armies later in the war. This use of specialist units had ample precedent in the American light-infantry tradition. Sniping during siege operations also had earlier precedent; McLaws had recognized the importance of rifle-muskets in siege operations as early as the siege of Yorktown in the spring of 1862.[39]

The proximity of works and the static nature of operations during the siege accentuated the importance of sharpshooting. Humphreys thought it noteworthy that some of the 2nd Corps's trench lines before Petersburg in the fall of 1864 stood as close as two hundred yards from the Confederate works. During the new phase of continuous operations that began in the spring of 1864, opposing armies would regularly face each other separated by such short distances. If we take two hundred yards as a rough minimum distance between two trench lines, then that distance by itself already exceeds by far the effective range of a smoothbore for sniping (fifty yards).[40] The increased use of fieldworks led to the growing importance of the rifle-musket's increased accuracy, but this does not mean that that increased accuracy had led to the fieldworks in the first place.

Both armies even managed to improve their proficiency in assault tactics. During the Army of Northern Virginia's last offensive action of any significance, the attack on Fort Stedman in late March 1865, Maj. John B. Gordon's picked assault force actually scored some early local successes. The Confederates did their best to achieve tactical surprise, using picked men to clear away obstructions and infiltrate the Federal pickets. Like the assault plans of Upton at Spotsylvania and Burnside at the Crater, supporting Confederate troops received orders to widen the prospective breach in the Federal lines by fanning out along the captured trenches. Once again, following a technique going at least as far back as C. F. Smith at Fort Donelson, some of the lead Confederate troops made their assaults with unloaded muskets. Despite the real success of Gordon's elaborate preparations and plans, the wretched condition of his troops hampered the attacks. Some units could not resist plundering captured Federal camps for supplies, reminiscent of the early-war failures of discipline among Federal troops at Belmont and Confederate soldiers at Shiloh. While those troops had been demoralized by inadequate seasoning and training, these Confederates suffered from months of grinding siege operations.[41]

The attack proved strategically barren, however. After Petersburg's eventual evacuation, Grant conducted a masterful pursuit of Lee where he managed to capture an entire opposing field army, a nearly unique feat for the war. A well-conducted pursuit, much hard marching, and the rise of mobile cavalry armed with repeating arms helped make this achievement possible. The Federal cavalry after Gettysburg, and earlier in the western theater, had evolved into a force that used its horses for greater mobility but frequently fought on foot, although saber charges remained in use. When combined with the Spencer repeater, these new dragoon tactics created a potent offensive striking force for the Union army. Brig. Gen. James Harrison Wilson made the Spencer carbine, a breech-loading repeater with a rate of fire two-to-three times greater than previous cavalry arms, the standard Federal cavalry arm in 1864. The heavy logistical demands of cavalry horses remained a limiting factor on their effectiveness, however, and these reforms came about too late in the war to have a decisive effect.[42] After all, the great failing of the Union cavalry in the Overland campaign was its failure to competently conduct screening and reconnaissance functions (Sheridan *chose* to neglect his task) that predated the rise of Spencer-armed cavalrymen fighting as shock troops.

In sum, the capture of Lee's army resulted for the most part from the attrition Grant inflicted on Lee with line infantry and artillery units over the course of the previous year. The commanding Union general may not have originally aimed to achieve his ends through such means, but the siege did at least allow Grant to maintain the initiative by forcing Lee to remain in a static position that the Confederate commander himself knew to be doomed.[43] In the end, it proved enough to gain the Union a decisive victory. With the surrender of Lee's army, and the unwillingness of the Confederate leadership to resort to a true guerrilla strategy, the war could now finally accelerate to a desultory close, after four long years.

EPILOGUE

★ ★ ★

On March 14, 1881, Maj. Gen. Emory Upton, hero of Spotsylvania, and one of the most esteemed officers of the postwar U.S. Army, shot himself in his room at the Presidio near San Francisco. Various factors probably contributed to Upton's suicide—his wife's death eleven years before, problems with severe headaches, and a profound sense of professional failure at this point in his career.[1] Despite, or, perhaps because of his sterling combat record during the Civil War, Upton found the postwar regular army's return to isolated constabulary functions especially unsatisfying. Upton's exhortations to reform the American military establishment along what he perceived to be a Prussian model fell mostly on deaf ears during his own lifetime, and it would not be until Secretary of War Elihu Root's momentous reforms after the Spanish-American War that his ideas would find any sort of fruition. In the meantime, the postwar U.S. Army demobilized into a constabulary force of twenty-five thousand men fighting Indians on the frontier and supervising Reconstruction in the former states of the Confederacy. As it did during the antebellum period, the American service conducted its constabulary functions while maintaining a basic expertise in nation-state warfare, but until the Spanish-American War, such a conflict would never arise. Nothing akin to the Civil War would exercise the army's officers until the world wars of the twentieth century.

Despite the important role the antebellum old army played in the radical changes the Civil War wrought, its own postwar history revealed as many continuities as discontinuities. The American Civil War was the crucible event, if there is any such thing, in the history of the United States. It destroyed slavery, more or less settled various deep-seated problems in the definition of American nationhood, and set the stage in many ways for the country's rise to global prominence in the following century.

Upton's suicide showed, however, how little things had changed for the regulars. For an officer who had begun his career on a stage as grand as any professional soldier could dream of, the return to the obscurities of Indian fighting or Reconstruction-era police work must have been especially disorientating.

Like many supremely competent military professionals, Upton could be unforgiving, and his harsh criticisms of American military policy after the war reflected that mind-set. Nevertheless, he did not call for revolutionary reforms. Upton argued for an expansible regular army, rotation between staff and line positions, a comprehensive program of education for officers, and a reformed general staff no longer completely preoccupied with logistics and administrative issues. Upton's proposals fit within the broad confines of previous professional thinking, and his system of National Volunteers did not depart drastically from Calhoun's expansible army plan. Even the postwar tactical reforms Upton himself supervised, including the introduction of single-rank tactics, had important roots in the gradual dispersal of infantry formations that had occurred over the course of the antebellum period.

Upton's ideas lived on beyond his death, and an uncompleted manuscript giving a historical justification for his reforms circulated within the army. Root drew off of these ideas for his crucial post–Spanish-American War reforms, which included the creation of a European-style general staff, an enlarged regular army, extensive provision for officer education, rotation between staff and line, and greater federal supervision over the National Guard. Root supervised the publication of Upton's manuscript, and through it, the conqueror of Doles's Salient acquired a posthumous life of sorts, as the American army prepared itself for world power status.[2]

Upton in his own life thus represented the complex relationship between the regular army and the American societies it served. On the one hand, as an institution, the old army inhabited the margins of American history — but that marginal and isolated status also contributed to the regulars' powerful influence in wartime. The gradual decline of the militia system, along with the inherently complex nature of nation-state warfare, allowed the old army during the antebellum period to monopolize specialized military expertise, even while it toiled away on the unforgiving frontier.

This exclusive possession of professional military knowledge, whose creation we saw in the three decades before the Mexican War, made possible the striking military successes of that conflict. The political consequences of those military victories pushed the question of slavery's status in the Mexican cession to the foreground of American politics, making possible in turn the eventual outbreak of the Civil War. The scarcity of military expertise available in both sections then forced the old army's leadership cadre to positions of high command in both contending armies. During the war, both the Union and Confederate armies did their best to adapt an institutional legacy inherited from that antebellum army to the new and challenging circumstances of the Civil War. This mixed inheritance, for all its flaws, proved better than no patrimony at all, and both the Union and Confederate armies never entirely escaped the legacies left to it by the antebellum old army.

Viewed from this perspective, Upton's suicide seems all the more tragic. For all its faults, the old army had supervised the creation of armies of unprecedented—in American terms—size in a short period of time, a professional achievement in and of itself. After supervising the regulated killing of nation-state warfare, the regulars also helped prevent the war from becoming an even more violent insurgency—questions regarding the nature of freedom, especially in relation to African Americans, would continue to vex American history—but at least the question of states' rights and Federal supremacy had essentially been settled. Instead of focusing on the failures of American military policy, Upton could have easily talked about its achievements.

Perhaps the part of Upton that made him such an excellent military professional—his pride, ambition, and unforgiving view of incompetence—made him in the end profoundly unsuited to the hard-won peace he had helped achieve. One of the premiere products of antebellum old army professionalism, an excellent battlefield commander who became a military writer and thinker of some note, seems to have found the relative quiet of a frontier garrison a deeply dispiriting existence. Thankfully, Sherman, who as a cadet had repudiated the academy's idealization of the engineers, and Grant, who had stumbled along in indifferent mediocrity at West Point, both proved better suited to living in the post–Civil War world. But it is Lee's reaction to that world that proved to be the most important. He decided that if he could not fight the way the old army had taught him wars should be fought—by uniformed armies regulated by a disciplined chain of command—then he would not fight at all. The same military ethic that made peace so unsatisfying to Upton made it the only available alternative to Lee at the close of the Appomattox campaign. The old army thus served both in war and in peace.

EPILOGUE

NOTES

Abbreviations

AGO   Records of the Office of the Adjutant General, Record Group 94, National
        Archives, Washington, D.C.

ANC   *Army and Navy Chronicle*

OR   United States. War Department. *The War of the Rebellion: A Compilation
        of the Official Records of the Union and Confederate Armies.* 128 vols.
        Washington, D.C.: Government Printing Office, 1880–1901.

RJCCW United States Congress. Joint Committee on the Conduct of the War. *Report
        of the Joint Committee on the Conduct of the War.* 3 vols. Washington, D.C.:
        Government Printing Office, 1863.

WPTP   West Point Thayer Papers, Special Collections, United States Military
        Academy Library, West Point, N.Y.

Introduction

1. Edward Alexander, *Fighting for the Confederacy*, 532.

2. Lincoln, *Collected Works of Abraham Lincoln*, 8:332.

3. In short, the seeming invulnerability of guerrillas to large field armies because of their ability to evade contact can also be a crippling weakness.

I follow the general outlines of Gallagher's concise treatment of the guerrilla option in Gallagher, *Confederate War*, 123–27, 140–44. On the issue of international recognition, many Confederate political leaders knew how important French assistance was to the successful outcome of the American Revolution and had high hopes for acquiring foreign aid from Great Britain and France. For the decidedly undesirable consequences of guerrilla war, see Fellman, *Inside War*.

4. The United States Military Academy at West Point, New York, was the U.S. Army's most important institution during the antebellum period. About 75 percent of regular army officers in 1860 were West Point graduates. See Morrison, "*Best School in the World*," 15.

The term "regular army" refers to the small professional military the United States maintained in peacetime during the nineteenth century. For the antebellum period, I use the term interchangeably with the phrase "old army," which is far more elastic and which army officers and historians have used in varying manners. One historian, Edward M. Coffman, has sagely remarked that "the Old Army is the army that existed before the last war." See Coffman, *Old Army*, vii. For my own purposes, old army refers to the regular army that existed from the end of the War of 1812 in 1814 to the outbreak of the American Civil War.

To use one convenient index of the old army's importance to the management of Civil War armies, consider these figures: former regular army officers constituted 43.9 percent of general officers of all grades in the Union army and 36.7 percent of Confederate generals. Former regulars made up roughly two-thirds of officers ranking major general and above in both armies. See Skelton, *American Profession of Arms*, 361, 446 n. 4. This is even more astonishing when one realizes that West Point graduated per class around forty to fifty cadets a year during the antebellum period.

5. The Confederacy was by no means immune to frictions at the highest levels of civilian and military leadership. The destructive feud between Jefferson Davis and Joseph Johnston is perhaps the most important example, although this feud is better traced to questions of personality, as opposed to professional culture and political ideology. Davis, after all, was himself a graduate of West Point, and a highly professional secretary of war in the 1850s.

6. For better or for worse, McClellan's regular army loyalists made up the largest coherent faction, roughly one-half, of the corps commanders of the Army of the Potomac. In the Union army, corps commanders were major generals who commanded army corps that totaled between 10,000 and 30,000 men, and which were the crucial building blocks of larger field armies. See Taaffe, *Commanding the Army of the Potomac*, 2–3, 215.

7. On the importance of the antebellum army's quartermaster corps to northern military mobilization, see Mark Wilson, *The Business of Civil War*, 2, 35–36. For the profound importance of basic close-order drill and army administration, see McMurry, *Two Great Rebel Armies*, 92–93, 104–5.

8. Grimsley, "Continuing Battle of Gettysburg," 185, 187. Grimsley defines "'pure' battle history" (what I term tactical history) as "history in which the command, operational, and tactical dimensions are strongly foregrounded and the political, social, and cultural dimensions are dealt with in passing or avoided altogether. Pure battle history has its place — and contrary to what some may believe, it is difficult to do well — but like any other kind of history it needs to fit into a larger context and extend a larger dialogue."

Much of this work focuses on tactics, defined by one Civil War–era military authority as "the art of handling troops." This seems an apt definition when applied to drill manuals, which were essentially standardized procedures for moving troops from one point to another in various types of formation and organization. This work does focus on a few discrete tactical episodes at some length, the most important being Upton's assault on Doles's Salient. Such a treatment is clearly an example of tactical history, while my analysis of the evolution of the manuals themselves might be best described as the *history of tactics*, as opposed to *tactical history*. Tactics still must be distinguished from "strategy," however, defined by the same authority as "the art of concerting a plan of campaign, combining a system of military operations determined by the end to be attained, the character of the enemy, the nature and resources of the country, and the means of attack and defence." In a modern professional military, such issues tend to be governed by formal systems of military doctrine, which in turn require well-articulated ideas about different levels of military operations (hence the modern distinction between the operational and strategic levels of war). As a study of an institution that lacked anything comparable to this body of knowledge, I have decided to retain only the distinction between tactics and strategy. Strategy in the Civil War tended to be the purview of individual commanders, who, lacking a set doctrine, made their own decisions in conjunction with their superiors about larger campaign objectives. Also, as a study of, more than anything else, an institution, this work will tend to focus on the narrower world of the *history of tactics*, and how those tactics were then used in specific circumstances. Strategic issues are, however, inherently unavoidable. See H. Scott, *Military Dictionary*, 601, 574.

9. For a different emphasis on the importance of Civil War generals, see Gallagher, "Generals." Gallagher's essay can be seen in many ways as an intellectually coherent defense of the best elements of "Battles and Leaders" history. For a different and perceptive disquisition on the ethical implications of writing Civil War history, see Ayers, "Worrying about the Civil War."

10. It is no coincidence that the current standard one-volume military history of the war by academic authors is titled *How the North Won*. See Hattaway and Jones, *How the North Won*.

11. Fuller, *Generalship of Ulysses S. Grant*, viii, 358 (quotation), 365; Liddell Hart, *Sherman*, vii, 81 (quotation), 125–26, 262–63. The most important early scholarly argument for the primacy of the rifle-musket and entrenchments is in Wagner, *Organization and Tactics*, 265–72.

Herman Hattaway and Archer Jones explicitly compare the quality of military leadership during the American Civil War with western-front commanders during World War I. See Hattaway and Jones, *How the North Won*, 692–94.

For an excellent discussion of both Liddell Hart's and Fuller's treatments of the Civil War, see Luvaas, *Military Legacy of the Civil War*, 212–25.

For American scholarship in this vein, see, for example Catton, *Army of the Potomac*, 29, 235–42; Nevins, *War for the Union*. Two of Nevins's subtitles in his multivolume history are especially revealing, "The Improvised War, 1861–1862," and "The Organized War, 1863–1864." In another essay, Catton described Grant as "the modern man emerging; beyond him, ready to come on the stage, was the great age of steel and machinery. . . . Lee might have ridden down from the old age of chivalry, lance in hand, silken banner fluttering over his head. Each man was the perfect champion of his cause, drawing both his strengths and his weaknesses from the people he led." Catton, "Grant and Lee," 204–5. For a contrasting view, see Gallagher, "An Old-Fashioned Soldier."

On the whole issue of total war, see Förster and Nagler, *On the Road to Total War*. For perhaps the strongest critique of the "total war" thesis, see Grimsley, *Hard Hand of War*, 4–5, 219.

12. Liddell Hart, *Sherman*, vii; Fuller, *Generalship of Ulysses S. Grant*, viii.

13. Weller, "Civil War Minie Rifles," 36, 38. The best of the revisionist school's work can be found in Hess, *Union Soldier in Battle*, 54–72. For the work that started it all, see

Griffith, *Battle Tactics of the Civil War*, 67, 147, 190. Nosworthy takes a moderately revisionist position in Nosworthy, *Bloody Crucible of Courage*, 647–48. Grimsley has pointed out, however, that the earlier rifle-musket consensus seems to still reign supreme in college textbooks. See Grimsley, "Continuing Battle of Gettysburg," 186. For the best recent defense of the previous consensus, see Glatthaar, "Battlefield Tactics." For a perspective and critique of Griffith that focuses less on the range issue, see Haughton, *Training, Tactics and Leadership*, 8–9. Although Haughton here focuses too much on Griffith's account of Civil War fire fights, his focus on questions of training and tactics is commendable.

Griffith used range figures from a very thin database of sources, but his conclusions did find support in Grimsley's more thorough statistical analysis of range figures in the *Official Records*. See Grimsley, "Surviving Military Revolution," 76.

14. McWhiney and Jamieson, *Attack and Die*, 50; Nosworthy, *Bloody Crucible of Courage*, 87–95. The only full-dress treatment of pre–Mexican War tactics is in the relevant chapters of Osterhoudt, "Evolution of U.S. Army Assault Tactics."

15. I prefer more-modest criteria for determining whether a battle was decisive; namely, did a battle have a significant effect on the overall strategic situation? This should include a consideration of politics and public opinion. This is admittedly far more vague than a standard centered on the complete and total destruction of an army in the field, but total annihilation is too rare an achievement in military history to use it as a useful measure of a battle's importance. For a treatment that plays down the importance of the rifle-musket but does vigorously argue for the indecisiveness of Civil War battle, see Hess, *Union Soldier in Battle*, 54–60.

Much to his credit, Edward Hagerman also pays a good deal of attention to the problem of coordinating units on a Civil War battlefield. See Hagerman, *American Civil War and the Origins of Modern Warfare*, 86, 271. Still, Hagerman remains very much committed to the rifle-musket modernization school.

Chapter 1

1. Skelton, *American Profession of Arms*, xv–xvi. Skelton's work is the leading study of American military professionalism in this period. There are many different definitions of professionalism. See, for example, Huntington, *Soldier and the State*, 8–10; Skelton, *American Profession of Arms*, 88; Teitler, *Genesis of the Professional Officers' Corps*, 8. In my own view, a working definition military professionalism should focus on specialized training and education, a self-conscious professional awareness of vocation, and reasonably long lengths of service.

2. Cunliffe, *Soldiers and Civilians*, 154–56, 597, 168. On the astonishing and important quality of this achievement, see Mark Wilson, *The Business of Civil War*, 36.

3. On the lasting importance of Washington's and Hamilton's ideas, see Kohn, *Eagle and Sword*, 48.

4. When I speak of American military policy, I refer to the actions of the federal government, as embodied in legislation passed by Congress and the actions of responsible executive branch officials. For a summary of the militia ideal, see Cunliffe, *Soldiers and Civilians*, 31–43. On the close connection between military organization and western

Civilians, 31–43. On the close connection between military organization and western

European state formation, see Tilly, "Reflections on the History of European State-Making," 42.

5. On the mixed character of the southern campaign, see Higginbotham, *War of American Independence*, 374–75, 382.

6. Bailyn, *Ideological Origins of the American Revolution*, 61–63; Cunliffe, *Soldiers and Civilians*, 40–42.

7. Martin and Lender, *A Respectable Army*, 127. It should be pointed out that calculated threats are very different from a real coup d'etat. On this important distinction and the episode's importance as a whole, see Kohn, *Eagle and Sword*, 36–39. Also see Higginbotham, *George Washington and the American Military Tradition*, 63, 98–100.

8. John Fitzpatrick, *Writings of George Washington*, 26:374–75. For two historians' treatments of Washington's "Sentiments," see Kohn, *Eagle and Sword*, 45–47; Weigley, *Towards an American Army*, 10–14. The Continental army was not a true regular army, because it was disbanded after the end of the Revolution.

9. Weigley, *Towards an American Army*, 13–16. Congress also authorized a pseudo-regular force, the First American regiment of seven hundred men, to be recruited through militia contributions from various states. In 1785 the force was regularized by moving to three-year enlistment independent of the militia, but the force proved woefully inadequate. See Millett and Maslowski, *For the Common Defense*, 91–92.

10. Weigley, *Towards an American Army*, 19–21; Millett and Maslowski, *For the Common Defense*, 95–98.

11. Weigley, *Towards an American Army*, 22. The expansible army concept had been anticipated in Washington's "Sentiments on a Peace Establishment."

12. Syrett, *Papers of Alexander Hamilton*, 24:70–73.

13. Ibid., 22:358. Hamilton was complaining specifically about the practice of allowing officers to be detached from their regiments to serve as aides-de-camp, without in turn making provision for their duties to be filled in their companies in their absence. Problems with officers serving on detached staff duties would bedevil the old army throughout the antebellum period.

Sherman also later used the metaphor of a military "machine." See Sherman, *Memoirs*, 877.

14. John Fitzpatrick, *Writings of George Washington*, 26:397. For Hamilton's comments on the same problem in 1798, see Syrett, *Papers of Alexander Hamilton*, 22:363.

Holden, "Origins of the United States Military Academy," 203–4, 209–10, 212; Molloy, "Technical Education and the Young Republic," 176–77, 180. On the early American reliance on French engineers, see ibid., 156–58. For some Revolutionary-era complaints by American officers of excessive favors given to foreign officers, see Higginbotham, *War of American Independence*, 214–15.

15. Molloy, "Technical Education and the Young Republic," 187–88, 212–13, 239–41. Quotations in ibid., 309, 241–42.

16. Ambrose, *Duty, Honor, Country*, 30–32; Molloy, "Technical Education and the Young Republic," 280–84, 292–98.

17. Millett and Maslowski, *For the Common Defense*, 110–11; Winfield Scott, *Memoirs*, 1:63.

18. Timothy Johnson, *Winfield Scott*, 43–46, 83; Kieffer, *Maligned General*, 27;

Weigley, *History of the United States Army*, 131. It should be pointed out that Brown was himself originally a militia officer, if a quick-learning one who stayed in the regular army after the war. The American desire to emulate European discipline had gone as far back as Washington. See Higginbotham, *George Washington and the American Military Tradition*, 32–33.

19. Winfield Scott, *Memoirs*, 1:65–67, 71; Kieffer, *Maligned General*, 39. Riall had been captured.

20. See, for example, Christopher [VanDeventer] to Sylvanus Thayer, June 4, 1816, WPTP. On the ambiguities of the issue of foreign expertise in this and other cases, see Dupuy, *Where They Have Trod*, 95–97, 100–101. For a more positive opinion of the use of foreign engineers, see William McRee to Joseph G. Swift, January 8, 1817, WPTP. On Simon Bernard, see Hunter and Dooley, *Claudius Crozet*, 19–20.

21. [Joseph G. Swift] to Sylvanus Thayer, March 30, 1815, WPTP. On McRee's career, see Dupuy, *Where They Have Trod*, 60–62.

22. Sylvanus Thayer to Joseph G. Swift, October 10, 1815; [Joseph G. Swift] to Sylvanus Thayer, March 30, 1815; Sylvanus Thayer to Joseph G. Swift, February 12, [1817], WPTP; Dupuy, *Where They Have Trod*, 92–93.

23. Sylvanus Thayer to [Joseph G. Swift], August 12, 1816; William McRee to Joseph G. Swift, December 18, 1816, WPTP. On the usefulness of models, also see William McRee to Joseph G. Swift, September 14, 1816, WPTP.

24. William McRee to Joseph G. Swift, January 8, 1817, WPTP (emphasis added); Allen Johnson and Dumas Malone, *Dictionary of American Biography*, 223.

25. Sylvanus Thayer to George Graham, August 28, 1817, WPTP; Molloy, "Technical Education and the Young Republic," 369–70. Molloy overstates Renwick's Francophilia, see James Renwick to Joseph Gardiner Swift, May 13, 1816, Joseph Gardiner Swift Papers.

26. Hunter and Dooley, *Claudius Crozet*, 16–17, 22–30, 125–26; Molloy, "Technical Education and the Young Republic," 370–71. The French faculty at West Point was not universally liked — Jared Mansfield, professor of Natural and Experimental Philosophy, had a distinct distaste for his French colleagues.

27. Winfield Scott to James Monroe, June 20, 1815 [copy]; Winfield Scott to James Monroe, September 28, 1815 [copy], Winfield Scott Papers; Elliott, *Winfield Scott*, 196–97; Mansfield, *Life of General Winfield Scott*, 148–49; Winfield Scott, *Memoirs*, 1:157–58.

28. Winfield Scott to James Monroe, September 28, 1815 [copy], Winfield Scott Papers; James Renwick to Joseph Gardiner Swift, July 30, 1815, January 4, 1816, Joseph Gardiner Swift Papers.

29. Winfield Scott, *Memoirs*, 1:205–6. Compare, for example, Adjutant General's Horse Guards, *General Regulations and Orders*, 87, with Winfield Scott, *General Regulations*, 30 [16.1]. There is also a rough concordance in the organization of the earlier sections of both regulations, although Scott's system of articles is far more detailed and laid out. On camp layouts, compare Gay de Vernon, *Treatise on the Science of War and Fortification*, pl. VI, fig. 4, and Winfield Scott, *General Regulations*, pl. III; O'Connell, "Origins of Modern Management," 57, 60; Winfield Scott to John C.

Calhoun, September 2, 1818, in U.S. Congress, *American State Papers*, Military Affairs, 2:199–200.

30. Scott during his time in Europe had in fact visited some of the European officers — mostly Frenchmen — who had served with the Americans during the Revolution. See Winfield Scott, *Memoirs*, 1:160.

31. Winfield Scott to James Monroe, November 18, 1815 [copy], Winfield Scott Papers; James Renwick to Joseph Gardiner Swift, July 30, 1815, May 13, 1816, Joseph Gardiner Swift Papers; ibid., 1:162–67. For Renwick's opinion that another war with Great Britain was likely, see James Renwick to Joseph Gardiner Swift, January 4, 1816, Joseph Gardiner Swift Papers.

32. Molloy, "Technical Education and the Young Republic," 388–91. Quotation from Sylvanus Thayer to [George Graham], August 29, 1817, WPTP.

33. Alexander Macomb to Sylvanus Thayer, August 22, 1822, WPTP; Molloy, "Technical Education and the Young Republic," 396–97. Citing French practice in its military schools proper (as opposed to the Polytechnique, which also trained civil engineers and scientists), Capt. T. Wolf Tone in his report to Swift after the War of 1812 believed that a nonengineering officer need have only the scientific and technical skills of arithmetic, geometry as far as conic sections, algebra, trigonometry, and good skills in drawing and mapmaking. T. Wolf Tone, "Notes on the Military Schools of St. Germain and Fontainbleu," Joseph Gardiner Swift Papers.

34. Sylvanus Thayer to Joseph G. Swift, April 14, 1818, WPTP.

35. Morrison, *"Best School in the World,"* 23–25; Skelton, *American Profession of Arms*, 138, 182.

36. William H. Crawford to Richard M. Johnson, December 27, 1815, in U.S. Congress, *American State Papers*, Military Affairs, 1:636; John C. Calhoun to John W. Taylor, December 12, 1820, in *Papers of John C. Calhoun*, 5:480–91 (quotation of Calhoun from 484).

37. Risch, *Quartermaster Support of the Army*, 184; Watson, "Professionalism, Social Attitudes, and Civil-Military Accountability," 679–80.

38. Risch, *Quartermaster Support of the Army*, 196, 201, 210, 213–14, 218.

The Subsistence Bureau continued to exist until 1912, when a new "Quartermaster Corps" absorbed the functions of the Pay, Subsistence, and Quartermaster Departments. A Clothing Bureau also existed from 1832 to 1841. Seacoast fortifications were the responsibility of the Engineers, although the Quartermaster Bureau later became responsible for sheds and buildings designed to store public property at coastal forts. The Quartermaster Bureau always maintained jurisdiction over strictly military roads throughout the antebellum period and sometimes even participated in internal improvement projects of a nonmilitary character, although the creation of the Corps of Topographical Engineers in 1836 relieved it of some of its road-building burdens.

39. Ibid., 184–85; Mark Wilson, *The Business of the Civil War*, 2, 35, 40, 65–71 (quotation from 66). Goff, *Confederate Supply*, 8–10.

40. For the historical context of the Western staff system, see Hittle, *Military Staff*. Lee himself cited French methods when he called for reforms in staff organization to help with the difficult management of large Civil War armies. See Freeman, *Lee's Dispatches*, 81–82.

41. The battle of Königgrätz between Austria and Prussia in 1866 saw 440,000 to 460,000 troops present, which was a slightly larger number than the troops present at Leipzig in 1813 during the final phase of the Napoleonic Wars. A Napoleonic corps usually numbered 20,000 to 30,000 men. See Van Creveld, *Command in War*, 105, 61. Hittle has a somewhat more critical view of the American staff system. See Hittle, *Military Staff*, 184–87.

42. Hittle, *Military Staff*, 33, 132.

43. On significant similarities in terminology from the Revolutionary period, see ibid., 171; Risch, *Quartermaster Support of the Army*, 1–2. On the separation of artillery and engineer branches in the American service, see Winfield Scott, *General Regulations*, 87.

44. Griffith, *Military Thought in the French Army*, 144–46; Hittle, *Military Staff*, 53, 62–65, 103–4; Winfield Scott, *General Regulations*, 85 [44.4], 89 [45.3], 87 [44.14], 89–90 [45].

45. Hittle, *Military Staff*, 98–99, 146–47; Winfield Scott, *General Regulations*, 162–309 [66–73]; Skelton, *American Profession of Arms*, 131, 233.

46. Joel R. Poinsett and Jefferson Davis were the only two other secretaries of war of any real quality during the whole antebellum period after Calhoun's departure.

Chapter 2

1. Even during the Mexican War, American cavalrymen never possessed the high level of training necessary to conduct true, Old World–style heavy cavalry charges with the *arme blanche* ("cold steel"). Nevertheless, in addition to necessary frontier duties on the Great Plains, American horse-soldiers during the Mexican War provided screening and reconnaissance functions that every orthodox nation-state army needs on campaign. See Starr, *The Union Cavalry*, 1:53–54.

2. Emory Upton also commented on the different military performances turned in by United States forces during the War of 1812 and the Mexican War. See Upton, *Military Policy of the United States*, 222.

3. Skelton, *American Profession of Arms*, 306.

4. The first generation of American reformers had field experience during the War of 1812, of course.

5. Crackel, "Battle of Queenston Heights," 40; Osterhoudt, "Evolution of U.S. Army Assault Tactics," 28. Congress had also authorized a Battalion of Mounted Rangers in 1832, which became the First Dragoons the next year. See Watson, "Professionalism, Social Attitudes, and Civil-Military Accountability," 461. Artillery will be dealt with at more length later in this chapter.

6. Crackel, "Battle of Queenston Heights," 51–52; Hindman, "The New Infantry Tactics, No.1," *ANC* 1 (October 15, 1835): 332. Hindman gives a reasonably complete historical account of the evolution of American infantry tactics from the Revolution until Scott's tactics of 1835.

7. Crackel, "Battle of Queenston Heights," 55–56; Watson, "Professionalism, Social Attitudes, and Civil-Military Accountability," 388.

8. Winfield Scott to General [Alexander] Macomb, July 2, 1835, New York, Winfield Scott Papers. The army also distributed through general orders corrections

for typographical errors in the first printing of the 1835 tactical manual along with supplemental instructions to adapt the manual of arms to new percussion-lock muskets. See General Orders No. 66, October 7, 1837, and General Orders No. 44, October 30, 1844, AGO. For a low opinion of American officers' knowledge of the 1825 tactics, see Clairfait, "The New Infantry Tactics," *ANC* 1 (March 19, 1835): 95.

9. Osterhoudt, "Evolution of U.S. Army Assault Tactics," 33–34; Watson, "Professionalism, Social Attitudes, and Civil-Military Accountability," 388–90, 403–4; Gardner, *Compend of the United States System of Infantry Exercise*, viii; Rogers, *British Army of the Eighteenth Century*, 73–74; Ross, *From Flintlock to Rifle*, 160–61; Riling, *Von Steuben and His Regulations*, 6; United States, War Department, *Rules and Regulations for the Field Exercise and Manœuvres of Infantry* [1815], 6. On early American and European criticism of the three-rank system, which may have influenced von Steuben's decision to use two-ranks, see Peterkin, *Exercise of Arms*, 10–11. The Blue Book itself represented an amalgam of French, British, Prussian, and American colonial practice (ibid., 16).

10. For the step rates, see Table 1.

11. D. H. Galk to Ch. L. Rourse, October 15, 1824, S 110 1824; Winfield Scott to C. Van De Venter, November 9, 1824, S 377 (18) 1824, Letters Received by the Secretary of War; Watson, "Professionalism, Social Attitudes, and Civil-Military Accountability," 389–90.

12. Osterhoudt criticizes the light infantry sections for repetitive duplication of line tactics and the absence of skirmish drill. See Osterhoudt, "Evolution of U.S. Army Assault Tactics," 38. The 1825 tactical manual does in fact give instruction on extending into a loose order, that is, those involving skirmishers. See United States, War Department, *Infantry Tactics* [1825], 266–72 [1722–57].

13. Rogers, *British Army of the Eighteenth Century*, 70–73. It should be pointed out that a distinction is sometimes made between "riflemen," armed with rifles proper, and "light infantry," who were not armed with rifles but a lighter and more compact version of the standard line-infantry musket. Both types of troops emphasized the same open-order tactics and aimed fire, which I simply call "light infantry tactics."

14. Ross, *From Flintlock to Rifle*, 55–56, 67, 92, 136–37, 83–84 n. 15. Instructions for light infantry would be added in the 1831 revision of the 1791 tactical manual (ibid., 160–61).

15. Ibid., 67, 150. The French also had adopted skirmishing tactics partly out of necessity, because the untrained levies of the Revolution had not had the requisite training for ancien régime linear tactics.

The march rates of the 1792 British Regulations probably match British practice throughout the eighteenth century. See Rogers, *British Army of the Eighteenth Century*, 76. The figures for the British 1792 tactics are the following: ordinary step of 30 inches at 75 steps per minute ([Great Britain], War Office, *Rules and Regulations* [1792], 6 [S.6]), quick step at 108 per minute (ibid., 13 [S.16]), and quickest step at 120 per minute (ibid., 14 [S.17]). Note that the Blue Book did use the same pace as the British ordinary step and had no provision for a quickest step, in effect making quickest time the same as quick time.

On Gardner, see Heitman, *Historical Register*, 1:445; Allen Johnson and Dumas

Malone, *Dictionary of American Biography*, 141. Gardner, interestingly enough, was also a political associate of Calhoun and edited a newspaper after he left the service.

16. Gardner, *Compend of the United States System of Infantry Exercise*, xii–xiv, 197–98.

17. United States, War Department, *Infantry Tactics* [1825], 244 [1573], 251 [1623], 252–54 [1627–37], 266–72 [1722–57], 8 [13], 59 [356], 296 [1906, 1910], 126 [803]; Hindman, "The New Infantry Tactics, No. IV," *ANC* 2 (February 4, 1836): 78. In American practice, the battalion was the primary tactical unit, while the regiment was the primary organizational unit. In other words, when I refer to battalions in a tactical context, the term should be seen as equivalent to "regiment." Only in 1861 did the regular army add in principle multibattalion regiments structured on the European depot system.

18. Ross, *From Flintlock to Rifle*, 160–61. For another example of the opening and extension of the French tactics, also note the increased intervals between battalions in columns by battalions in mass noted in Hindman, "New Infantry Tactics, No. VI," *ANC* 2 (March 10, 1836): 154.

Winfield Scott, *Infantry Tactics* [1835], 2:212 [1674–75], 2:220 [1710–14], 2:194 [1585], 2:196–97 [1595–96]; United States, War Department, *Infantry Tactics* [1825], 266 [1723].

19. See Table 1. The change in step rates did not go un-noticed; "Hindman" defended it on the grounds of needing to conform to the new French tactics, Hindman, "The New Infantry Tactics, No. IV," *ANC* 2 (February 4, 1836): 78.

Winfield Scott, *Infantry Tactics* [1835], 1:132 [562], 2:189–90 [1567–68]; United States, War Department, *Infantry Tactics* [1825], 244–45 [1577]. For an example of the problems with double time, see Sommers, *Richmond Redeemed*, 45.

20. See Table 1. McWhiney and Jamieson, *Attack and Die*, 50. It should be pointed out that Hardee's tactics also made more common use of double quick time and the run.

21. Clairfait, "The New Infantry Tactics, No. 5," *ANC* 1 (April 23, 1835): 133–34; "Light Infantry," *ANC* 2 (April 14, 1836): 235; Young Fogram, "The New Infantry Tactics," *ANC* 1 (August 27, 1835): 277; Cooke, *Scenes and Adventures in the Army*, 87. Also see Philo-Clairfait, "The New Infantry Tactics," *ANC* 2 (April 14, 1836):, 234–35. For another indication that light infantry instruction did actually make it into the field, see Watson, "Professionalism, Social Attitudes, and Civil-Military Accountability," 458.

22. Clairfait, "The New Infantry Tactics," *ANC* 1 (March 19, 1835): 95.

Clairfait, "The New Infantry Tactics, No. 2," *ANC* 1 (March 26, 1835): 101. In light of Clairfait's advocacy of light infantry methods in the rough American wilderness, he must be drawing a link between the two-rank formation's more open order and American frontier conditions. For another critique of the three-rank formation, see Young Fogram, "The New Infantry Tactics," *ANC* 1 (July 30, 1835): 247.

23. Hindman, "The New Infantry Tactics, No. I," *ANC* 1 (October 15, 1835): 332–33; Hindman, "The New Infantry Tactics, No. V," *ANC* 2 (February 11, 1836): 91; Hindman, "The New Infantry Tactics, No. II," *ANC* 1 (October 22, 1835): 340–41. For long excerpts of the report of the French commission that revised the 1791 French tactical manual, see Hindman, "The New Infantry Tactics, No. III," *ANC* 1 (October 29, 1835): 348–49;

Hindman, "New Infantry Tactics, No. IV," *ANC* 2 (February 4, 1836): 76–78; Hindman, "New Infantry Tactics, No. V," *ANC* 2 (February 11, 1836): 90–91; Hindman, "New Infantry Tactics, No. VI," *ANC* 2 (March 10, 1836): 153–56; Hindman, "New Infantry Tactics, No. VII," *ANC* 2 (March 17, 1836): 170–72.

24. Hindman, "The New Infantry Tactics, No. II," *ANC* 1 (October 22, 1835): 340–41; Philo-Clairfait, "The New Infantry Tactics," *ANC* 2 (April 14): 1836, 234. It should be remembered that firing in infantry formations of more than one rank required provisions to prevent the rear ranks from firing into their comrades in front of them. In two ranks, the problem is dealt with by having rear-rank soldiers step to the side so that their muskets point through an interval in between their front-rank comrades. See, for example, United States, War Department, *Infantry Tactics* [1825], 36 [199]). With three ranks, that expedient no longer works, so the front rank kneels if all three ranks fire. See Winfield Scott, *Infantry Tactics* [1835], 1:52–54 [211–21]. Or the rear rank loads muskets for the center rank (ibid., 1:69–70 [291–298]). Even then, injuries in the front rank from the discharge of rear-rank muskets were all too common.

25. Watson, "Professionalism, Social Attitudes, and Civil-Military Accountability," 407.

26. Hindman, "New Infantry Tactics, No. V," *ANC* 2 (February 11, 1836): 91; Joseph G. Totten to J. R. Poinsett, April 18, 1840, Joseph Gilbert Totten Papers. For the elaborate process by which the new French tactics had been developed, see Griffith, *Military Thought in the French Army*, 124–25. Nevertheless, Griffith sees the new French tactics as excessively conservative.

27. Dastrup, *King of Battle*, 62–64.

28. Ibid., 64–69; Watson, "Professionalism, Social Attitudes, and Civil-Military Accountability," 452–56, 392, 398–401.

29. The technical terminology for artillery had an unfortunate tendency to change over time and varied between different countries' services (see, e.g., Henry J. Hunt to Robert Anderson, November 28, 1854, Robert Anderson Papers), but for our own purposes, field artillery refers to mobile artillery designed to be used on the battlefield, as opposed to heavy or foot artillery, which garrisoned seacoast fortifications. Following American practice, the terms light and horse artillery are used interchangeably (Dastrup, *King of Battle*, 46) — this was essentially field artillery with all the cannoners mounted on horse. In normal field artillery, only the drivers are mounted, and the rest of a crew either marches or, in some cases, rides on top of the caissons (the boxes towed behind guns, which contain each gun's supply of ammunition). The obvious advantage of horse artillery was its greater mobility. Finally, it should be noted that because of funding shortages, American units that were officially designated as horse or light artillery frequently did not have enough horses to actually mount all the cannoners (Watson, "Professionalism, Social Attitudes, and Civil-Military Accountability," 464).

Cullum, *Biographical Register*, 1:22. Anderson was instructor of artillery from 1835 to 1837, while Knowlton held the same post after Anderson's relief until 1844.

30. Dastrup, *King of Battle*, 66–67, 69–70; Cullum, *Biographical Register*, 1:189. Ringgold had also earned a brevet for gallantry during the Seminole War. He was killed in action in the battle of Palo Alto during the Mexican War.

31. Robert Anderson to Capt. Samuel Cooper, May 1837 [copy]; Benjamin Huger to Robert Anderson, February 27, 1840, Robert Anderson Papers; General Orders No. 13, March 14, 1840, AGO; Anderson, *Instruction for Field Artillery*, I; Abram Eustis to Robert Anderson, June 22, 1840; Minor Knowlton to Robert Anderson, April 20, 1840; Robert Anderson to Samuel Ringgold, May 4, 1840 [copied on the back of Knowlton letter dated April 20, 1840]; Samuel Ringgold to Robert Anderson, May 18, 1840, Robert Anderson Papers; General Orders No. 46, August 19, 1841, AGO. The publication date printed on the title page of the 1840 tactical manual is 1839, but the text of Poinsett's order must have been added after the pages were first printed and before the volumes were bound.

32. Maj. L. Whiting to Robert Anderson, May 4, 1840; Miner Knowlton to Robert Anderson, April 20, 1840, Robert Anderson Papers; Gaines quoted in Watson, "Professionalism, Social Attitudes, and Civil-Military Accountability," 342. For perceptive comments on American officers as "patriots as well as cosmopolitans," see ibid., 339–40.

On the warm relations between Knowlton and Anderson, see Minor Knowlton to Robert Anderson, August 21, 1840; B. R. Alden to Robert Anderson, February 9, 1842; Minor Knowlton to Robert Anderson, February 19, 1842, Robert Anderson Papers.

33. Abram Eustis to Robert Anderson, July 6, 1839, Robert Anderson Papers; Anderson, *Instruction for Field Artillery*, 10, 106–7; United States, War Department, *Instruction for Field Artillery* [1845], 69–70, 51. A system of cavalry, infantry, and artillery tactics, using similar, or "assimilated," commands, would not be achieved until 1874. See Jamieson, *Crossing the Deadly Ground*, 9.

34. Abram Eustis to Robert Anderson, July 14, 1840; 1st Lt. William P. Bainbridge to Robert Anderson, September 24, 1841; Morris J. Miller to Robert Anderson, November 12, 1841; Robert Anderson to Winfield Scott, January 16, 1841 [copy], Robert Anderson Papers. The harmonization of the artillery tactics with the new cavalry tactics was, of course, approved by the board. For another officer's interest in this point, see John Macrae Washington to Robert Anderson, December 16, 1841, copied extract written on James Duncan to Robert Anderson, December 21, 1841, ibid. In contrast, Abram Eustis cautioned against making change simply for the sake of making changes, see Abram Eustis to Robert Anderson, January 27, 1842, ibid.

On the review of drafts, see Capt. J. Dimick to Robert Anderson, December 27, 1841; James Duncan to Robert Anderson, December 21, 1841; Capt. William G. Freeman to Robert Anderson, February 7, 1842; Minor Knowlton to Robert Anderson, May 8, 1842; C. F. Smith to Robert Anderson, November 22, 1842; C. F. Smith to Robert Anderson, November 25, 1842; Minor Knowlton to Robert Anderson, August 22, 1842; F. Taylor to Robert Anderson, August 30, 1842, Robert Anderson Papers.

35. General Orders No. 38, June 17, 1843; General Orders No. 38, September 27, 1844, AGO; 1st Lt. E. Deas to Robert Anderson, July 10, 1843; Minor Knowlton to Robert Anderson, February 10, 1844; R. Jones to Robert Anderson, March 29, 1844; Robert Anderson to Capt. Cooper [copy], May 1837, Robert Anderson Papers; Birkhimer, *Historical Sketch*, 306.

36. Watson, "Professionalism, Social Attitudes, and Civil-Military Accountability," 464; General Orders No. 21, April 1, 1842; General Orders No. 65, October 12, 1842;

General Orders No. 10, March 25, 1844, AGO. My assumption is that "mounted companies" refers to the light or horse artillery, because the other provisions refer to "fixed" and "field" batteries.

37. Watson, "Professionalism, Social Attitudes, and Civil-Military Accountability," 462, 464. Note that the first American horse-trooper regiments were designated as dragoons, which meant that they carried firearms and normally fought while dismounted. Dragoons are essentially mounted infantry. True heavy cavalry on the European model relies on the "shock" of a charge by mounted horsemen using the *arme blanche* ("cold steel"). Shock cavalry could still be effective during the Napoleonic Wars and was in many ways indispensable for exploiting weak points in an enemy's line, or for turning a retreat into a rout, but increasingly effective infantry weapons would reduce the effectiveness of this arm throughout the nineteenth-century and into the early decades of the twentieth. Nevertheless, horsemen were still useful for reconnaissance and screening duties, their primary role during the Civil War. However, by war's end, mounted Union troopers equipped with repeating breech-loading rifles became a sort of super-dragoon. I will follow American practice in using the term "dragoon" and "cavalry" interchangeably, but it should be realized that this is something of a misnomer.

William Eustis to John Bell, May 10, 1841, E 32 1841; Proceedings of the Boards for establishing a System for the Cavalry Instructions, F 6 1841 ENCL, AGO.

38. S. Cooper to Adjutant General, August 9, 1839, P 187 1839; Philip Kearny to Joel Poinsett, October 16, 1839, K 140 1839; Lt. Philip Kearny to Lieut. Comdt. Michaux, October 12, 1839, K 140 1839 ENCL, AGO.

39. Joel Poinsett to Adjutant General, November 26, 1840, P 287 1840; Lewis Cass to John G. Spencer, February 20, 1842, C 99 1842; William Eustis to Joel Poinsett, October 23, 1839, E 109 1839 [ENCL]; L. Beall, W. Hardee, and W. Newton to Secretary of War, October 7, 1841, B 596 1841; Philip Kearny to Joel Poinsett, October 16, 1839, K 140 1839, AGO. It should be remembered that West Pointers learned only how to *read* French.

40. Watson, "Professionalism, Social Attitudes, and Civil-Military Accountability," 466, 459; United States, War Department, *Instruction for Field Artillery* [1845], 69–70.

41. Quoted in Freeman, *Lee*, 3:8.

Chapter 3

1. Bill, *Rehearsal for Conflict*.

2. Even the most recent scholarly attempt to look at the Mexican War and Civil War causation uses as its counterfactual not an American defeat but the election of Henry Clay in 1844 and the total absence of a war in the first place. See Kornblith, "Rethinking the Coming of the Civil War," pars. 63–67. Also see Bright and Geyer, "Where in the World Is America?," 77–78. Bright and Geyer make no mention of how the United States' victory was anything but inevitable.

3. Bauer, *Mexican War*, 397–98.

4. Justin Smith, *War with Mexico*, 1:105–6, 440; Winders, *Mr. Polk's Army*, 9; *The Times*, April 5, 1845; Tayloe and Watson, *In Memoriam*, 113–14.

5. Quoted in Justin Smith, *War with Mexico*, 1:107; DePalo, *Mexican National Army*, 35–38.

6. Grant in his memoirs recalled of his small force, "A more efficient army for its number and armament, I do not believe ever fought a battle than the one commanded by General Taylor in his first two engagements on Mexican — or Texan soil." See Grant, *Memoirs*, 50.

7. Bauer, *Mexican War*, 37–40; Bauer, "Battles on the Rio Grande," 63–65.

8. Bauer, "Battles on the Rio Grande," 67–73; Justin Smith, *War with Mexico*, 1:465.

9. Justin Smith, *War with Mexico*, 1:172, 175.

10. George Smith and Charles Judah, *Chronicles of the Gringos*, 68. In his report to the chief engineer, Lt. Jeremiah Mason Scarritt also makes explicit reference to the use of skirmishers.

Bauer, "Battles on the Rio Grande," 78; Bauer, *Mexican War*, 60–62, 82; General Viscount Wolseley quoted in Adams, *Our Masters the Rebels*, 71. Adams cited this quote in relation to the Confederate victory at Bull Run.

11. Coffman, *Old Army*, 137–38, 193; Justin Smith, *War with Mexico*, 1:166, 173.

12. Johannsen, *To the Halls of the Montezuma*, 114–21. Johannsen puts more emphasis than I do on Taylor's place as a "romantic" hero.

13. Justin Smith, *War with Mexico*, 1:198–200.

14. Bauer, *Zachary Taylor*, 215; Justin Smith, *War with Mexico*, 1:352–53.

15. Bauer, *Mexican War*, 93–101; Justin Smith, *War with Mexico*, 1:501, 550. Bauer is less scathing on Taylor's performance, although he describes Taylor's assaults on September 21 "as poorly executed as any action by American forces during the war outside California." See Bauer, *Mexican War*, 96.

16. Bauer, *Zachary Taylor*, 185–87; Bauer, *Mexican War*, 77–78, 232–35.

17. Justin Smith, *War with Mexico*, 1:352–54, 362–63, 368–69, 547–48.

18. Ibid., 1:379–83; Bauer, *Mexican War*, 209–10, 217. For a detailed American order of battle, see Justin Smith, *War with Mexico*, 1:555–56.

19. Justin Smith, *War with Mexico*, 1:384, 392.

20. Wool's comment in George Smith and Charles Judah, *Chronicles of the Gringos*, 99; Bauer, *Mexican War*, 215; Justin Smith, *War with Mexico*, 1:395.

21. Taylor quoted in Bauer, *Mexican War*, 214.

22. On early problems with logistical support, see ibid., 84; George Smith and Charles Judah, *Chronicles of the Gringos*, xv. In historical terms, the conquests of California and New Mexico were not inconsiderable events, and although fascinating in and of themselves, those campaigns bore no resemblance to or influence on the major set-piece battles of the Civil War.

23. Bauer, *Mexican War*, 241–52; Justin Smith, *War with Mexico*, 2:29–30. Smith also points out that both regular division commanders, Worth and Twiggs, preferred a frontal assault, as opposed to a siege.

24. Justin Smith, *War with Mexico*, 2:39; Bauer, *Mexican War*, 261–68. On Robles's misgivings about the position, see Justin Smith, *War with Mexico*, 2:45, 348.

25. Bauer, *Mexican War*, 270.

26. Ibid., 282–86. Smith gives a somewhat more positive portrayal of Scott's conduct during his feud with Trist. See Justin Smith, *War with Mexico*, 2:128–29.

Ibid., 2:93; Bauer, *Mexican War*, 274. Scott himself had told Washington he needed twenty thousand men, which Marcy had promised him to be available by the end of June. See Justin Smith, *War with Mexico*, 2:371. The term "divisions" is also more fictive than real—in reality, these were really brigade-sized units. Bauer sees Quitman as probably the best of the volunteer generals, while most historians have not seen much value in Pillow's military skills. See Bauer, *Mexican War*, 75.

27. Bauer, *Mexican War*, 274, 288; DePalo, *Mexican National Army*, 126–27; Justin Smith, *War with Mexico*, 2:73, 89. Bauer gives a figure of thirty thousand for the Mexican forces.

28. Bauer, *Mexican War*, 288–93, 299; Justin Smith, *War with Mexico*, 2:107.

29. Bauer, *Mexican War*, 294–300; Justin Smith, *War with Mexico*, 2:116.

30. Bauer, *Mexican War*, 300–301; Justin Smith, *War with Mexico*, 2:117–18.

31. Bauer, *Mexican War*, 301, 307–11.

32. Ibid., 311–12; Justin Smith, *War with Mexico*, 2:149–53; G. T. Beauregard to John L. Smith [copy], September 20, 1847, Beinecke Library; DePalo, *Mexican National Army*, 135–37.

33. Bauer, *Mexican War*, 313–17; Justin Smith, *War with Mexico*, 2:155–56, 409.

34. Bauer, *Mexican War*, 318–21; Justin Smith, *War with Mexico*, 2:162–63. For quotations, see Bauer, *Mexican War*, 318.

35. Levinson, *Wars within War*, 57–59, 86; Robert Anderson to D. L. Clinch, November 30, 1846, Robert Anderson Papers; Bauer, *Mexican War*, 378–88, 371–74.

36. The small and mixed forces that fought in New Mexico and California are not large enough to be truly called field armies.

37. Myers, *Mexican War Diary of George B. McClellan*, 18; Timothy Johnson, *A Gallant Little Army*, 269. On frictions between regulars and volunteers, see Bauer, *Mexican War*, 83, 101–2, 147, 220–21. On the implications of volunteer abuses of Mexican civilians for regular army officers during the Civil War, see Bradley and Dahlen, *From Conciliation to Conquest*, 5, 79–83.

38. Johannsen, *To the Halls of the Montezumas*, 43. For a contemporary recognition of Ringgold's professionalism, see Peterson, *Military Heroes of the War with Mexico*, 161–63. For more-florid treatments of Ringgold's death, see Johannsen, *To the Halls of the Montezumas*, 124–27. And even Peterson, who was obviously willing to praise Ringgold for his role in the creation of the American artillery arm, admired Taylor so much that he absurdly claimed Buena Vista "in one sense, the cause of all our subsequent triumphs"; Peterson, *Military Heroes of the War with Mexico*, 139.

39. Justin Smith, *War with Mexico*, 2:98; George to Alfred Sully, n.d., folder no. 29, Alfred Sully Papers; [P.] G. T. Beauregard to John L. Smith, September 20, 1847, WA MSS S-2000, Un3127, Beinecke Library. For the use of marksmen in the urban fighting at Monterrey, see Justin Smith, *War with Mexico*, 1:258. On sniping during the assault on Chapultepec, see Bauer, *Mexican War*, 317. On the use of skirmishers by both Americans and Mexicans at Monterrey, see Justin Smith, *War with Mexico*, 1:242, 245. The use of sniping against the defenders of a fortification during the assault on Chapultepec bore a rough similarity to the Civil War sniping that started in earnest during the siege of Yorktown in 1862. See Nosworthy, *Bloody Crucible of Courage*, 370; Oeffinger, *A Soldier's General*, 141. On the general lessons the regulars drew, see McWhiney and Jamieson, *Attack and Die*, 27–40.

Chapter 4

1. Because the North ended up retaining control over the federal government, one would think that it would be the section least hostile to the extension of federal military power. The fact that significant numbers of northerners during the Civil War era were profoundly hostile to standing-army coercion shows just how powerful Anglo-American antimilitarism remained.

2. Hughes, *General William J. Hardee*, 42–43.

3. Bruce, *Lincoln and the Tools of War*, 32, 70; Nevins, *War for the Union*, 1:361–63, 369; U.S. Army Ordnance Department, *Reports of Experiments with Small Arms*, 3, 6–7. For antebellum debates over the role of the breechloader, see Carl Davis, *Arming the Union*, 107–21.

4. U.S. Army Ordnance Department, *Reports of Experiments with Small Arms*, 105, 108, 102.

5. Weller, "Civil War Minie Rifles," 36–38.

6. Hughes, *General William J. Hardee*, 47–48; William J. Hardee to Edwin V. Sumner, May 23, 1854 [rough], H 250 1854, AGO; Samuel Cooper to Jefferson Davis, July 28, 1854, W 287 1854, AGO. As far as I know, the chasseur manual never included a third volume going beyond the School of the Battalion.

7. Silas Casey to Samuel Cooper, December 14, 1854, C 562 1854, AGO. The order is reprinted on the frontispiece of Hardee's *Rifle and Light Infantry Tactics*. Willard, *Comparative Value of Rifled and Smooth-Bored Arms*, 12–13.

8. Silas Casey to Samuel Cooper, December 14, 1854, C 562 1854, AGO; Silas Casey to Jefferson Davis, October 28, 1854, C 490 1854; General Orders No. 2, February 28, 1857, AGO.

9. Todd, *American Military Equipage*, 1:118–19; Hardee, *Rifle and Light Infantry Tactics* [1855], 1:13 [51]. Saber bayonets could be used as short swords by themselves and included a hilt, while socket bayonets were designed to be used only when fitted to a musket.

10. William J. Hardee, "Infantry Tactics—Detailed Programme," Curriculum Study, 1858–59, series 15, 4b, box 1, Records of the Academic Board. No practical drills in the "evolutions of the line" could be conducted at West Point, because the cadets could muster only an understrength battalion. Hardee also retained instruction in the third volume of Scott in his proposed curriculum during the 1860 curricular review. See Hardee, "Programme of a course of instruction in the Department of tactics, prepared in accordance with a resolution of the Board 'appointed to revise the programme of studies at the Military Academy,'" Board of Officers—Curriculum Revision, Jan.–April 1860, part 1, series 15, 4b, box 1, Records of the Academic Board. For an example of an attempt to use Scott's third volume in addition to Hardee's light infantry manual during the Civil War, see William B. Hazen to Jas. A. Fry, January 7, 1862, pp. 359–60, William B. Hazen Papers.

11. Silas Casey to Samuel Cooper, December 14, 1854, C 562 1854, AGO; McWhiney and Jamieson, *Attack and Die*, 50. For other contemporaneous documents that make no mention of adopting the double quick time to compensate for the increased range of the rifle-musket, see W. H. T. Walker to S. Cooper, November 16, 1854, W 479 1854, and

C. M. Wilcox to Samuel Cooper, November 17, 1854, W 483 1854 filed w/ W 364 1846, AGO.

12. Silas Casey to Samuel Cooper, December 14, 1854, C 562 1854, AGO; Silas Casey to Jefferson Davis, October 28, 1854, C 490 1854, ENCL-3, AGO.

13. George W. Cushing to "My dear Folks," November 5, 1854, George W. Cushing to mother, November 11, 1854 [in section addressed to "Sam"], George William Cushing Letters; George D. Bayard to Esther Bayard, October 7, 1854, George Dashiell Bayard Papers.

14. Hardee even made requests for the actual uniform and equipment of the Chasseurs à Pied. See William J. Hardee to Thomas S. Jesup, June 14, 1854, enclosed in W. G. Freeman to T. S. Jesup and H. K. Craig, June 29, 1854, H 217 1854, AGO. On the French tactical system as a whole, see Griffith, *Military Thought in the French Army*, 109, 127–30.

Heth, *System of Target Practice*; McClellan, *Manual of Bayonet Exercise*; Willard, *Manual of Target Practice*; Diary, August 24, 28–29, 1850, Ct. D5, George B. McClellan Papers. For references to bayonet fencing, see the entries for September 11, October 28, November 4–6, 10, 13, 15, and 18.

15. McClellan, *Report of Captain George B. McClellan*, 44, 42. Also see McClellan's excerpts of the Russian infantry tactics, whose comments on skirmishing correspond roughly to French and American thought and practice. Ibid., 158–59.

It is unclear how common post schools and libraries were, but at least a few did indeed exist. See Coffman, *Old Army*, 175–76. The movement to provide for a soldiers' home for old enlisted soldiers during the antebellum period did certainly owe something to European precedent and practice. See newspaper clipping from the *Daily Delta*, Sunday, March 12, 1848, Container 1 [332], Robert Anderson Papers.

On the Delafield Commission, see Moten, *Delafield Commission*. This commission was an observer mission sent to assess the Crimean War. It included Maj. Richard Delafield of the Engineers, Maj. Alfred Mordecai of the Ordnance Department, and Capt. George B. McClellan of the Cavalry. On the question of the rifle-musket and the Crimean War, see ibid., 198.

16. Kelton does not specifically refer to the term "rifle-musket," but the high level of accuracy required demands its use in these exercises and that presumably is what the cadets used for target practice. John C. Kelton, "Programme of the Course of instruction for the department of small arms," Curriculum Study, 1858–59, series 15, 4b, box 1, Records of the Academic Board.

Kelton's ideas were not actually unprecedented in the American service; 1st. Lt. Henry C. Wayne, the master of sword when the academic board had proposed a five-year course in 1844, had advocated the introduction of "such gymnastic exercises as would tend to develop that physical energy and activity necessary to render an officer an efficient leader, as well as director of his men, in all emergencies; such as the lodgement and uses of scaling hooks, ropes, ladders &c. &c." He also called for bayonet exercise, citing European practice. See Henry C. Wayne to J. A. Thomas, December 26, 1844, "Adjutant's Circular 13 Dec 1844 and Dept. Head's replies thereto (Dec 1844) concerning early proposals for FIVE YEAR COURSE," series 15, 4b, box 2, Records of the Academic Board.

17. Willard, *Manual of Target Practice*, 71–72.

18. Ibid., 74–80. See, for examples, Hardee, *Rifle and Light Infantry Tactics* [1855], 1:197 [129], 1:200–1 [141–43], 1:213 [201].

19. Keegan, *Face of Battle*, 154–60; Willard, *Manual of Target Practice*, 78.

20. Wilcox, *Rifles and Rifle Practice*, 173.

21. Ibid., 243–45 (quotation from 244).

The mix of British and French organizational terms in American military practice and writing can lead to some confusion. Following British practice, the fundamental organizational unit of the American army in this period was the regiment, generally ten companies of a hundred men each. However, following French practice, the primary tactical unit referred to in drill manuals was the battalion, which generally was the same thing as the regiment but called by a different name.

22. Ibid., 245, 37, 175–76; C. M. Wilcox to Samuel Cooper, November 17, 1854, W 483 1854 filed w/ W 364 1846, AGO. In the published version of Hardee's tactics, corporals are posted in the first rank with privates in the rear, so Wilcox's complaints may have had some effect. Hardee, *Rifle and Light Infantry Tactics*, 1:6[8].

23. Wilcox, *Rifles and Rifle Practice*, 245–46; C. M. Wilcox to Samuel Cooper, November 17, 1854, W 483 1854 filed w/ W 364 1846, AGO. Curiously enough, Wilcox's official comments on Hardee's tactics in 1854 actually argued that the new tactics could serve as the manual for both light and line infantry.

The only explicit antebellum American citation I have seen of increased step rates as a means of coping with the rifle-musket can be found in R.E.C., "Modern Tactics," 16. Even this author, however, still operated very much in the chasseur tradition when he declared his commitment to bayonet fencing (18). Although the author predicted an increase in the use of fieldworks, he still did not totally discount the role of cavalry (19). One historian has identified R.E.C. as Raleigh Edward Colston, an instructor at the Virginia Military Institute. See Nosworthy, *Bloody Crucible of Courage*, 88. For French ideas about quicker movement rates as a means of compensating for the rifle-musket, see Griffith, *Military Thought in the French Army*, 129. The fact remains, however, that official American discussion of the question never explicitly saw increased movement rates as a means of overcoming the increased range of the rifle-musket. Furthermore, American movement rates had always been peculiarly swift since before the Mexican War.

24. Wilcox, *Rifles and Rifle Practice*, 246–47. For a treatment that understates Wilcox's recognition of the reduced effectiveness of artillery and cavalry, see McWhiney and Jamieson, *Attack and Die*, 56–58.

25. Wilcox, *Rifles and Rifle Practice*, 248, 242–46 (emphasis in original).

26. Ibid., 237–38.

27. Ibid., 238; Willard, *Manual of Target Practice*, 69. On the problem of preventing ammunition waste, see Wilcox, *Rifles and Rifle Practice*, 242.

28. W. S. Ketchum to Samuel Cooper, September 21, 1859, K 63 1859; W. S. Ketchum to Samuel Cooper, May 20, 1860, K 25 1860, AGO. Ketchum's commentary on Hardee's tactics was also premised in large part on the distinction between rifle-armed riflemen and musket-armed light infantry.

29. Report of Academic Board to Col. J. G. Totten, February 7, 1845, vol. 4, pp. 48–50

(quotation from 50), Staff Records; Minority Report, February 12, 1845, vol. 4, pp. 52–56
(quotation from 55), Staff Records; Morrison, *"Best School in the World,"* 115–20. The
five-year course was more than a little controversial. Most of the academic board called
for its removal in 1858, but Secretary of War John Floyd reinstated the curriculum in
1859. A commission headed by Jefferson Davis and staffed by various military authorities, including respected old army professionals, also supported the retention of the
five-year course. However, the breakout of war settled the issue in 1861, with the four-
year course returning. See ibid., 123–25. Furthermore, some officers remained dissatisfied with the professional content of the five-year academy curriculum. Maj. William
H. Emory, for example, later made proposals for instruction in the "Art of War" that
included grand tactics, strategy, and a fair amount of historical instruction. See "Course
of Instruction in the Art of War," April 24, 1860, Board of Officers—Curriculum
Revision, Jan–April 1860, part 1, series 15, 4b, box 1, Records of the Academic Board.
This document even includes a lesson covering, in part, the "Use of Riflemen, Indians
and other irregular auxiliaries."

30. John B. Floyd, January 30, 1860, Board of Officers—Curriculum Revision, Jan.–
April 1860, part 2, series 15, 4b, box 1, Records of the Academic Board. Also see D. H.
Mahan, "Replies to Question accompanying Resolution of Jan. 21 & 23, 1860," February
17, 1860, Board of Officers—Curriculum Revision, Jan.–April 1860, part 1, series 15, 4b,
box 1, section B, pp. 2–3, Records of the Academic Board; John B. Floyd, January 5, 1860,
"Instructions for the Board appointed to revise the programme of instruction at the
Military Academy . . . ," Board of Officers—Curriculum Revision, Jan.–April 1860, part
2, series 15, 4b, box 1, Records of the Academic Board. On the regulars and the militia,
see, for example, B. F. Edwards to Sylvester Churchill, July 18, 1857, Correspondence Re.
Proposed Drill Manual Folder, Sylvester Churchill Papers.

31. Richard Delafield to R. E. DeRussy, February 7, 1859, Curriculum Study, 1858–
59, series 15, 4b, box 1, Records of the Academic Board; D. H. Mahan, "Replies to
Question accompanying Resolution of Jan. 21 & 23, 1860," February 17, 1860, Board of
Officers—Curriculum Revision, Jan.–April 1860, part 1, series 15, 4b, box 1, section B,
p. 2, Records of the Academic Board; D. H. Mahan, "Replies to Question accompanying
Resolution of Jan. 21 & 23, 1860," February 17, 1860, Board of Officers—Curriculum
Revision, Jan.–April 1860, part 1, series 15, 4b, box 1, section A, p. 2, Records of the
Academic Board. For Mahan's committee report recommending the dissolution of
the five-year course, see D. H. Mahan, Committee Report, September 4, 1858, vol. 6,
353–362, Staff Records.

32. Starr, *The Union Cavalry*, 1:53–54. The most important result from the Delafield Commission's observation mission in the Crimea was the adoption of the twelve-
pounder Napoleon gun-howitzer. See Moten, *Delafield Commission*, 180–81. Container 8
of the Robert Anderson Papers includes letters written by artillery officers to Anderson
on the subject of the artillery school that reopened at Fort Monroe in 1859.

Chapter 5

1. I also counted as loyal individuals who made public professions of loyalty to the
Union, even if they did not serve in a military capacity. Most of the individuals counted,
however, did serve in uniform.

2. Morrison, *"Best School in the World,"* 80–81, 129–30; Schaff, *The Spirit of Old West Point*, 145–48; Ball, *Army Regulars*, 83. Schaff described himself as "born and bred in a family some of whose ties were Southern and all of whose political views were sympathetic" (147–48).

3. On the distinction between partisan and political, see Skelton, *American Profession of Arms*, 282–83.

4. Coakley, *Federal Military Forces in Domestic Disorders*, 97, 101; Winfield Scott to William C. Preston, December 14, 1832, reprinted in Winfield Scott, *Memoirs*, 1:241; Timothy Johnson, *Winfield Scott*, 91, 108–9.

5. Coakley, *Federal Military Forces in Domestic Disorders*, 110–19. For another instructive example of Scott's philosophy of using a policy "at once moderate & firm" to defuse frontier frictions, see his instructions regarding threats of a possible Texan invasion of New Mexico, Winfield Scott to Bvt. Col. J. [James] Monroe, August 6, 1850, War Department, Winfield Scott Papers.

6. Furniss, *Mormon Conflict*, 197, 201–3, 211–12, 215, 217–18, 221, 225.

7. Sumner quoted in Ball, *Army Regulars*, 177; Coakley, *Federal Military Forces in Domestic Disorders*, 158–59. It should be noted that Davis was distinctly partial toward the proslavery forces. Coakley argues that Sumner was more or less impartial in his treatment of the pro- and antislavery factions (ibid., 171–72). Durwood Ball concurs with Coakley on Sumner's impartiality (Ball, *Army Regulars*, 176). On Sumner in the secession winter, see ibid., 190, 195.

8. Philip St. George Cooke to Colonel S. Cooper, June 18, 1856, reprinted in United States, War Department, *Report of the Secretary of War*, 48–49. Also see Coakley, *Federal Military Forces in Domestic Disorders*, 157.

9. Philip St. George Cooke to Daniel Woodson, September 2, 1856, reprinted in United States, War Department, *Report of the Secretary of War*, 91–92; Ewy, "United States Army in the Kansas Border Troubles," 399–400; Coakley, *Federal Military Forces in Domestic Disorders*, 163.

10. Coakley, *Federal Military Forces in Domestic Disorders*, 162, 164–65; Philip St. George Cooke to George Deas, August 31, 1856, in United States, War Department, *Report of the Secretary of War*, 89; Ball, *Army Regulars*, 176.

11. Philip St. George Cooke to George Deas, September 5, 1856, in United States, War Department, *Report of the Secretary of War*, 103; Rodenbough, *From Everglade to Cañon*, 184.

12. Cooke, *Scenes and Adventures in the Army*, 40. The episode is supposed to have occurred in 1829, two years after his graduation from the academy.

13. Coakley, *Federal Military Forces in Domestic Disorders*, 156, 163.

14. Ball, *Army Regulars*, 183–84. Regulars were, of course, much more aggressive toward Indians, for a variety of reasons — political, racial, and cultural — but I separate the regular army's Indian-fighting role from its forays into law enforcement and civil administration among whites.

15. Coakley, *Federal Military Forces in Domestic Disorders*, 165–67.

16. Ibid., 168–72 (quotation from 168).

17. Ibid., 175–88.

18. Ball, *Army Regulars*, 177, 182, 185–87.

19. Magruder went as far as serving in the Army of the Potomac during the Peninsula campaign. He went on leave of absence on August 3, 1862, and resigned his commission on October 1. He then joined the Confederate service and was killed at Gettysburg (Cullum, *Biographical Register,* 2:414–15). Cullum lists Stith as serving on detached service through much of 1861, but as dismissed on September 25, 1861. He then joined the Confederate cause (ibid., 2:435–36). Meade actually served as part of the Sumter garrison but immediately resigned his commission afterward on May 1 and joined the Confederate service (ibid., 2:675). On Emory, see Ball, *Army Regulars,* 192–94.

20. W. T. H. Brooks to father, April 28, 1861, William T. H. Brooks Papers.

21. On Mordecai, see Skelton, *American Profession of Arms,* 355.

22. Assuming as a rough measure that the average USMA graduate was twenty-one years of age at graduation, a 1830 grad would have been fifty-one in 1860. As a point of comparison, Robert E. Lee graduated in 1829, Stonewall Jackson in 1846, Ulysses S. Grant in 1843, and William T. Sherman in 1840. Lee was, compared to his contemporary generals, something of an old man during the Civil War — all other things being equal, relative youthfulness was advantageous for a Civil War general.

23. Seniority was the primary determinant for promotion in the old army. However, brevet ranks were given out for meritorious conduct, and in my database I have made no distinction between regular and brevet ranks.

Jefferson Davis (USMA 1828), Albert Sidney Johnston (USMA 1826), and Joseph Eggleston Johnston (USMA 1829) were the generals. I have included Davis even though he declined his brigadier's commission, because my use of rank is as a proxy for achievement in the regular army. The Unionist colonels were John J. Abert, John J. Abercrombie, Lorenzo Thomas, Edmund B. Alexander, Dennis Hart Mahan, Dixon S. Miles, Washington Seawell, William H. C. Bartlett, Philip St. George Cooke, and Henry H. Lockwood. Note that I have considered professors at either West Point or the United States Naval Academy as being equivalent to colonels — D. H. Mahan and William H. C. Bartlett for the former, Henry H. Lockwood for the latter. I have felt justified in doing this because the academies played such an important role in their respective services, although the Naval Academy at this time had a weaker footing. Nevertheless, Lockwood was one of the Naval Academy's most prominent early instructors and would go on to become a brigade commander at Gettysburg. See Todorich, *The Spirited Year,* 57–59, 77–78, 199. The Confederate colonels were Edward G. W. Butler, Robert E. Lee, and Jones M. Withers.

Using data drawn from only officers still in the U.S. Army in 1861, Skelton finds rank to be a minor factor in the decision of serving officers to resign and join the Confederacy, except for field-grade and general officers (Skelton, *American Profession of Arms,* 355–56). My own data are different in that they include all living West Point graduates, as opposed to those still in the regular army in 1860.

24. McKinney, *Education in Violence,* 82, 85–93. Simon Cameron, Lincoln's first secretary of war, had doubts about Thomas's loyalty early in the war. See Hattaway and Smith, "Thomas, George Henry," *American National Biography Online.*

Thomas later claimed that he had warned Winfield Scott of David Twiggs's plans to surrender the Department of Texas. See Van Horne, *George H. Thomas,* 20.

25. McKinney, *Education in Violence*, 86, 88 (quotation). On the issue of Thomas's wavering, also see Piatt, *General George H. Thomas*, 82–83.

26. McKinney, *Education in Violence*, 88–89; Wilbur Thomas, *General George H. Thomas*, 133; Van Horne, *George H. Thomas*, 28.

After the war, Mrs. Thomas recalled that Thomas had written her that, "turn it every way he would, the one thing was uppermost, his duty to the government of the United States," quoted in McKinney, *Education in Violence*, 89.

Thomas's decision must have come after Virginia's secession on April 17 in response to Lincoln's call for volunteers, although Van Horne is not explicit in giving the timing as such.

27. Van Horne, *George H. Thomas*, 26–27; Cleaves, *Rock of Chickamauga*, 67; George H. Thomas to A. A. Draper, March 22, 1865, A. A. Draper Letters.

28. Hartsuff quoted in Wilbur Thomas, *General George H. Thomas*, 134. On the conservatism of the antebellum regular army officer corps as a whole, see Skelton, *American Profession of Arms*, 350.

29. George H. Thomas to A. A. Draper, March 4, 1865, A. A. Draper Letters. On Sherman's southern sympathies, see Royster, *Destructive War*, 126–27.

30. Coppée, *General Thomas*, 23, 27–28; McKinney, *Education in Violence*, 91. On the importance of family considerations, see Skelton, *American Profession of Arms*, 357.

31. James Maget to Elizabeth Thomas, Southampton County, February 7, 1848, Mss2/M2723/a/1, Virginia Historical Society; O'Connor, *Thomas*, 111; McKinney, *Education in Violence*, 90–93, 473; Cleaves, *Rock of Chickamauga*, 306–7; Einolf, *George Thomas*, 87–88; O'Connor, *Thomas*, 115–16; Wilbur Thomas, *General George H. Thomas*, 133; Piatt, *General George H. Thomas*, 84–85.

32. Warner, *Generals in Blue*, 496–97; [William H. Terrill] to William Rufus Terrill, May 13, 1861 [copy], Alexander Dallas Bache Papers. Whatever the merits of the family tradition, there is some evidence that Terrill was given duty in the West out of deference to his Virginian family. See A. D. Bache to G. W. Cullum, May 20, 1861, Alexander Dallas Bache Papers.

On Gibbon (including the source of the quotation), see Taaffe, *Commanding the Army of the Potomac*, 198. E. Porter Alexander's brief reference to Gibbon as "a despicable traitor" in a personal letter to his wife in the summer of 1862 also shows that many southerners expected the most famous commander of the Iron Brigade to follow his native state. See Edward Porter Alexander to Bessie [Alexander], June 13, 1862, Edward Porter Alexander Papers.

33. Emory Thomas, *Bold Dragoon*, 95 (includes quotation of Stuart); Young, *The West of Philip St. George Cooke*, 322, 328, 346.

34. Young, *The West of Philip St. George Cooke*, 322–24 (quotations from 323 and 324).

35. P. St. George Cooke to *Washington National Intelligencer*, June 6, 1861, in Frank Moore, *Rebellion Record*, 2:171–72. I was unable to locate the original document, but I have no reason to doubt the letter's authenticity.

36. Timothy Johnson, *Winfield Scott*, 223; Winfield Scott, *Memoirs*, 2:610–11. For one

reference to Scott's Unionism in relation to the Compromise of 1850, see Winfield Scott to [Charles Ferguson] Smith, March 13, 1850, New York, Winfield Scott Papers.

37. Quoted in Timothy Johnson, *Winfield Scott*, 224–25 (quotation from 224); Winfield Scott, *Memoirs*, 2:614–15; Cooling, *Military during Constitutional Crisis*, 37, 46–47.

38. Winfield Scott, *Memoirs*, 1:248.

39. Potter, *Lincoln and His Party*, 360–63; Freeman, *Lee*, 1:437; Timothy Johnson, *Winfield Scott*, 226, 233. I am following Potter's argument that Lincoln had originally hoped to give up Fort Sumter but stay firm on Fort Pickens (358–59). On Scott's conservative and conciliatory Unionism, also see his letter of March 3 to Seward, reprinted in Winfield Scott, *Memoirs*, 2:625–28. On Scott's reluctance to reinforce the two forts, see "Notes on Military Matters," April 4, 1861, HM 41701, Edward Davis Townsend Papers.

40. J. W. Jones, *Personal Reminiscences*, 137; Lee quoted in Nolan, *Lee Considered*, 33.

41. Nolan, *Lee Considered*, 37. For the text of the standard army oath, as given in the Articles of War, see Art. 10 of the Articles of War in United States, War Department, *Regulations for the Army*.

42. Freeman, *Lee*, 1:438, 429; Ball, *Army Regulars*, 192; Skelton, *American Profession of Arms*, 357. After Twiggs took over command of the Department of Texas, Lee was in effect on leave at Arlington.

43. Pryor, *Reading the Man*, 292–93.

44. My analysis of Cullum counted fourteen Lower South West Pointers who stayed with the Union. How many were "true" southerners is open to question—six had associations of some sort with non-southern locales, either as their birthplaces or their residences at the time of appointment. We do not have enough biographical data to make firm conclusions with regard to the group as a whole. A northern state of residence may not, after all, indicate any real shedding of a southern identity. Because some northern-born officers ended up in the Confederate service because of family ties and connections with the South, I have simply assumed that such cases more or less washed each other out.

45. Edward Alexander, *Fighting for the Confederacy*, 27–28; Warner, *Generals in Blue*, 419–20, 657 n. 553; Cullum, *Biographical Register*, 2:668. Alexander was also stunned when he heard that 2nd Lt. Thomas G. Baylor and 1st Lt. Robert Williams, both Virginians, had stayed loyal to the Union. Edward Porter Alexander to wife, June 4, 1861, Edward Porter Alexander Papers.

46. Lee quoted in Freeman, *Lee*, 4:279.

Chapter 6

1. Fellman, *Inside War*; Gallagher, *Confederate War*, 123–27, 140–44; Macky, *Uncivil War*, 22. Mackey attributes a more important role to guerrillas than I do.

2. Eugene Carr to father, January 28, 1862, Eugene A. Carr Papers.

3. Eugene Carr to father, June 7, 1863, Eugene A. Carr Papers. Carr could still find some humor in stories of soldiers' misbehavior, but when he later wrote of one toward the end of the war, he still made clear his intentions to hold his men to higher standards

of behavior. See Eugene Carr to Mary P. Maguire, March 14, 1865, Eugene A. Carr Papers. Carr also declared his intention to execute Confederates found with exploding bullets, who he believed violated civilized norms of warfare.

Alfred Sully to [?], December 15, 1862; Alfred Sully to [?], June 24, 1861, Alfred Sully Papers. Sully actually excelled at Indian fighting, so it is possible he did not have an inherent distaste for all constabulary duty. Executing those sorts of duties against white Americans, as opposed to Indian peoples, however, may have given him special unease, especially considering his restrained McClellanite instincts.

4. Dowdey, *Wartime Papers of Robert E. Lee*, 689; Edward Porter Alexander to wife, March 18, 1862, Edward Porter Alexander Papers.

5. It must be pointed that old army men themselves realized their dearth of experience in the management of large units. See, for example, Lee's comments in a letter in March 1863, *OR*, ser. 4, vol. 2, 448. Also see McDowell's statement in *RJCCW* 2:38.

6. *OR*, ser. 1, vol. 2, 671, 721; "What Sort of Fighting," *Charleston Mercury*, May 30, 1861.

7. The naiveté of the armies that fought First Bull Run is a virtual staple of Civil War history. Both standard battle studies follow this motif. See William Davis, *Battle at Bull Run*, xii–xiii; Hennessy, *First Battle of Manassas*, 128–29. Marcus Cunliffe's prologue to his fine study of American military culture, *Soldiers and Civilians*, is an excellent treatment of the aura of romantic glory that surrounded the contending armies before the battle. See Cunliffe, *Soldiers and Civilians*, 3–27. Cunliffe focuses on the variegated and ambiguous nature of American martial culture. This includes in his view the professional tradition represented by West Point and the regular army, which he pointedly refuses to privilege over the competing traditions of citizen-soldier virtue and pacifist antimilitarism. See especially ibid., 281–82.

Moore's comments in *OR*, ser. 4, vol. 1, 422. For a similar document from August, see *OR*, ser. 4, vol. 1, 561. *OR*, ser. 4, vol. 2, 728. Fahs, *Imagined Civil War*, 93–94, 110, 118–19; Sherman, *Memoirs*, 877.

8. J. B. Jones, *Rebel War Clerk's Diary*, 1:18, 51; "The Confederate Army," *Richmond Enquirer*, April 27, 1861; "What Sort of Fighting," *Charleston Mercury*, May 30, 1861. Also see Greene, *Civil War Petersburg*, 67.

9. Fahrney, *Horace Greeley and the Tribune*, 83–85; Nevins, *War for the Union*, 1:210–11, 214–15; Crawford, *William Howard Russell's Civil War*, 74, 83; *New York Daily Tribune*, July 2, 1862; "The Real Issue," *New York Daily Tribune*, July 1, 1861; "Just Once," *New York Daily Tribune*, July 25, 1861; Harry Williams, "Attack upon West Pointers during the Civil War," 493. Williams's article is the best single survey of radical Republican hostility toward West Point. For a wider perspective on congressional opposition to the academy during the war, which was not always directly linked to the radicals, see Lisowski, "Future of West Point."

10. Freeman, *Lee*, 1:492; Dowdey, *Wartime Papers of Robert E. Lee*, 15; Oeffinger, *A Soldier's General*, 88; Dowdey, *Wartime Papers of Robert E. Lee*, 27; *OR*, ser. 1, vol. 51, pt. 1, 369–70.

11. Sherman to Thomas Ewing Jr., May 23, 1861; Sherman to Ellen Ewing Sherman, June 12, 1861, in Simpson and Berlin, *Sherman's Civil War*, 91, 102–3; Rosecrans to wife, July 18, 1861, box 59, folder 8, William Rosecrans Papers; *OR*, ser. 1, vol. 2, 721.

12. *New York Times*, May 1, 1861; "superior beings" quoted in William Davis, *Battle at Bull Run*, 112; Freeman, *Lee*, 1:468–69; "The Confederate Army," *Richmond Enquirer*, April 27, 1861; J. B. Jones, *Rebel War Clerk's Diary*, 1:53.

13. On the relationship between prowess on the drill field and unit pride, see Weitz, "Drill, Training, and the Combat Performance," 280.

Howe, *Passages from the Life of Henry Warren Howe*, July 14, 1861; Bratton, *Letters of John Bratton*, March 1, 1861; Piston and Hatcher, *Wilson's Creek*, 114–15. Steen had been an officer appointed from civil life during the Mexican War who had received a brevet for gallantry during the conflict. He left the service after the war's end, but returned to the old army with another appointment from civil life in 1852 and served until the outbreak of the Civil War in 1861. See Heitman, *Historical Register*, s.v. "Steen, Alexander Early."

14. Michie, *Life and Letters of Emory Upton*, 42–46. It should be pointed out, however, that in the North, the federal government refused to disperse regular army officers among the volunteer regiments from the war's initial outbreak because of fears of wrecking the regular army as an institution, which still had responsibilities on the frontier. For an early criticism of this policy, see Upton, *Military Policy*, 235–36. Also see Kreidberg and Henry, *History of Military Mobilization*, 97.

William Davis, *Battle at Bull Run*, 21; Freeman, *Lee*, 1:493–94; McMurry, *Two Great Rebel Armies*, 99–104; Piston and Hatcher, *Wilson's Creek*, 8, 10, 72, 94, 115. One Union officer even reported some target practice in his regiment. See Favill, *Diary of a Young Officer*, 23. For a practice range for Confederate troops in Missouri, see Piston and Hatcher, *Wilson's Creek*, 117. On training time, see Haughton, *Training, Tactics and Leadership*, 54.

On the use of Citadel cadets to drill South Carolina regiments, see William Davis, *Battle at Bull Run*, 26. On a specific VMI example, see Edward Porter Alexander to wife, June 29, 1861, Edward Porter Alexander Papers. For the role of southern military schools in general, see Allardice, "West Points of the Confederacy." Allardice's article is a fine piece on the topic, but he overstates the importance of southern military schools. The importance of West Pointers did not simply derive from what they studied at the academy, but also on the experience many gained from service in the regular army, and the fact that the academy was one part of a larger military institution. Furthermore, many of these academies focused on the scientific, as opposed to the military, aspects of their curricula. See Green, "Books and Bayonets," 6–7, 79, 90–91.

15. "The Correspondence of Thomas Reade Rootes Cobb," 182–83; Ingraham, *Elmer E. Ellsworth*, 7, 12, 65.

16. Ingraham, *Elmer E. Ellsworth*, 89; [Ellsworth], *Zouave Drill Book*, 41–42 [1–6]; Hardee, *Rifle and Light Infantry Tactics* [1855], 171–75 [1–12], [15–21]; Ingraham, *Elmer E. Ellsworth*, 92; Bradley and Dahlen, *From Conciliation to Conquest*, 33. Ingraham, however, downplays frictions between Ellsworth and the regulars.

17. Hardee, *Rifle and Light Infantry Tactics* [1855], 196 [125–26]; [Ellsworth], *Zouave Drill Book*, 54 [105–6].

18. John Smith, *Nineteenth Regiment of Maine Volunteer Infantry*, 293. On the importance of skirmishers maintaining a "good general alignment" in order to give confidence to one another and not stall an advance, see Sherman, *Memoirs*, 886.

19. Cunliffe, *Soldiers and Civilians*, 20, 248.

20. Ingraham, *Elmer E. Ellsworth*, 130. Also see "Ellsworth's Fire Zouaves," and "Wilson's Fighting Men," *Harper's Weekly*, May 18, 1861, 311; Wise quoted in J. B. Jones, *Rebel War Clerk's Diary*, 1:18; Moseley, "American Civil War Infantry Tactics," 193.

21. William Davis, *Battle at Bull Run*, 30; Warner, *Generals in Gray*, 56–57; Robert Anderson to Duncan L. Clinch, November 30, 1846, Robert Anderson Papers.

22. Fitzhugh, "The Times and the War," 2–4.

23. "Extempore Warfare," *Charleston Mercury*, June 13, 1861. It should also be pointed out that, in American practice at least, saber bayonets were usually attached only to rifles as opposed to the longer musket (either rifled or smoothbore). The article's reference to "good long muskets" seems to clearly indicate that it understood the distinction between the longer musket and the shorter rifle, but the reference to saber bayonets seems to be just another sign of somewhat misinformed editorial opinion. Warner, *Generals in Gray*, 28–29; William Davis, *Battle at Bull Run*, 51 (quotation), 66.

24. Fitzhugh, "The Times and the War."

25. Fitzhugh, "Reflections on the Conduct of the War," 429–30.

26. "Modern Warfare," 82; *OR*, ser. 1, vol. 2, 476.

27. Fitch, *Annals of the Army of the Cumberland*, 271; Bergeron, *Civil War Reminiscences*, 66; Mark Wilson, *The Business of Civil War*, 2, 35, 65–71; Goff, *Confederate Supply*, 8–10.

28. I have drawn on William Davis, *Battle at Bull Run*, and Hennessy, *First Battle of Manassas*, for the basic battle narrative.

29. William Davis, *Battle at Bull Run*, 146.

30. Col. Israel B. Richardson, a brigade commander in Tyler's division, used a battalion of light infantry composed of forty picked men from each of his four regiments as scouts in front of his line of march. See *OR*, ser. 1, vol. 2, 312. For an example of skirmishers' probing, see William Davis, *Battle at Bull Run*, 116. Also see *OR*, ser. 1, vol. 2, 369, 375, 383, 405, 488. On aimed fire, see *OR*, ser. 1, vol. 2, 494, 540, 543, 547. Skirmishers did not limit their role to probing and reconnaissance on the enemy; aimed fire was designed to inflict losses. Aimed fire also need not be conducted at long ranges. Confederate sharpshooters in the Henry House were only sixty yards away from the nearest one of Ricketts's guns on Henry Hill. See Hennessy, *First Battle of Manassas*, 78–79. Finally, it must be remembered that long-range fire was not always effective, even if it did occur as early as this battle; see, for example, ibid., 111. For examples of volley fire, see William Davis, *Battle at Bull Run*, 119; Hennessy, *First Battle of Manassas*, 80–81.

31. William Davis, *Battle at Bull Run*, 172–74, 212–13; *OR*, ser. 1, vol. 2, 482. Also see one report of Jackson on Henry Hill instructing his men to allow the Federals to close within fifty yards and then conduct a bayonet countercharge in Hennessy, *First Battle of Manassas*, 79. On Stuart's charge, see ibid., 80–82.

32. William Davis, *Battle at Bull Run*, 129; *OR*, ser. 1, vol. 2, 379; Hennessy, *First Battle of Manassas*, 80.

33. Hennessy, *First Battle of Manassas*, 58–60; Favill, *Diary of a Young Officer*, 33;

Sherman to Ellen Ewing Sherman, July 19, 1861, in Simpson and Berlin, *Sherman's Civil War*, 119; *OR*, ser. 1, vol. 2, 407. Also see Glatthaar, *General Lee's Army*, 62.

34. William Davis, *Battle at Bull Run*, 192; Hennessy, *First Battle of Manassas*, 126.

35. *OR*, ser. 1, vol. 2, 353, 358, 369; William Davis, *Battle at Bull Run*, 217; *OR*, ser. 1, vol. 2, 390.

36. *RJCCW*, 2:147; *OR*, ser. 1, vol. 2, 494; Hennessy, *First Battle of Manassas*, 112; *OR*, ser. 1, vol. 2, 523, 545; Warner, *Generals in Gray*, 146; Hennessy, *First Battle of Manassas*, 69–70, 101. On the instinctual propensity for soldiers to head for cover, see Hess, *Union Soldier in Battle*, 81. Kershaw may have been a volunteer, but he had a high respect for the old army, which he referred to in his report.

37. William Davis, *Battle at Bull Run*, 150–51, 154; *OR*, ser. 1, vol. 2, 169–70; Hennessy, *First Battle of Manassas*, 5.

38. Hennessy, *First Battle of Manassas*, 83.

39. William Davis, *Battle at Bull Run*, 203; Hennessy, *First Battle of Manassas*, 77–78; Robertson, "First Bull Run," 101.

40. *RJCCW*, 2:176; Bauer, *Mexican War*, 216.

41. *RJCCW*, 2:171; Gibbon, *Artillerist's Manual*, 401, 389; "Modern Warfare," 77. Late in the war, at least some Federal officers called for supports of two hundred infantrymen per battery. See General Orders No. 14, April 7, 1864, Artillery Brigade HQ, Henry Jackson Hunt Papers.

42. *OR*, ser. 1, vol. 2, 378–79; *RJCCW*, 2:173. Also see the corroborating testimony of 2nd Lt. Horatio B. Reed, Griffin's chief of caissons, ibid., 2:220.

43. *RJCCW*, 2:174, 2:213; Hennessy, *First Battle of Manassas*, 79. One must also remember that the Confederate artillery at First Bull Run benefited from old army expertise. Jackson, a former artillerist, had deployed his artillery on Henry Hill with a practiced professional eye. See ibid., 70.

44. Many historians would also cite Federal numerical superiority, but most Civil War battles were usually fought by armies of roughly comparable size. It was certainly an advantage to have superior numbers, but the simple counting of bodies ignores all the other factors that go into operating an army such as training, leadership, and morale. For example, while Federal forces possessed a general numerical superiority at most battles, the Union practice of raising new regiments as opposed to rebuilding veteran units with recruits frequently diluted much of this advantage. Frequent problems with expiring enlistments also reduced the effectiveness of superior Federal numbers during several crucial campaigns, including the Antietam, Chancellorsville, and Overland campaigns.

Chapter 7

1. Andrew Humphreys, *Virginia Campaign*, 4. For a stimulating treatment of McClellan's influence, see Adams, *Our Masters the Rebels*, 98–103.

2. Neely, *Union Divided*, 66; Fahrney, *Horace Greeley and the Tribune*, 86–91. On Raymond's more positive attitude toward military science, see, for example, "The Advance into Virginia — Necessity of Prudence and Economy of Life," *New York Times*, June 15, 1861. Procurement and recruitment are, of course, very different things. See Mark Wilson, *The Business of Civil War*, 31–32.

3. Dwight, *Life and Letters of Wilder Dwight*, 97–98 (quotation), 10; Favill, *Diary of a Young Officer*, 41, 49.

4. *OR*, ser. 1, vol. 2, 334; Crawford, *William Howard Russell's Civil War*, 94; *RJCCW*, 2:142–43, 2:245, 2:211; Shannon, *Organization and Administration of the Union Army*, 1:186–87. Also see Michie, *Life and Letters of Emory Upton*, 53.

5. Woodward, *Mary Chesnut's Civil War*, 401; Scheibert, *A Prussian Observes the American Civil War*, 37; *Daily Richmond Examiner*, July 24, 1861; J. B. Jones, *Rebel War Clerk's Diary*, 1:66. Jones was not so overly sanguine himself. See his entries on pp. 68, 77–78. On Confederates' later recognition of their previous complacency, see Fremantle, *Three Months in the Southern States*, 84.

6. Scheibert, *A Prussian Observes the American Civil War*, 36–37; *Daily Richmond Examiner*, September 27, 1861, February 3, 1862.

7. *Daily Richmond Examiner*, October 11, 1861; Dowdey, *Wartime Papers*, 80.

8. *Daily Richmond Examiner*, January 8, 1862; Crabtree and Patton, "*Journal of a Secesh Lady*," 189. Edmonston had no special animus against professionals; she defended Johnston as a "master of strategy" in the same diary entry. For other negative comments on Lee, see ibid., 169.

Freeman, *Lee*, 1:576–77, 602. Freeman points out that Lee may have been somewhat deceived by his experience during the Mexican War, where Scott's efficient staff could manage operations of far greater complexity.

Troops were eager and anxious for battle as late as Shiloh. See Frank and Reaves, "*Seeing the Elephant*," 72–78.

9. Taylor, "Boyce-Hammond Correspondence," 349–50; *Daily Richmond Examiner*, April 15, 1862. For another scathing comment on "red-tape West Point," see J. B. Jones, *Rebel War Clerk's Diary*, 1:87.

10. Woodward, *Mary Chesnut's Civil War*, 361, 391–92. Reflecting the sometimes-contradictory ideas of northern and southern advocates of martial enthusiasm, McCord also praised Stonewall Jackson for his aggressiveness, not realizing that Jackson also subscribed to West Point notions of rigid discipline. For another comment critical of West Pointers, see ibid., 374 [June 10]. On corps commanders, see Van Creveld, *Command in War*, 97–98.

11. Pollard, *First Year of the War*, 179, 191, 315, 251. According to the book's prefaces, Pollard's book was first completed in July 1862, but he reissued a revised and corrected version in September. On Pollard's life, see Risley, "Pollard, Edward Alfred," *American National Biography Online*. Pollard probably helped John M. Daniel with the newspaper's editorials.

12. *Daily Richmond Examiner*, June 10, 1862; Harsh, *Confederate Tide Rising*, 18–19, 27–28.

13. Dowdey, *Wartime Papers of Robert E. Lee*, 184. For a strong representative of historians who criticize Lee for excessive aggressiveness, see Nolan, *Lee Considered*, 78–89.

14. *OR*, ser. 4, vol. 2, 129–31; Sherman, *Memoirs*, 879.

15. Emory Thomas, *Confederate Nation*, 120–44.

16. Gary Wilson, "Diary of John S. Tucker," 5, 11.

17. Prokopowicz, *All for the Regiment*, 47–48, 50–51; Miller, *Training of an Army*, 71–74.

Scheibert, *A Prussian Observes the American Civil War*, 57; Thomas Fry Tobey to John Fry Tobey, December 20–22, 1862, Thomas Fry Tobey Papers.

Even for veteran units, drill could serve as a useful way of rehabilitating a unit battered by heavy action. See, for example, John Smith, *Nineteenth Regiment of Maine Volunteer Infantry*, 260, on drill in veteran units during the winter of 1864–65, and comments from Scheibert in the same page cited above. For terse late-war references to drill in a veteran Confederate unit, see "Rebel Diary, Covering the Battle of the Wilderness, Spotsylvania, Cold Harbor, etc., 1864," February 1, 1864 [p. 8], April 7, 9, and 21, 1864, [pp. 16, 18], May 4, 1864 [p. 20], and August 31, 1864 [p. 40], John Codman Ropes Papers. On an enthusiastic drill competition involving the hard-bitten 31st Illinois, originally commanded by the citizen-soldier Logan, in the winter of 1863–64, see Morris, Hartwell, and Kuykendall, *31st Regiment Illinois Volunteers*, 81. For an account of bayonet practice, target shooting, and skirmish drill (called in this case Zouave drill) in the winter of 1862–63 and later, see 155th Regimental Association, *Under the Maltese Cross*, 123, 223–26, 338. Unsurprisingly, this regiment was originally in a division commanded by the old army man A. A. Humphreys, and was later associated with regulars in Sykes's division. On brigade, battalion, division, and skirmish drills in a 6th Corps unit the following winter, see Fisk, *Hard Marching Every Day*, 155.

18. On the institutional advantages the Union should have received from inheriting the regular army establishment, particularly with regard to staff work, see Freeman, *Lee*, 2:236.

Shannon, *Organization and Administration of the Union Army*, 1:184; McClellan, *McClellan's Own Story*, 97; Grant, *Memoirs*, 187. Also see Upton, *Military Policy*, 235–36; Reese, *Sykes' Regular Infantry Division*, 43; McClellan, *Report on the Organization and Campaigns of the Army of the Potomac*, 51–52.

19. Goff, *Confederate Supply*, 55. For examples of drilling during this period, see Kundahl, *Confederate Engineer*, 92, 102. *Daily Richmond Examiner*, November 29, 1861.

20. For the best treatment of training in any western army, see Prokopowicz, *All for the Regiment*, 46–54. For one regiment's experience with extensive drill at Camp Nevin in Buell's department, see Cope, *Fifteenth Ohio*, 40, 47. Also see Morris, Hartwell, and Kuykendall, *31st Regiment Illinois Volunteers*, 19–20, 26, 41. For the western Confederate army, see Haughton, *Training, Tactics and Leadership*, 52–55.

McMurry, *Two Great Rebel Armies*, 93–95, 99–103. According to one contemporary estimate, VMI cadets drilled fifteen thousand men who later served in the Army of Northern Virginia during the spring and early summer of 1861, *OR*, ser. 4, vol. 3, 1093.

Hughes, *Battle of Belmont*, 70–71, *Daily Missouri Republican*, November 10, 1861; Cooling, *Forts Henry and Donelson*, 86–87; Shannon, *Organization and Administration of the Union Army*, 1:184–85.

21. For some examples of the general ignorance of officers, see Prokopowicz, *All for the Regiment*, 51. On the 31st Illinois, see Morris, Hartwell, and Kuykendall, *31st Regiment Illinois Volunteers*, 19. For the parade ground dispute, see Hughes, *Battle of Belmont*, 40. For the ditch quotation, see Scott, *The Story of a Cavalry Regiment*,

16. For examples of evening schools for officers, see Best, *History of the 121st New York State Infantry*, 33; [Rowe], *Sketch of the 126th Regiment*, 8. For references to officers having to first learn the drill themselves, see Horrall, *History of the Forty-second Indiana Volunteer Infantry*, 95; Child, *History of the Fifth Regiment*, 31. The 5th New Hampshire even had recitations on siege craft, see ibid., 37. Also see Regimental Orders No. 1, September 16, 1861, p. 292; Regimental Orders No. 2, September 17, 1861, p. 292; Regimental Orders No. 22, November 11, 1861, p. 314; General Orders No. 2, 19th Brigade, January 8, 1862, p. 360, William B. Hazen Papers. For the abnormally sophisticated system of recitations that Hazen used, including readings in Jomini and Napier, see General Orders No. 2, 2nd Brigade, Readyville, Tenn., March 4, 1863, p. 421. For a Confederate example of recitations, see Edward Porter Alexander to wife, June 29, 1861, Edward Porter Alexander Papers.

22. Shannon, *Organization and Administration of the Union Army*, 1:186–91. The system of examination boards was far from foolproof, or even adequate, but it was better than nothing. For examples of various defects, see Starr, *Union Cavalry*, 1:149–53. For the figures on expulsions in the Army of the Potomac, see Wert, *Sword of Lincoln*, 36. For examples of syphilis and drunkenness, see Col. Wm. Blaisdell to Brig. Gen. Joseph Hooker, November 15th, 1861, box I, folder E; Col. Charles K. Graham to Brig. Gen D. Sickles, December 19, 1861, box II, folder D, Joseph Hooker Military Papers. The Hooker papers include extensive documentation of discipline problems in a Civil War division, resulting in large part from alcohol consumption. For a reference to the use of boards in the western Federal armies, see Regimental Orders No. 36, December 15, 1861, p. 328, William B. Hazen Papers. In Hazen's regiment, the spate of resignations that shortly followed the establishment of the boards seems to indicate that they were effective in his regiment. See William B. Hazen to C. P. Buckingham, January 3, 1862, p. 337, William B. Hazen Papers.

On Confederate boards of examination, see *OR*, ser. 4, vol. 1, 1122–23. For an example of the boards actually having some effect, see Bergeron, *Civil War Reminiscences*, 50, 52. For a late reference to their use, see "Rebel Diary, covering the Battle of the Wilderness, Spottsylvania [*sic*], Cold Harbor, etc., 1864," March 2, 1864, p. 12, John Codman Ropes Papers. For Scheibert's comments, see Scheibert, *A Prussian Observes the American Civil War*, 57.

23. Skelton, *American Profession of Arms*, 48–49, 193; Freeman, *Lee's Lieutenants*, 3:200; Cunliffe, *Soldiers and Civilians*, 281.

24. Sherman, *Memoirs*, 559; Sherman to Philemon B. Ewing, April 21, 1864, in Simpson and Berlin, *Sherman's Civil War*, 625.

25. Beatie, *McClellan Takes Command*, 168–71, 177.

26. Taaffe, *Commanding the Army of the Potomac*, 215–18; Alexander S. Webb to father, May 12, 1863, Alexander S. Webb Papers. Like many other regulars, Webb attributed the army's problems to political generals.

On the Napoleonic system of command and control, with corps commanders given enough leeway to complete their tasks, but army headquarters also retaining enough control to coordinate the army as a whole, see Van Creveld, *Command in War*, 96–102. Sherman commented in his memoirs that "the corps is the true unit for grand campaigns and battle, should have a full and perfect staff, and every thing requisite for separate action, ready at all times to be detached and sent off for any nature of service. The general in command should have the rank of lieutenant-general, and should be, by experience and education, equal to any thing in war." See Sherman, *Memoirs*, 876–77.

27. Special Order No. 54, Division HQ, Hall's Hill, Va., February 9, 1862, pp. 131–32 (quotation); Thomas G. Hoyt to Morris, No. 44, n.d.; Fred F. Locke to Col. T. B. W. Stockton, No. 79, January 5, 1862, Division HQ, Halls Hill, Va.; Stockton to T. Hoyt, No. 111, March 1, 1862, Regimental HQ, Halls Hill, Va.; General Orders No. 29, November 14, 1861, Regimental HQ, Hall's Hill, Va., p. 20; Special Orders No. 36, October 30, 1861, 3rd Brigade HQ, Porter's Division, Army of the Potomac, p. 67; General Orders No. 25, November 21, 1861, Porter's Division HQ, Hall's Hill, Va., p. 82; Circular, November 21, 1861, 3rd Brigade HQ, Porter's Division, Hall's Hill, Va., pp. 82–83; Special Orders No. 48, November 25, 1861, 3rd Brigade HQ, Hall's Hill, Va., p. 85; Circular, n.d. 3rd Brigade HQ, Porter's Division, Hall's Hill, Va., pp. 89–90, Sixteenth Michigan Infantry Regimental Letter, Order, and Guard Report Book, AGO; General Orders No. 7, January 29, 1862, Regimental HQ, Camp Griffin, Va., Regimental Letter and Order Book, Fifth Vermont Infantry Regimental Letter & Order Book; Circular, Regimental HQ, Camp Griffin, Va., February 7, 1862; General Orders No. 8, Regimental HQ, Camp Griffin, Va., March 5, 1862, Third Vermont Infantry Regimental Descriptive Letter, Endorsement, & Order Book, AGO; Fisk, *Hard Marching Every Day*, 14; Blake, *Three Years in the Army of the Potomac*, 33; Child, *History of the Fifth Regiment*, 31, 33. For a brief secondary treatment, see Wert, *Sword of Lincoln*, 33–34. Also see Beatie, *McClellan Takes Command*, 281–82.

Regimental Orders No. 22, November 11, 1861, p. 314, William B. Hazen Papers. Later in the war, as a brigade commander, Hazen instituted the addition of target practice. See Orders, 2nd Brigade, 2nd Division, 21st Army Corps, Manchester, Tenn., July 29, 1863, p. 451. In his order book, there is also a record of skirmish drill on the brigade level, although it seems reasonable to think that Hazen also used skirmish drill when a regimental commander. See General Orders No. 20, 19th Brigade, February 10, 1862, p. 372; General Orders No. 28, 19th Brigade, February 27, 1862, p. 378; General Orders No. 39, 19th Brigade, April 17, 1862, p. 389. The spotty nature of Civil War infantry training is even found in Hazen's brigade, where as late as 1864, he complains about his soldiers' poor marksmanship and knowledge of target practice. See Circular, Brigade HQ, April 26, 1864, pp. 557–58. Hazen's emphasis on drill continued after his promotion to division command. See General Orders No. 44, September 16, 1864, Second Division, 15th Corps, p. 34. For another reference to limited target practice in a western regiment in December 1862, see R. Scott, *History of the 67th Regiment Indiana*, 12–14. For an example of target practice that seemed to do some good, see Marshall, *History of the Eighty-third Ohio*, 48.

28. For an example of larger unit drill using "skeleton battalions," see Special Orders No. 21, October 18, 1861, 3rd Brigade HQ, Porter's Division, Army of the Potomac, p. 28/52, Sixteenth Michigan Infantry Regimental Letter, Order, and Guard Report Book, AGO. Also see Child, *History of the Fifth Regiment*, 27, 32.

On sham battles, see Wert, *Sword of Lincoln*, 36; Beatie, *McClellan Takes Command*, 403. For more accounts and examples, see Herdegen and Murphy, *Four Years with the Iron Brigade*, 35–36, 38–39.

Beatie, *McClellan Takes Command*, 283. For another positive comment of a review, see Hyde, *Following the Greek Cross*, 35–36. For examples of conditioning with military equipage, see Herdegen and Murphy, *Four Years with the Iron Brigade*, 13–14; Child, *History of the Fifth Regiment*, 33; Reese, *Sykes' Regular Infantry Division*, 81–83. Later in the war in 1863, one soldier wrote of entire divisions drilling. See Fisk, *Hard Marching Every Day*, 111.

29. William T. Sherman to John Sherman, May 20, 1861, May 22, 1861, May 24, 1861, in Simpson and Berlin, *Sherman's Civil War*, 88–90, 92. It is telling that even Sherman thought the relatively small (by European standards) number of troops in Mexico to qualify as "large masses."

30. *OR*, ser. 1, vol. 3, 289; on defective Federal arms at Belmont in general, see Hughes, *Battle of Belmont*, 22. On exchanging, see, for example, Frank and Reaves, *"Seeing the Elephant,"* 148; Sears, *Landscape Turned Red*, 149; Gary Wilson, "Diary of John S. Tucker," 13, *OR*, ser. 1, vol. 11, pt. 1, 945; Horrall, *History of the Forty-second Indiana Volunteer Infantry*, 165–66; Blackford, *Letters from Lee's Army*, 159. Grant claimed in his memoirs that the capture of sixty thousand Confederate arms at Vicksburg was a boon to the Union, because "the small-arms of the enemy were far superior to the bulk of ours." See Grant, *Memoirs*, 384–85.

31. Cooling, *Forts Henry and Donelson*, 185; Greenwalt, "A Charge at Fort Donelson," 345; William Smith, "Operations before Fort Donelson," 41; Wainwright, *Diary of Battle*, 252. For another reference to the dangers of pausing an attack to return fire from slight cover, see Fiske, *Mr. Dunn Browne's Experiences*, 54.

32. Historians have generally been far more interested in Morgan L. Smith's use of an open-order charge by successive rushes at Donelson, where troops tried to use cover and advance in successive spurts while laying down a covering fire. See, for example, McWhiney and Jamieson, *Attack and Die*, 102, Cooling, *Forts Henry and Donelson*, 191, *OR*, ser.1, vol. 7, 239; Wallace, "Capture of Fort Donelson," 1:424. Wallace in his *Battles and Leaders* account called these methods "Zouave practice"; *OR*, ser. 1, vol. 52, pt. 1, 8.

33. For the best overview of the battle, from which I have drawn extensively, see Krick, "Men Who Carried This Position."

On the strength of the position, see ibid., 188–89; Barziza, *The Adventures of a Prisoner of War*, 27; Nicholas Davis, *Chaplain Davis and Hood's Texas Brigade*, 77; Polley, *Hood's Texas Brigade*, 47. Quotation in Barziza, *The Adventures of a Prisoner of War*, 27. This a reprint of a letter originally attributed to August 1, 1862.

Krick, "Men Who Carried This Position," 192, 195, 207–8; Harold Simpson, *Gaines' Mill to Appomattox*, 87; Barry, "Three Glorious Regiments," 103; Nicholas Davis, *Chaplain Davis and Hood's Texas Brigade*, 83, 88; Polley, *Hood's Texas Brigade*, 46–47; Hood, *Advance and Retreat*, 26; Yeary, *Reminiscences of the Boys in Gray*, 77; Polley, *Soldier's Letters*, 54–55, 299.

Note that Barry claims the regiment never lost fire discipline, as does Crozier. See Crozier, "Private with General Hood," 557; Polley also generally has the Texans maintaining complete fire discipline (Polley, *Hood's Texas Brigade*, 52, 59, but compare that with 65), as does Hood himself (*Advance and Retreat*, 27). However, I follow Krick's account, because, as excellent as the Texan troops were, it seems better to assume less rather than more fire discipline at this point in the war.

34. Nicholas Davis, *Chaplain Davis and Hood's Texas Brigade*, 86–87; Hood, *Advance and Retreat*, 26; Yeary, *Reminiscences of the Boys in Gray*, 815; Nicholas Davis, *Chaplain Davis and Hood's Texas Brigade*, 80; Coles, *History of the 4th Regiment, Alabama Volunteer Infantry*, 31, 47.

35. Griffith, *Battle Tactics of the Civil War*, 137–40.

36. Ibid., 189–90. For some examples of clichéd appeals to the bayonet from regulars, see Nosworthy, *Bloody Crucible of Courage*, 594–95.

37. Edwin Stanton to Horace Greeley, February 19, 1862, in Ingersoll, *Life of Horace Greeley*, 401.

38. *New York Herald*, February 28, 1862.

39. On the Iowa regiments, see *OR*, ser. 1, vol. 10, pt. 1, 287–88.

Connelly, *Army of the Heartland*, 151; Daniel, *Cannoneers in Gray*, 9, 16, 42.

On the arms and equipage of both armies, see Daniel, *Shiloh*, 94, 106–8. On the Enfield, see *OR*, ser. 1, vol. 4, 430, vol. 53, 228. For an example of flintlocks at Shiloh among confederate troops, see *OR*, ser. 1, vol. 10, pt. 1, 575. On Federal arms, see, for example, Olney, "Battle of Shiloh," 579. On the Confederate side, see, for example, Bergeron, *Civil War Reminiscences*, 40.

For Bragg's quotation, see *OR*, ser. 1, vol. 10, pt. 1, 12.

40. Olney, "Battle of Shiloh," 583; *OR*, ser. 1, vol. 10, pt. 1, 318, 214. It should be pointed out that Olney thought this helped nerve his regiment for coming action. For an example of a similar phenomenon at Stones River, see Stewart, "Battle of Stone River," 13. On the general problem of poor fire discipline, see Hess, *Union Soldier in Battle*, 80–81; Frank and Reaves, "*Seeing the Elephant*," 134–35.

41. Abernethy, *Private Elisha Stockwell*, 18. Stockwell also described a comrade misloading his musket during the battle. See ibid., 23. On soldiers loading muskets with multiple cartridges, see Noe, *Perryville*, 203. For this problem at Gettysburg, see Laidley, "Breech-Loading Musket," 69. Contrast this with the veteran fire discipline in Stockwell's regiment in 1864. See Abernethy, *Private Elisha Stockwell*, 133. Firing into the air with one's eyes closed was a perennial problem with raw troops; for an example at Antietam, see Fiske, *Mr. Dunn Browne's Experiences*, 9. On how poor fire discipline should have warned the Federals of the Confederate advance, see Daniel, *Shiloh*, 129; Roman, *Military Operations of General Beauregard*, 1:282; Roland, *Albert Sidney Johnston*, 2:319; *OR*, ser. 1, vol. 10, pt. 1, 512; Haughton, *Training, Tactics and Leadership*, 67.

42. *OR*, ser. 1, vol. 10, pt. 1, 469–70, 512; Daniel, *Shiloh*, 173, 191, 200–201; Houston, "Shiloh Shadows," 329–31; Bergeron, *Civil War Reminiscences*, 33–34; Hughes, *Battle of Belmont*, 130; Morris, Hartwell, and Kuykendall, *31st Regiment Illinois Volunteers*, 24. Also see Haughton, *Training, Tactics and Leadership*, 68–69, and Glatthaar, *General Lee's Army*, 466.

43. Daniel, *Shiloh*, 132, 118–23; Brooks Simpson, *Ulysses S. Grant*, 129; Hood, *Advance and Retreat*, 131. Hood's diatribe against earthworks was in many ways profoundly misguided, and helps explain his disastrous command of the Army of the Tennessee in 1864, but it certainly reflects a real school of thought in the old army. Furthermore,

it should be pointed out that this mentality helped the Confederates gain a striking victory over entrenched Federals at Gaines's Mill later that spring. Also see Stephen D. Lee's reprinted letter on ibid., 138–39.

On Johnston's disappointing performance, also see Connelly, *Army of the Heartland*, 158–60. On Johnston and Beauregard, see Roland, "P. G. T. Beauregard," 50–52. For a more generous assessment, see Hattaway and Jones, *How the North Won*, 164–69.

44. *OR*, ser. 1, vol. 10, pt. 1, 203, 241, 393, 317–18.

OR, ser. 1, vol. 10, pt. 1, 353, 172. On sharpshooting, also see ibid., 341, 448, 513; Daniel, *Shiloh*, 169; Daniel, *Cannoneers in Gray*, 27–28. At Fort Donelson, Federal forces even included a specialized regiment of sharpshooters. See Cooling, *Forts Henry and Donelson*, 117, 140; Coffin, *My Days and Nights on the Battle-field*, 86; Morris, Hartwell, and Kuykendall, *31st Regiment Illinois Volunteers*, 34. For an example after the battle near Corinth in May, see Daniel, *Cannoneers in Gray*, 40.

The column-by-division was not some sort of magical formation always appropriate to every situation, or even to this one. Willich's use of the column came under some criticism. See Daniel, *Shiloh*, 285. The point is, however, that some officers knew of the formation and used it on occasion.

OR, ser. 1, vol. 10, pt. 1, 202. Sniping also occurred at other early battles before the near universal adoption of static trench lines during the war's last years. For example, Lee himself nearly fell to a sharpshooter's rifle at Second Manassas. See Hennessy, *Return to Bull Run*, 226. Upton, while commanding an artillery brigade at Antietam, also commented on about a dozen deliberate attempts by Confederate sharpshooters to shoot him down. See Michie, *Life and Letters of Emory Upton*, 63.

45. For newspaper anger at the bungling at Shiloh, see, for example, Moore, *Rebellion Record: A Diary of American Events*, 4:387, 397, and Brooks Simpson, *Ulysses S. Grant*, 136–38. On the *Tribune* and press reaction in general, see Sears, *To the Gates of Richmond*, 160–61.

46. See, for example, Cohen, *Supreme Command*, 31.

47. McClellan, unfortunately, never made the necessary efforts to assure Lincoln of Washington's safety. With its powerful fortifications and a garrison, the Federal capital stood in no real military danger, but McClellan's unwillingness to explain the issue properly to Lincoln caused all sorts of problems. See Rafuse, *McClellan's War*, 202–3; Sears, *George B. McClellan*, 170–71, 175–79, 187–91.

48. Dowdey, *Wartime Papers of Robert E. Lee*, 184; Freeman, *Lee*, 2:110; Freeman, *Lee's Lieutenants*, 1:202. Seven Pines was in effect Johnston's only trial of this strategy. It is an interesting question as to whether Johnston might have tried another spoiling attack on McClellan similar to Lee's strike at Mechanicsville. However, Johnston's own passive performances during the Vicksburg and Atlanta campaigns would seem to argue otherwise. For a negative treatment of Johnston's prospects, see Gallagher, "A Civil War Watershed," 20.

49. Sears, *To the Gates of Richmond*, 154–55; Woodward, *Mary Chesnut's Civil War*, 387.

50. For a succinct treatment of the need to institute corps-level organization in the army, see Freeman, *Lee's Lieutenants*, 1:670–71.

On the high Unionist expectations of victory versus low Confederate morale before the Seven Days, see Gallagher, "A Civil War Watershed," 19–20. It must be acknowledged, however, that Lee suffered grievously in the butcher's bill — twenty thousand casualties — while Federal forces lost sixteen thousand men. See Hattaway and Jones, *How the North Won*, 199.

51. Quotation in Fahrney, *Greeley and the Tribune*, 101. On the deleterious role of partisan conflict with regard to debates over military strategy, see Neely, *Union Divided*, 176. Adams, *Our Masters the Rebels*, 126–27. On the negative consequences of disputes within the Federal high command between professional and political generals, see Goss, *War within the Union High Command*, 161–64.

Chapter 8

1. Frequently left out in this narrative is the successful frontal assault on Missionary Ridge, which serves as a bookend in this treatment. For some representative examples, see the rifle-musket historians and critics of Lee's aggressive strategy cited in Gallagher, "An Old-Fashioned Soldier," 159–62.

2. Hennessy, *Return to Bull Run*, 436; Hess, *Union Soldier in Battle*, 58–60; Prokopowicz, *All for the Regiment*, 4–6.

3. *OR*, ser. 1, vol. 12, pt. 3, 474; Herman Haupt to Mrs. Haupt, July 17, 1862, Herman Haupt Papers. Haupt disapproved of *both* McClellan and Pope.

4. Hennessy, *Return to Bull Run*, 189–90, 364, 458–59.

5. Sears, *Landscape Turned Red*, 187–88, 198–99.

6. Hartwig, "Who Would Not Be a Soldier," 144–47; Sherman, *Memoirs*, 879. For another contemporary preference to fill up veteran regiments, as noted by a highly competent officer, see William B. Hazen to John Brough, July 31, 1864, pp. 609–10, William B. Hazen Papers. For a rebuttal, see Griffith, *Battle Tactics of the Civil War*, 94–95. Also, Federal practice allowed state authorities to appoint regimental officers (i.e., ranks below general-grade). See Beatie, *McClellan Takes Command*, 227–28. On the 1864 example, see John Smith, *Nineteenth Regiment of Maine Volunteer Infantry*, 244; Noe, *Perryville*, 82–83, 203, 209–10, 250, 274. On Confederate manpower policy, see *OR*, ser. 4, vol. 1, 1096, 1103; *OR*, ser. 4, vol. 3, 96.

7. Hartwig, "Who Would Not Be a Soldier," 162–63; Sears, *Landscape Turned Red*, 287–89; Croffut and Morris, *Military and Civil History of Connecticut*, 271. For one example of the importance of drill, see the excellent performance of the 17th Michigan which had begun forming in May 1862 and had been drilled during the summer before being mustered into service officially on August 21. Although the regiment had no actual combat experience, it performed well at Fox's gap. See Hartwig, "Who Would Not Be a Soldier," 155–56.

8. Harsh, *Taken at the Flood*, 39–40; Sears, *Landscape Turned Red*, 139, *OR*, ser. 1, vol. 19, pt. 1, 262.

9. Harsh, *Taken at the Flood*, 38, 41; Bohannon, "Dirty, Ragged, and Ill-Provided For," 101–2, 130–32; Sears, *Landscape Turned Red*, 70–71, 175–76, 286. A. P. Hill's division (3,300 men, not counting stragglers lost in the forced march to Sharpsburg) arrived later in the day, of course.

10. Sears, *Landscape Turned Red*, 296; Gallagher, "Confederate Reaction to the Maryland Campaign," 31–33, 4–5; McPherson, *Battle Cry of Freedom*, 858. One must

remark, however, that the Union forces lost 25 percent of men engaged, while the Confederates lost 31 percent. For the campaign as a whole, the capture of the Harpers Ferry garrison made the ledger appear more respectable for the Confederates — fourteen thousand Confederates versus twenty-seven thousand Federals. See Sears, *Landscape Turned Red*, 309.

11. Gallagher, "Confederate Reaction to the Maryland Campaign," 34.

12. Alfred Sully to [?], May 12, 1861, Alfred Sully Papers. The Joint Committee also would not have approved of Sully's respectful disagreement with southern-born officers over the legitimacy of leaving the service, his willingness to pay one of those officers for a horse, or the nephew Sully had in the Confederate service. See Alfred Sully to [?], July 12, 1861, and Alfred Sully to [?], January 22, 1863, Alfred Sully Papers.

Congressional Republicans did not make completely implausible accusations; Porter shared with his chief an arrogance toward civilian and military superiors that was both unmilitary and dangerously close to outright insubordination, but Second Bull Run's leading student, John Hennessy, has convincingly argued that John Pope held the most blame for that crushing Federal defeat (Hennessy, *Return to Bull Run*, 469).

Stone's case reflects far more harshly on Republican advocates of a more vigorous war effort. Stone was a local commander during the early engagement at Ball's Bluff, an unfortunate fiasco blown out of proportion because of its early date in the war, before the country had become better inured to the mercurial fortunes of war. Stone's only fault seems to have been his misinterpretation of a poorly worded order of McClellan, but Stanton and the committee ruined Stone's career and reputation, in addition to imprisoning him for six months without specifying the charges proffered against him — namely vague and unsupported accusations of treason. Lincoln seems to have been ignorant and ill informed of the whole sordid affair, but neither did the episode reflect well on McClellan, who let Stone twist in the wind to protect his own position. For that reason, Stone eventually turned on his chief, which suited the committee just as well, because it hoped to use his testimony during the 1864 elections against Little Mac. Nevertheless, although McClellan's conduct was anything but heroic, the real blame for this unfortunate witch-hunt should center on both Stanton and the committee. See Tap, *Over Lincoln's Shoulder*, 62–77. On Ball's Bluff itself, see Sears, *George B. McClellan*, 120–22.

For an example of abolitionist distaste and suspicion of McClellan, see Lawson, *Patriot Fires*, 152–53.

13. On doubts among moderate and conservative Republicans, see Rable, *Fredericksburg! Fredericksburg!*, 49–50.

14. Fehrenbacher and Fehrenbacher, *Recollected Words of Abraham Lincoln*, 209. Lincoln probably should have chosen Maj. Gen. Joseph Hooker, who succeeded Burnside after the disaster at Gettysburg. Lincoln had many good reasons to not appoint Hooker, who had his own failing as a general and was guilty of scheming for advantage, but Hooker was still a better choice than Burnside.

15. Hess, *Field Armies and Fortifications*, 146–47, 155, 159, 161–63, 170–71, 308–9; Hagerman, *Origins of Modern Warfare*, 116–17, 122–25; O'Reilly, *The Fredericksburg Campaign*, 43; Sorrel, *Recollections of a Confederate Staff Officer*, 125.

16. Hagerman, *Origins of Modern Warfare*, 55–56, 116, 297; *RJCCW*, 1:366; Sherman, *Memoirs*, 249.

17. O'Reilly, *The Fredericksburg Campaign*, 135–38, 196–97, 505. For an excessively revisionist, if still useful, rehabilitation of Burnside, see Marvel, "Making of a Myth."

18. *RJCCW*, 1:668. On Humphreys' assault, I have relied heavily on O'Reilly, *The Fredericksburg Campaign*, 401–10, and Reardon, "Forlorn Hope."

19. *OR*, ser. 1, vol. 21, 433; *RJCCW*, 1:668. On the general importance of officers leading by example on the battlefield, see Hess, *Union Soldier in Battle*, 120–21. Humphreys was also fully aware of how difficult it would be for his raw troops to mount a bayonet charge. See Andrew Humphreys, "General Humphreys at Gettysburg," 356. For references to premature firing and the confusion caused by earlier lines of battle on the ground, see Philip Welsh to mother, December 19, 1862, reprinted in Ted Alexander, *126th Pennsylvania*, 128. There were even accusations of the broken Federal line firing *through* Humphreys's new assault lines. See [Rowe], *Sketch of the 126th Regiment*, 18. For another example of attacking troops unable to advance beyond a swale occupied by fragments of previous Federal assaults, see *OR*, ser. 1, vol. 21, 233, and O'Reilly, *The Fredericksburg Campaign*, 318.

20. *OR*, ser. 1, vol. 21, 284; O'Reilly, *The Fredericksburg Campaign*, 317; Child, *History of the Fifth Regiment*, 155.

21. *RJCCW*, 1:653.

22. O'Reilly, *The Fredericksburg Campaign*, 408, 412; Rable, *Fredericksburg! Fredericksburg!*, 261. Humphreys later served as a very efficient chief of staff for the Army of the Potomac. See Hennessy, "I Dread the Spring," 72–73.

23. Andrew Humphreys, "General Humphreys at Gettysburg," 353.

24. *OR*, ser. 1. vol. 16, pt. 1, 1115; Noe, *Perryville*, 208–13.

25. Alfred Sully to [?], November 19, 1862, Alfred Sully Papers. Sully also expressed disapproval of Lincoln's movement toward a policy of abolition.

Thomas Fry Tobey to John Fry Tobey, December 20–22, 1862; Thomas Fry Tobey to Carrie, March 21, 1863; Thomas Fry Tobey to Father, March 21, 1863, Thomas Fry Tobey Papers. Sully also sighed, "Oh that McClellan were here," after the disaster at Fredericksburg. See Alfred Sully to [?], December 15, 1862, Alfred Sully Papers; Nathaniel Weede Brown to Albert M. Given, December 23, 1862, 133rd Pennsylvania [typescript], Book 74, Fredericksburg and Spotsylvania National Military Park, Fredericksburg, Va. On McClellan's popularity, see Greene, "Morale, Maneuver, and Mud," 177, 191.

26. Newton and Cochrane were agents of a larger movement to restore McClellan to command led by Maj. Gen. William B. Franklin, head of the Left Grand Division in Burnside's reorganization of the Army of the Potomac into three super-corps, and Maj. Gen. William F. Smith, chief of the Sixth Corps, which was part of Franklin's Grand Division. On the politicking to remove Burnside, see Sears, "Revolt of the Generals," 139–57. On the Mud March's crucial effect on morale, see Greene, "Morale, Maneuver, and Mud," 205, and O'Reilly, *The Fredericksburg Campaign*, 486–88. On Burnside's administrative failures, see Hennessy, "We Shall Make Richmond Howl," 1–4.

27. Hennessy, "We Shall Make Richmond Howl," 9–11; Sears, *Chancellorsville*,

15–16. For veteran commentary on Hooker's strengths as an organizer, see John Smith, *Nineteenth Regiment of Maine Volunteer Infantry*, 39. For another reference to Hooker's skills as an administrator, see [Rowe], *Sketch of the 126th Regiment*, 26. Hooker's reorganization of the army also included a continuation of McClellan's program of reviews, drills, and target practice. See 155th Regimental Association, *Under the Maltese Cross*, 126.

28. Sears, *Chancellorsville*, 32–38, 109–10. On logistical problems, also see Goff, *Confederate Supply*, 78–81, 88.

29. Sears, *Chancellorsville*, 103–4, 132–33, 150; Marcus, *New Canaan Private*, 36–37; Hagerman, *Origins of Modern Warfare*, 131–33, 314, n. 54; Hennessy, "We Shall Make Richmond Howl," 12–13, 18, 23–24; Sears, *Chancellorsville*, 67–70. Hennessy also considered Hooker's disbanding of Burnside's Grand Divisions a mistake, although I see the issue as less clear-cut. On the importance of Confederate artillery superiority, see ibid., 332–33. On Confederate artillery organization, also see Edward Alexander, *Fighting for the Confederacy*, 104–5.

30. Freeman, *Lee*, 2:514. On the new respect for works, see the suggestive comments and quotations in Gallagher, "The Yanks Have Had a Terrible Whipping," 73. Hess also describes Chancellorsville as the "pivot point in the development of field fortifications in the East," where past experience led to a new willingness in both eastern armies to construct fieldworks. See Hess, *Field Armies and Fortifications*, 309.

On the Federal works, see Sears, *Chancellorsville*, 236, 238; Marcus, *New Canaan Private*, 30–33; Catton, *Glory Road*, 195; United States, Joint Committee on the Conduct of the War, *Army of the Potomac*, 126; On Hooker's May 1 orders to his army, including Howard's Eleventh Corps, to entrench, see Sears, *Chancellorsville*, 226; *OR*, ser. 1, vol. 25, pt. 2, 328; *OR*, ser. 1, vol. 25, pt. 1, 199. Unfortunately for the Federals, Howard's 11th Corps on the Federal right flank did not entrench, which helped lead to Jackson's successful flank attack. It should be remarked in Hooker's defense that he was stunned for a time by a cannonball that hit his headquarters the crucial morning of May 3.

For a more positive view of Hooker's performance, see Sears, *Chancellorsville*, 437–38.

31. Bearss, *Campaign for Vicksburg*, 2:670; *OR*, ser. 1, vol. 24, pt. 2, 136.

32. Bearss, *Campaign for Vicksburg*, 2:672–74; *OR*, ser. 1, vol. 24, pt. 2, 138. On the effects felt from the heavy skirmishing fire, see Rose, "Sixty-first Tennessee Infantry," 575–76; Eugene A. Carr to father, June 7, 1863, Eugene A. Carr Papers.

33. Bearss, *Campaign for Vicksburg*, 3:761, 765, 772, 806–7, 810. Also see Morris, Hartwell, and Kuykendall, *31st Regiment Illinois Volunteers*, 69; Crooke, *Twenty-first Regiment of Iowa Volunteer Infantry*, 80–81, 83; and Saunier, *History of the Forty-seventh Regiment Ohio*, 146–48. Saunier, in terms he believed complimentary, called one of Sherman's storming parties the "Forlorn Hope."

Lawler also comments on Grant's overconfidence, which he felt understandable in light of the signal successes up to that point. See Eugene A. Carr to father, June 7, 1863, Eugene A. Carr Papers.

34. Bearss, *Campaign for Vicksburg*, 3:814–15; Hagerman, *Origins of Modern Warfare*, 203–4. Hagerman has compared this attack to Morgan L. Smith's well-known

attack by rushes at Donelson. See ibid., 204; McWhiney and Jamieson, *Attack and Die*, 102.

35. Bearss, *Campaign for Vicksburg*, 3:859–60.

36. Hess, *Pickett's Charge*, 31–33, 22–23, 117, 136, 390–91. On artillery's general weakness as an offensive arm, see Naisawald, *Grape and Canister*, xvii. On the Confederate failure to coordinate the bombardment properly, see Edward Alexander, *Fighting for the Confederacy*, 251.

Also note that Grimsley has pointed out that Hess's treatment of the attack, where Federal troops had wide fields of fire that would have allowed them to use the longer range of the rifle-musket, shows that Civil War soldiers still preferred to mass their fire at ranges of less than two hundred yards. See Grimsley, "Continuing Battle of Gettysburg," 186–87.

37. Oeffinger, *A Soldier's General*, 216. Whether the charges were true is irrelevant for our analytical purposes; it is simply significant that Longstreet could make the argument that all these measures should be expected from a competent commander. In the resulting court martial, McLaws was vindicated. See ibid., 44.

38. Cozzens, *Shipwreck of Their Hopes*, 248–62, 273, 286–87; McDonough, *Chattanooga*, 181–85, 205; *OR*, ser. 1, vol. 31, pt. 2, 278. There is at least one example of shock tactics used, where a regiment received orders to hold its fire during the assault (ibid., 309), but such methods were not terribly important in this context. Dead space was a safe area for attacking troops created at the base of an elevation by the inability of pieces at the crest to depress sufficiently to cover all the terrain below it.

39. Hagerman, *Origins of Modern Warfare*, 222–25 (quotation from 224).

Chapter 9

1. Hattaway and Jones, *How the North Won*, 489–96. Both concede that Grant's plans are "almost entirely implicit" (496).

2. Ibid., 509; *OR*, ser. 1, vol. 32, pt. 2, 481. For a similar example of Hattaway and Jones's confusing Grant's confidence in Sherman's abilities with an abstract commitment to the superiority of the tactical defensive, see Hattaway and Jones, *How the North Won*, 638, and *OR*, ser. 1, vol. 39, pt. 3, 239. In contrast, Jamieson and McWhiney see Grant as almost stubbornly committed to the tactical offensive. See McWhiney and Jamieson, *Attack and Die*, 107. On Grant's and Sherman's trust in one another, see Glatthaar, *Partners in Command*, 152.

Another document Hattaway and Jones cite, a letter from Grant to Halleck dated February 12, 1862, *OR*, ser. 1, vol. 32, pt. 2, 375 (note that Hattaway and Jones' citation is incorrect) only contains Grant's statement that "If we move against Longstreet with an overwhelming force he will simply fall back toward Virginia until he can be re-enforced or take up an impregnable position." The quotation refers specifically to Longstreet's situation in East Tennessee and should not be seen as a general judgment on the impregnability of Civil War armies in general. See Hattaway and Jones, *How the North Won*, 489, 499.

3. Hagerman, *Origins of Modern Warfare*, 244–45, 264 (quotation). Grant quotation in *OR*, ser. 1, vol. 36, pt. 1, 13. For another interpretation of Grant's strategy that downplays the role of attrition, see Brooks Simpson, "Great Expectations," 8.

4. Grant's original operational plan for the Army of the Potomac to conduct a sixty-thousand-man raid through southeastern Virginia and North Carolina did indeed hope to target railroads and deprive the South of both supplies and slave labor in the region. See Hattaway and Jones, *How the North Won*, 512–15.

5. Grant, *Memoirs*, 166–67.

6. *OR*, ser. 1, vol. 33, 395; *OR*, ser. 1, vol. 31, pt. 3, 430. It is revealing that Hagerman used the term "erratic" to describe Grant's behavior, which when viewed from his modernization perspective does seem inconsistent — a focus on Grant's concern with maintaining the initiative, in contrast, does not need to assume that Grant's actions were somehow confused or irrational.

7. Quoted in Neely, "Wilderness and the Cult of Manliness," 59–60; *OR*, ser. 1, vol. 46, pt. 1, 11.

8. Blackford, *Letters from Lee's Army*, 246.

9. Brooks Simpson, *Ulysses S. Grant*, 274–77.

10. Ibid., 352–53.

11. *New York World*, August 4, 1864; Brooks Simpson, *Ulysses S. Grant*, 353, 408–9; Tap, *Over Lincoln's Shoulder*, 239.

12. Zornow, *Lincoln and the Party Divided*, 110, 112–16; Waugh, *Reelecting Lincoln*, 140; Simon, *Papers of Ulysses S. Grant*, 12:16–17. Greeley would have preferred a candidacy of either Grant, Butler, or, extraordinarily enough, Sherman.

13. J. W. Jones, *Personal Reminiscences*, 40; Brooks Simpson, "Great Expectations," 4–5; Freeman, *Lee's Dispatches*, 254. For a contemporaneous, if less definitive, account by Lee of the importance of holding the Rapidan line and not being pushed back to Richmond, see *OR*, ser. 1, vol. 33, 1283. On the possibility of winning the war by only maintaining the investments of Richmond and Atlanta, see Samuel R. Curtis to Henry B. Curtis, August 17, 1864, CU 56, Samuel Ryan Curtis Papers.

14. Brooks Simpson, "Great Expectations," 30–31; Hattaway and Jones, *How the North Won*, 694.

15. R. Curtis to Henry B. Curtis, September 4, 1862, CU 32; Samuel R. Curtis to Henry B. Curtis, June 1, 1863, CU 39; Samuel R. Curtis to Henry B. Curtis, September 20, 1863, CU 42; Samuel R. Curtis to Henry B. Curtis, October 19, 1863, CU 44, Samuel Ryan Curtis Papers. On Curtis's biography, see Heitman, *Historical Register*, 1:347. For Curtis's politics, see Shea, "Curtis, Samuel Ryan," *American National Biography Online*.

16. Rhea, "Union Cavalry in the Wilderness," 125–26, 129–30. More generally, Rhea denies that Lee actually trapped Grant in the Wilderness, describing him as "merely the fortunate beneficiary of sloppy Federal planning and reconnaissance." See Rhea, *Battle of the Wilderness*, 443; Rhea, *Battles for Spotsylvania*, 314–15.

17. For the attack on Doles's Salient, I have relied heavily on Rhea, *Battles for Spotsylvania*, 168–77.

Best, *History of the 121st New York State Infantry*, 31, 128; *OR*, ser. 1, vol. 36, pt. 1, 667; Fisk, *Hard Marching Every Day*, 220–21; Terry Jones, *Civil War Memoirs of Captain William J. Seymour*, 121; Henry Thomas, *History of the Doles-Cook Brigade*, 77.

The modern reconstruction of the tree line, based on early postwar surveys, indicates a considerably shorter distance for the size of the field that needed to be crossed than the available written evidence. For example, it is roughly 120 yards between the extant Confederate works and the modern monument at the edge of the reconstructed tree line. I measured this distance with a measuring wheel, while John Cummings of Spotsylvania, Virginia, informed me of what he saw as the basic accuracy of the modern reconstruction. One Federal diary reports a distance of 330 yards (May 10, 1862, Anonymous Diary Excerpt, Fifth Wisconsin Regiment), while the usually perceptive Fisk reports an improbable figure of 100 rods, or 550 yards (Fisk, *Hard Marching Every Day*, 220). One Confederate account claimed that at one place, the Federals went "undiscovered within thirty yards of the Breastworks" (Roberts, "Wilderness and Spotsylvania," 68–69). Upton in his official report gave a figure of 200 yards (*OR*, ser. 1, vol. 36, pt. 1, 667). This is supported by Henry Thomas, *History of the Doles-Cook Brigade*, 76–77, 478. The second reference is to a figure of more than 200 but less than 250 yards.

Upton's attack at Rappahannock Station the previous November set some precedent for this famous assault. There, Upton's much smaller assault with only one brigade benefited from a hill that allowed the regiments to form up their assault columns under cover within two hundred yards of the Confederate works. The absence of daylight during the assault, along with a false shouted order by Upton to units he did not possess, also demoralized the Confederate defenders. See Best, *History of the 121st New York State Infantry*, 100–102; Morse, *Personal Experiences*, 54–55; Ambrose, *Upton and the Army*, 24–25.

18. *OR*, ser. 1, vol. 36, pt. 1, 667; Scheibert, *A Prussian Observes the American Civil War*, 41–42. Scheibert was only referring specifically to the Confederates he observed, but his description in my view also applies to Federal attacks.

19. Best, *History of the 121st New York State Infantry*, 129–30; Fisk, *Hard Marching Every Day*, 297. Also see Henry Thomas, *History of the Doles-Cook Brigade*, 478. This Confederate account, while recording "a yell," also stated that the attacking Federals "never made any halt."

20. Rhea, *Battles for Spotsylvania*, 166–68, 176; David Fitzpatrick, "Emory Upton," 105–7; Rhea, *Battles for Spotsylvania*, 215; *OR*, ser. 1, vol. 36, pt. 2, 629; Tyler, *Recollections of the Civil War*, 169; Rhea, *Battles for Spotsylvania*, 223–25, 313–14; Matter, *If It Takes All Summer*, 185–88. It should also be pointed out that the Federals benefited from Lee's mistake in withdrawing his artillery from the Mule Shoe.

Barlow, "Capture of the Salient," 247, 253–54, 258. Also see Black, "Reminiscences of the Bloody Angle," 423.

21. Rhea, *Cold Harbor*, 313–17, 364; John Smith, *Nineteenth Regiment of Maine Volunteer Infantry*, 188. Also see Wainwright, *Diary of Battle*, 405. Rhea also revises downward Federal losses at Cold Harbor. For the Overland campaign as a whole, he counts fifty-five thousand Federal casualties versus thirty-three thousand Confederate losses. Percentage-wise, Lee still lost more than Grant. Rhea, *Cold Harbor*, 393.

22. And neither are they required for the Confederacy to win its independence. Lee quite nearly wore northern public opinion down into a possibly fatal torpor during the Overland campaign by simply bleeding the Army of the Potomac white. Lee himself may have always aimed for the complete destruction of the Army of the Potomac, but the more modest achievement of a reasonably clear battlefield victory during either

the Antietam or Gettysburg campaigns might have had a deleterious effect on northern morale similar to the Overland campaign's gruesome losses. Furthermore, putting too much weight on Lee's inability to obliterate the Army of the Potomac in open combat obscures the failings of the Army of Tennessee, which never carried its own weight in the Confederate cause.

23. Rhea, *Battles for Spotsylvania*, 315–16, 322–23; Rhea, *Cold Harbor*, 393; Taaffe, *Commanding the Army of the Potomac*, 218. This is not to say that the Army of Northern Virginia's commanders were infallible, only that they overmatched their opponents in the Army of the Potomac. Both armies would see their respective command cadres decimated by casualties during the Overland campaign, and their rank and file jaded by the carnage, but because both armies deteriorated at roughly constant rates, they continued to maintain a rough equilibrium in competence.

24. Hennessy, "I Dread the Spring," 86. Sears, *Controversies and Commanders*, xv; Brooks Simpson, *Ulysses S. Grant*, 285–86. Simpson also makes it clear that Grant took great pains to avoid ruffling the feathers of the proud eastern army and that, although there was a real division between the two, it should not be overstated. For another review of the Army of the Potomac's mixed first impression of Grant, see Hennessy, "I Dread the Spring," 93–94. On the reaction of the eastern officer corps to Pope, see Hennessy, *Return to Bull Run*, 13.

25. Rhea, *Battle of the Wilderness*, 432; Rhea, *Battles for Spotsylvania*, 317–18; Andrew Humphreys, *Virginia Campaign*, 83 n. 1. Problems with divided command in the Army of the Potomac persisted until the final campaign of the war in the spring of 1865. See Sears, "Gouverneur Kemble Warren and Little Phil," 265.

26. Richard Sommers's comments on tactics during Grant's offensive in late September apply just as well to other frontal assaults throughout the war. In his words, "Yet it was not whether an army was in an offensive or a defensive posture that ulti- mately determined the outcome — any more than did deployment of tactics. The determining factor was not availability of force but co-ordination of force. The attacks that succeeded — whatever their deployment or tactics — did so because they were well co-ordinated. . . . Such lack of co-ordination was a sure way to doom an attack or to nullify the many advantages of the defense. . . . Virtually the only chance for overcom- ing all these defensive advantages was for attackers to co-ordinate potential power into actual force simultaneously applied. That principle of co-ordination, more than any other, explains the outcome of virtually all the fighting during the Fifth Offensive." See Sommers, *Richmond Redeemed*, 429–30.

27. Meade in his own testimony emphasized the raw and untested status of Ferraro's division, although he may also have doubted its abilities for racial reasons. See United States, Joint Committee on the Conduct of the War, *Battle of Petersburg*, 127. Fears of a Radical backlash in case of a failure at the crater were not entirely groundless. Some Radicals frowned on the use of African American troops not for any lack of faith in their military abilities, but in the Confederacy's openly avowed refusal to treat captured black troops as prisoners of war, with all the associated protections of that status. See Tap, *Over Lincoln's Shoulder*, 189. In the best tactical study of the war, Michael A. Cavanaugh and William Marvel emphasize frictions between Burnside and Meade. See Cavanaugh and Marvel, *Battle of the Crater*, 117.

Marvel, *Burnside*, 390–409, 411–12; Brooks Simpson, *Ulysses S. Grant*, 360–67. Not too much should be made of Ferrero's original well-thought-out assault plan for his United States Colored Troops division, because his training program was obstructed by demands on his division to perform fatigue duty. See Robertson, "From the Crater to New Market Heights," 179–80, 187. In my view, the freshness of Ferraro's division would have given it a far higher chance of success than Ledlie's badly led and spent division.

28. Hennessy, "I Dread the Spring," 77–80. The army's rank and file had also decided to, at the very least, tolerate emancipation as a legitimate war aim.

Whatever Meade's faults, he was not a disruptive intriguer. For example, he refused to participate in various conspiracies among the Army of the Potomac's corps commanders after Chancellorsville to pressure Lincoln to replace Hooker with himself. See Sears, "Revolt of the Generals," 160.

On civil-military tensions, see Tap, *Over Lincoln's Shoulder*, 175, 181–82; Brown, *Retreat from Gettysburg*, 260, 287, 326. Brown is deeply sympathetic to the challenges Meade faced after Gettysburg. Meade's unpopularity also factored into Grant's decision to send Sheridan rather than Meade to the Valley to contend with Jubal Early. See Glatthaar, "Grant and the Union High Command," 47–48.

29. For a more brooding analysis of McClellanite caeserism in the Army of the Potomac, see Adams, *Our Masters the Rebels*, 118–19.

30. On the vexations of McClernand, see Brooks Simpson, *Ulysses S. Grant*, 205.

31. On the poisoned and politicized relationship between Joseph Johnston and Jefferson Davis, and an interpretation that emphasizes internal Confederate division to a greater degree, see Symonds, "No Margin for Error."

32. Neely, "Wilderness and the Cult of Manliness," 65–66, 69.

33. Brooks Simpson, *Ulysses S. Grant*, 172–73, 251–53, 268–77. On Richmond's general importance, see Sommers, *Richmond Redeemed*, 1–2.

34. Eugene A. Carr to father, August 16, 1861, Eugene A. Carr Papers.

35. Weber, *Copperheads*, 176–77.

36. Grimsley, *Hard Hand of War*, 222–23; Van Creveld, *Supplying War*, 7–8, 27–28, 37–38, 73–74; Campbell, *When Sherman Marched North from the Sea*, 5–6. Glatthaar, unlike Campbell, argues that Sherman's march had debilitating effects on Confederate morale. See Glatthaar, *General Lee's Army*, 449–50.

37. Hagerman, *Origins of Modern Warfare*, 282–83. On the much improved state of the Army of the Potomac's logistics, see Hennessy, "I Dread the Spring," 72.

38. Glatthaar, *General Lee's Army*, 444–48; letter reprinted in Henry Humphreys, *Andrew Atkinson Humphreys*, 249. It should be pointed out, however, that Grant's operations before Richmond and Petersburg did involve various sustained attempts to take Confederate works or turn his opponents' flanks, in addition to desultory and static sniping between entrenched troops. In this sense, the active operations of the Overland campaign never really ended until Appomattox. Those who argue that Grant engaged in a strategy of attrition thus have a somewhat better basis than Hattaway and Jones's heavy emphasis on attacks on logistical resources in the countryside. On conceiving of the siege as containing a large number of minicampaigns, see Sommers, *Richmond Redeemed*, xii.

39. This issue of basic competence should not be underestimated. For example, the April 2, 1864, assault of Maj. Gen. Horatio G. Wright's 6th Corps on Lee's lines to take advantage of Sheridan's victory at Five Forks involved substantial amounts of preparation, with abatis cleared and the assault troops given careful instructions. See Andrew Humphreys, *Virginia Campaign*, 363–65.

On entrenching and skirmishing, see Edward Alexander, *Fighting for the Confederacy*, 346, 370–71; Edward Porter Alexander to Father, May 29, 1864; Edward Porter Alexander to wife, June 10, 1864, Edward Porter Alexander Papers; 155th Regimental Association, *Under the Maltese Cross*, 281. On the taxing nature of siege warfare outside Petersburg, also see ibid., 309–10. Similar operations had been in effect during Vicksburg's siege. For a Federal account of those operations, see Marshall, *History of the Eighty-third Ohio*, 89–91.

See, for an example of a Confederate sharpshooter unit, Sommers, *Richmond Redeemed*, 330. The Union 5th Corps used a specialist battalion of sharpshooters equipped with telescopic sights for sniping during the siege of Petersburg. See 155th Regimental Association, *Under the Maltese Cross*, 354, 492–93. An intermediate step was to detail companies for sharpshooting duty. See June 6, 1864, Anonymous Diary Excerpt, Fifth Wisconsin Regiment. For other examples of the use of specialist sharpshooter units, see General Order No. 16, March 11, 1863, Walthall's Brigade HQ, Camp near Shelbyville, Tenn., p. 67, Order Book, 24th and 29th Mississippi Volunteers, 1862–63; General Order No. 6, Division HQ, January 28, 1863, Special Orders No. 79, June 2, 1863, Brigade HQ, p. 51, Order Book, 23rd North Carolina Regiment; General Order No. (12) 73(73), March 5, 1863, Brown's Brigade HQ, p. 90, Orders Received and Issued, Col. J. W. Newman's Battalion of Tennessee Volunteers. More generally on the Army of Tennessee, see Haughton, *Training, Tactics and Leadership*, 84–86. For an early western Federal example from 1862 shortly after Shiloh, see Glatthaar, "Evans Family of Ohio," 340; Oeffinger, *A Soldier's General*, 141.

One old army veteran—but not a West Pointer—Col. George L. Willard, even called for the restriction of rifled arms to specialist skirmisher units, and the use of smoothbores for line infantry. Willard had in fact been the author of a standard target practice manual before the war. See Willard, *Comparative Value of Rifled and Smooth-Bored Arms*, 12–13; Willard, *Manual of Target Practice*.

40. Henry Humphreys, *Andrew Atkinson Humphreys*, 265. Such close and constant quarter combat also existed in the West during the Atlanta campaign. See, for example, Horrall, *History of the Forty-second Indiana Volunteer Infantry*, 221–22, 232. During the siege of Vicksburg, Federal strong points with artillery were within one hundred to two hundred yards of the Confederate works, with pickets even closer to one another. See Morris, Hartwell, and Kuykendall, *31st Regiment Illinois Volunteers*, 70–71. Soldiers also manned positions in forward rifle pits and picket outposts, of course, but one must remember that smoothbore muskets were only really effective for sniping at ranges of fifty yards or less. It should be remembered that the effective range of volley fire against opposing units in close order was a very different matter than firing on individual man-sized targets. For a rare example of sharpshooting at five hundred to six hundred yards, see Morris, Hartwell, and Kuykendall, *31st Regiment Illinois Volunteers*, 117.

41. Trudeau, *Last Citadel*, 335–36, 338, 340–41. Confederate staff work also seems to

have improved by this time, despite various failures. See Krick, *Staff Officers in Gray*, 7. On various Federal attempts to crack the tactical nut of earthworks, see Sommers, *Richmond Redeemed*, 427–28. On earlier Confederate problems with plundering during the campaign, see ibid., 297.

42. Starr, *The Union Cavalry*, 1:438–39, 2:69–71, 3:590–94; Griffith, *Battle Tactics of the Civil War*, 179–88. Because of problems with training, quality of mounts, and terrain, classic shock cavalry with the saber never had a chance to play a major role in the American Civil War. On the limited importance of cavalry as a raiding force, see Mackey, *Uncivil War*, 194.

43. Grant's use of a strategy of attrition also does not mean that the old image of "Grant the Butcher" is at all accurate. See Sommers, *Richmond Redeemed*, 423–24. On the benefits of the new repeater-armed cavalry, see Griffith, *Battle Tactics*, 186–88.

Epilogue

1. Ambrose, *Upton and the Army*, 150.

2. Ibid., 101–3, 120–21, 151–59; Jamieson, *Crossing the Deadly Ground*, 9–10.

BIBLIOGRAPHY

Manuscript Collections

Boston, Massachusetts
    Howard Gottlieb Archival Research Center, Boston University
        John Codman Ropes Papers, BB15, Military Historical Society of
            Massachusetts Collection
Carlisle, Pennsylvania
    United States Army Military History Institute
        William T. H. Brooks Papers
        Eugene A. Carr Papers
        Sylvester Churchill Papers
        William B. Hazen Papers
Chapel Hill, North Carolina
    Southern Historical Collection, University of North Carolina Library
        Edward Porter Alexander Papers
Fredericksburg, Virginia
    Fredericksburg and Spotsylvania National Military Park
        Anonymous Diary Excerpt [typescript], Fifth Wisconsin Regiment, Book 32
        Nathaniel Weede Brown to Albert M. Given, December 23, 1862 [typescript],
            133rd Pennsylvania, Book 74
Los Angeles, California
    Special Collections Library, University of California, Los Angeles
        William S. Rosecrans Papers
New Haven, Connecticut
    Beinecke Rare Book and Manuscript Library, Yale University
        G. T. Beauregard to John L. Smith [copy], September 20, 1847, Western
            Americana Collection
        Alfred Sully Papers, Western Americana Collection
        Thomas Fry Tobey Papers, Yale Collection of American Literature
    Yale University Library, Manuscripts and Archives
        Herman Haupt Papers
        Alexander S. Webb Papers

Richmond, Virginia

    Virginia Historical Society

        James Maget to Elizabeth Thomas, Southampton County, February 7, 1848,
            Mss2/M2723/a/1

San Marino, California

    The Huntington Library

        Samuel Ryan Curtis Papers, 1826–66

        Joseph Hooker Military Papers, 1861–64

        Edward Davis Townsend Papers, 1761–1928

Washington, D.C.

    Library of Congress

        Robert Anderson Papers

        Henry Jackson Hunt Papers

        George B. McClellan Papers

    National Archives

        Records of the Office of the Adjutant General, Record Group 94

            Book Records of Volunteer Union Organizations

                Fifth Vermont Infantry Regimental Letter & Order Book

                Sixteenth Michigan Infantry Regimental Letter, Order, and Guard
                    Report Book

                Third Vermont Infantry Regimental Descriptive Letter, Endorsement,
                    & Order Book

            General Orders and Circulars of the War Department and Headquarters
                of the Army, 1809–60, Microfilm M1094

            Letters Received by the Office of the Adjutant General (Main Series),
                1822–60, Microfilm M567

        Records of the Office of the Secretary of War, Record Group 107

            Letters Received by the Secretary of War (Main Series), 1801–70, Microfilm
                M221

        War Department Collection of Confederate Records, Record Group 109

            Order Book, 23rd North Carolina Regiment, October 1862–February 1865,
                Ch. II, vol. 262

            Order Book, 24th and 29th Mississippi Volunteers, 1862–63, Ch. VIII,
                Vol. 98

            Orders Received and Issued, Col. J. W. Newman's Battalion of Tennessee
                Volunteers, 1862–64, Ch. VIII, vol. 340

West Point, New York

    United States Military Academy Library

        Archives (Record Group 404)

            Cadet Cards Arranged by State

            Records of the Academic Board

            Staff Records

        Special Collections

            Alexander Dallas Bache Papers

            George Dashiell Bayard Papers

George William Cushing Letters
A. A. Draper Letters
Winfield Scott Papers
Joseph Gardiner Swift Papers
Joseph Gilbert Totten Papers
West Point Thayer Papers

Newspapers

Charleston Mercury
Daily Richmond Examiner
Harper's Weekly
New York Daily Tribune
New York Herald
New York Times
New York World
Richmond Enquirer

Printed Sources

155th Regimental Association. *Under the Maltese Cross: Antietam to Appomattox, The Loyal Uprising in Western Pennsylvania, 1861–1865*. Pittsburg: 155th Regimental Association, 1910.

Abernethy, Byron R. *Private Elisha Stockwell, Jr. Sees the Civil War*. Norman: University of Oklahoma Press, 1958.

Adams, Michael C. C. *Our Masters the Rebels: A Speculation on Union Military Failure in the East, 1861–1865*. Cambridge, Mass.: Harvard University Press, 1978.

Adjutant General's Office. Horse Guards. *General Regulations and Orders for the Army*. London: W. Clowes, 1811.

Alexander, Edward Porter. *Fighting for the Confederacy: The Personal Recollections of General Edward Porter Alexander*. Edited by Gary W. Gallagher. Chapel Hill: University of North Carolina Press, 1989.

Alexander, Ted, ed. *The 126th Pennsylvania*. Shippensburg, Pa.: Beidel Printing House, 1984.

Allardice, Bruce. "West Points of the Confederacy: Southern Military Schools and the Confederate Army." *Civil War History* 43 (December 1997): 310–31.

Ambrose, Stephen. *Duty, Honor, Country: A History of West Point*. Baltimore: Johns Hopkins University Press, 1966.

———. *Upton and the Army*. Baton Rouge: Louisiana State University Press, 1964.

Anderson, Robert. *Instruction for Field Artillery Horse and Foot Translated from the French and Arranged for the Service of the United States*. Philadelphia: R. P. Desilver, 1839.

Ayers, Edward L. "Worrying about the Civil War." In *What Caused the Civil War?: Reflections on the South and Southern History*, 103–30. New York: W. W. Norton, 2005.

Bailyn, Bernard. *The Ideological Origins of the American Revolution*. Enl. ed. Cambridge, Mass.: Harvard University Press, 1992.

Ball, Durwood. *Army Regulars on the Western Frontier, 1848–1861*. Norman: University of Oklahoma Press, 2001.

Barlow, Francis Channing. "Capture of the Salient May 12 1864." In *The Wilderness Campaign: May–June 1864*. Vol. 4 of *Papers of the Military Historical Society of Massachusetts*, 243–62. 1905. Reprint, Wilmington, N.C.: Broadfoot Publishing, 1989.

Barry, William E. "Three Glorious Regiments." In *Unveiling and Dedication of Monument to Hood's Texas Brigade . . .*, edited by F. B. Chilton, 102–5. Houston: F. B. Chilton, 1911.

Barziza, Decimus et Ultimus. *The Adventures of a Prisoner of War: 1863–1864*. Edited by R. Henderson Shuffler. Austin: University of Texas Press, 1964.

Bauer, K. Jack. "The Battles on the Rio Grande: Palo Alto and Resaca de la Palma, 8–9 May 1846." In *America's First Battles, 1776–1965*, edited by Charles E. Heller and William A. Stofft, 57–80. Lawrence: University Press of Kansas, 1986.

———. *The Mexican War, 1846–1848*. Bison Book ed. Lincoln: University of Nebraska Press, 1992.

———. *Zachary Taylor: Soldier, Planter, Statesman of the Old Southwest*. Baton Rouge: Louisiana State University Press, 1985.

Bearss, Edwin Cole. *The Campaign for Vicksburg*. 3 vols. Dayton, Ohio: Morningside, 1985–86.

Beatie, Russel H. *McClellan Takes Command, September 1861–February 1862*. Vol. 2 of *Army of the Potomac*. Cambridge, Mass.: Da Capo Press, 2004.

Bergeron, Arthur W., Jr. *The Civil War Reminiscences of Major Silas T. Grisamore, C.S.A.* Baton Rouge: Louisiana State University Press, 1993.

Best, Isaac O. *History of the 121st New York State Infantry*. Chicago: Published by Lieut. Jas. H. Smith, 1921.

Bill, Alfred Hoyt. *Rehearsal for Conflict: The War with Mexico, 1846–1848*. New York: Alfred A. Knopf, 1947.

Birkhimer, William E. *Historical Sketch of the Organization, Administration, Matérial, and Tactics of the Artillery, United States Army*. Washington, D.C.: James J. Chapman, 1884.

Black, John D. "Reminiscences of the Bloody Angle." In *Glimpses of the Nation's Struggle: Fourth Series; Papers Read before the Minnesota Commandery of the Military Order of the Loyal Legion of the United States, 1892–1897*, 420–36. 1898. Reprint, Wilmington, N.C.: Broadfoot Publishing, 1992.

Blackford, Charles Minor, III, ed. *Letters from Lee's Army; or, Memoirs of Life in and out of the Army in Virginia during the War between the States*. Compiled by Susan Leigh Blackford. New York: Charles Scribner's Sons, 1947.

Blake, Henry N. *Three Years in the Army of the Potomac*. Boston: Lee and Shepard, 1865.

Bohannon, Keith S. "Dirty, Ragged, and Ill-Provided For: Confederate Logistical Problems in the 1862 Maryland Campaign and Their Solutions." In *The Antietam Campaign*, edited by Gary W. Gallagher, 101–42. Chapel Hill: University of North Carolina Press, 1999.

Bradley, George C., and Richard L. Dahlen. *From Conciliation to Conquest: The*

Sack of Athens and the Court-Martial of Colonel John B. Turchin. Tuscaloosa: University of Alabama Press, 2006.

Bratton, John. *Letters of John Bratton to His Wife*. Privately published, 1942.

Bright, Charles, and Michael Geyer. "Where in the World Is America? The History of the United States in the Global Age." In *Rethinking American History in a Global Age*, edited by Thomas Bender, 63–99. Berkeley: University of California Press, 2002.

Brown, Kent Masterson. *Retreat from Gettysburg: Lee, Logistics, and the Pennsylvania Campaign*. Chapel Hill: University of North Carolina Press, 2005.

Bruce, Robert V. *Lincoln and the Tools of War*. Indianapolis: Bobbs-Merrill, 1956.

Calhoun, John C. *The Papers of John C. Calhoun*. Edited by W. Edwin Hemphill. 28 vols. Columbia: University of South Carolina Press, 1959–2003.

Campbell, Jacqueline Glass. *When Sherman Marched North from the Sea: Resistance on the Confederate Home Front*. Chapel Hill: University of North Carolina Press, 2003.

Catton, Bruce. *The Army of the Potomac: Glory Road*. Garden City, N.Y.: Doubleday, 1952.

———. "Grant and Lee: A Study in Contrasts." In *The American Story: The Age of Exploration to the Age of the Atom*, edited by Earl Schenck Miers, 202–5. Great Neck, N.Y.: Channel Press.

Cavanaugh, Michael A., and William Marvel. *The Petersburg Campaign: The Battle of the Crater; "The Horrid Pit," June 25–August 6, 1864*. 2nd ed. Lynchburg, Va.: H. E. Howard, 1989.

Child, William. *A History of the Fifth Regiment New Hampshire Volunteers in the American Civil War, 1861–1865*. Bristol, N.H.: R. W. Musgrove, 1893.

Cleaves, Freeman. *Rock of Chickamauga: The Life of General George H. Thomas*. Norman: University of Oklahoma Press, 1948.

Coakley, Robert W. *The Role of Federal Military Forces in Domestic Disorders, 1789–1878*. Washington, D.C.: Center of Military History, 1988.

Coffin, Charles Carleton. *My Days and Nights on the Battle-Field*. Boston: Estes and Lauriat, 1887.

Coffman, Edward M. *The Old Army: A Portrait of the American Army in Peacetime, 1784–1898*. New York: Oxford University Press, 1986.

Cohen, Eliot A. *Supreme Command: Soldiers, Statesmen, and Leadership in Wartime*. New York: Free Press, 2002.

Coles, Robert T. *From Huntsville to Appomattox: R. T. Coles's History of the 4th Regiment, Alabama Volunteer Infantry, C.S.A., Army of Northern Virginia*. Edited by Jeffrey D. Stocker. Knoxville: University of Tennessee Press, 1996.

Connelly, Thomas Lawrence. *Army of the Heartland: The Army of Tennessee, 1861–1862*. Baton Rouge: Louisiana State University Press, 1967.

Cooke, P[hilip] St. G[eorge]. *Scenes and Adventures in the Army; or, Romance of Military Life*. 1857. Reprint, New York: Arno Press, 1973.

Cooling, Benjamin Franklin. *Forts Henry and Donelson: The Key to the Confederate Heartland*. Knoxville: University of Tennessee Press, 1987.

———, ed. *The Military during Constitutional Crisis: The Secession Winter*. Vol. 19

of *The New American State Papers: Military Affairs*. Wilmington, Del.: Scholarly
Resources, 1979.

Coppée, Henry. *General Thomas*. New York: D. Appleton, 1893.

Cope, Alexis. *The Fifteenth Ohio Volunteers and Its Campaigns: War of 1861–5*.
Columbus, Ohio: Published by author, 1916.

"The Correspondence of Thomas Reade Rootes Cobb, 1860–1862." *Publications of the
Southern History Association* 11 (May 1907): 147–85.

Cozzens, Peter. *The Shipwreck of Their Hopes: The Battles for Chattanooga*. Urbana:
University of Illinois Press, 1994.

Crabtree, Beth G., and James W. Patton, ed. *"Journal of a Secesh Lady": The Diary
of Catherine Ann Devereux Edmondston, 1860–1866*. Raleigh: North Carolina
Division of Archives and History, 1979.

Crackel, Theodore J. "The Battle of Queenston Heights, 13 October 1812." In
America's First Battles, 1776–1965, edited by Charles E. Heller and William A.
Stofft, 33–56. Lawrence: University Press of Kansas, 1986.

Crawford, Martin, ed. *William Howard Russell's Civil War: Private Diary and
Letters, 1861–1862*. Athens: University of Georgia Press, 1992.

Croffut, W. A., and John M. Morris. *The Military and Civil History of Connecticut
during the War of 1861–65*. New York: Ledyard Bill, 1868.

Crooke, George. *The Twenty-first Regiment of Iowa Volunteer Infantry: A Narrative
of Its Experience in Active Service, Including a Military Record of Each Officer,
Non-commissioned Officer, and Private Solider of the Organization*. Milwaukee:
King, Fowle, 1891.

Crozier, Granville H. "A Private with General Hood." *Confederate Veteran*, December
1917, 556–58.

Cullum, George W. *Biographical Register of the Officers and Graduates of the U.S.
Military Academy at West Point, N.Y., from Its Establishment, in 1802, to 1890, with
the Early History of the United States Military Academy*. 3rd rev. and extended ed.
3 vols. Boston: Houghton, Mifflin, 1891.

Cunliffe, Marcus. *Soldiers and Civilians: The Martial Spirit in America, 1775–1865*.
Boston: Little, Brown, 1968.

Daniel, Larry J. *Cannoneers in Gray: The Field Artillery of the Army of Tennessee*.
Rev. ed. Tuscaloosa: University of Alabama Press, 2005.

———. *Shiloh: The Battle That Changed the Civil War*. New York: Simon & Schuster,
1997.

Dastrup, Boyd L. *King of Battle: A Branch History of the U.S. Army's Field Artillery*.
Fort Monroe, Va.: Office of the Command Historian, United States Army Training
and Doctrine Command, 1993.

Davis, Carl L. *Arming the Union: Small Arms in the Civil War*. Port Washington, N.Y.:
National University Publications, 1973.

Davis, Nicholas A. *Chaplain Davis and Hood's Texas Brigade: Being an Expanded
Edition of the Reverend Nicholas A. Davis's The Campaign from Texas to
Maryland, with the Battle of Fredericksburg (Richmond, 1863)*. Edited by Donald
E. Everett. Baton Rouge: Louisiana State University Press, 1999.

Davis, William C. *Battle at Bull Run: A History of the First Campaign of the Civil War.*
    Baton Rouge: Louisiana State University Press, 1977.

Dean, Eric T. "'We Live under a Government of Men and Morning Newspapers':
    Image, Expectation, and the Peninsula Campaign of 1862." *Virginia Magazine of
    History and Biography* 103 (Winter 1995): 5–28.

DePalo, William A., Jr. *The Mexican National Army, 1822–1852.* College Station: Texas
    A&M University Press, 1997.

Dowdey, Clifford, ed. *The Wartime Papers of Robert E. Lee.* 1961. Reprint, New York:
    Da Capo Press, n.d.

Duane, William. *A Hand Book for Infantry: Containing the First Principles of
    Military Discipline, Founded in Rational Method.* 1812. 9th ed. Philadelphia:
    Printed for the author, 1814.

[———]. *The System of Infantry Discipline: According to Regulations Established
    for the Army of the United States.* N.p., 1814.

Dupuy, R. Ernest. *Where They Have Trod: The West Point Tradition in American
    Life.* New York: Frederick A. Stokes, 1940.

Dwight, Wilder. *Life and Letters of Wilder Dwight: Lieut.-Col. Second Mass. Inf. Vols.*
    Boston: Ticknor, 1868.

École du soldat et de peloton. Vol. 1 of *Réglement concernant l'exercice et les manœu-
    vres de l'infanterie de première aout 1791.* 3 vols. Libraire pour l'Art Militaire.
    Paris: Chez Anselin, 1825.

Einolf, Christopher J. *George Thomas: Virginian for the Union.* Norman: University
    of Oklahoma Press, 2007.

Elliott, Charles Winslow. *Winfield Scott: The Soldier and the Man.* New York:
    Macmillan, 1937.

[Ellsworth, Elmer E.] *Zouave Drill Book: French Bayonet Exercise and Skirmisher's
    Drill, as Used by Col. Ellsworth's Zouaves, with over Thirty Illustrations, to
    Which Is Added a Portrait and Biography of the Late Col. Elmer E. Ellsworth.*
    Philadelphia: King & Baird, 1861.

Ewy, Marvin. "The United States Army in the Kansas Border Troubles, 1855–1856."
    Kansas Historical Quarterly 32 (1966): 385–400.

Fahrney, Ralph Ray. *Horace Greeley and the Tribune in the Civil War.* Cedar Rapids,
    Iowa: Torch Press, 1936.

Fahs, Alice. *The Imagined Civil War: Popular Literature of the North and South,
    1861–1865.* Chapel Hill: University of North Carolina Press, 2001.

Favill, Josiah Marshall. *The Diary of a Young Officer, Serving with the Armies of
    the United States during the War of the Rebellion.* Chicago: R. R. Donnelley &
    Sons, 1909.

Fehrenbacher, Don E., and Virginia Fehrenbacher. *Recollected Words of Abraham
    Lincoln.* Stanford: Stanford University Press, 1996.

Fellman, Michael. *Inside War: The Guerrilla Conflict in Missouri during the
    American Civil War.* New York: Oxford University Press, 1989.

Fisk, Wilbur. *Hard Marching Every Day: The Civil War Letters of Private Wilbur
    Fisk, 1861–1865.* Edited by Emil Rosenblatt and Ruth Rosenblatt. Lawrence:
    University Press of Kansas, 1992.

Fiske, Samuel W. *Mr. Dunn Browne's Experiences in the Army: The Civil War Letters of Samuel W. Fiske.* Edited by Stephen W. Sears. New York: Fordham University Press, 1998.

Fitch, John. *Annals of the Army of the Cumberland: Comprising Biographies, Descriptions of Departments, Accounts of Expeditions, Skirmishers, and Battles; Also Its Police Record of Spies, Smugglers, and Prominent Rebel Emissaries.* 1864. Reprint, Mechanicsburg, Pa.: Stackpole Books, 2003.

Fitzhugh, George. "Reflections on the Conduct of the War." *De Bow's Review, Agricultural, Commercial, Industrial Progress and Resources* 31, nos. 4–5 (1861): 427–35.

———. "The Times and the War." *De Bow's Review, Agricultural, Commercial, Industrial Progress and Resources* 31, no. 1 (1861): 1–13.

Fitzpatrick, David John. "Emory Upton: The Misunderstood Reformer." Ph.D. diss., University of Michigan, 1996.

Fitzpatrick, John C., ed. *Writings of George Washington.* 39 vols. Washington, D.C.: Government Printing Office, 1931–44.

Förster, Stig, and Jörg Nagler, eds. *On the Road to Total War: The American Civil War and the German Wars of Unification, 1861–1871.* Cambridge: Cambridge University Press, 1997.

Frank, Joseph Allen, and George A. Reaves. *"Seeing the Elephant": Raw Recruits at the Battle of Shiloh.* New York: Greenwood Press, 1989.

Freeman, Douglas Southall. *Lee's Dispatches: Unpublished Letters of General Robert E. Lee, C.S.A to Jefferson Davis and the War Department of the Confederate States of America, 1862–65.* New ed. New York: G. P. Putnam's Sons, 1957.

———. *Lee's Lieutenants: A Study in Command.* 3 vols. New York: Charles Scribner's Sons, 1942–44.

———. *R. E. Lee: A Biography.* 4 vols. New York: Charles Scribner's Sons, 1934–35.

Fremantle, Arthur James Lyon. *Three Months in the Southern States: April–June, 1863.* 1864. Reprint, Lincoln: University of Nebraska Press, 1991.

Fuller, J. F. C. *The Generalship of Ulysses S. Grant.* London: John Murray, 1929.

Furniss, Norman F. *The Mormon Conflict, 1850–1859.* New Haven: Yale University Press, 1960.

Gallagher, Gary W. "A Civil War Watershed: The 1862 Richmond Campaign in Perspective." In *The Richmond Campaign of 1862: The Peninsula and the Seven Days*, edited by Gary W. Gallagher, 3–27. Chapel Hill: University of North Carolina Press, 2000.

———. *The Confederate War.* Cambridge, Mass.: Harvard University Press, 1997.

———. "The Net Result of the Campaign Was in Our Favor: Confederate Reaction to the Maryland Campaign." In *The Antietam Campaign*, edited by Gary W. Gallagher, 3–43. Chapel Hill: University of North Carolina Press, 1999.

———. "An Old-Fashioned Soldier in a Modern War? Lee's Confederate Generalship." In *Lee and His Army in Confederate History*, 151–90. Chapel Hill: University of North Carolina Press, 2001.

———. "'Upon Their Success Hang Momentous Interests': Generals." In *Why the Confederacy Lost*, edited by Gabor S. Boritt, 79–108. New York: Oxford University Press, 1992.

———. "The Yanks Have Had a Terrible Whipping: Confederates Evaluate the Battle of Fredericksburg." In *Lee and His Army in Confederate History*, 51–82. Chapel Hill: University of North Carolina Press, 2001.

Gardner, C. K. *Compend of the United States System of Infantry Exercise and Manœuvres; Also, the Best System Extant for Light Infantry and Riflemen.* New York: William A. Mercein, 1819.

[Gay de Vernon, Simon François.] *A Treatise on the Science of War and Fortification: Composed for the Use of the Imperial Polytechnick School, and Military Schools; and Translated for the War Department, for the Use of the Military Academy of the United States; to Which Is Added a Summary of the Principles and Maxims of Grand Tactics and Operations.* Atlas. Translated by John Michael O'Connor. New York: J. Seymour, 1817.

Gibbon, John. *The Artillerist's Manual, Compiled from Various Sources, and Adapted to the Service of the United States.* New York: D. Van Nostrand, 1860.

Glatthaar, Joseph T. "Battlefield Tactics." In *Writing the Civil War: The Quest to Understand*, edited by James M. McPherson and William J. Cooper Jr., 60–80. Columbia: University of South Carolina Press, 1998.

———. "Duty, Country, Race, and Party: The Evans Family of Ohio." In *The War Was You and Me: Civilians in the American Civil War*, edited by Joan E. Cashin, 332–57. Princeton: Princeton University Press, 2002.

———. *General Lee's Army: From Victory to Collapse.* New York: Free Press, 2008.

———. *Partners in Command: The Relationships between Leaders in the Civil War.* New York: Free Press, 1994.

———. "U. S. Grant and the Union High Command during the 1864 Valley Campaign." In *The Shenandoah Valley Campaign of 1864*, edited by Gary W. Gallagher, 34–55. Chapel Hill: University of North Carolina Press, 2006.

Goff, Richard D. *Confederate Supply.* Durham, N.C.: Duke University Press, 1969.

Goss, Thomas J. *The War within the Union High Command: Politics and Generalship during the Civil War.* Lawrence: University Press of Kansas, 2003.

Grant, Ulysses S. *Memoirs and Selected Letters: Personal Memoirs of U. S. Grant, Selected Letters, 1839–1865.* New York: Library of America, 1990.

[Great Britain. War Office.] *Field Exercise and Evolutions of the Army, as Revised in 1833.* London: W. Clowes and Sons, [1833].

[Great Britain.] War Office. Adjutant-General's Office. *Rules and Regulations for the Formations, Field-Exercise, and Movements of His Majesty's Forces.* Whitehall: T. Egerton at the Military Library, 1808.

Green, Jennifer R. "Books and Bayonets: Class and Culture in Antebellum Military Academies." Ph.D. diss., Boston University, 2002.

Greene, A. Wilson. *Civil War Petersburg: Confederate City in the Crucible of War.* Charlottesville: University of Virginia Press, 2006.

———. "Morale, Maneuver, and Mud: The Army of the Potomac, December 16, 1862–January 26, 1863." In *The Fredericksburg Campaign: Decision on the Rappahannock*, edited by Gary W. Gallagher, 171–228. Chapel Hill: University of North Carolina Press, 1995.

Greenwalt, John G. "A Charge at Fort Donelson, February 15, 1862." In vol. 2 of *War*

253

★

Papers: Being Papers Read before the Commandery of the District of Columbia,
edited by Military Order of the Loyal Legion of the United States, 335–50.
Reprint, Wilmington, N.C.: Broadfoot Publishing, 1993.

Griffith, Paddy. *Battle Tactics of the Civil War*. 1987. Reprint, New Haven: Yale
University Press, 1989.

———. *Military Thought in the French Army, 1815–1851*. Manchester: Manchester
University Press, 1989.

Grimsley, Mark. *The Hard Hand of War: Union Military Policy toward Southern
Civilians, 1861–1865*. Cambridge: Cambridge University Press, 1995.

———. "Review Essay: The Continuing Battle of Gettysburg." *Civil War History* 49
(June 2003): 181–87.

———. "Surviving Military Revolution: The U.S. Civil War." In *The Dynamics
of Military Revolution, 1300–2050*, edited by MacGregor Knox and Williamson
Murray, 74–91. Cambridge: Cambridge University Press, 2001.

Hagerman, Edward. *The American Civil War and the Origins of Modern Warfare:
Ideas, Organization, and Field Command*. Bloomington: Indiana University
Press, 1988.

Hardee, W[illiam] J. *Rifle and Light Infantry Tactics*. 2 vols. 1855. Reprint,
Philadelphia: J. B. Lippincott, 1856.

Harsh, Joseph L. *Confederate Tide Rising: Robert E. Lee and the Making of Southern
Strategy, 1861–1862*. Kent, Ohio: Kent State University Press, 1998.

———. *Taken at the Flood: Robert E. Lee and Confederate Strategy in the Maryland
Campaign of 1862*. Kent, Ohio: Kent State University Press, 1999.

Hartwig, D. Scott. "Who Would Not Be a Soldier: The Volunteers of '62 in the
Maryland Campaign." In *The Antietam Campaign*, edited by Gary W. Gallagher,
143–68. Chapel Hill: University of North Carolina Press, 1999.

Hattaway, Herman, and Archer Jones. *How the North Won: A Military History of the
Civil War*. Urbana: University of Illinois Press, 1983.

Hattaway, Herman, and Michael D. Smith. "Thomas, George Henry." *American
National Biography Online*. February 2000. <http://www.anb.org/articles/04
/04-009873.html>. June 24, 2008.

Haughton, Andrew. *Training, Tactics and Leadership in the Confederate Army of
Tennessee: Seeds of Failure*. London: Frank Cass, 2000.

Heitman, Francis B. *Historical Register and Dictionary of the United States Army,
from Its Organization, September 29, 1789, to March 2, 1903*. 2 vols. Washington,
D.C.: Government Printing Office, 1903.

Hennessy, John J. *The First Battle of Manassas: An End to Innocence, July 18–21, 1861*.
Lynchburg, Va.: H. E. Howard, 1989.

———. "I Dread the Spring: The Army of the Potomac Prepares for the Overland
Campaign." In *The Wilderness Campaign*, edited by Gary W. Gallagher, 66–105.
Chapel Hill: University of North Carolina Press, 1997.

———. *Return to Bull Run: The Campaign and Battle of Second Manassas*. New
York: Simon & Schuster, 1993.

———. "We Shall Make Richmond Howl: The Army of the Potomac on the Eve

of Chancellorsville." In *Chancellorsville: The Battle and Its Aftermath*, edited by
Gary W. Gallagher, 1–35. Chapel Hill: University of North Carolina Press, 1996.

Herdegan, Lance, and Sherry Murphy, eds. *Four Years with the Iron Brigade: The
Civil War Journal of William Ray, Co. F, Seventh Wisconsin Infantry*. Cambridge,
Mass.: Da Capo Press, 2002.

Hess, Earl J. *Field Armies and Fortifications in the Civil War: The Eastern Campaigns,
1861–1864*. Chapel Hill: University of North Carolina Press.

———. *Pickett's Charge — The Last Attack at Gettysburg*. Chapel Hill: University of
North Carolina Press, 2001.

———. *The Union Soldier in Battle: Enduring the Ordeal of Combat*. Lawrence:
University Press of Kansas, 1997.

Heth, Henry. *A System of Target Practice: For the Use of Troops When Armed with the
Musket, Rifle-Musket, Rifle, or Carbine*. Philadelphia: Henry Carey Baird, 1858.

Higginbotham, Don. *George Washington and the American Military Tradition*.
Athens: University of Georgia Press, 1985.

———. *The War of American Independence: Military Attitudes, Policies, and
Practice, 1763–1789*. Reprinted with new preface. Boston: Northeastern University
Press, 1983.

Hittle, J. D. *The Military Staff: Its History and Development*. 3rd ed. Harrisburg, Pa.:
Stackpole, 1961.

Holden, Edward S. "Origins of the United States Military Academy, 1777–1802."
In *Addresses and Histories*. Vol. 1 of *The Centennial of the United States
Military Academy at West Point, New York: 1802–1902*, 201–22. Washington, D.C.:
Government Printing Office, 1904.

Hood, J. B. *Advance and Retreat: Personal Experiences in the United States and
Confederate States Armies*. Edited by Richard N. Current. Bloomington: Indiana
University Press, 1959.

Horrall, S. F. *History of the Forty-second Indiana Volunteer Infantry*. Chicago:
Donahue & Henneberry, 1892.

Houston, Sam, Jr. "Shiloh Shadows." *Southwestern Historical Quarterly* 34 (April
1931): 329–33.

Howe, Henry Warren. *Passages from the Life of Henry Warren Howe, Consisting of
Diary and Letters Written during the Civil War, 1816–1865. A Condensed History of
the Thirtieth Massachusetts Regiment and Its Flags, Together with the Genealogies
of the Different Branches of the Family*. Lowell, Mass.: Courier-Citizen Company
Printers, 1899.

Hughes, Nathaniel Cheairs, Jr. *The Battle of Belmont: Grant Strikes South*. Chapel
Hill: University of North Carolina Press, 1991.

———. *General William J. Hardee: Old Reliable*. Baton Rouge: Louisiana State
University Press, 1965.

Humphreys, Andrew A. "The Army of the Potomac: General Humphreys at
Gettysburg." *Historical Magazine* 5, 2nd ser. (June 1869): 353–56.

———. *The Virginia Campaign of 1864 and 1865: The Army of the Potomac and the
Army of the James*. 1883. Reprint, New York: Da Capo Press, 1995.

Humphreys, Henry H. *Andrew Atkinson Humphreys: A Biography*. Philadelphia: John C. Winston, 1924.

Hunter, Robert F., and Edward L. Dooley Jr. *Claudius Crozet: French Engineer in America, 1790–1864*. Charlottesville: University Press of Virginia, 1989.

Huntington, Samuel P. *The Soldier and the State: The Theory and Politics of Civil-Military Relations*. Cambridge, Mass.: Harvard University Press, 1957.

Hyde, Thomas W. *Following the Greek Cross; or, Memories of the Sixth Army Corps*. Boston: Houghton, Mifflin, 1894.

Ingersoll, Lurton D. *The Life of Horace Greeley*. 1873. Reprint, New York: Beekman Publishers, 1974.

Ingraham, Charles A. *Elmer E. Ellsworth and the Zouaves of '61*. Chicago: University of Chicago Press, 1925.

Jamieson, Perry D. *Crossing the Deadly Ground: United States Army Tactics, 1865–1899*. Tuscaloosa: University of Alabama Press, 1994.

Johannsen, Robert W. *To the Halls of the Montezumas: The Mexican War in the American Imagination*. New York: Oxford University Press, 1985.

Johnson, Allen, and Dumas Malone, eds. *Dictionary of American Biography*. 21 vols. New York: Charles Scribner's Sons, 1928–37.

Johnson, Timothy D. *A Gallant Little Army: The Mexico City Campaign*. Lawrence: University Press of Kansas, 2007.

———. *Winfield Scott: The Quest for Military Glory*. Lawrence: University Press of Kansas, 1998.

Jones, J. B. *A Rebel War Clerk's Diary at the Confederate States Capital*. Vol. 1. Philadelphia: J. B. Lippincott, 1866.

Jones, J. Williams. *Personal Reminiscences of General Robert E. Lee*. 1874. Reprint, Richmond, Va.: United States Historical Society Press, 1989.

Jones, Terry L., ed. *The Civil War Memoirs of Captain William J. Seymour: Reminiscences of a Louisiana Tiger*. Baton Rouge: Louisiana University Press, 1991.

Keegan, John. *The Face of Battle*. 1976. Reprint, New York: Penguin Books, 1978.

Kieffer, Chester L. *Maligned General: The Biography of Thomas Sidney Jesup*. San Rafael, Calif.: Presidio Press, 1979.

Kohn, Richard H. *Eagle and Sword: The Federalists and the Creation of the Military Establishment in America, 1783–1802*. New York: Free Press, 1975.

Kornblith, Gary J. "Rethinking the Coming of the Civil War: A Counterfactual Exercise." *Journal of American History* 90 (June 2003). <http://www.historycooperative.org/journals/jah/90.1/kornblith.html>. October 22, 2007.

Kreidberg, Marvin A., and Merton G. Henry. *History of Military Mobilization in the United States Army, 1775–1945*. Washington, D.C.: Department of the Army, 1955.

Krick, Robert E. L. "The Men Who Carried This Position Were Soldiers Indeed: The Decisive Charge of Whiting's Division at Gaines's Mill." In *The Richmond Campaign of 1862: The Peninsula and the Seven Days*, edited by Gary W. Gallagher, 181–216. Chapel Hill: University of North Carolina Press, 2000.

———. *Staff Officers in Gray: A Biographical Register of the Staff Officers in the*

Army of Northern Virginia. Chapel Hill: University of North Carolina Press, 2003.

Kundahl, George G. *Confederate Engineer: Training and Campaigning with John Morris Wampler*. Knoxville: University of Tennessee Press, 2000.

Lacroix, Irenée Amelot de. *Rules and Regulations for the Field Exercise, and Manoeuvres of the French Infantry, Issued August 1, 1791*. 3 vols. Boston: T. B. Wait, 1810.

Laidley, T. T. S. "Breech-Loading Musket." *United States Service Magazine* 3 (January 1865): 67–70.

Lawson, Melinda. *Patriot Fires: Forging a New American Nationalism in the Civil War North*. Lawrence: University Press of Kansas, 2002.

Levinson, Irving W. *Wars within War: Mexican Guerrillas, Domestic Elites, and the United States of America, 1846–1846*. Canada: Irving W. Levinson, 2005.

Liddell Hart, B. H. *Sherman: Soldier, Realist, American*. New York: Dodd, Mead, 1929.

Lincoln, Abraham. *The Collected Works of Abraham Lincoln*. Edited by Roy P. Basler. 9 vols. New Brunswick, N.J.: Rutgers University Press, 1953.

Lisowski, Lori A. "The Future of West Point: Senate Debates on the Military Academy during the Civil War." *Civil War History* 34 (March 1988): 5–21.

Luvaas, Jay. *The Military Legacy of the Civil War: The European Inheritance*. Chicago: University of Chicago Press, 1959.

Mackey, Robert R. *The Uncivil War: Irregular Warfare in the Upper South, 1861–1865*. Norman: University of Oklahoma Press, 2004.

Mansfield, Edward D. *The Life of General Winfield Scott, Embracing His Campaign in Mexico*. New York: A. S. Barnes, 1848.

Marcus, Edward, ed. *A New Canaan Private in the Civil War: Letters of Justus M. Silliman, 17th Connecticut Volunteers*. New Canaan, Conn.: New Canaan Historical Society, 1984.

Martin, James Kirby, and Mark Edward Lender. *A Respectable Army: The Military Origins of the Republic, 1763–1789*. Wheeling, Ill.: Harlan Davidson, 1982.

Marshall, T. B. *History of the Eight-third Ohio Volunteer Infantry: The Greyhound Regiment*. Cincinnati: Eighty-third Ohio Volunteer Infantry Association, 1912.

Marvel, William. *Burnside*. Chapel Hill: University of North Carolina Press, 1991.

———. "The Making of a Myth: Ambrose E. Burnside and the Union High Command at Fredericksburg." In *The Fredericksburg Campaign: Decision on the Rappahannock*, edited by Gary W. Gallagher, 1–25. Chapel Hill: University of North Carolina Press, 1995.

Matter, William D. *If It Takes All Summer: The Battle of Spotsylvania*. Chapel Hill: University of North Carolina Press, 1988.

McClellan, George B. *Manual of Bayonet Exercise: Prepared for the Use of the Army of the United States*. Philadelphia: Lippincott, Grambo, 1852.

———. *McClellan's Own Story: The War for the Union, the Soldiers Who Fought It, the Civilians Who Directed It, and His Relations to It and Them*. New York: Charles L. Webster, 1887.

———. *Report on the Organization and Campaigns of the Army of the Potomac:*

257
★

To Which Is Added an Account of the Campaign in Western Virginia, with Plans of Battle-Fields. New York: Sheldon, 1864.

───. *Report of the Secretary of War, Communicating the Report of Captain George B. McClellan, (First Regiment United States Cavalry,) One of the Officers Sent to the Seat of War in Europe in 1855 and 1856.* Senate Ex. Doc. No. 1, Special Session. Washington, D.C.: A. O. P. Nicholson, 1857.

McDonough, James Lee. *Chattanooga: A Death Grip on the Confederacy.* Knoxville: University of Tennessee Press, 1984.

McKinney, Francis F. *Education in Violence: The Life of George H. Thomas and the History of the Army of the Cumberland.* Detroit: Wayne State University Press, 1961.

McMurry, Richard M. *Two Great Rebel Armies: An Essay in Confederate Military History.* Chapel Hill: University of North Carolina Press, 1989.

McPherson, James M. *Battle Cry of Freedom: The Civil War Era.* 1988. New York: Ballantine Books, 1989.

McWhiney, Grady, and Perry D. Jamieson. *Attack and Die: Civil War Military Tactics and the Southern Heritage.* University: University of Alabama Press, 1982.

Michie, Peter S. *The Life and Letters of Emory Upton.* New York: D. Appleton, 1885.

Miller, William J. *The Training of an Army: Camp Curtin and the North's Civil War.* Shippensburg, Pa.: White Mane Publishing, 1990.

Millett, Allan R., and Peter Maslowski. *For the Common Defense: A Military History of the United States of America.* Rev. ed. New York: Free Press, 1994.

"Modern Warfare." *De Bow's Review, Agricultural, Commercial, Industrial Progress and Resources* 31 (July 1861): 77–85.

Molloy, Peter Michael. "Technical Education and the Young Republic: West Point as America's École Polytechnique, 1802–1833." Ph.D. diss., Brown University, 1975.

Moore, Frank. *The Rebellion Record: A Diary of American Events, with Documents, Narrative, Illustrative Incidents, Poetry, Etc.* 11 vols. New York: D. Van Nostrand, 1861–68.

Morris, W. S., L. D. Hartwell Jr., and J. B. Kuykendall. *History 31st Regiment Illinois Volunteers: Organized by John A. Logan.* 1902. Reprint, Carbondale: Southern Illinois University Press, 1998.

Morrison, James L. *"The Best School in the World": West Point; The Pre–Civil War Years, 1833–1866.* Kent, Ohio: Kent State University Press, 1986.

Morse, F. W. *Personal Experiences in the War of the Great Rebellion, from December, 1862, to July, 1865.* Albany: n.p., 1866.

Moseley, Thomas Vernon. "Evolution of the American Civil War Infantry Tactics." Ph.D. diss., University of North Carolina at Chapel Hill, 1967.

Moten, Matthew. *The Delafield Commission and the American Military Profession.* College Station: Texas A&M University Press, 2000.

Myers, William Starr. *The Mexican War Diary of George B. McClellan.* Princeton: Princeton University Press, 1917.

Naisawald, L. VanLoan. *Grape and Canister: The Story of the Field Artillery of the Army of the Potomac, 1861–1865.* 2nd ed. Mechanicsburg, Pa.: Stackpole Books, 1999.

Neely, Mark E., Jr. *The Union Divided: Party Conflict in the Civil War North.*
Cambridge, Mass.: Harvard University Press, 2002.

————. "Wilderness and the Cult of Manliness: Hooker, Lincoln, and Defeat." In
Lincoln's Generals, edited by Gabor S. Boritt, 51–78. New York: Oxford University
Press, 1994.

Nevins, Allan. *The War for the Union.* 4 vols. New York: Charles Scribner's Sons,
1959–71.

Noe, Kenneth W. *Perryville: This Grand Havoc of Battle.* Lexington: University Press
of Kentucky, 2001.

Nolan, Alan T. *Lee Considered: General Robert E. Lee and Civil War History.* Chapel
Hill: University of North Carolina Press, 1991.

Nosworthy, Brent. *The Bloody Crucible of Courage: Fighting Methods and Combat
Experience of the Civil War.* New York: Carroll & Graf Publishers, 2003.

O'Connell, Charles F., Jr. "The United States Army and the Origins of Modern
Management, 1818–1860." Ph.D. diss., Ohio State University, 1982.

O'Connor, Richard. *Thomas: Rock of Chickamauga.* New York: Prentice-Hall, 1948.

Oeffinger, John C., ed. *A Soldier's General: The Civil War Letters of Major General
Lafayette McLaws.* Chapel Hill: University of North Carolina Press, 2002.

Olney, Warren. "The Battle of Shiloh with Some Personal Reminiscences." *Overland
Monthly Devoted to the Development of the Country,* June 1885, 577–89.

*Ordonnance du roi du 22 juillet 1845 sur l'exercice et les manoeuvres des bataillons de
chasseurs a pied, 1re partie.* Paris: Librairie Militaire de J. Dumaine, 1854.

O'Reilly, Francis Augustin. *The Fredericksburg Campaign: Winter War on the
Rappahannock.* Baton Rouge: Louisiana State University Press, 2003.

Osterhoudt, Henry Jerry. "The Evolution of U.S. Army Assault Tactics, 1778–1919:
The Search for Sound Doctrine." Ph.D. diss., Duke University, 1986.

Peterkin, Ernest W. *The Exercise of Arms in the Continental Infantry: Being a Study
of the Manual of the Firelock … Displayed in 1,000 Photographic and Artistic
Plates.* Bloomfield, Ontario: Museum Restoration Service, 1989.

Peterson, Charles J. *The Military Heroes of the War with Mexico with a Narrative
of the War.* Philadelphia: William A. Leary, 1848.

Piatt, Donn. *General George H. Thomas: A Critical Biography, with Concluding
Chapters by Henry V. Boynton.* Cincinnati: Robert Clarke, 1893.

Piston, William Garrett, and Richard W. Hatcher III. *Wilson's Creek: The Second
Battle of the Civil War and the Men Who Fought It.* Chapel Hill: University of
North Carolina Press, 2000.

Pollard, Edward A. *The First Year of the War: Corrected and Improved Edition.*
Richmond, Va.: West & Johnston, 1862.

Polley, J. B. *Hood's Texas Brigade: Its Marches Its Battles Its Achievements.* New York:
Neale Publishing, 1910.

————. *A Soldier's Letters to Charming Nellie.* New York: Neal Publishing, 1908.

Potter, David Morris. *Lincoln and His Part in the Secession Crisis.* New Haven: Yale
University Press, 1942.

Prokopowicz, Gerald J. *All for the Regiment: The Army of the Ohio, 1861–1862.* Chapel
Hill: University of North Carolina Press, 2001.

Pryor, Elizabeth Brown. *Reading the Man: A Portrait of Robert E. Lee through His Private Letters*. New York: Viking, 2007.

Rable, George C. *Fredericksburg! Fredericksburg!* Chapel Hill: University of North Carolina Press, 2002.

Rafuse, Ethan S. *McClellan's War: The Failure of Moderation in the Struggle for the Union*. Bloomington: Indiana University Press, 2005.

Reardon, Carol. "The Forlorn Hope: Brig. Gen. Andrew A. Humphreys's Pennsylvania Division at Fredericksburg." In *The Fredericksburg Campaign: Decision on the Rappahannock*, edited by Gary W. Gallagher, 80–112. Chapel Hill: University of North Carolina Press, 1995.

R.E.C. "Modern Tactics." *Southern Literary Messenger* 26 (January 1858): 1–20.

Reese, Timothy J. *Sykes' Regular Infantry Division, 1861–1864: A History of Regular United States Infantry Operations in the Civil War's Eastern Theater*. Jefferson, N.C.: McFarland, 1990.

Rhea, Gordon C. *The Battle of the Wilderness, May 5–6, 1864*. Baton Rouge: Louisiana State University Press, 1994.

———. *The Battles for Spotsylvania Court House and the Road to Yellow Tavern, May 7–12, 1864*. Baton Rouge: Louisiana State University Press, 1997.

———. *Cold Harbor: Grant and Lee, May 26–June 3, 1864*. Baton Rouge: Louisiana State University Press, 2002.

———. "Union Cavalry in the Wilderness: The Education of Philip H. Sheridan and James H. Wilson." In *The Wilderness Campaign*, edited by Gary W. Gallagher, 106–35. Chapel Hill: University of North Carolina Press, 1997.

Riling, Joseph R. *Baron Von Steuben and His Regulations Including a Complete Facsimile of the Original Regulations for the Order and Discipline of the Troops of the United States*. Philadelphia: Ray Riling Arms Books, 1966.

Risch, Erna. *Quartermaster Support of the Army: A History of the Corps, 1775–1939*. Washington, D.C.: Center of Military History, 1989.

Risley, Ford. "Pollard, Edward Alfred." *American National Biography Online*. February 2000. <http://www.anb.org/articles/16/16-01304.html>. June 24, 2008.

Roberts, James W. "The Wilderness and Spotsylvania, May 4–12, 1864: Narrative of a Private Soldier." *Quarterly Periodical of the Florida Historical Society* 11 (October 1932): 58–76.

Robertson, William Glenn. "First Bull Run, 19 July 1861." In *America's First Battles, 1776–1965*, edited by Charles E. Heller and William A. Stofft, 81–108. Lawrence: University Press of Kansas, 1986.

———. "From the Crater to New Market Heights: A Tale of Two Divisions." In *Black Soldiers in Blue: African American Troops in the Civil War Era*, edited by John David Smith, 169–99. Chapel Hill: University of North Carolina Press, 2002.

Rodenbough, Theo F., ed. *From Everglade to Cañon with the Second Dragoons (Second United States Cavalry): An Authentic Account of Service in Florida, Mexico, Virginia, and the Indian Country, Including the Personal Recollections of Prominent Officers*. New York: D. Van Nostrand, 1875.

Rogers, H. C. B. *The British Army of the Eighteenth Century*. London: George Allen & Unwin, 1977.

Roland, Charles P. *Albert Sidney Johnston: Soldier of Three Republics.* 2 vols. Austin: University of Texas Press, 1964.

———. "P. G. T. Beauregard." In *Leaders of the Lost Cause: New Perspectives on the Confederate High Command*, edited by Gary W. Gallagher and Joseph T. Glatthaar, 43–70. Mechanicsburg, Pa.: Stackpole Books, 2004.

Roman, Alfred. *The Military Operations of General Beauregard in the War between the States, 1861 to 1865.* 2 vols. New York: Harper & Row, 1884.

Rose, J. G. "Sixty-First Tennessee Infantry." In *The Military Annals of Tennessee. Confederate. First Series: Embracing a Review of Military Operations, with Regimental Histories and Memorial Roles*, edited by John Berrien Lindsley, 573–82. Nashville: J. M. Lindsley, 1886.

Ross, Steven. *From Flintlock to Rifle: Infantry Tactics, 1740–1866.* 2nd ed. London: Frank Cass, 1996.

[Rowe, David Watson]. *A Sketch of the 126th Regiment Pennsylvania Volunteers: The Comrades.* Chambersburg, Pa.: Cook & Hays, 1869.

Royster, Charles. *The Destructive War: William Tecumseh Sherman, Stonewall Jackson, and the Americans.* New York: Alfred A. Knopf, 1991.

Saunier, Joseph A., ed. *A History of the Forty-seventh Ohio Veteran Volunteer Infantry, Second Brigade, Second Division, Fifteenth Army Corps, Army of the Tennessee.* Hillsboro, Ohio: Lyle Printing, [1903].

Schaff, Morris. *The Spirit of Old West Point, 1858–1862.* Boston: Houghton, Mifflin, 1907.

Scheibert, Justus. *A Prussian Observes the American Civil War: The Military Studies of Justus Scheibert.* Edited by Frederic Trautmann. Columbia: University of Missouri Press, 2001.

Scott, H. L. *Military Dictionary: Comprising Technical Definitions; Information on Raising and Keeping Troops; Actual Service . . .* New York: D. Van Nostrand, 1864.

Scott, R. B. *The History of the 67th Regiment Indiana Infantry Volunteers, War of the Rebellion.* Bedford, Ind.: Herald Book and Job, 1892.

Scott, Winfield. *General Regulations for the Army; or, Military Institutes.* Philadelphia: M. Carey and Sons, 1821.

———. *Infantry Tactics; or, Rules for the Exercise and Manoeuvres of the United States Infantry.* 1835. New ed. 3 vols. New York: Harper & Brothers, 1861.

———. *Memoirs of Lieut.-General. Scott, LL.D.* 2 vols. New York: Sheldon, 1864.

Scott, Wm. Forse. *The Story of a Cavalry Regiment: The Career of the Fourth Iowa Veteran Volunteers from Kansas to Georgia, 1861–1865.* 1892. Reprint, Iowa City: Camp Pope Bookshop, 1992.

Sears, Stephen W. *Chancellorsville.* Boston: Houghton Mifflin, 1996.

———. *Controversies and Commanders: Dispatches from the Army of the Potomac.* Boston: Houghton Mifflin, 1999.

———. *George B. McClellan: The Young Napoleon.* New York: Ticknor & Fields, 1988.

———. "Gouverneur Kemble Warren and Little Phil." In *Controversies and Commanders: Dispatches from the Army of the Potomac*, 253–87. Boston: Houghton Mifflin, 1999.

———. *Landscape Turned Red: The Battle of Antietam.* New Haven, Conn.: Ticknor & Fields, 1983.

———. "The Revolt of the Generals." In *Controversies and Commanders: Dispatches from the Army of the Potomac,* 131–66. Boston: Houghton Mifflin, 1999.

———. *To the Gates of Richmond: The Peninsula Campaign.* New York: Ticknor & Fields, 1992.

Shannon, Fred Albert. *The Organization and Administration of the Union Army, 1861–1865.* Vol. 1. Cleveland: Arthur H. Clark Company, 1928.

Shea, William L. "Curtis, Samuel Ryan." *American National Biography Online.* February 2000. <http://www.anb.org/articles/04/04-00287.html>. June 24, 2008.

Sherman, William Tecumseh. *Memoirs of General W. T. Sherman.* New York: Library of America, 1990.

Simon, John Y., ed. *The Papers of Ulysses S. Grant.* Vol. 12. Carbondale: Southern Illinois University Press, 1984.

Simpson, Brooks D. "Great Expectations: Ulysses S. Grant, the Northern Press, and the Opening of the Wilderness Campaign." In *The Wilderness Campaign,* edited by Gary W. Gallagher, 1–35. Chapel Hill: University of North Carolina Press, 1997.

———. *Ulysses S. Grant: Triumph over Adversity, 1822–1865.* Boston: Houghton Mifflin, 2000.

Simpson, Brooks D., and Jean V. Berlin, eds. *Sherman's Civil War: Selected Correspondence of William T. Sherman, 1860–1865.* Chapel Hill: University of North Carolina Press, 1999.

Simpson, Harold B. *Gaines' Mill to Appomattox: Waco and McLennan County in Hood's Texas Brigade.* 2nd ed. Waco, Tex.: Texian Press, 1988.

Skelton, William B. *An American Profession of Arms: The Army Officer Corps, 1784–1861.* Lawrence: University Press of Kansas, 1992.

———. "The Commanding General and the Problem of Command in the United States Army, 1821–1841." *Military Affairs* 34 (December 1970): 117–22.

Smith, George Winston, and Charles Judah, eds. *Chronicles of the Gringos: The U.S. Army in the Mexican War, 1846–1848: Accounts of Eyewitnesses and Combatants.* Albuquerque: University of New Mexico Press, 1968.

Smith, John Day. *The History of the Nineteenth Regiment of Maine Volunteer Infantry, 1862–1865.* Minneapolis: Great Western Printing Company, 1909.

Smith, Justin H. *The War with Mexico.* 2 vols. 1919. Reprint, Gloucester, Mass.: Peter Smith, 1963.

Smith, William Farrar. "Operations before Fort Donelson." *Magazine of American History with Notes and Queries* 15 (January–June 1886): 20–43.

Smyth, Alexander. *Regulations for the Field Exercise, Manœuvres, and Conduct of the Infantry of the United States, Drawn up and Adapted to the Organization of the Militia and Regular Troops.* Philadelphia: T. & G. Palmer, 1812.

Sommers, Richard J. *Richmond Redeemed: The Siege at Petersburg.* Garden City, N.Y.: Doubleday, 1981.

Sorrel, G. Moxley. *Recollections of a Confederate Staff Officer.* Edited by Bell Irvin Wiley. Jackson, Tenn.: McCowat-Mercer Press, 1958.

Starr, Stephen Z. *The Union Cavalry in the Civil War.* 3 vols. Baton Rouge: Louisiana State University Press, 1979–85.

Stewart, R. B. "The Battle of Stone River, as Seen by One Who Was there." *Blue and Gray* 5 (January 1895): 10–14.

Symonds, Craig L. "No Margin for Error: Civil War in the Confederate Government." In *The Art of Command in the Civil War,* edited by Steven E. Woodworth, 1–16. Lincoln: University of Nebraska Press, 1998.

Syrett, Harold C., ed. *The Papers of Alexander Hamilton.* 27 vols. New York: Columbia University Press, 1961–87.

Taaffe, Stephen R. *Commanding the Army of the Potomac.* Lawrence: University Press of Kansas, 2006.

Tap, Bruce. *Over Lincoln's Shoulder: The Committee on the Conduct of the War.* Lawrence: University Press of Kansas, 1998.

Tayloe, Phoebe Warren, and Winslow M. Watson. *In Memoriam: Benjamin Ogle Tayloe.* Washington, D.C.: Winslow M. Watson, 1872.

Taylor, Rosser H. "Boyce-Hammond Correspondence." *Journal of Southern History* 3 (August 1937): 348–54.

Teitler, Gerke. *The Genesis of the Professional Officers' Corps.* Beverly Hills, Calif.: Sage Publications, 1977.

Thomas, Emory. *Bold Dragoon: The Life of J. E. B. Stuart.* New York: Harper & Row, 1986.

———. *The Confederate Nation: 1861–1865.* New York: Harper & Row, Publishers, 1979.

Thomas, Henry W. *History of the Doles-Cook Brigade . . .* Atlanta: Franklin Printing and Publishing Company, 1903.

Thomas, Wilbur. *General George H. Thomas: The Indomitable Warrior.* New York: Exposition Press, 1964.

Tilly, Charles. "Reflections on the History of European State-Making." In *The Formation of National States in Western Europe,* edited by Charles Tilly, 3–83. Princeton: Princeton University Press, 1975.

Todd, Frederick P. *American Military Equipage, 1851–1872.* Vol. 1. 1974. Reprint, New York: Charles Scribner's Sons, 1980.

Todorich, Charles. *The Spirited Years: A History of the Antebellum Naval Academy.* Annapolis, Md.: Naval Institute Press, 1984.

Trudeau, Noah Andre. *The Last Citadel: Petersburg, Virginia, June 1864–April 1865.* Boston: Little, Brown, 1991.

Tyler, Mason Whiting. *Recollections of the Civil War: With Many Original Diary Entries and Letters Written from the Seat of War, and with Annotated References.* Edited by William S. Tyler. New York: G. P. Putnam's Sons, 1912.

United States. *The Public Statutes at Large of the United States of America.* 8 vols. Boston: Charles C. Little and James Brown, 1845–67.

United States Army Ordnance Department. *Reports of Experiments with Small Arms for the Military Service, by Officers of the Ordnance Department.* Washington, D.C.: A. O. P. Nicholson, Public Printer, 1856.

United States Congress. *American State Papers: Documents, Legislative and*

Executive, of the Congress of the United States . . . 28 vols. Washington, D.C.: Gales and Seaton, 1832–61.

United States Congress. Joint Committee on the Conduct of the War. [*Army of the Potomac.* In] *Report of the Joint Committee on the Conduct of the War at the Second Session Thirty-eighth Congress.* Vol. 1. Washington, D.C.: Government Printing Office, 1865.

———. *Battle of Petersburg.* In *Report of the Joint Committee on the Conduct of the War at the Second Session Thirty-eighth Congress.* Vol. 1. Washington, D.C.: Government Printing Office, 1865.

———. *Report of the Joint Committee on the Conduct of the War.* 3 vols. Washington, D.C.: Government Printing Office, 1863.

United States War Department. *Cavalry Tactics.* Vol. 1. Washington, D.C.: J. and G. S. Gideon, 1841.

———. *Infantry Tactics; or, Rules for the Exercises and Manoeuvres of the Infantry of the U.S. Army.* Washington, D.C.: Davis & Force, 1825.

———. *Instruction for Field Artillery, Horse and Foot.* Baltimore: Joseph Robinson, 1845.

———. *Regulations for the Army of the United States, 1857.* New York: Harper & Brothers, [1857].

———. *Report of the Secretary of War.* Senate Executive Document No. 5. Serial Set No. 876, Vol. 3, pt. 2. 34th Congress, 3rd Session. Washington, D.C.: A. O. P. Nicholson, 1857.

———. *Rules and Regulations for the Field Exercise and Manœuvres of Infantry, Compiled and Adapted to the Organization of the Army of the United States, Agreeably to a Resolve of Congress, Dated December, 1814.* New York: T. & W. Mercein, 1815.

———. *The War of the Rebellion: A Compilation of the Official Records of the Union and Confederate Armies.* 128 vols. Washington, D.C.: Government Printing Office, 1880–1901.

Upton, Emory. *The Military Policy of the United States.* Washington, D.C.: Government Printing Office, 1904.

Van Creveld, Martin. *Command in War.* Cambridge, Mass.: Harvard University Press, 1985.

———. *Supplying War: Logistics from Wallenstein to Patton.* Cambridge: Cambridge University Press, 1977.

Van Horne, Thomas B. *The Life of Major-General George H. Thomas.* New York: C. Scribner's Sons, 1882.

Wagner, Arthur L. *Organization and Tactics.* 7th ed. Kansas City, Mo.: Franklin Hudson Publishing, 1906.

Wainwright, Charles S. *A Diary of Battle: The Personal Journals of Colonel Charles S. Wainwright, 1861–1865.* Edited by Allan Nevins. New York: Harcourt, Brace & World, 1962.

Wallace, Lew. "The Capture of Fort Donelson." In vol. 1 of *Battles and Leaders of the Civil War,* edited by Robert Underwood Johnson and Clarence Clough Bell, 398–429. 1887. Reprint, Secaucus, N.J.: Castle, n.d.

Warner, Ezra J. *Generals in Blue: Lives of the Union Commanders*. Baton Rouge: Louisiana State University Press, 1964.

———. *Generals in Gray: Lives of the Confederate Commanders*. Baton Rouge: Louisiana State University Press, 1959.

Watson, Samuel J. "Professionalism, Social Attitudes, and Civil-Military Accountability in the United States Army Officer Corps, 1815–1846." Ph.D. diss., Rice University, 1996.

Waugh, John C. *Reelecting Lincoln: The Battle for the 1864 Presidency*. New York: Crown Publishers, 1997.

Weber, Jennifer L. *Copperheads: The Rise and Fall of Lincoln's Opponents in the North*. New York: Oxford University Press, 2006.

Weigley, Russell F. *History of the United States Army*. Enl. ed. Bloomington: Indiana University Press, 1984.

———. *Towards an American Army: Military Thought from Washington to Marshall*. New York: Columbia University Press, 1962.

Weitz, Mark A. "Drill, Training, and the Combat Performance of the Civil War Soldier: Dispelling the Myth of the Poor Soldier, Great Fighter." *Journal of Military History* 62 (April 1998): 263–89.

Weller, Jac. "Civil War Minie Rifles Prove Quite Accurate." *American Rifleman* 119, no. 7 (1971): 36–40.

Wert, Jeffrey D. *The Sword of Lincoln: The Army of the Potomac*. New York: Simon & Schuster, 2005.

Wilcox, C. M. *Rifles and Rifle Practice: An Elementary Treatise upon the Theory of Rifle Firing, Explaining the Causes of Inaccuracy of Fire, and the Manner of Correcting It*. New York: D. Van Nostrand, 1859.

Willard, G. L. *Comparative Value of Rifled and Smooth-Bored Arms*. [1863]. N.p.: Cornell University Library Digital Collections, n.d.

———. *Manual of Target Practice for the United States Army*. 1858. Reprint, Philadelphia: J. P. Lippincott, 1862.

Williams, Harry. "The Attack upon West Pointers during the Civil War." *Mississippi Valley Historical Review* 25 (March 1939): 491–504.

Wilson, Gary, ed. "The Diary of John S. Tucker: Confederate Soldier from Alabama." *Alabama Historical Quarterly* 43 (Spring 1981): 5–33.

Wilson, Mark R. *The Business of Civil War: Military Mobilization and the State, 1861–1865*. Baltimore: Johns Hopkins University Press, 2006.

Winders, Richard Bruce. *Mr. Polk's Army: The American Military Experience in the Mexican War*. College Station: Texas A&M University Press, 1997.

Woodward, C. Vann, ed. *Mary Chesnut's Civil War*. New Haven: Yale University Press, 1981.

Yeary, Mamie. *Reminiscences of the Boys in Gray, 1861–1865*. Dallas: M. E. Church, South, 1912.

Young, Otis E. *The West of Philip St. George Cooke*. Glendale, Calif.: Arthur H. Clarke, 1955.

Zornow, William Frank. *Lincoln and the Party Divided*. Norman: University of Oklahoma Press, 1954.

INDEX

Adjutant General, 28, 29, 31, 48, 51, 79, 87

Alexander, Edward Porter, 1, 110, 113, 220 (n. 32), 221 (n. 45)

Allabach, Peter H., 167, 168, 170

Alvarez, Juan, 70

American Revolution, 3, 17, 23, 49, 54, 199 (n. 3); Blue Book of, 26, 39; political goals after, 12–13. *See also* Continental army

Ampudia, Pedro de, 57, 59, 61, 62

Anderson, George T., 99

Anderson, Robert, 95, 108, 123, 210 (n. 32); artillery tactics and, 47, 48–50, 72, 209 (n. 29)

Antietam, 160–61, 162–63, 164–65, 186, 189, 232 (n. 44), 233 (n. 9); casualties, 163, 233–34 (n. 10); entrenchments and, 158, 165

Antimilitarism, 11, 12, 97, 135, 189, 214 (n. 1)

Appomattox, 1, 8, 98, 122, 187, 198, 241 (n. 38)

Arista, Mariano, 57, 59

Arkansas toothpick. *See* Bowie knife

Army and Navy Chronicle, 43

Army Bill (1818), 26

Army of Northern Virginia, 172, 242 (n. 39); 6th Alabama, 162; Antietam, 161, 162–63, 165, 186, 233 (n. 9), 233–34 (n. 10); artillery, 165, 171, 174–75, 237 (n. 36); casualties, Antietam, 163, 233–34 (n. 10); casualties, Overland Campaign, 180, 239 (n. 21), 240 (n. 23); casualties, Seven Days battles, 232–33 (n. 50); command system, strength of, 135, 186, 187, 240 (n. 23); drill for volunteers, 141, 142, 227 (n. 20); entrenchments and, 156, 165, 173; final defeat, 178, 194, 195; Fredericksburg, 165, 166–68; Gettysburg, 174–75, 186, 237 (n. 36); Lee's leadership, 133, 135, 156, 162, 186, 187; military superiority of, 134–35, 171; morale, 135, 154, 156; organizational weakness, 162–63, 171, 174–75, 186, 233 (n. 9), 237 (n. 36); Richmond and, 1862, 134–35, 154–55, 156; Second Bull Run, 160, 165; Seven Days battles, 134, 156, 175, 186, 232–33 (n. 50); Spotsylvania, 184–85, 238–39 (n. 17), 239 (nn. 18–19); strategy of attrition and, 178, 180, 191. *See also* Chancellorsville

Army of Tennessee, 9, 63, 121, 165, 189–90, 231–32 (n. 43), 239–40 (n. 22); artillery, 152, 175, 237 (n. 38); Missionary Ridge, 175–76

Army of the Cumberland, 126, 175, 176

Army of the Potomac: 1st Corps, 161, 162; 2nd Corps, 166, 167, 168, 185, 189, 193; 5th Corps, 163, 188, 193;

1st Louisiana battalion, 128; 2nd
South Carolina, 130; 4th Alabama,
150; 4th Texas, 149–50, 167, 173,
230–31 (n. 33); 8th Virginia, 130; 9th
Tennessee, 169; 18th Georgia, 149,
150; 33rd Virginia, 128, 129; artillery,
1, 110, 127, 130, 131, 148–49, 152, 173;
artillery tactics, 132, 133, 144, 225
(n. 43); assault tactics, 168–69, 174–
76, 194; cavalry in, 93, 110, 128, 133;
citizen-soldier and, ideal of, 112, 117,
141; citizen-soldiers as raw recruits of,
120, 155, 161, 171; citizen-soldiers vs.
regulars, 75, 120, 139, 153, 226 (n. 10);
Confederate state, giving legitimacy
to, 3, 199 (n. 3); conscription, 117,
137, 141, 143, 171; discipline of, 2,
143, 144, 159, 226 (n. 10), 228 (n. 22);
drill for volunteers, 121, 141, 143,
144, 227 (n. 17); final defeat, 163, 177,
195; lack of action, late 1861, 137–41;
Mexican War, future generals of in,
63, 64, 66, 68–69, 103, 140, 226 (n. 8);
morale, 9, 173, 174, 176, 194, 232–33
(n. 50); nation-state type of war,
commitment to, 2, 94, 118; old army
influence, 1–2, 8, 10, 53, 76, 84–87,
94, 96, 119, 124–26, 135–36, 145, 198,
223 (n. 14), 225 (n. 43); pillaging, 153,
194; political goals, 4, 190, 200 (n. 5),
241 (n. 31); railroads, use of, 171, 177,
193, 238 (n. 4); romanticism of, 118,
121, 125; slaves, arming, 1, 2; small
arms, 148, 152, 230 (n. 30), 231 (n. 39);
southern officers of, 91, 96, 151, 221
(n. 44); staff/logistical organization, 9,
27, 32, 75, 135, 143, 156, 162–63, 193,
242–43 (n. 41); in western theater, 9,
96, 106, 121, 143–44, 148, 155, 175.
See also Army of Northern Virginia;
Army of Tennessee; Big Black Bridge;
Bull Run, First; Civil War; Guerrilla
warfare; Missionary Ridge; Perryville,
Ky.; Richmond; Seven Days battles;
Shiloh; West Point

Continental army: antimilitarism and,
12, 189; disbandment, 15, 203 (n. 8);
French army influence, 14, 17, 23, 203
(n. 14), 205 (n. 30); light infantry tac-
tics, 41; mutinies, 14–15, 94, 203 (n. 7);
as regulars, 14, 40, 203 (n. 8)
Contreras. *See* Padierna
Cooke, John Esten, 106
Cooke, John Rogers, 106
Cooke, Julia Turner, 106
Cooke, Philip St. George, 43–44, 123, 218
(n. 12); Kansas and, 97–98, 99–100; as
West Point southerner in Union army,
93, 102–3, 106–7, 108, 109, 219 (n. 23)
Corpus Christi, Tex., 56, 58, 59
Cowskin Prairie, 120
Crater, the, 181, 188, 194, 240–41 (n. 27)
Crawford, William H., 25
Crimean War, 76, 86; Delafield
Commission, 82, 89, 147, 215 (n. 15),
217 (n. 32)
Cross, Edward E., 167
Crozet, Claudius, 21
Cullum, George W., 92
Cumming, Alfred, 96
Curtis, Samuel R., 182–83
Cushing, George William, 81

Davis, Jefferson, 101, 218 (n. 7); as
Confederate leader, 63, 121, 140, 155,
182, 190, 200 (n. 5), 241 (n. 31); Lee
and, 155, 182, 190; in Mexican War,
63; as secretary of war, 75, 78, 79, 81,
85, 97, 200 (n. 5), 206 (n. 46); as West
Pointer, 2, 63, 110, 139, 200 (n. 5),
216–17 (n. 29), 219 (n. 23)
Davis, Nicholas A., 150
Dearborn, Henry, 18
De Bow's Review, 124–25, 132
Delafield, Richard, 89, 215 (n. 15)
Delafield Commission, 82, 89, 147, 215
(n. 15), 217 (n. 32)
Democratic Party, 62, 98, 163, 164, 170,
180, 182, 189; McClellan and, 4, 151,
154, 156, 157, 181, 191

common and quick-time, 8, 39, 41, 42–43, 44, 46, 77, 80–81, 86, 207–8 (n. 15), 208 (nn. 19–20), 216 (n. 23); tactical boards, 39–40, 80–82; tactical manuals for, 5, 8, 36, 37–38, 39–40, 41–46, 52, 78–81, 83, 206 (n. 6), 206–7 (n. 8), 207 (nn. 9, 12), 216 (n. 28); tactical manuals for, during Civil War, 38, 43, 46, 150–51, 178–79, 214 (n. 10); tactics, 37–40, 41–46, 71, 81, 208 (n. 17); target practice, 76, 77, 79, 82, 83, 87, 89, 142, 215 (n. 16), 229 (n. 27), 242 (n. 39); three-rank formation, 42, 44, 45, 46, 207 (n. 9), 209 (n. 24); training programs, 16, 52, 87–89, 147; two-rank formation, 39, 41, 42, 44, 45, 46, 85, 207 (n. 9), 208 (n. 22), 209 (n. 24); weapons technology and, 36, 76, 77–82, 86–87, 123, 124, 158–59; Wilcox's rifles treatise and, 84–87, 125. *See also* Army of Northern Virginia; Army of Tennessee; Army of the Potomac; Bayonets; British army; Bull Run, First; Confederate armies; French army; Hardee's Infantry Tactics; Napoleonic Wars; Rifle-muskets; Union armies

Infantry School of Practice, Jefferson Barracks, 38, 52

Iron Brigade, 106, 132, 220 (n. 32)

Jackson, Andrew, 12, 23, 25, 34, 56; Jacksonian Revolution and, 19; nullification crisis and, Charleston, 94–95, 108

Jackson, Thomas J. "Stonewall," 119, 120–21, 160, 186, 236 (n. 30); First Bull Run and, 127, 128, 130, 224 (n. 31), 225 (n. 43); Fredericksburg, 166, 171; as West Pointer, 140, 219 (n. 22), 226 (n. 10)

Jamieson, Perry D., 8, 81, 86

Jayhawkers, 101

Jefferson, Thomas, 16–17

Jesup, Thomas S., 18–19, 26–27

Johannsen, Robert W., 73

Johnston, Albert Sidney, 96, 154, 219 (n. 23)

Johnston, Joseph Eggleston, 120–21, 226 (n. 8); Army of Tennessee, command, 165; First Bull Run and, 125, 126, 127, 130, 133; Jefferson Davis and, 200 (n. 5), 241 (n. 31) ; as old army, 125, 219 (n. 23); Richmond and, 1862, 155, 232 (n. 48); Seven Pines, 156, 232 (n. 48); Sherman's Atlanta campaign and, 192, 232 (n. 48); Shiloh and, 153–54, 231–32 (n. 43)

Jones, Archer, 177, 178, 182

Jones, J. B., 118, 120, 138, 226 (n. 5)

Julian, George, 181

Kansas, 93, 94, 95; U.S. Army actions in, 96–101, 218 (n. 7)

Kearny, Philip, 51, 52

Kelton, John C., 83, 87, 215 (n. 16)

Kennesaw Mountain, 192

Kershaw, J. B., 130, 225 (n. 36)

Ketchum, W. S., 87, 216 (n. 28)

Keyes, Erasmus D., 88, 129

Kimmel, Manning M., 101

Knowlton, Minor, 47, 48–49, 209 (n. 29), 210 (n. 32)

Knox, Henry, 15

Knoxville, Tenn., battle of, 110, 175

Lacroix tactics, 38, 44

Lallemand, H., 47

Lances, 42, 51, 63, 83, 84. *See also* Bayonets; Sabers

Lane, James, 112

Law, Evander M., 149, 150

Lawler, Michael K., 172, 173

Lawrence, Kans., 99

Lecompton, Kans., 97, 98, 100

Ledlie, James H., 188, 240–41 (n. 27)

Lee, Robert E., 119, 142, 189, 232 (nn. 44, 48), 239 (n. 20), 242 (n. 39); aggressiveness, 134, 140, 226 (n. 13); Antietam and, 158, 161, 162–63, 186,

McLaws, Lafayette, 119, 175, 193, 237 (n. 37)
McLemore, O. K., 150
McPherson, James B., 174
McRee, William, 19–21, 22
McWhiney, Grady, 8, 81, 86
Meade, George G., 145, 146, 158, 166, 168, 183, 187, 188, 240–41 (n. 27); Gettysburg and, 189, 190, 241 (n. 28)
Meade, Richard K., 101, 219 (n. 19)
Meridian expedition, 177–78
Mexican army, 34, 75; casualties, 66, 69; cavalry, 55, 63; Monterrey and, 61–62; at Rio Grande, 56–57, 59–60; San Patricios (American deserters) and, 69; Vera Cruz campaign and, 64–72, 213 (n. 27)
Mexican guerrillas, 60, 72, 73, 123
Mexican War, 8, 33, 105, 140, 147, 223 (n. 13); armistice, after Churubusco, 70; armistice, after Monterrey, 61–62; armistice, final, 72; British observers of, 55–56, 59; Buena Vista, 62–64, 70, 72, 103, 131, 213 (n. 38); California and New Mexico and, small-scale expeditions, 64, 147, 212 (n. 22), 213 (n. 36); Cerro Gordo and, 66, 67, 70, 212 (n. 24); Churubusco and, 69, 70; citizen-soldiers as volunteers in, 15, 60–61, 63, 66–67, 72; citizen-soldiers vs. regulars, 72–73, 74, 116, 213 (n. 37); financial costs, 55; First Bull Run compared with, 130–31; Mexican advantages in, 55–56; Mexico City and, 62, 64, 66, 67–68, 70–72; Monterrey and, 60, 61–62, 70, 103, 212 (n. 15), 213 (n. 39); nation-state type of war and, 36, 37, 64; Palo Alto and, 57, 60, 61, 74, 130, 131, 132, 209 (n. 30); Resaca de la Palma and, 57–59, 60, 61; Rio Grande and, 56–60; small-unit engagement in, 60, 64; U.S. Army casualties in, 55, 57, 69, 70, 71; U.S. Army divisions, 67, 212–13 (n. 26); U.S. Army engineers, 57, 64, 66, 68, 70; U.S. Army forms small regular army for, 12, 55, 230 (n. 29); U.S. Army officer objections to, 93, 164; U.S. Army staff organization in, 35, 72, 159; U.S. Army success in, 11, 34, 46, 54–55, 59, 72, 75, 206 (n. 2), 211 (n. 2); U.S. Army training for, 56, 61, 212 (n. 6); Vera Cruz campaign, 55, 62, 64–72, 212–13 (n. 26); Vera Cruz siege, 64, 66, 212 (n. 23). *See also* Artillery; Cavalry; Infantry; Mexican army
Mexico, 34, 55–56, 62, 67
Mexico City, 62, 64, 66, 67, 68, 70–72
Militias, 77, 95, 130, 166, 197, 203–4 (n. 18); citizen-soldier and, ideal of, 3, 12, 13–14, 60; Confederate partisans, 121, 123–24; in Kansas, 98–101; vs. regulars, 13–14, 15, 40, 41, 55, 67, 73, 75, 88, 203 (n. 9); in War of 1812, 12, 18, 19, 67
Mine Run, 158
Minié ball, 5, 76, 77, 78, 158
Minié rifle, 80, 85
Missionary Ridge, 9, 159, 175–76, 233 (n. 1)
Missouri, 100, 112, 182
Missouri state guard, 120, 121
Mobile, Ala., 188, 191
Model 1855 Rifle-Musket, 79–80
Model 1855 Springfield rifle-musket, 78, 80
Model 1863 Springfield rifle-musket, 7
Monroe, James, 23
Monterrey, 60, 61–62, 70, 103, 212 (n. 15), 213 (n. 39)
Moore, Thomas, 117
Morales, Juan, 64
Mordecai, Alfred, 88, 102, 109–10, 215 (n. 15)
Mormon expedition, 96, 100, 116
Mott, Gershom, 185
Mounted School of Instruction, Carlisle Barracks, 51
Mudd, John J., 172

3–4, 5, 199–200 (n. 4); regulars vs. citizen-soldiers, 12–13, 15, 36, 37, 40, 56,
74; sectional tensions within, 1850s,
91–94, 96–97, 99, 100–101; seniority
just before Civil War, 102, 219 (n. 23);
Spanish-American War, reforms
of after, 197; staff organization, 12,
26, 28, 31, 32–33, 35, 37, 197, 203
(n. 13); standardized procedures for,
23, 25–27; swearing oaths of loyalty,
103, 109, 111, 221 (n. 41); Unionism
of, 1850s, 92, 93, 97, 101, 104–5, 110,
220 (n. 28). *See also* Artillery; Cavalry;
Indian wars; Infantry; Mexican War;
Quartermaster Bureau; U.S. Congress;
War of 1812; West Point
United States Colored Troops, 94, 240–41
(n. 27). *See also* Union armies
U.S. Congress: Congressional Joint
Committee on the Conduct of the
War, 164, 234 (n. 12); military educa-
tion and, 17; U.S. Army, funding cuts,
12, 47, 91; U.S. Army, legislation, 12,
15–16, 25, 26, 31, 203 (n. 9), 206 (n. 5);
war goals between Revolution and
Civil War, 13, 202–3 (n. 4)
United States Military Academy at West
Point. *See* West Point
United States Military Philosophical
Society, 18
U.S. Navy, 15, 17, 23, 66
U.S. War Department, 16, 22, 44, 52, 75,
79, 101; artillery tactics, 48, 50–51,
210 (n. 31). *See also* Secretaries of War
Upton, Emory, 92, 183–85, 194, 196, 197,
198, 206 (n. 2), 238–39 (n. 17)

Valencia, Gabriel, 68, 69
Van Buren, Martin, 95
Van Horne, Thomas B., 103–4, 220
(n. 26)
Van Rensselaer, Stephen, 18
Vera Cruz, 64, 66, 212 (n. 23)
Vera Cruz campaign, 55, 60, 62, 64–72,
212–13 (n. 26), 213 (n. 27)

Vicksburg, 173–74, 183, 242 (n. 40)
Vicksburg campaign, 112, 172–74, 178,
189, 190, 192, 230 (n. 30), 236 (n. 33),
236–37 (n. 34); Big Black Bridge,
172–73, 174
Vincennes, France, 82, 84
Virginia, 105, 106, 107, 108, 110; secession, 103, 109, 220 (n. 26)
Virginia Military Institute, 22, 103, 121,
123, 143

Wadsworth, Decius, 17
Walker, Robert J., 100
Wallace, Lew, 154
War of 1812, 53, 64, 66, 206 (n. 4);
Buffalo camp of instruction (1814)
and, 38; Canadian border campaigns,
18, 19; infantry tactics and, 37, 38,
41, 74; New Orleans, battle of, 12, 23;
Queenston, battle of, 18, 19, 67; Treaty
of Ghent (1814), 35; U.S. Army professionalization after, 5, 8, 11, 12, 19, 54,
55, 72, 74, 197, 202 (n. 1); U.S. Army
shortcomings during, 9, 11, 23, 25, 33,
35, 46, 206 (n. 2); Washington, D.C.,
fall of, 12, 18, 23, 36; West Point after,
11, 17, 18, 20, 24–25
Washburne, Elihu, 181
Washington, D.C.: fall of, War of 1812,
12, 18, 23, 36; safety of in 1862, 155,
232 (n. 47)
Washington, George, 12, 13, 16, 17, 24;
establishment of regular army and,
14–15
Wayne, Anthony, 15–16
Weapons technology, 18, 46, 50, 75,
206–7 (n. 8); bowie knife, 123;
breechloaders, 77, 87, 194, 211 (n. 37);
"Burton bullet," 78; Confederate
vs. Union, 148, 152, 230 (n. 30);
development in 1840s and 1850s, 47;
gun-howitzer, twelve-pounder, 89, 217
(n. 32); minié ball, 5, 76, 77, 78, 158;
Minié rifle, 80, 85; as morale-booster,
9, 86–87; muzzle-loading muskets,

285

★